Laws of the Postcolonial

Law, Meaning, and Violence

The scope of Law, Meaning, and Violence is defined by the wide-ranging scholarly debates signaled by each of the words in the title. Those debates have taken place among and between lawyers, anthropologists, political theorists, sociologists, and historians, as well as literary and cultural critics. This series is intended to recognize the importance of such ongoing conversations about law, meaning, and violence as well as to encourage and further them.

Series Editors:

Martha Minow, Harvard Law School
Elaine Scarry, Harvard University
Austin Sarat, Amherst College

Narrative, Violence, and the Law: The Essays of Robert Cover, edited by Martha Minow, Michael Ryan, and Austin Sarat

Narrative, Authority, and Law, by Robin West

The Possibility of Popular Justice: A Case Study of Community Mediation in the United States, edited by Sally Engle Merry and Neal Milner

Legal Modernism, by David Luban

Surveillance, Privacy, and the Law: Employee Drug Testing and the Politics of Social Control, by John Gilliom

Lives of Lawyers: Journeys in the Organizations of Practice, by Michael J. Kelly

Unleashing Rights: Law, Meaning, and the Animal Rights Movement, by Helena Silverstein

Law Stories, edited by Gary Bellow and Martha Minow

The Powers That Punish: Prison and Politics in the Era of the "Big House," 1920–1955, by Charles Bright

Law and the Postmodern Mind: Essays on Psychoanalysis and Jurisprudence, edited by Peter Goodrich and David Gray Carlson

Russia's Legal Fictions, by Harriet Murav

Strangers to the Law: Gay People on Trial, by Lisa Keen and Suzanne B. Goldberg

Butterfly, the Bride: Essays on Law, Narrative, and the Family, by Carol Weisbrod

The Politics of Community Policing: Rearranging the Power to Punish, by William Lyons

Laws of the Postcolonial, edited by Eve Darian-Smith and Peter Fitzpatrick

Laws of the Postcolonial

Edited by
Eve Darian-Smith
and
Peter Fitzpatrick

Ann Arbor
THE UNIVERSITY OF MICHIGAN PRESS

Published in the United States of America by
The University of Michigan Press
Manufactured in the United States of America
⊗ Printed on acid-free paper

2002 2001 2000 1999 4 3 2 1

A CIP catalog record for this book is available from the British Library.

Library of Congress Cataloging-in-Publication Data

Laws of the postcolonial / edited by Eve Darian-Smith and Peter Fitzpatrick.
p. cm. — (Law, meaning, and violence)
Includes bibliographical references and index.
ISBN 0-472-10956-1 (alk. paper)
1. Legal polycentricity. 2. Multiculturalism—Law and legislation. 3. Postcolonialism. 4. Cultural relativism. 5. Culture and law. I. Darian-Smith, Eve, 1963– II. Fitzpatrick, Peter, 1941– III. Series.
K236 .L39 1999
340—dc21 98-51222
CIP

Contents

Acknowledgments vii

Laws of the Postcolonial: An Insistent Introduction 1
Peter Fitzpatrick and Eve Darian-Smith

Part 1. Postcolonialism in Theory

Approaching Anxiety: The Insistence of the Post-colonial in the Declaration on the Rights of Indigenous Peoples 19
Colin Perrin

Passions Out of Place: Law, Incommensurability, and Resistance 39
Peter Fitzpatrick

A Moral Geography of Liberty: John Stuart Mill and American Free Speech Discourse 61
Paul A. Passavant

Part 2. The Persistence of the Colonial

Francisco de Vitoria and the Colonial Origins of International Law 89
Antony Anghie

Islamic Law and English Texts 109
John Strawson

The View from the International Plane: Perspective and Scale in the Architecture of Colonial International Law 127
Annelise Riles

Part 3. The Postcolonial Without

Subalternity and International Law: The Problems of Global Community and the Incommensurability of Difference 145
Dianne Otto

An Ontological Approach to Constitutionalism in Sri Lanka: Contingency and the Failure of Exclusion 181
Roshan de Silva

Postcolonialism: The Emperor's New Clothes? 203
Jeannine Purdy

Part 4. The Postcolonial Within

Rites of Passage into the Global Village 233
Rolando Gaete

From Law to Popular Justice: Beyond Antinomialism 249
Alan Norrie

Rabies Rides the Fast Train: Transnational Interactions in Postcolonial Times 277
Eve Darian-Smith

Contributors 301

Index 303

Acknowledgments

For a collection which so extensively questions the civility of the West, it is apt and even necessary to mention the agreeable exception of the University of Michigan Press and especially those with whom we as editors have had the great pleasure of working, Charles Myers and Kevin Rennells. We have also been blessed with our authors. During the various transformations of this project, they were almost unfailingly responsive and supportive. Thanks to Sarah Kyambi for so generously providing such a generous index.

Eve Darian-Smith
Peter Fitzpatrick

Laws of the Postcolonial: An Insistent Introduction

Peter Fitzpatrick and Eve Darian-Smith

Introducing Postcolonialism to Law

While postcolonialism may be the least attended "post," it is hardly a deserted one. Even as poststructuralism and postmodernism become paradoxically established, postcolonialism persists in its marginality and subversion.[1] Far from being diminished in this, postcolonialism would lay claim to a large and expansive range of reference, something abundantly attested to by the concerns of this collection. The diversity of these concerns appears irredeemable. They sweep over vast geographies and chronologies. They amply accommodate several imperial and religious systems. And all the while they maintain an intense engagement with many matters of current intellectual significance—with questions of alterity and identity, with community and globalism, with racism's now protean forms, and, in a way above all, with the centrality of law to all this.

Such seeming promiscuity of concerns lends point and drama to the cohering theme of this volume. It is by now close to a truism in the literature of postcolonialism, and elsewhere, that European or Western identity is constituted in opposition to an alterity that it has itself constructed. Identity is so formed in a defining exclusion of certain existent peoples accorded characteristics ostensibly opposed to that identity—savages and barbarians, or even those of the West less occidental than they should be. What is less remarked, and what initiates the defining moment of postcolonialism, is that the exclusion of these "others" is intrinsically antithetical to the West's arrogation of the universal to itself since this arrogation would require the inclusion within the West of those very others excluded in its constitution. The postcolonial—that is, the person subjected in this process—is thus torn between exclusion as something radically different to the West and the demand to join and become the same as it. In the result, the identity of the postcolonial is ever unresolved and fractured. Postcolonialism pivots to a considerable extent around this irresolute identity. In this present collection, however, there is a shift toward the counterpart of this postcolonial identity within the West itself.

For us, the gist of postcolonialism lies in this shift. It is the West that contrarily excludes and includes in the primal assertion of its own identity. The impelling irresolution is within a West that is excluding yet encompassing. In other words, this collection is always about an occidental "us," here and now, and then only in that perspective is it about "them" out there. The diversity of the collection then lends cogency to this occidental orientation of postcolonialism. Such uses of diversity are most obvious in indicating the pervasion of postcolonialism within the West. More pointedly, the revelation in the essays presented here of similarity in the very variety of postcolonialism's occidental involvement indicates that postcolonialism is integral to the West.

So postcolonialism, in our view, exists in an ambivalent belonging to the West. It speaks of the West and in a way comes from it. But postcolonialism is a disruption or fracturing of the West. It is not to be contained by the West. As such, it cannot be "part" of the West. It must speak from beyond a West that, in a sense, originates it. All of which does not involve our occupying some position secured apart from the West. We do not even remotely presume to stand in a place of "the other," to speak for "the subaltern."[2] Rather, we would say that postcolonialism does not lodge in any assured place. While we do assert that postcolonialism is a determinate position (we could hardly purport to have a collection about it otherwise), that position cannot exist in isolated fixity. To be, and to be secured, the position must be ever responsive to all that lies beyond it. Postcolonialism, then, and as Bhabha constantly puts it, is "in between" these two impossibilities of ultimate fixity and ultimate responsiveness.[3]

It is in this capacious in-between that we would also locate law. That location is illustrated and much elaborated in the collection, but for now we could lend it some familiarity through noting an ambivalence in the rule of law. Conventionally, the rule of law imports assured stability and ultimacy of determination. But for law to rule, it must also embrace the opposite attributes. Law must be ever responsive and indeterminate, capable of extending to the infinite variety that constantly confronts it. This opposition within law is reflected in the plangent irresolution of debates in jurisprudence, philosophy, and the social sciences over what law may be—debates that divide implacably between law's quality of autonomous determination and its supine dependence on forces to which it must relate and give way. We would argue, in part, that this irresolution itself is "the answer" (at last!) to the question of what law may be—or at least "law" as a rule of law confronted by what we could figuratively call the double demand of an occidental modernity: the demand for an assured position integrated with a responsiveness to all that is beyond a position. This is a demand that is now to be met without resort to erstwhile solutions of a transcendent kind. The ever incipient resolution of this modernity's double demand becomes law. "Here the impossible union / Of spheres of existence is actual."[4]

But in all this we also, of course, claim too much. Law is only one occupant, one purported resolution, of the fractured "in-between." We could get a little closer to its specificity by suggesting that, in law's dynamic, determination seeks to predominate over responsiveness. The opposite could be said, for instance, of poetry. But law is not alone in its inclination toward determination. Mapping is an example akin to law. So, there remains an imperative to delineate the specificity of law's occupation of the "space" in between. And it is in response to this imperative that the collection seeks to show how law comes to "be" precisely in that space. Here again we claim a virtue for the collection's diversity—in its wide-ranging instantiations of law's so coming to be, in its not relying on some anterior singularity such as the nation-state to lend law a spurious coherence. This collection is not, then, a quest for some "complete" accounting for law's specificity. It is a placing of law in and through the space in between.

The relative modesty of this project could also be aligned with postcolonialism in their both opposing modernist claims to sufficiency. Postcolonialism took much of its initial impetus in its rejection of colonialist and developmentalist appropriations of the universal. Its rejection of the unashamedly imperial is obvious enough. There was also a more difficult, if no less intense, rejection of those who opposed imperialism but still advanced agendas of revelation and liberation that subsumed "the native" in all-including explanations and inexorable teleologies of their own. Escape from the pall of one universalism could only be had by fleeing to the embrace of another.

To illustrate this in legal equivalence, postcolonialism would not only oppose those who perceived law as a great civilizing mode of colonization or as an instrument of development or of modernization. It would also have to oppose critics of these perceptions who would account for law and for those whom it oppresses in encompassing schematas such as those offered by neo-Marxism. Even when these extended to the affirmation of difference—to the seeming irreducibility of the colonized, the peasant, and such—these differences were always triggered and sustained by a containing imperative usually issuing from some straitened version of Western capitalism.[5] Self-evidently, postcolonialism will not deny all valency to such critical views.[6] It would, however, deny their claims to completeness and finality.

Introducing Law to Postcolonialism

We cannot take this spotting of legal equivalence very far into the range of postcolonialism itself. Engagements between law and postcolonialism have been infrequent if stunning.[7] The lack of engagement is both astonishing and understandable. "Astonishing" because postcolonialism is now the main mode in which the West's relation to its "other" is critically explored, and law has been to the forefront of that very relation. Yet the lack is also understandable because the engagement between law and postcolonialism would drastically disrupt legal academic renditions of the relation—disrupt not just the persistent orthodoxy of law and development, but also the newly settled consensus around two frequent concerns of this collection—legal globalization and international human-rights discourse. We will now take one of these ways of seeing law in a world and, in departing from it, bring postcolonialism to bear on a legal artifact. The orthodoxy of law and development, despite seemingly devastating onslaughts on it, is still wearily available for this purpose,[8] but the other two have now surpassed it in significance. Globalization would be a large fish to land, but it is also a slippery one in its theoretical adroitness. It could not be dealt with adequately and briefly. That leaves international human-rights discourse as the doubtless unsuspecting target, suffused as it still is in a certain primal virtue. Its relative immunity from criticism[9] may be due to international human rights only recently taking on a large practical significance as an instrument of occidental assertion. Even so, human rights were well positioned for this elevated destiny, having long since become, in Gong's cogent assessment, the "new" standard replacing civilization as the criterion for dividing and judging the world.[10] Perhaps, however, it is more a matter of human rights joining and enlivening the standard of civilization for this purpose, a role that has also been played by notions of development and modernization. There is a constant search for new legitimation here because, as we will now show, this is territory that cannot be securely settled.

We will take as exemplary of the genre Rhoda E. Howard's vigorous defense of international human rights against "cultural absolutism."[11] Her argument could be readily replicated in the literature, but the ostensible robustness of its delivery does facilitate summary. Howard, as is usual, presents human rights as a universal good implacably opposed to and by a relativism that she calls cultural absolutism. It is never exactly clear what these human rights may be. They are ideals, matters of principle, "transcendent ethical norms" not tied to palpable "practice" (317, 338). They can thus exist in a "universal" dimension. But they are also something quite different. They subsist factually in what it is to be human. They have some empirical location in their issuing from the West, even if they can now extend beyond it. They are associated integrally with individualism, liberalism, and, occasionally, social democracy. But neither these particular qualities nor the claim to be universal and transcendent and such is exclusive to human rights. Such rights, in Howard's account, are left in almost complete vacuity and given no specific and positive content. "Almost complete" because Howard provides a few examples of particular types of behavior, such as "polygynous marriage," which are said to have no relevance to human rights (337). The indefinite implication is that there are specific requirements relevant to human rights. But just what these may be is not revealed, even though this could, in one way, be readily done since provisions claiming to embody human rights obviously do exist. If specific examples are advanced, however, they particularly locate human rights and shatter the claim to universality. An actually existing human right is an embroiled entity. The politics and modes of its making, of its discursive justifications, of its application or nonapplication are all indistinguishable from what it "is." While we could hardly deny that the idea of human rights with its tremendous force assumes some position apart from its instantiations, the content and conditions attending that position are not averted to by Howard because leaving that position vacant is central to her scheme of things.

We could approach this vacuity through a conundrum involved when talking about human rights in general—a conundrum embedded in the summary so far of Howard's views. The assertion or the effective existence of human rights depends on their not being observed, and Howard's account brims with nonobservance, usually located in "third world" or "non-Western societies." But if human rights inhere, as they do for Howard, in being human—in behaving or aspiring as a human being—then those who do not behave in accordance with or aspire to human rights must not be human. Alternatively, if they are human, then the rights cannot be. So they have to be human and inhuman at the same time. The resulting irresolution, as we shall now see, both underpins and undermines human rights.

Intimations of some such difficulty surfacing in Howard's text are accompanied by strident affirmations that human rights are abstract and universal ideals and not connected to the exigency of "practice." But how may the ethereal, unconnected universal speak? How could it ever palpably present itself and remain abstract and universal? And even if it could speak to us, how could we, who can only come from within what is universal, ever hear it, ever stand apart from it and perceive it as universal? These are venerable insuperabilities attending the claim to the universal, but they are rendered poignant here because Howard contradictorily does and must claim that human rights are particularly located. The chosen location is the West.

We can now unravel how Howard bestows a paradoxically particular content on universal human rights by observing that cultural absolutism, far from being merely in chasmic opposition to the human universal, comes to its aid, becomes its necessary supplement, and makes its vacuous silence garrulous with meaning. And we could begin to show how this is done by observing the travesty role in which Howard casts Said's *Orientalism,* an apt invocation since this work informs many of the enquiries in the present collection.[12] Howard elliptically calls on Said to produce an Orient that instances cultural absolutism (327). This is appropriate enough. The Orient has long been presented in terms that Howard associates with cultural absolutism—presented as "unchanging," inert, and self-contained (327). But Said is saying much more. He sees the West constructing this Orient in an oppositional reference to itself. The West's meaning to itself comes through the West's "setting itself off from the Orient as a sort of surrogate and even underground self."[13] In a similar way, we will now argue, the identity of universal human rights comes from their being set against cultural absolutism. That identity is thus endowed negatively and vacuously. As a result, it is not tied to any positive ascription that would counter its claim to the universal.

As a general conception, universal human rights derived from the negation of a positive and excessive particularity. Cultural absolutism exalts an impossible particular, one, for Howard, completely contained within a culture-bound, closed, exclusionary, traditional, authoritarian, status-ridden, static, "pure and inviolable community" (325). Since "cultural absolutism is the antithesis of human rights" (325), one has only to read off a redemptive contrary to cultural absolutism in order to find out what human rights are. They are, for a start, "not culture-bound" (320). Indeed, they escape the trammels of culture altogether through their superceding cultural particularity—through their being "transcultural" or able to "transcend culture-boundedness" (321). In formative contrast to the inequalities of status in traditional societies and to their fixed ascription of roles, human rights are "held equally by every individual by virtue of his or her humanity" (315). Human rights are integral to liberalism, democracy, individualism, and progressive change, all of which happen to be typified by the West. In this, they are explicitly set against the static and pervasive dominance by community or the state in less happy climes. Above all, human rights are "supreme" and "fundamental" (318, 322), marking the place we all will or should come to. Cultural absolutism, in contrast, can only confer identity on societies in their distinct particularity. The most that can be hoped for such a scene is that these societies will "change" and come to conform more to the universal in human rights even while carrying the consolation that "many aspects of culture, such as kinship patterns, art or ritual, have nothing to do with human rights and can be safely preserved, even enhanced, when other rights-abusive practices are corrected" (332, 337). Contradiction now intrudes since these societies are now envisaged as changing but are supposed to be static. They are to move alacritously toward the universal, yet remain torpidly apart from it.

The story so far is that the idea of human rights is constituted in a negative reflection of qualities that it rejects or excludes, but these are not qualities that may be allowed to stay compliantly beyond some conclusively secured realm of human rights. If the idea of human rights results always from a negative rejection of certain qualities, then that rejection must be constantly or repeatedly sustained. For this to happen, the rejected qualities must be ever proximate to the human rights they serve to form. They must always affront and disturb human rights. Conveniently, in their heroic assertion, human rights sedulously provoke that which affronts and disturbs. This necessary proximity is utterly assured. Conceiving human rights does not involve the rejection of qualities that are simply "out there" and apart that then have to be brought into proximity. The rejected qualities themselves belong to human rights but are excluded in order to make a certain idea of human rights coherent and consistent. So, for Howard, human rights are universal but come from a particular place, the West (335). They are transcendent ideals not tied to practice, yet they are of the "real" and exist "in . . . practice" (335). Human rights exist in the aspiration of every individual member of humanity, yet concretely only "most people" want them (322). Human rights are intrinsically set against "the pure and inviolable community" formed in "the exclusion of outsiders," yet they themselves assert a "supreme" and "fundamental" commonality through such an exclusion (321–25). The list could go on.

We can confirm this contrapuntal dynamic forming the identity of human rights by showing how the identity dissolves when the dynamic fails. The last third of Howard's essay contains a radical departure from the argument we have so far engaged with. That argument set human rights "antithetically" against cultural absolutism. Howard sees this cultural absolutism as taking on especially alarming dimensions because of a now rampant "communitarianism." She so ardently espouses the liberalism and individualism typifying human rights because they counter cultural absolutism and communitarianism. But when Howard seeks to accommodate the standard criticism that "universal" human rights enshrine occidental values, she does recognize the vices of "unbridled individualism" in the West, and she does recognize that "liberalism in North America is overly individualistic" (333, 336). "Communitarian features" of society can then perform a meliorative function, and indeed "both in practice and in theory, we need to reconcile the communitarian and the individualist account of society" (332). This is all very well, but human rights took identity as individualistic because they opposed that which has now to be "reconciled" with individualism. In the soup of reconciliation it cannot be clear how much, if any, individualism will survive the admixture. There is nothing to stop individualism disappearing into communitarianism or to prevent their both forming something quite different to either. No matter what, the crucial identity of universal human rights as individualistic can blithely disappear. In sum, those offensive qualities rejected in the making of a coherent idea of universal human rights were and remain within human rights, and when these qualities are explicitly recognized as within, the idea dissolves.

This "return of the repressed" also comes about in another way that is more oblique but just as subversive. In constructing an idea of universal human rights, certain qualities were pitted against it—qualities intrinsically offensive, opposed, or "antithetical" to that idea. Once the universal is admitted into the equation, the opposition is ineluctable, since anything opposing the omnipresent universal can only be of another dimension and absolutely apart from it. But if the rejected qualities were absolutely apart, they could not relate or be proximate to universal human rights and serve to constitute them. Relation is essential. The universal, however, can relate only by bringing everything to itself. Anything ostensibly outside it must be already within it.

So, in Howard's plot, there now occurs a miraculous transformation. The excluded, who were at first in their traditional, static, status-bound state absolutely beyond the pale, are now touched by the universal and bidden to become the same as it. They can now "change," occupy some position on a continuum and eventually conform to universal human rights. After all, "Westerners" themselves were "primitives whose societies underwent centuries of social change" (328). How is such a stunning shift effected? Quite simply by taking those offensive qualities of the excluded that once objectively opposed human rights and changing them into subjective misperceptions of foolish Western observers, such as "romantic" anthropologists. People like this, but no longer Howard now, present the excluded as "unchanging," "pure, idealized," "holistic," and typified by a distinct and uniform "culture" (326–27). What Howard once described as traditional now becomes distanced in quotation marks as "traditional" (327). This shift allows her to say that it is the oppressively misguided observers who "impose" identity on the excluded and prevent their joining the universal dispensation of human rights (327, 329). The perverse anthropologist is not quite so potent as all this would suggest, however. Scenes are presented where Canute-like anthropologists attempted to hold back the tide of an inexorable Westernization (326, 329). There is always and everywhere "change" and "progress" toward universal human rights (332–35), toward a condition that is idealized, essentialized, absolutized, invariant, holistic—all those qualities excluded to constitute human rights in the first place.

We have now come full circle, and it is time to draw these postcolonial perceptions of human rights to a close. In abrupt summary, we can say that postcolonialism holds apart what the discourse of universal human rights would oppressively unite. To take one of Howard's duplexities, the problem postcolonialism has with human rights is not that they are universal ideals or that they have a particular practical purchase, or even that they contain both these qualities. The problem lies in these two things being made to correspond to each other. "Universal" human rights correspond to some particular practice somewhere. The obvious contradiction is resolved by making the location of that practice transcendently exemplary. The practice can then correspond to the universal ideal. And that practice, trailing clouds of its universal glory, is definitively situated in the West.

The constitution of the postcolonial "subject" follows inexorably from this conjunction of opposites.[14] Lying outside the particularized universality of the West, the postcolonial can only be absolutely beyond and completely antithetical to occidental virtue. Yet the West's universalized particularity would contrarily assert that the postcolonial must connect with and be the same as it. The irresolution, the very unachievability of occidental identity, along with the other offensive qualities incompatible with the West's self-constitution, are all cast onto savages and other postcolonials—something the collection amply instances.

The Contributions

Nowhere has occidental othering been better illustrated than in Colin Perrin's contribution, one that provides a theoretical impetus for much of the collection. Like all the essays in the initial section, "Postcolonialism in Theory," Perrin's engages with a specific legal artifact and derives his theoretical perspectives from that engagement. The artifact here is the United Nations Declaration on the Rights of Indigenous Peoples. The attaching of "international human rights" to the postcolonial throws up an ambivalence in the notion of indigenous peoples and thence in the Declaration itself—an ambivalence that Perrin unerringly traces to an unresolved occidental conception of modernity. In extending the work of Said and of Bhabha, he accounts for this ambivalence and limit by working through ideas of nation and the international. These ideas do not serve only as examples, they are integral to the Declaration itself and to Perrin's deconstruction of it.

The engagement with ambivalence is sustained in Fitzpatrick's essay, which traces a specific conjunction of "law and incommensurability" in the work of Diderot. This exercise highlights the formation of a civilized occidental law in its incommensurable difference to the ways of "savage" places. But that very incommensurability in its own terms proves to be inconceivable. In its very failure, it reveals the savagery that subsists within law. Law is thence revealed as the "impossible union" of savagery and civilization. The essay then moves on to situations of "savage" resistance that intimate this impossibility, this irresolution in law. They also indicate how this irresolution provides openings for resistance in and through law.

One reviewer of the manuscript described Paul Passavant's essay as "a gem." We could say that in its polished surface we see political theory uncovering the assumptions of that "free-speech discourse" which is enshrined in the Constitution of the United States. But in the essay's luminous depth there is more. By way of another debt to Said, this chapter shows how the "paradigm of free speech," associated with John Stuart Mill, becomes identified with the practices of the United States and is thence encapsulated as a universal right of freedom of speech. Both the practices and the "Millian paradigm" are produced in their difference to a backward and speechless non-West. Passavant ends by emphasizing the relevance of this analysis in the current international scene.

The roots of that relevance can be found in Antony Anghie's tracing "the colonial origins of international law" in a chapter that aptly begins the second part of the collection, dealing with "the persistence of the colonial." That most civilized and virtue-laden of artifacts, international law, is linked to its origin in one of its ancestor figures, the sixteenth-century Spanish jurist, Francisco de Vitoria. Anghie's account is never less than telling, but it is particularly so in Vitoria's being on the side supportive of "the Indian" in contemporary debates over how to treat the inhabitants of what is now called Central and South America. It was in an attempt to resolve the issues in debate that Vitoria developed central tenets of international law such as the doctrine of sovereignty. Almost needless to say, this was not done by way of elevation of the Indians but by constituting them in terms compatible with their subsequent treatment under colonial rule and international law.

A comparable shaping of the colonized is revealed in John Strawson's monumental conjoining of "Islamic law and English texts." A frequent criticism of Said's *Orientalism* is that, by showing how the Orient is occidentally constructed, he presents us with a West that is unshakable in its omnipotence.[15] There is a point to that criticism, but Strawson's rich history explicitly supports Said and reveals that there was indeed a hugely effective constructing power involved here. The reduction and shaping of Islamic law through the "English texts" not only fitted it to European perceptions and uses but also set the terms in which Islamic law is still commonly viewed.

A dimension of identity-formation underlying the situations so epochally plotted by Anghie and Strawson is brought to a pointed focus in Annelise Riles's enthralling case study of claims to land in what was then the British colony of Fiji. These were claims adjudicated in 1923 that involved the right of citizens of the United States who had been shipwrecked in Fiji to acquire land there. What seemed to be an intensely local, even remote issue assumed international dimensions in the involvement of the British and United States governments. Riles deftly shows how, as a matter of "perspective," the "international plane" came to be seen as above and containing a local and a "national" plane. But she also brings out the contingency of that international plane, and, in a disturbingly pertinent way, she indicates how it can readily inhabit the literature of postcolonialism itself.

The remaining two sections of the collection do relate the question of perspective to postcolonialism. Although both sections focus on a postcolonialism brought to bear on the West, the first concentrates on manifestations of the postcolonial outside of the West's customary ambit, while the other section identifies and explores manifestations of the postcolonial within that ambit. Of course, the remaining chapters are arranged in terms of that powerful conventional divide, not to affirm, but to problematize it.

Dianne Otto looks at the efforts within the United Nations of the

"Group of 77" third world states to change the international economic order and its accompanying international law. To account for the failure of these efforts, she creatively combines two seemingly distinct viewpoints—one derived from the agenda for decolonization that goes with the Charter of the United Nations and the other derived from the struggles of Indian nationalists for independence from the British. Otto works through this combination to show that the Group of 77, by relying on European systems of knowledge, denied the relevance of contrary postcolonial experience. Otto then brings another creative combination into play. By drawing on the Indian subaltern studies group, she links this type of failure with intimations of its resistant reversal.

A companionate reversal is then actually employed by Roshan de Silva in his portrayal of postcolonial themes within "the ontological schema of the 1972 Constitution of the Republic of Sri Lanka." Postcolonialism's theoretical themes come largely from the West, and de Silva intensely evokes them here. But what they do in this setting is to inform, rather than constitute, a postcolonial analytic acutely extracted from the Sinhalese Buddhist cosmology. Its self-creating claim to construct identity, as well as its failure to achieve this, produced a dynamic that ultimately explains the making and operation of key sections of the Sri Lankan constitution.

A no less striking shift is advocated by Jeannine Purdy through her questioning whether postcolonialism is doing any more than clothing or obscuring ancient oppressions. In doing this, she would add a distinct yet supportive voice to a line of recent criticism that sees postcolonialism as elevating cultural and ideational factors and thereby diminishing the perception of persistent colonial and neocolonial violence and economic exploitation.[16] Purdy then provides accounts of such violence and exploitation trenchant enough to ensure that her point is not forgotten. Quite apart from their sustaining her argument, these studies are significant in their own right.

In initiating the final section, "The Postcolonial Within" the West, Rolando Gaete takes us straight into the belly of the beast. There he finds a dyspeptic tension between two "gravitation centers," one putting human rights in a "transcultural" orientation, the other demanding that human rights take account of cultural relativism—a demand usually seen as issuing from the third world but that Gaete locates within a postcolonial "global village." Unlike that reduction of human rights to one "center" that we deconstructed earlier in this introduction, Gaete innovatively accepts the tension and from it extracts the alluring conception of an "alternative" human rights.

Alan Norrie then confronts a tension that assumes the same proportions. Formal, rational, and general law in the West has long been set against an informal, popular, and particular "justice" prototypically located in the third world. Intriguingly, the academic literature has failed to produce an agreed border between the two. Norrie imaginatively moves beyond the dichotomy by locating each side of it in its "particular" setting. Formal occidental legality can then be seen as historically specific and popular justice as law "differently formed" rather than informal. This step beyond the dichotomy then opens possibilities denied by it. For example, it becomes possible to challenge the idea that "informal," community-based justice denies individual rights.

Darian-Smith's closing chapter is an omnium-gatherum of postcolonial themes brought to bear on an occidental national and legal identity. The disruptive point of entry to the identity is the building of the channel tunnel between England and France. Closely observed English reactions to this dangerous intrusion reveal the divisions and instabilities in a national and legal identity often taken to be the epitome of self-containment and calm assurance. There is a suggestive similarity between what makes for the identity and what makes for its disruption. Trains, again closely observed, provide one instance. In their national and imperial histories, British trains symbolized an existential security. But now the train has become treacherous and semiforeign, broaching a previously inviolate island boundary and bringing within it a phantasmagoria of alterity.

In all, we hope that our "laws of the postcolonial" have not only introduced a new understanding to several significant legal artifacts but that these artifacts, so considered, reveal something of the law, the impelling nature, of postcolonialism itself.

NOTES

1. For a broad sampling of the literature on postcolonialism see Patrick Williams and Laura Chrisman, eds., *Colonial Discourse and Postcolonial Theory: A Reader* (New York: Columbia University Press, 1994): Padmini Mongia, ed., *Contemporary Postcolonial Theory: A Reader* (London: Arnold, 1996); and Ian Chambers and Lidia Curti, eds., *The Postcolonial Question* (London: Routledge, 1996). These collections as well as ours deal, of course, with postcolonialism as

an academic discipline. They cover the colonial situation and what came after it. They are not confined to what is temporally "post" the colonial.

2. See Gayatri Chakravorty Spivak, "Can the Subaltern Speak?" in *Marxism and the Interpretation of Culture,* ed. Cary Nelson and Lawrence Grossberg (Urbana: University of Illinois Press, 1988).

3. See, e.g., chapter 6 of Homi K. Bhabha, *The Location of Culture* (London: Routledge, 1994). To emphasize: what is in between is always unsettled and unresolved. There is not here a simple and settled combination of these impossibilities.

4. T. S. Eliot, "Dry Salvages," in the *Four Quartets,* in, for example, *Collected Poems, 1909–1962* (London: Faber, 1974), 213.

5. See Peter Fitzpatrick, "Law, Plurality, and Underdevelopment," in *Legality, Ideology, and the State,* ed. David Sugarman (London: Academic Press, 1983).

6. Postcolonialism will depend on these things not just for determinate elements in its position but also for the perception of all that would impinge on, challenge, and change its position.

7. See, e.g., Bernard Cohn, "The Command of Language and the Language of Command," in *Subaltern Studies IV: Writings on South Asian History and Society,* ed. Ranajit Guha (Delhi: Oxford University Press, 1985); and Ranajit Guha, "Chandra's Death, " in *Subaltern Studies V: Writings on South Asian History and Society,* ed. Guha (Delhi: Oxford University Press, 1987).

8. See Anthony Carty, ed., *Law and Development* (Aldershot: Dartmouth, 1992).

9. The unsurpassed critical engagement is Colin Perrin, "Breath from Nowhere: Justice and Community in the Event of Human Rights," Ph.D. diss., University of Kent at Canterbury, 1996.

10. G. W. Gong, *The Standard of "Civilization" in International Society* (Oxford: Clarendon Press, 1984), 18.

11. Rhoda E. Howard, "Cultural Absolutism and the Nostalgia for Community," *Human Rights Quarterly* 15 (1993): 315. Page numbers in the text refer to this work.

12. Edward Said, *Orientalism* (New York: Vintage, 1978).

13. Ibid., 3, 6.

14. See Bhabha, *The Location of Culture,* chap. 3.

15. He offered something of a corrective later by emphasizing that such constructions existed along with resistance by colonized peoples: Edward Said, *Culture and Imperialism* (London: Chatto and Windus, 1993). He does this, however, without pursuing its implications for his original constructionist claim.

16. For an influential instance see Aijaz Ahmad, *In Theory: Classes, Nations, Literatures* (London: Verso, 1992).

Part 1

Postcolonialism in Theory

Approaching Anxiety: The Insistence of the Postcolonial in the Declaration on the Rights of Indigenous Peoples

Colin Perrin

Keep watch over absent meaning.

Maurice Blanchot

The postcolonial may be understood, I shall argue, in terms of a certain excess; something like the excess of a modernity which persists rather than disappears in an onslaught of incredulity,[1] or that of a dead God whose presence rather than absence is assured by the announcement of that death, or perhaps of the "West" which, despite its deconstruction, somehow manages to elude its demise. This is, however, less a condition of inertia than, as Nancy has indicated, one of paralysis.[2] It is the paralysis of an anxiety felt in the effort to seize a word which refuses to come to mind and which, even more, that effort seems only to push farther away; where a decision simultaneously must but cannot be made, in the gaping extension of what ought to have been just a moment of indecision.[3] In these senses, the persistence of a present which, by rights, ought to have passed—an insistence of the past in the present—will be the concern of this paper.

These anxieties of ineffability and indecision will be explored in a reading of the United Nations Draft Declaration on the Rights of Indigenous Peoples.[4] They will, moreover, be elaborated in the context

An earlier version of this essay appeared in a Special Issue on Law and Postcolonialism, edited by Eve Darian-Smith and Peter Fitzpatrick in *Law and Critique* 6, no. 1 (1995). Reprinted by permission of Deborah Charles Publications.

of a recurrent movement in Homi Bhabha's articulations of the postcolonial.[5] In his psychoanalytically informed characterization of an ambivalent and disjunctive modernity, Bhabha strives to upset the certainties of self and other, of the West and the rest. He repeatedly evokes an anxiety in the assertion of identity and pursues its unsettling traces upon the narrative or referential distance which would secure the distinction between us and them. His concern is with a colonial otherness which can neither be established nor disestablished; "not the Colonialist Self or the Colonized Other but the disturbing distance in-between." As "quite literally, difficult to place,"[6] this otherness opens up the self, rather than closes it down. In the failure of distance and in the anxiety of proximity, coherence and consistency are undermined rather than underlined.

> man tethered to, *not* confronted by, his dark reflection, the shadow of colonized man that splits his presence, distorts his outline, breaches his boundaries . . . and divides the very time of his being.[7]

From this perspective, indeterminacy and insufficiency are prized open in order to dislodge the certainties of a colonial encounter between those with power and those without as well as its documentation as a violence characterized in the unilateral construction and exclusion of others. My intention here is to shift the emphasis away from the standard constructivist analyses which have provided the impetus for an apparently endless stream of similarly inspired accounts of Modernity, Law, the Nation, the West, and so on. This shift, educed in and against the familiarity of Said's *Orientalism* and Anderson's *Imagined Communities,* is elaborated throughout the essay in an approach to the Declaration on the Rights of Indigenous Peoples. This shift will, furthermore, be pursued in a way which implicates the certainties not only of selves and others, but of their consideration in critical thought.

In this respect, my focus is upon an anxious moment which nevertheless pervades the Declaration as it encounters the problem of "placing" indigenous peoples. The Declaration comes across itself as its own other in the difficult contiguity of indigenous peoples and the nation.[8] Article 5 of the Declaration states that,

> Every indigenous individual has the right to a nationality

and then in Article 9, "indigenous peoples and individuals" are ascribed

> the right to belong to an indigenous community or nation, in accordance with the traditions and customs of the nation concerned.

This reference to the nation as both indigenous, in the sense of first nations, and modern, in the sense of nation-states, (dis)locates indigenous peoples; as citizens of both an indigenous and a modern nation,[9] they occupy "two places at once."[10] It is in this splitting or doubling that the nation exhibits the trace of an anxiety, and it is upon this trace that the following discussion elaborates.

Here, my concern is less with an otherness which is excluded and more with an otherness which can never be. The postcolonial insists upon a difficult relationship, upon the excess of an ambivalent in-between. It insists upon the anxiety of an otherness which is both approached and approaching; which is too close as soon as it is close enough.

The Problem of Colonial Origins

Edward Said's *Orientalism* takes its methodological inspiration from Foucault's characterization of discourse.[11] Said documents a complicity between the production of knowledge about the Orient and its colonial deployment. As distinct and exotic, he argues, the Orient is an Occidental construction. Three criticisms of this account are most often repeated, and I shall argue that they all indicate a single but pervasive problem.

The first criticism concerns an equivocation in the ontological status of the Orient itself. Said defines Orientalism as the work done by Orientalists who teach, write, or research about "the Orient." Orientalism also concerns the making of a distinction between " 'the Orient' and (most of the time) 'the Occident.' " It is further characterized as "a corporate institution for dealing with the Orient itself."[12] Centrally, the problem is with Said's supposition in two of these definitions that something called "the Orient" provides a referent upon which Orientalism goes to work. In the other, however, the Orient appears, not as the referent for an Orientalist discourse, its raw material, but rather as its product. Said is equivocal, therefore, regarding an Orient which comes before or after discourse; as something distorted and misrepresented by it or, alternatively, as something produced by it.[13]

The second and third criticisms concern the status of "power" and "resistance" in Said's argument. Clifford suggests that "Said's work frequently relapses into the essentializing modes it attacks." Young adds that Said cannot separate himself from the "coercive structures he is describing" and, therefore, "finds himself repeating them." For Ahmad also, Said reinforces a silencing of the Orient to the extent that he examines "the history of Western textualities about the non-West quite in isolation from how these textualities might have been received, accepted, modified, challenged, over-thrown."[14] The problems outlined here are, however, not as distinct as they have been presented. Said's equivocations regarding the referential status of the Orient must be read along with an ambivalence toward both the power of Orientalist discourse and the possibility of "the Orient's" resistance.

Said wishes to present a rigorously Foucauldian account, whereby the Orient is wholly constructed by the Occident. Accordingly, power is attributed entirely to an Orientalist discourse, and there is no possibility of any reference to another Orient. The problem, however, is that Said's analysis is impossible given such a scenario. In some sense Orientalism must fail to construct the Orient, if only in order for Said himself to recognize it as a construction.

Foucault contends that discourse is "more" than a set of signs, and he locates this more not "anterior to discourse" and not "beyond discourse . . . [but] at the level of discourse itself." To the extent that discourses appear less as systems of reference and more "as practices which systematically form the objects of which they speak,"[15] discourse itself becomes a methodological confinement. Its utility is premised upon and limited by the forbidden reference to something outside itself. Conventionally, the constructivist appropriation of discourse responds with a familiar formula; the thing/other is constructed "in the interests" of the discourse/self. For Said, "European culture *gained* in strength and identity by setting itself off against the Orient."[16] Recourse to this "gain" or something similar has become a hallmark of constructivism. The theory is well known; the self is confirmed, reaffirmed, bolstered, or whatever, in its construction of the other and its difference.

From here, the criticisms of Said's account of Orientalism may be understood. Centrally, Said misses the ambivalent character of this "gain," and as he fails to identify it as a difficult moment within an Orientalist discourse, it splits his own; the reference to a gain is supposed to explain both the beginning and the end of Orientalism, its cause and its effect. This failure is unsurprising given Said's methodological preferences. Foucault never really accounts for the "more" of discourse,[17] and neither does Said. "At the level of discourse itself" Said's analysis is condemned to a circular reflection upon a situation which must, in some sense, already be established. In Foucault's terms, if the appearance of the object owes everything to discourse, then discourse itself must be specified before the object's appearance. Similarly, Said cannot account for the making of a distinction between the Occident and the Orient, as he must presuppose both an Occident which carries it out and, according to the reciprocity of the argument, an Orient before its own construction. The problems of power and resistance within Said's account thereby appear as direct manifestations of what he must presuppose, that "the imaginative examination of things Oriental was based more or less exclusively upon a sovereign Western consciousness out of whose unchallenged centrality an Oriental world emerged."[18]

In his claims to document not just the perpetuation of Orientalism, but its emergence, Said must, however, simultaneously avoid these presuppositions. He consequently offers the contrary description of a prediscursive absence of occidental selves and Oriental others: Orientalism *makes* a distinction; "the Orient is not an inert fact of nature. It is not merely *there*, just as the Occident itself is not just *there* either."[19]

Said's failure both to address and to avoid the indeterminacy of an Orientalist origin ensures its return as an equivocation throughout his analysis.[20] He both must and must not refer to an Orient outside of its construction. What Said overlooks, and what this equivocation indicates, is an ambivalence within Orientalism itself.[21] Both the construction and the constructivist account rely upon a closure of the problem of enunciation, of the undecidability of their origins. The latter is revealed, however, in the circular and repetitive character of the former. In Orientalism's assertions of an essential Orient and in Said's assertions of its construction, the power of Orientalism and the power that Said attributes to it appear similarly uncertain. In both cases, these assertions of closure betray the anxiety of an opening. Orientalism and Said's account of it "must owe nothing to the movement which makes [them] appear," although, necessarily, they "cannot operate without disclosing [themselves]."[22]

With this focus, the power which Foucault attributes to discourse becomes uncertain, as the recourse to a "gain" reveals an ambivalence in the constructivist procedure. Foucault's "more" of discourse must *also* be read as a "less" in an unsettling of the proposition that:

> In a quite *constant* way, Orientalism depends for its strategy on [a] flexible positional superiority, which puts the Westerner in a whole series of possible relationships with the Orient without *ever* losing him the upper hand.[23]

Rather, Orientalism betrays the desperate activity of a "Western consciousness" which may, more productively, be regarded as less concerned with the assertion of a constant superiority and more with the anxious attempt to conceal its fissility.

I want to pursue this shift of emphasis through two movements in the Declaration on the Rights of Indigenous Peoples: first, a movement "from construction to its failure" and second, a movement "from the other to the double." The shift, in both cases, hinges upon a certain anxiety.

From Construction to Its Failure

The Declaration itself does not contain a definition of indigenous people, although a previous United Nations study offers the following description, which the chairperson-rapporteur of the UN Working Group on Indigenous Populations suggests should be taken as a "working definition."[24]

> Indigenous communities, peoples and nations are those, which having a historical continuity with pre-invasion and pre-colonial societies that developed on their territories, consider themselves distinct from other sectors of the societies now prevailing in those territories or parts of them. They form, at present, non-dominant sectors of society and are determined to preserve, develop and transmit to future generations their ancestral territories, and their ethnic identity, as the basis for their continued existence as peoples.[25]

Here, "indigenousness" is considered distinct in the reference to "ancestral territories" and "ethnic identity," both of which are figured as indicative of a continuity, a bond of blood and soil, to a time and a place before colonization. There is much at stake in the preservation of this bond which, the author of the report stresses, "no-one should be permitted to destroy."[26]

The distinctive character of an indigenous relationship to the land is repeated everywhere. "'Mother Earth' is the core of their culture, the provider of everyday material needs and spiritual sustenance as well."[27] This relationship is "close," "historic," and "harmon[ious]." It is a "special relationship . . . basic to their existence as such and to all their beliefs, customs, traditions and culture," such that "the entire relationship between the spiritual life of indigenous peoples and Mother Earth . . . has a great many deep-seated implications."[28] Moreover, the Declaration itself assures indigenous peoples "the right to maintain and strengthen their distinctive spiritual and material relationship with the lands . . . [etc.] which they have traditionally owned or otherwise occupied or used."[29]

The purity and immediacy of this relationship is reproduced in the description of a distinctive indigenous ethnicity/culture. As "descendants of the original inhabitants of many lands," indigenous peoples exhibit a "distinct personality,"[30] one which is repeated throughout the Declaration. Indigenous peoples have "distinct political, economic, social and cultural characteristics" and "distinctive juridical customs, traditions, procedures and practices." They have "the right to maintain and develop their distinct identities," they are "distinct peoples," and so on.[31]

These assertions seem to offer the possibility of a focus upon the construction, exclusion, and exoticization of colonized or indigenous others[32] in which the declaration of their distinct character assigns indigenous peoples a "location" outside of modernity. The Declaration deploys a distinction analogous to that to which Said refers in order to clarify Orientalism, and, on this account, indigenous peoples are similarly essentialized. Such an approach is, however, inadequate. The Declaration cannot be regarded as simply complicit with the exclusion of indigenous peoples, and neither can it be considered according to a straightforward effort to include them. Indigenous peoples are "hard to place" simply here (inside) or there (outside), and it is the terms of inclusion and exclusion, in which indigenous peoples are approached colonially or critically, that are rendered difficult here.

The constructivist analysis fails to register, as Said himself does, the ambivalence which pertains to the *act* of "constructing" indigenous peoples and, correlatively, to the origins of the Declaration itself. According to Bhabha, what is missed is the enunciative moment of "construction," and, indeed, its centrality is indicated precisely to the extent that these assertions of the distinctive character of indigenous peoples are contained in a *declaration* of indigenous rights.[33]

This declarative aspect is analogous to the ambivalence which I have located in the "gain" that Said attaches to Orientalism. Insofar as there is the possibility of merely a declaration, an already established situation is described: indigenous peoples are distinct. Insofar as a declaration is necessary, however, in its enunciation, a somewhat different origin is implied; where the distinctiveness of indigenous peoples is not established at all. The indication, therefore, is of the undecidable status of a distinction which the Declaration fails both to conceal and resolve.

In the compulsive repetition of the distinctive qualities of indigenous peoples, of the mysterious and unknowable character of their bonds to blood and soil, the anxiety which pertains to this undecidability emerges. Against Said's detection of the settled violence which essentializes an Oriental stereotype and his description of a mutually beneficial intimacy between knowledge and power, my concern is with the less secure relationship between the failures of knowledge and the fragility of power. The stereotype must be understood as "a complex, ambivalent, contradictory mode of representation, as anxious as it is assertive." More precisely,

> the stereotype is a form of knowledge and identification that vacillates between what is always "in place," already known, and something that must be anxiously repeated.[34]

It is not simply the case that the assertion, as a statement of fact, indicates, to the extent that it is required, that what is asserted is false.[35] Rather, it is with its repetition that the failure to convince or to refer becomes apparent. In the assertion, enunciation, or declaration, in these very *acts,* what is said is, at the same time, undermined. It is in the ongoing demand for reassertion that a series of failed attempts to refer, to place the other or the object, reveals an anxiety.

In terms more general than those employed by Bhabha, Jean Baudrillard writes:

> When the real is no longer what it used to be . . . [t]here is a proliferation of myths of origin and signs of reality; of . . . objectivity and authenticity. There is an escalation of the true . . . a resurrection of the figurative where the object and substance have disappeared. And there is a panic stricken production of the real and the referential.[36]

The loss to which this panic responds and which it would "cover up" nevertheless provokes and is, therefore, revealed by it;[37] the referent no longer convinces, as it is invoked only in order to conceal its absence. For this reason, it must be constantly and obsessively repeated; it must be declared over and over again. In a panic response to the eternal return of their lack, the real and the true proliferate; what is always "in place," "already known," nevertheless needs to be repeatedly confirmed. "That in the malaise of anxiety we often try to shatter the vacant stillness with compulsive talk only proves the presence of the nothing."[38]

While the assertion of the stereotype and the production of the referent would seek to maintain the distance of their objects, the safety of a distinction between reality and its representation or between the self and its other, the anxious character of their enunciation betrays a more awkward and less certain predicament. The distinctiveness of indigenous peoples eludes the Declaration as its language fails to do justice to a distinctive bond to blood and soil: "Anxiety robs us of speech."[39] Consequently, the Declaration fails to locate indigenous peoples and the bond which defines them at a distance that would, on the constructivist account, secure the integrity of a modernity defined otherwise. In anxiety, "We can get no hold on things."[40] As such, indigenous peoples are not placed simply before or behind colonialism and modernity; this time is inimical to the writing of the Declaration; it is a "time immemorial" which is, therefore, not quite historical.[41]

In these respects, indigenous peoples appear to contest rather than confirm a progressive narrative of modernity. The undecidability of their place and time, the failure to establish and locate them at a determinate distance, reveals an "oppressive" anxiety,[42] one that "demonstrates the *proximity* not the loss of the object *qua* Real."[43] In Lacan's terms, this intrusion of the Real upsets the consistency of a reality in which the self and its discourse appear secure. For this reason, anxiety is an "altogether unsettling experience" in which "one feels ill at ease."[44] It signals the proximity of indigenous peoples not simply as a lack of modernity, but as a lack in modernity. It is the proximity of this lack which Heidegger evokes as the "presence" of the "nothing" and that, as the "appearance" of a certain absence of reality, provides the impetus for Baudrillard's referential panic.

From the Other to the Double

The assertion of the stereotype may, therefore, be read as the anxious response not to an other which strays too far, but to an other which comes too close.[45] In this proximity the status of the other, as determinately distinct from the self, becomes unclear. It is, moreover, this proximity which threatens to reveal the inconsistency of a self that, consequently, suffers the anxiety of a dissolution, a fracturing or a splitting.

For Bhabha "anxiety is the affective address of 'a world [which] reveals itself as caught up in the space between frames; a doubled frame or one that is split.'"[46] It is discernible in the ambivalence of the stereotype "between the frames" of an assertive distance and an anxious proximity, a difference and a likeness. It is discernible, I am suggesting, in a Declaration which seeks but fails to clarify the distinctiveness of indigenous peoples who remain "hard to place." It resides in the space between a lack of modernity and a lack in modernity; between the frames of the presence or absence of this distinctiveness and the distinction between modernity and indigenous peoples. In this original undecidability and in its return, "anxiety leaves us hanging."[47]

The ineffable character of indigenous bonds to blood and soil betrays, in the Declaration's failed attempts to clarify them, an indecision. As I have suggested, there is much at stake in the preservation of these bonds outside of the time and place of modernity. First: the confirmation of a modernity which would be defined against the contingency and particularity of indigenous peoples, of blood and soil. Second: the effacement of a modern colonial history which documents something other than the simple continuation of indigenous peoples and the continuity of their links to the land. These two possibilities are undermined, however, by the "insistence" of indigenous peoples understood according to, on the one hand, their continued self-recognition as indigenous peoples and, on the other, their claims to human rights. Indigenous peoples have been neither fully excluded nor fully included. In a sense, their indigenousness is sufficiently "present" for them to be able to claim rights, as well as sufficiently "absent" to make their claim to rights necessary.[48]

As such, the insistence of indigenous peoples and their insistence upon rights is, necessarily, the insistence of a problem for modernity and for the Declaration.[49] In this ambivalence, modernity is revealed as not, in a sense, modern at all. Modernity is considered here in its inclusiveness, in its claim to accommodate the plurality of cultures, differences, and so on. This accommodation is, however, possible only on the basis of the exclusion of the particularity and contingency to which a modern rationality and formality are opposed. In a double sense, therefore, the insistence of indigenous peoples reveals the insufficiency of modernity as it fails both to exclude and to accommodate them.

On the basis of this double relation, moreover, the emphatic consideration of indigenous peoples as distinct, rather than simply different, may be understood.[50] Theirs is, it seems, both an excess and a lack of difference; a distinctiveness which brings them too close to modernity as soon as they are close enough. An ambivalent relationship toward this excess-lack, the double impulse to include and exclude indigenous peoples, to place them here or there, becomes apparent in the encounter between indigenous peoples and the nation. In Lacan's terms, this encounter is for the nation an encounter with the Real; the point at which the nation confronts its own impossibility, the inherent limit which doubles/splits it. It refers to what Bhabha has named an "unhomely" moment.[51] Here, the proximity of indigenous peoples threatens to reveal that the lack of/in modernity attributed to them is, rather, (dis)located within the nation itself.

At this point, I repeat a movement which is itself repeated throughout Bhabha's texts: "not Self and Other but the 'otherness' of the Self."[52] This is the moment of a failed distance, where the narrative coherence of modernity is interrupted by the return of its undecidable origin; where modernity and the nation appear tethered to, rather than confronted by, an excess which cannot be consigned to the past. This is a further elaboration of the shift which I have pursued throughout, and it hinges upon the anxiety of a failed construction that is repeated, an inability to locate the other, thereby breaching the boundary, and distorting the outline, of the self. Most succinctly, the failure of this (external) boundary reveals it as an (internal) limit.[53]

Importantly, the origin is marked by a *lack* of clarity, and the anxiety of its return does not, indeed could not, threaten an already established consistency; rather, it threatens to reveal an inconsistency which is only precariously concealed. The proximity of indigenous peoples is anxious not because they threaten to upset some kind of already secure community with the insecurity carried by their previously excluded difference, but because they threaten to reveal the fact that this difference, which ought to have been excluded, never was. As such, their proximity "brings out" rather than "brings in" an undecidability with which the nation is already too familiar.

The Nation and Its Origins

It is precisely the nation's difficult relationship to the "excesses" of blood and soil which offers the location of this undecidability. The origin of the modern nation is figured in the dissolution of such ties and their replacement with its own rational forms of citizenship, of rights, and so on. What I want to suggest here is, once again, that things are not so clear. This origin and the awkward relationship between the nation and its blood and soil insist as a problem for the nation and for any approach to it.

Just as Said stumbles over the origins of Orientalism and its founding (in)distinction, so theorists of the nation encounter something similar. The issue is that of a cut or a distinction which remains problematic; one that, once made, must be immediately undone or, alternatively, one that can never be made and which must be repeatedly redone.

In his account of nations as imagined communities, Anderson rebukes Gellner for implying that "true communities exist which can be advantageously juxtaposed to nations." Gellner, Anderson argues, commits the fallacy of "assimilat[ing] 'invention' to 'fabrication' and 'falsity' rather than to 'imagining' and 'creation.'" Anderson's argument is premised upon a Foucauldian refusal to ascribe an a priori truth or falsity to nations: "Communities are to be distinguished, not by their falsity/genuineness, but by the style in which they are imagined."[54]

Anderson's argument is, however, closer to Gellner's than he would concede. In his assertion that "all communities larger than primordial villages of face-to-face contact (and perhaps even these) are imagined,"[55] Anderson introduces the possibility of an exception. Despite a refusal to endow "face-to-face" communities with the authenticity which Gellner bestows upon his "putative folk culture,"[56] Anderson's account depends upon their referential status. Without an already established referent for community, it is immediately unclear that what is being imagined is, in fact, a community at all. Anderson's invocation of a national style, for example, presupposes something to be styled or, slightly differently, something according to which the various national styles may be so characterized, as different manifestations of the same thing.[57] The reference to "primordial face-to-face" communities recalls the immediacy and purity characteristic of the representations of indigenous peoples in and around the Declaration. This immediacy can only be imagined in the national context, and it is in this imagination that Anderson locates the difference of the nation.[58]

With his addition of parentheses, however, Anderson equivocates. In a movement similar to that which I have examined in Said's analysis of Orientalism, Anderson also makes and unmakes a cut.[59] He makes it in order to specify the nation but unmakes it in order to avoid the essentialism which he identifies in Gellner's conceptualization. It is, furthermore, not the case that the nation can be defined simply against the primordialism of face-to-face communities. While the nation is distinguished as imagined, it is nevertheless imagined as a community. In this demand for continuity and discontinuity, the status of the distinction between the nation and face-to-face communities appears undecidable. This indecision, moreover, indicates the point at which Anderson is unable to extricate himself and his analysis from the problematic status of this distinction for the nation itself.

Claims to the nation's modernity and to the empty form of its imaginings are persistently interrupted by an apparently inevitable repetition: the "excessive" reference to blood and soil. The modern promise/threat of the infinitely accommodating nation is shadowed by the nationalist threat/promise of a congruence between ethnicity and the nation—the nation itself as pure and immanent community. The indeterminate status of the nation accords with that of the concept, as face-to-face communities and the primordial bond to blood and soil can neither be fully excluded from the nation nor fully included. As a lack of "nation-ness" and a lack within it, these bonds cannot be consigned to the past; they appear, rather awkwardly, before and beyond the nation, as both lacking and excessive.

The representation of indigenous peoples and their distinctiveness in these terms ensures that they are also located both in front of and behind the nation and its modernity. In this respect, they too offer a referential guarantee. Indigenous peoples are "the stewards of 99% of the world's genetic resources,"[60] they are "the keepers of human variety."[61] Similarly, they "exercise a vital stewardship over the Earth's resources and environment," they are "the keepers of nature."[62]

Necessarily, however, these links to blood and soil must be forgotten as well as remembered. The other side of this future promise resides, as I have indicated, in the insistence of blood and soil at the level of the nation itself. In this context, the difficulty is elicited by the claims of indigenous peoples to determine themselves. It is in the face of these claims that the nation's inability to exclude a relation to blood and soil is exposed. In the persistent and "excessive" repetition of these bonds, the nation remains insufficiently modern, and it remains, moreover, unable to accommodate the difference of indigenous peoples.

The proximity of indigenous peoples and their claims to self-determination do not threaten to introduce the immanence of a relation to blood and soil which would upset the consistent modernity of the nation. Rather, anxiety is induced insofar as this relation persists within the nation itself. As the nation contains the contrary imperatives, to be both modern and a community, it is not the case that the nation is simply insufficiently modern. The anxiety here indicates not "a lack of determination but rather the essential impossibility of determining."[63] Community is precisely what must be left behind, but what also cannot be, and, as such, the full realization of the nation would also be its dissolution. The "limit" of the modern nation must, therefore, be understood as unsurpassable; as a line which crosses the nation, redrawing itself every time it is crossed.[64]

The nation's anxiety is evident in the expression of a concern "that the use of the term 'peoples' would have implications under international law";[65] "that the draft declaration should recognize the right of indigenous people to self-determination but that that concept ha[s] to be made subordinate to the concept of unity and territorial integrity of States."[66] The anxiety evoked by indigenous claims to self-determination may be clarified precisely at this point: "Many States . . . are fearful of separatist tendencies that could lead to a national dis-integration." The encounter between indigenous peoples and the nation is "Real" in the exposure of a certain lack of unity and integrity, of a splitting within the nation already; this encounter is anxious as it reveals the precarious situation of the nation irremediably crossed with cultural difference.

With the proximity of indigenous peoples "the boundary that secures the cohesive limits of the Western nation . . . turn[s] into a contentious *internal* liminality."[67] The nation is not confronted with either a memory or its forgetting, but rather with the difficulty of Renan's obligation to forget.[68] "It is this forgetting . . . that constitutes the beginning of the nation's narrative."[69] It is a forgetting which the Declaration is obliged to perform in the attempt to restore a progressive narrative to modernity, to avoid the difficulty of a colonial origin and, moreover, its insistence in the present. As hard to place, indigenous peoples are ascribed two places.

> The liminality of the western nation is the shadow of its own finitude: the colonial space played out in the imaginative geography of the metropolitan space; the repetition or return of the margin of the postcolonial migrant to alienate the holism of history. The postcolonial space is now "supplementary" to the metropolitan centre; it stands in a subaltern, adjunct relation that doesn't aggrandize the *presence* of the west but redraws its frontiers in the menacing, agonistic boundary of cultural difference that never quite adds up, always less than one nation and double.[70]

It is the opening of a time and space in the "holism of history" and in the "presence of the west" which marks, in this context, the unsettling shift of emphasis that I have traced as a supplement to constructivism.

Here, indigenous peoples attest less to a formative and exclusionary violence of modernity and the nation, and more to its failure. They evoke the memory of "something that never ceases to be forgotten,"[71] and, as such, their insistence is, at the same time, an insistence of the postcolonial; the dislocated expression of a colonialism which can neither be remembered nor forgotten; the paralyzed and anxious persistence of an excess that cannot quite be consigned to the past.

NOTES

Thanks to Vikki Bell for her comments. Thanks to Peter Fitzpatrick for his comments and for all his encouragement and support. Thanks also to Michael Anderson for the suggestions and generosity out of which this paper originated.

1. J.-F. Lyotard, *The Postmodern Condition: A Report on Knowledge,* trans. G. Bennington and B. Massumi (Manchester: Manchester University Press, 1984), xxiv, 37. Despite the standard interpretation, it is not clear that for Lyotard this "incredulity" or "loss of credibility" entails the simple disappearance of metanarratives.

2. J.-L. Nancy, *The Birth to Presence* (Stanford: Stanford University Press, 1993), 50.

3. J. Derrida, in "Force of Law: The 'Mystical Foundation of Authority,'" in *Deconstruction and the Possibility of Justice,* ed. D. Cornell et al. (New York: Routledge, 1992), 20, 24, considers the impossibility and the imperative of an "anxiety-ridden moment of suspense" as an undecidability lodged "in every event of decision." Also compare M. Foucault, "The Anxiety of Judging," in *Foucault Live* (New York: Semiotext(e), 1989), 157–78.

4. The complete text of the Declaration is contained in the 1993 *Report of the Working Group on Indigenous Populations* (UN Doc. E/CN.4/Sub.2/1993/29). Further references will be to article numbers only. At the time of (re)writing, the final text (still) remains to be adopted by the higher organs of the United Nations, and it is possible that it may change. For a discussion of the legal issues as well as background to the working group and the drafting of the text, see the chapters on indigenous peoples in J. Crawford, ed., *The Rights of Peoples* (Oxford: Clarendon Press, 1989); P. Thornberry, *International Law and the Rights of Minorities* (Oxford: Clarendon Press, 1991); and H. Hannum, *Autonomy, Sovereignty, and Self-Determination: The Accommodation of Conflicting Rights* (Philadelphia: University of Pennsylvania Press, 1992).

5. Much of Bhabha's (earlier) work has been brought together in *The Location of Culture* (London: Routledge, 1994).

6. Ibid., 45, 62.

7. Ibid., 44. Compare Foucault's claim in *The Order of Things* (London: Routledge, 1970), 326, that modern "man" is endlessly pursued by his "double"; (his) thought discovering, "both in itself and outside itself . . . an unthought which it contains entirely, yet in which it is also caught."

8. It is only in this "final" draft of the Declaration that any mention of the nation has appeared.

9. See Article 32.

10. Bhabha, *The Location of Culture,* 62.

11. E. Said, *Orientalism* (London: Penguin, 1978), 3

12. Ibid., 2, 3.

13. Said responds to some of his critics in "Orientalism Reconsidered," in *Europe and Its Others,* ed. F. Barker et al. (Colchester: University of Essex Press,

1984), 14. He reaffirms here that "the line separating Occident from Orient . . . is less a fact of nature than it is a human production, which I have called imaginative geography." Said's argument that this distinction is "produced" is considered below. His reference to imaginative geography recalls Benedict Anderson's conceptualization of the nation in *Imagined Communities,* 2d ed. (London: Verso, 1991) as well as its problems: see my later discussion.

14. J. Clifford, *The Predicament of Culture* (Cambridge: Harvard University Press, 1988), 271; R. Young, *White Mythologies: Writing History and the West* (London: Routledge, 1990), 127; A. Ahmad, *In Theory: Classes, Nations, Literatures* (London: Verso, 1992), 172–73. Resistance provides the focus for Said's *Culture and Imperialism* (London: Chatto and Windus, 1993). He argues, "Never was it the case that the imperial encounter pitted an active Western intruder against a supine or inert non-Western native" (xii). The difficult engagement between this proposition and the argument of *Orientalism* is avoided, however, as Said adds that the more recent study is "not just a sequel of *Orientalism* but an attempt to do something else."

15. M. Foucault, *The Archaeology of Knowledge,* trans. A. M. Sheridan Smith (London: Tavistock, 1972), 48, 49.

16. Said, *Orientalism,* 3; emphasis added.

17. See, however, the discussion in H. Dreyfus and P. Rabinow, *Michel Foucault: Beyond Structuralism and Hermeneutics* (London: Harvester Wheatsheaf, 1982), 45–58, which considers this "more" in relation to speech act theory. See also n. 33.

18. Said, *Orientalism,* 8.

19. Ibid., 4.

20. Said's own reflections upon "origins" are contained in *Beginnings: Intention and Method* (New York: Basic Books, 1975). Said mentions the "interplay between the new and the customary without which . . . a beginning cannot really take place" (xiii), but he tends toward the "decidability" of this problem through its formulation as merely an issue of combination.

21. The ambivalence of Orientalism provides the basis for Bhabha's own critique of Said, in *The Location of Culture,* 71–73. On his account, however, it resides in the split between a discursive economy of, on the one hand, "manifest" knowledge, and, on the other, "latent" desire. Furthermore, the problem for Bhabha is not that Said fails to recognize this ambivalence but that he overlooks its implications by assimilating it to the unity of a discursive "intention."

22. C. Lefort, *The Political Forms of Modern Society* (Cambridge: Polity, 1986), 204, 212.

23. Said, *Orientalism,* 7; emphasis added.

24. UN, *Report of Working Group,* 15.

25. J. R. Martinez-Cobo, *Study of the Problem of Discrimination against Indigenous Populations* (UN Doc. E/CN.4/Sub.2/1983/21/Add.8 1983), 5.

26. Ibid., 67.

27. This quotation and those following (unless otherwise indicated) are taken from publicity materials surrounding United Nations' activities with

respect to indigenous peoples (UN Docs. DP1/1248–98045, DP1/1293–98051, DP1/1294–98054, 1993).

28. Martinez-Cobo, *Problem of Discrimination,* 26.

29. Article 25.

30. Martinez-Cobo, *Problem of Discrimination,* 13.

31. Articles 4, 33, 8, 7.

32. Indigenous peoples have been repeatedly approached from this perspective. See, for example, S. Diamond, *In Search of the Primitive: A Critique of Civilization* (New York: Transaction Books, 1974); and, classically, T. Todorov, *The Conquest of America: The Question of the Other* (New York: Harper and Row, 1984).

33. S. Žižek, in *Enjoy Your Symptom* (London: Routledge, 1992), 97, considers the specific character of "declarations" with reference to speech act theory. Declarations are unique as they seek to "bring . . . about a new state of things in the world . . . *by presenting . . . this state as already accomplished.*" Compare P. Bourdieu, in *Language and Symbolic Power,* ed. J. B. Thompson (Cambridge: Polity, 1991), 128: "The *performative* utterance, the political pre-vision, is in itself a pre-diction which aims to bring about what it utters."

34. Bhabha, *The Location of Culture,* 70, 66.

35. My concern is only with certain kinds of assertion. See the discussion in Dreyfus and Rabinow, *Michel Foucault,* as well as n. 33.

36. J. Baudrillard, *Simulations,* trans. Paul Foss, Paul Patton, and Philip Beitchman (New York: Semiotext(e), 1983), 12–13.

37. Compare Lefort, *Political Forms,* 211: "that which is sought but cannot be attained is . . . a certainty . . . a referent whose very loss lies at the origin."

38. M. Heidegger, "What Is Metaphysics?" in *Basic Writings,* ed. D. Farrell-Krell (London: Routledge, 1993), 101. My approach here is not particularly derived from Heidegger. I am only "culling" from his text in order to further my own argument.

39. Ibid.

40. Ibid.

41. In the standard distinction between oral and literate cultures, the place and time of indigenous peoples has often been opposed to that of "writing." Martinez-Cobo, *Problem of Discrimination,* 7 and 60, describes how the "myths and beliefs" of indigenous peoples are transmitted generationally in a language that is "more than a means of communication" but, it seems, less as well. As he recommends, "Efforts must be made to preserve authentic indigenous tradition, history and institutions by compiling written records." In this respect, the Declaration itself refers, in Article 29, to "oral traditions" and, in Article 14, to "writing systems." The immediacy and transparency attributed to the "face-to-face" encounter of the speech relation distinguishes the indigenous community from something more modern/literate. Instructively here, Anderson, *Imagined Communities,* chap. 2, traces the development of the nation in the rise of print capitalism. The celebrated discussion is J. Derrida, *Of Grammatology,* trans. G. C. Spivak (Baltimore: John Hopkins, 1976), esp. part 2.

42. Heidegger, "What Is Metaphysics?" 101.

43. S. Žižek, *For They Know Not What They Do: Enjoyment as a Political Factor* (London: Verso, 1991), 126 (original emphasis).

44. Heidegger, "What Is Metaphysics?" 101. This phrase is the translation of *unheimlich*—which has been rendered elsewhere as "the uncanny"—the strangely or disturbingly familiar.

45. Compare Baudrillard in *The Transparency of Evil,* trans. James Benedict (London: Verso, 1993), 113: "The double haunts the subject like a subtle death, but a death forever being conjured away."

46. Bhabha, *The Location of Culture,* 214, citing S. Weber, *Return to Freud: Jacques Lacan's Dislocation of Psychoanalysis* (Cambridge: Cambridge University Press, 1991), 161.

47. Heidegger, "What Is Metaphysics?" 101.

48. The indecision of whether to "include" or to "exclude" indigenous peoples also has a historical dimension. It was a rejection of the assimilationist character of the International Labour Organization's "Convention concerning the Protection and Integration of Indigenous and Other Tribal and Semi-Tribal Populations in Independent Countries" (No. 107), 1957, which led to the revised "Convention Concerning Indigenous and Tribal Peoples in Independent Countries" (No. 169), 1989. See H. Berman, "The International Labour Organization and Indigenous Peoples," *International Court of Justice Review* 41 (1988). The practice and policy of assimilation undermines the assumption of a straightforward indigenous continuity; however, the failure of assimilation also problematizes the assertion of its simple interruption.

49. This problem is evident in the term *indigenous,* where the precolonial reference only arises in the situation of a nonindigenous presence. The difficult status of an origin that is both colonial and precolonial appears in the working definition of indigenous peoples as it (also) suggests *both* an indigenous continuity and its colonial interruption.

50. In different terms, Bhabha, *The Location of Culture,* 34–36, makes the distinction between cultural diversity, as that which is accommodated within a relativist frame, and cultural difference, as that which problematizes it. Žižek, *For They Know Not,* chap. 1, elaborates more generally upon the latter as the exception to the universal. As distinct, indigenous peoples are rendered exceptional, in Žižek's terms, or different, in Bhabha's. In both cases, their "location" is a problem.

51. Bhabha, *The Location of Culture,* 9–18, as another version of *unheimlich.*

52. Ibid., 44. Again, more generally, see S. Žižek, "Appendix: Beyond Discourse Analysis," in E. Laclau, *New Reflections on the Revolution of Our Time* (London: Verso, 1990), 249–60.

53. Žižek, *For They Know Not,* 109–12.

54. Anderson, *Imagined Communities,* 6.

55. Ibid.

56. E. Gellner, *Nations and Nationalism* (Oxford: Blackwell, 1983), 57.

57. The existence of this essence provides the "frame" for Bhabha's notion of diversity—see n. 50.

58. See also n. 41.

59. This movement is also evident in Anthony Smith's account of the nation. In his *National Identity* (London: Penguin, 1991), 12–15, Smith makes a distinction between "civic" and "ethnic" nations, although problems arise for him in that his central argument concerns the location of the origins of the nation in ethnicity. Inevitably, Smith is compelled to equivocate over his founding distinctions. He goes on to suggest that "the nation is a multi-dimensional concept, an ideal type . . . which concrete examples imitate in varying degrees," and elsewhere, "the nation has come to blend two sets of dimensions, the one civic . . . the other ethnic"—necessarily, however, he cannot fully dispose of these two types/models, adding, "in various proportions in particular cases."

60. See UN documents cited in n. 27.

61. *Choices: The Human Development Magazine* (New York: UN Publications), June 1993, 16. The phrase comes from a definition produced by the Worldwatch Institute.

62. Ibid., 17.

63. Heidegger, "What Is Metaphysics?" 100–101.

64. M. Foucault, "A Preface to Transgression" in *Language, Counter-Memory, Practice,* trans. Donald Bouchard and Sherry Simon, ed. D. F. Bouchard (Oxford: Blackwell, 1977), 32.

65. UN, *Report of Working Group,* 19. These implications being, of course, a right to self-determination.

66. Ibid., 17. In a repetition of its "doubling" of the nation, the Declaration is equivocal on this point. In Article 3, indigenous peoples are ascribed "the right of self-determination, [b]y virtue of [which] they are able to freely determine their political status." Later, however, in Article 31, this right is circumscribed; acquiring "a specific form" in terms of "the right to autonomy or self-government in matters relating to their internal or local affairs."

67. Bhabha, *The Location of Culture,* 149.

68. E. Renan, "What Is a Nation?" (1882), in *Nation and Narration,* ed. H. Bhabha (London: Routledge, 1990), 8–22.

69. Bhabha, *The Location of Culture,* 318.

70. Ibid., 160.

71. In *Heidegger and "the jews,"* trans. Andreas Michel and Mark S. Roberts (Minneapolis: University of Minnesota Press, 1990), 3, this is J.-F. Lyotard's characterization of the "immemorial."

Passions Out of Place: Law, Incommensurability, and Resistance

Peter Fitzpatrick

Who has caused this dredded parting???
To be out on scatterd places.

Song of Papuan workers

"The peasants," concludes Rév, "do not talk in the courtrooms."[1] There is concentrated irony in the aphorism. Without more, it could be yet another affirmation of the peasants' marginality, of their continuing displacement by more potent forms of organization. The aphorism comes, however, at the end of a study of how in Hungary's recent history resistance substantially changed what was that country's state-operated political and economic system, and this even before 1989. The peasants surreptitiously invaded a fortress of modernity and made much of it their own. This reversal of the standard historicist relegation of the peasantry does not seem to have been brought about by giving the peasant a voice or by some explicit accommodation of divergent interests. The peasant remained mute and the state, and its courts, remained insensate.

Why should the perception of such potent resistance prove so elusive? And how can it elude in particular a tentacular modernist administration? Because, so this chapter argues, modernity itself depends on its asserted incommensurability with certain recalcitrant "others"—others that it cannot therefore adequately recognize, others that are a constant and felt threat to its coherent and exclusive self-creation. Mod-

An earlier version of this essay appeared in a Special Issue on Law and Postcolonialism, edited by Eve Darian-Smith and Peter Fitzpatrick in *Law and Critique* 6, no. 1 (1995). Reprinted by permission of Deborah Charles Publications.

ern law, the argument continues, putatively resolves that fraught and anxious condition.

In this chapter, incommensurability is put in perhaps its best light—in its eighteenth-century invention by Herder and Diderot, when it was to counter the arrogations of an "enlightened" Europe and to deny it, in particular, the inherent capacity to know and to settle the world. But even then the precedents were not propitious. The Spanish had used their incommensurability with the populations of the Americas to reason that the supposed absence of property relations enabled them to occupy the land. Indeed, incommensurability was to become not just a prime justification for Europe's colonial extraversion but also a foundation for the identity of the European as exemplary of modernity. All of which provides an extended prelude to the last part of the chapter, which looks to the resolute notion of resistance, and to transformative resistances in the once-colonized world, as a way of confirming the centrality of incommensurability in figuring a contingent modernity and its law.

Incommensurability

There is an insistent impossibility of relation, an incommensurable divide, between the peasant and the court. The Hunts provide an elaborate illustration in their study of a state court in a region of Mexico and its attitude to the Indian peasantry.[2] Indians from the region simply did not bring cases to the court. Some from outside the region had done so. Indians could also be brought before the court, charged with criminal offenses. The court recognized issues only in terms foreign to the Indians. There were, for example, criminal cases of elopement. For the Mestizo elite of the region, elopement was a serious matter, presumably because it would avoid significant settlements of property. It was punished by the court with prison sentences ranging from six months to six years and with heavy fines. In the Indian view, elopement deserved only passing admonition. As for those cases exceptionally brought by Indians from outside the region, these were classified in terms of the national legal system and treated with a resulting inaptness. An action brought against a witch who was hired to bring rain but failed to do so was treated as one of fraud, and the fine imposed was far too light by the standards of Indian society. An application to the court for protection from accusations of having practiced witchcraft, a matter of the utmost seriousness for a society of this kind, was treated irrelevantly as a case of libel. More is involved here than a little cultural mismanagement. If we consider attempts to subject Indians to the court, it begins to look more like a matter of completely different ways of life. There was, for example, a manifest and radical divide between the Indians and a commodified world. The proffering by Indians of corn rather than money to pay a fine was mocked by officials. Indians would set aside coming to court as a witness if there were important agricultural tasks to perform. And one judge complained about Indian modes of argument taking too much time to be accommodated in court proceedings. For the court, social relations had to fit within time, whereas for Indians, it would seem, time fits within social relations.[3]

To provide a setting for this great divide, I will mention and then expand on instances taken from Pagden's alluring exploration of incommensurability in his *European Encounters with the New World.*[4] The legal analytics of Las Casas in the sixteenth century provide an instance of what became the Occident's orientation toward commensurability.

> God has given no man neither living nor dead (and that only through His goodness and through no worth of my own) so much experience and understanding of the facts and the Law natural, divine and human, as I have of the things of these Indians.[5]

The site of deific origin may now be differently occupied, but the impelling inclusion of "the Indian" within an occidental knowledge and a Law intrinsic to the universal has not. The inclusion has, however, been attended with a certain ambivalence. Hayden White, in describing the modes of perception of "the European settlers in the New World," finds

> two opposed, and ultimately contradictory, ways of conceiving the relationships between the Europeans and the natives. On the one hand, the natives were conceived to be *continuous* with the humanity on which Europeans prided themselves; and it was this mode of relationship that underlay the policy of proselytization and conversion. On the other hand, the natives could be conceived as simply existing *contiguously* to the Europeans, as representing either an inferior breed of humanity or a superior breed, but in any case as being essentially different from the European breed.[6]

In the "particular" completeness of the universal emanating from Europe, beings newfound and different were of necessity assigned to another realm. Yet the universal was also universal and had to be held capable of extending to these beings.

This ambivalence was revealingly resolved for some in the figure of the monster. The monster is both utterly outside yet a deformation of, or a combination with, that which is within.[7] The extravagant fantasy of these inventions—of such as monopodes and hippopods, to go no further than the feet—should not distract us from the fact that this was fantasy as operative truth, or at least as an effort to assert one, and it lent coherence and constancy to a reality in confrontation with what was novel and strange. Hence, explorers laid great emphasis on having seen the monsters. They endowed a certain palpability on the monster as that point of separation from yet connection with a new world that, without such mediation, could confute their own. Greater familiarity with the people of new worlds, including the familiarity of slaveholding and colonization, did not dispel the element of strangeness and separation but, rather, led to their refinement and more emphatic assertion.[8] And this comprehension of "otherness" was still charged by that occidental fiat of encompassing universality that rendered or could render everything commensurable and containable in its terms.

It was the operative effects of that encompassing claim, especially in colonization, that provoked, so Pagden finds, an apostatic incommensurability in one reach of the Enlightenment and its Romantic aftermath. Herder is the most seemingly straightforward. He insisted on an "absolute incommensurability," on cultures "remain[ing] absolute within their own compounds": so "the European has no idea of the boiling passions and imagination which glow in the negro's breast; and the Hindu has no conception of the restless desires that chase the European from one end of the world to the other."[9] As this quotation readily reveals, matters cannot be quite so simple. To single out "the negro" for "boiling passions" can hardly be divorced from a more explicitly imperial idiom then emerging in Europe. Quite apart from invidious distinctions, to say that "the negro" has "boiling passions" and to say that "the Hindu" is incapable of conceiving something are both overweening attributions that contravene the principle of absolute incommensurability itself. This indicates some difficulty if not impossibility in formulating the principle. Being set against universal assertion, the principle must be itself culturally located, in which case it becomes an instance of one culture making a definitive pronouncement about all other cultures—something that, of course, contravenes the principle. Further, the principle simply does not allow us to know that we cannot know other cultures. And, what is particularly delicious, it does not allow us to know that people of other cultures do not know us. Hence, perhaps, the space left for apostles of the incommensurable to elevate the savage sage who knows us better than we know ourselves. I will now consider a renowned instance of this knowledge.

The failure of incommensurability is a productive one, as I now hope to show in a more extensive engagement with Pagden's other main proponent of the incommensurable, Diderot, especially Diderot of the *Supplément* to Bougainville's voyage.[10] Pagden brings to the fore the Diderot of an "ultimate incommensurability" heightened in the divide between French and Tahitian society (141–43). Yet, for all the impossibility of knowing another culture, Diderot was not at all inhibited in drawing on and embellishing Bougainville's account of Tahiti. What is more, for much of the work Diderot adopts a Tahitian perspective. All of which could simply illustrate Diderot's famed inconsistency. Or it could be that the Tahitian perspective, especially as embodied in Diderot's sage, is merely a literary device, a type of authorial projection much favored at the time, where the superior naïf sees through the follies and frustrations of French society. Adopting the Tahitian perspective doubtless instances all these things, but, in my argument, it imports more. I will now delineate what that more may be and, in so doing, attempt to show how incommensurability is integral rather than opposed to the imperial arrogation of other cultures.

The challenge posed by Diderot's *Supplément* to such an outcome is particularly acute. The *Supplément* is usually considered to be a strong statement of Diderot's passionate opposition to slavery and colonialism and their destructive effects on other cultures.[11] Furthermore, the work is commonly seen as an elevation of a primal, idyllic, and erotically charged Tahitian society to a position of superiority from which the artifice and the social and sexual constrictions of the French could be revealed and derided. In one way, that view of the work is manifestly accurate, but the form of the work may make us hesitate before accepting it. In most of the *Supplément* Diderot adopts his favorite form of the dialogue, and in the dialogue the elevation of Tahitian society is much hedged about and even contradicted. This reveals, in my argument, not so much simple inconsistency but lines of irresolution that characterize occidental identity.

The elevation of the Tahitian perspective is most profoundly confirmed in its being able to speak of and encompass French society. The superiority of the Tahitians derives not just from their fresh intelligence but also from the irresistible attraction of their ways, especially their sexual spontaneity.[12] The source of these strengths was the Tahitian identification with nature that Diderot sees variously as instinctual or as the law of nature and, in either case, as more authentic and more basic than the legal and religious codes of France.[13]

The *bon sauvage* of Diderot's text remains, however, very much a savage, exhibiting all the traits that Europeans had come to see as antithetical to their very own being. Admittedly, Diderot's account here is, unlike most, not crudely condemnatory. Much like a latter-day ethnography, he understands the natives, confidently discerning their motivations and finding excuses for them. So, the sexually permissive Tahitians can be almost grimly utilitarian in their relations with Bougainville's enraptured sailors and chaplain, seeking as they do to increase the quantity and quality of an existing population short of males and less intelligent than the French.[14] There are good reasons given for murder and cannibalism as well (144–45, 149–50). But it was the eroticism and exoticism that counted for Diderot's audience and not, somehow, the explanations. Diderot also attributed savage traits without meliorative explanation to the state of nature in its Tahitian and other manifestations. Such a state was lawless and typified by excessive punishment and a violence, especially against women, that would be prohibited in French law; it could be a depraved, miserable, and monotonous existence in which idleness was preferred over work (149, 172–73, 181–82, 184).

In this reduced and reducing gaze, the very qualities that "naturally" gave the Tahitians a surpassing position begin to look small and contained. The penetrating vision of the naïve outsider can be rendered as ignorance and as consistent with an inability "really" to know "us."[15] "We," on the other hand, readily encompass "them." The very address of the *Supplément* is to us. We see them seeing us. The French are more intelligent than the Tahitians and—with their force, ambition, and even their evil—they envelop a Tahiti that is but "a remote recess of our globe."[16] For Tahiti to be brought into the ambit of the Occident, for it to be quite overwhelmed by its contrary, it is enough for

Bougainville to have touched it and to have enacted there a ritual of appropriation—the erection of a plaque asserting "this land is ours," described by the ever-perspicacious Tahitian sage as "the title of our future slavery."[17]

Thus far we have an impasse. The noble savage stands outside of and encompasses an occidental civilization, securing a position from which its deficiencies can be made visible and denounced. Yet the noble savage remains tied to base traits and is readily encompassed by a superior occidental civilization. This may be an instance of what has so often been discovered in the *Supplément* and elsewhere in Diderot—his inconsistency, his lightness and playfulness, his lack of commitment to a position.[18] To complicate matters, however, we could observe that these are the defining characteristics of Diderot's most famous character, Rameau's nephew, and the responsible and consistent interrogator of the nephew is usually taken to be the voice of Diderot himself. I will explore the impasse of the savage as encompassing yet encompassed by looking at *Rameau's Nephew* in the light of Hegel's use of it in the *Phenomenology of Spirit*.[19]

Hegel used Rameau's chameleon-like nephew to exemplify "self-alienated spirit." He instances the following accomplishment:

> He sang thirty tunes on top of each other and all mixed up: Italian, French, tragic, comic, of all sorts and descriptions, sometimes in a bass voice going down to the infernal regions, and sometimes bursting himself in a falsetto voice he would split the heavens asunder, taking off the walk, deportment and gestures of the different singing parts: in turn raging, pacified, imperious, scornful.[20]

In one way the nephew is dazzlingly omnicompetent, but in another, ignored by Hegel, he is frantic and pathetic, promiscuously responsive to the manifold of roles in natural and social existence, in "the state of a non-subject to which nothing is alien."[21] Lacking any consistent orientation, Rameau's nephew was, as the Diderot character put it after another kaleidoscopic performance, "better versed in good music than in good conduct."[22] As an ultimate criterion, "good conduct" bespeaks, in Hegel's terms, a "noble consciousness"—one that conforms, sometimes selflessly or heroically, to an authority set outside of itself as if to a universal power; nobility is thus alien to its own "being-for-itself." It is the "ignoble consciousness," such as that of Rameau's nephew, which asserts a "being-for-itself," which is always antagonistic to external authority, and which always seeks to bring the universal power under its own control.[23] The ignoble consciousness is not committed to anything. It has no content in its-self. Yet for Hegel that consciousness is an advance in the progression of Spirit. The ignoble self may remain alienated, but it is now self-alienated and as such autonomous and self-aware, able to bring together in itself the whole diversity of influences on it.[24] But at this point, Rameau's nephew can hardly remain an apt model for Hegel. Even if in his performances the nephew would sometimes intertwine the diverse parts "so as to preserve the connecting links and unity of the whole," that integration could not extend beyond the performance in hand.[25] The frantic, protean entity that is Rameau's nephew, in being existentially responsive to all things, cannot for long be anything. His own self, if such can be posited, is the source of endless dissociation and instability. "Nothing," says Diderot, "is less like him than himself."[26]

To supplement Hegel, we may return to the impasse of the savage as encompassing and encompassed via Hayden White's revelatory essay, "The Noble Savage Theme as Fetish." For a rootless European bourgeoisie of the eighteenth century "the idea of the Noble Savage" served "not to dignify the native, but rather to undermine the idea of nobility itself."[27] In this process, emphasis was placed on both the essential difference between the savage and the European, exemplified by the bourgeoisie, and on the containment of the savage within that difference.[28] Nobility becomes thence associated with an order that is fixed, backward, and passing. But this cannot be the whole story. The bourgeoisie did not manifest a purely ignoble consciousness but aspired to the marks and consequences of nobility, especially an enduring social hierarchy. The noble savage served here as an encompassing, pure indicator of a general humanity that was "naturally" stratified—and Diderot's idyllic Tahiti was indeed conveniently stratified.[29] In other words, the European not only rejected but also extended to and identified with the savage, for, after all, and as varying ideas of progress in both the eighteenth and the nineteenth centuries revealed, the European was once a savage too. More on this later. The analysis can for now be extended through Diderot's combining the *mauvais sauvage* and the noble. In this way, we can accommodate the largest supposed inconsistency in the *Supplément,* that distinctive eighteenth-century division between the elevation of nature and the elevation of civilization, and its laws. The outcome is a Diderot who is a precursor of European modes of thought more typical of the nineteenth, not to say the twentieth, century.[30]

Nature and its "general law" are relentless: their dictates fuse universal prescription with "pure instinct," and nothing "above or below" can detract from them.[31] "Civil man" is thus tied inextricably to nature.[32] Thus far, Diderot would seem to oppose the more usual view of his time, which exalted a civil culture in opposition to a savage nature. The primordial savagery of Tahiti was an authentic and happy state to be contrasted favorably with the artificiality of a French society that should be reformed to make itself and its laws accord more with the promptings and passions of nature.[33]

The same nature, however, if it knows no vice knows no virtue either.[34] Some of its passionate expressions are fit only for their savage site and would not sit well with the necessary morality of civil man. As we have already seen from the *Supplément*, the savage life was in ways nasty and brutish; it was also short.[35] To take an alarming instance from *Rameau's Nephew* of the passions misplaced:

> If the little brute were left to himself and kept in his native ignorance, combining the undeveloped mind of a child in the cradle with the violent passions of a man of thirty, he would wring his father's neck and sleep with his mother.[36]

The *Supplément* contributes its own Freudian prefiguring. There is an irreconcilable conflict between *le code de la nature* and *le code civil*, between being "a man" and "a citizen."[37] For there to be civilization, the passions of a happy savagery have to be contained and put in place. Its discontents are necessary ones. We must, as Diderot so often asserts, submit ourselves to the laws: "the laws, the laws; there is the sole barrier that one can erect against the passions of men."[38] The laws themselves are, for Diderot, the outcome of savagery transmuted or "decomposed."[39] Positioned in this way, law could then provide the fulcrum point of civilization, reconciling in itself civilization's universal arrogation with an incommensurable savagery. Law, emerging from savagery, could know, absorb, and deracinate the savage impulses, rendering savage contents of blood and soil, violence and nobility as universal and exemplary, and setting them in enduring opposition to a savagery henceforth condemned to the local and base.[40] In this now insuperable divide, the civilized must ultimately cleave to law. It does not matter whether the laws are good or, more likely, bad, whether they accord with nature's code, or whether they cause unhappiness, for if the laws are not obeyed, there will be no *moeurs,* and that is a "worse condition of a society."[41] For the creator of Rameau's ignoble, anomic nephew, law was the ultimate guarantor and repository of the civil. Law was a continuing assertion or a reinvention of a nobility before which the nephew's infinite variety would be necessarily curtailed. As a "code," a noble artifact, the law was universal in its prescription and located outside the particular subject who must conform to it and deny "being-for-itself."

So, although savagery and civil society are incommensurable, that very incommensurability, that impossibility of relating, is what sets them in relation. Yet that same incommensurability ensures that the relation is never fully achievable. It is never resolved. In a seeming paradox, the incommensurable and the relation are integral to each other. There is a complication to be added. Pagden reminds us that "since the late nineteenth century another interpretation [of incommensurability] has emerged. This claims that we—the cultures of the West—do not merely respond to the inescapable presence of the 'other': we actually construct him or her."[42] The Occident creates the savage other as part of its own self-creation and self-presentation. But it also creates that other as incommensurable with itself. The savage is distinct yet inextricable from occidental identity as it negatively provides the content of that identity. Occidental civilization is thus not tied positively or nobly to any fixed determination outside of itself. It can be-for-itself, protean and ignoble. This labile, unsettled identity can endure only if its negative impetus endures and only if what the identity may be or may ever be at any time can be productively contravened by its savage origin. "Barbarians," in Cavafy's terms, have to be constantly at "the frontier" in order to provide "some sort of solution."[43] Civilization in modernity is always threatened civilization. It has incessantly, and progressively, to be fought for and secured against an always-resurgent contrary of its own making. Being-for-itself thus depends upon a savage self-transgression—a transgression that is intrinsic to, yet always more than, what is transgressed. Such a transgression can be anticipated in an indefinite way but never in anticipation known either comprehensively or fixedly. Inevitably, it is a realm of mystery and infinite invention.[44]

This dangerous incommensurability was itself fixed within its own opposite—within the universal, commensurable collection of humanity. Even the base savage could be located in conjunction with occidental humanity because "we" were all the same, but with some of us, for good or ill, there was a containing, conflicting overlay of civilization that was ultimately preserved against savagery by the laws. For Diderot an incommensurable savagery persisted in civilized society and in its individual members, and, conveniently for the purposes of mystery and invention, the civilized can no longer have knowledge of their own incommensurable "pre-civil state."[45] That state persists, it thus became possible to say, "subconsciously." The encompassing sweep and the dominance of civilization, as well as its utter difference from savagery, were reassuringly confirmed by the ease with which, again for good or ill, savage cultures were subverted by it. Thus Bougainville's visit brings about "the eclipse" of a Tahitian society left in heavy expectation of what is to come.[46] Such a society, constructed as the occident's contrary, can only give way on civilized "contact" or alternatively triumph, as it also does, over the artifices of civilization.

This process of constructing identity leaves occidental law in a characteristically ambivalent position. Modern law is formed, along with civil society, in negation and has no enduring and positive content. Understandably, then, it fits well into an ignoble world. Law is part of society, it changes when society changes, and so on. Or, in another idiom, for law to rule it must be ever responsive and capable of extending to any situation. Yet modern law is also, as we saw, the fastness of nobility. It is that on which civil society ultimately relies. The rule of law assures order and stability, and so on. As such, law is autonomous and has an ultimate and necessary content that is officially, or nobly, determined.

The savage, including such variants as the barbarian and the peasant, takes on the burden of this irresolution in terms made familiar through their necessary repetition.[47] As different and coming incommensurably from beyond the range of Western civilization and its civilizing law, the savage is unknowable and mysterious. But as commensurably within that civilization's encompassing perception, as its own simple progenitor, the savage is transparent. The savage as different and without is irredeemable, but when called to be the same and included within, the savage becomes redeemable. Western civilization and its law, as changing and progressing and developing, surpass a savagery afflicted by stasis, iron rule, and inflexible order—a savagery that can never be otherwise than what it is. Yet the determined stability and beneficent order of occidental civilization and liberal legality are continually set about by the chaos of savagery and its mere spontaneity. The savage is feckless, incapable of sustaining any project, the antithesis of that which continues or endures. The savage, then, is inherently dissociated, called to be the same, yet repelled as different, bound in an infinite transition that requires it perpetually to attain what is intrinsically denied to it.

There remains a further service for the obliging savage and other like relicts to perform. The savage, as we have just seen, takes on the contrary characters of occidental law. It is the savage that thence becomes the site of essential irresolution and serves to constitute civilized law as its resolved and resolving opposite. The savage can for itself neither articulate nor adhere to a cohering project. This tormented figure can only assume some integral identity in abject submission to a resolving exteriority, whether traditional or natural or supernatural. Occidental law, then, takes on its assured civilizing mission in a negative constitution set against such a savagery. This particular rejection of the savage as unable to resolve itself, like the other rejections just mentioned, is accompanied by the demand that the savage also be included within a universal humanity. "We" thus become commensurate with the savage. For this demand of the universally human, what we have in common with the savage cannot be our persisting savagery since that savagery is still being rejected. It remains the antithesis of that civility on which human community is based. The universally human utterly and incommensurably repels savagery away from itself. Mere animality can serve the same oppositional purpose, and has done so. For common humanity, there has to be an acceptant, positive ascription to the savage, and that ascription is nobility. The rejected, ignoble savage is also the savage to be emulated in its nobility. There is something naturally, enduringly noble in our civilization, laws, values, human rights, and so on. Even while we hail these as protean instruments of progressive advance, we affirm in them something discretely and persistently elevated and fine. And while we passionately attach ourselves to these things as coming contingently from our particular place, we also endow them with a calm and transcendent exemplarity. So, law is supposed to be "general" and detached. "Law is not commensurate to passion."[48] Yet law is also "an object of passionate attachment."[49] It is the combining of such an exalted and encompassing nobility with a situated, ignoble force that "allows . . . the stentorian voice of the state to subsume the humble peasant voices which speak here in sobs and whispers."[50]

Resisting Savagery

The plan from here on is to derive some support for this account of incommensurability by somewhat replicating, if inverting, it in familiar concerns with resistance and transgression. Incommensurability may be introduced to resistance through Foucault's "theoretically unelaborated" notion of the latter.[51] Foucault, at least the Foucault whose ontological obsession was power, is usually seen to accord such a complete and pervasive reach to it as to preclude the possibility of resistance.[52] Power leaves "no spaces of primal liberty."[53] To the extent that it survives contact with power, resistance has a subordinate "role of adversary, target, support or handle in power relations"; it "is never in a position of exteriority in relation to power."[54] Yet power for Foucault does not just encompass resistance but is also encompassed by it—to use the language from the analysis of incommensurability. There can be a "strategic codification of . . . points of resistance that makes a revolution possible" and something within power impels resistance, thus making possible "an insurrection of subjugated knowledges" and "anti-authority struggles."[55] That resistant something, at times accorded a seemingly natural actuality as "the pleb" or "the body," is "inscribed" in relations of power "as an irreducible opposite."[56] But this resistance, either persisting in its opposition to power or even encompassing it, seems also to be outflanked by power, since resistance itself is created by "relations of power as their limit, their underside, their counter-stroke." Yet resistance is not ultimately contained by power—it is not "inexorably frustrated through being the compatriot of power."[57] The story could be continued, and later will be, in terms of Foucault's concern with transgression.

This alternation, so the argument now runs, can be replicated and in a way resolved through the literature on colonial and postcolonial resistance and on transgression. The academic literature on such resistance intrinsically marginalizes it even while according it sympathetic recognition. This work posits, implicitly or explicitly, an anterior order—as power, society, or hegemony, for example—and locates resistance as that which stands outside of, and opposed to, this order.[58] Resistance then becomes secondary or interstitial. It is about coping, the consumption of that which comes from elsewhere, the ingenuity of the weak, small escapes, the potency of the quotidian, persistence despite.[59] So, all people can do to resist "globalized production," for example, is to assert "human agency" at a "local level" and consume in distinctive ways.[60] More specifically, in characterizing "forms of peasant resistance" as "everyday," Scott instances

> the *ordinary* weapons of relatively powerless groups: footdragging, dissimulation, false-compliance, pilfering, feigned ignorance, slander, arson, sabotage, and so forth. These Brechtian forms of class struggle have certain features in common. They require little or no co-ordination or planning; they often represent a form of individual self-help; and they typically avoid any direct symbolic confrontation with authority or with elite norms.[61]

Such resistance always exists in relation to and within something else. Even when given a distinct identity, it remains less than something always surpassing it, plotted on "our" historical trajectory—traditional and atavistic, inchoate and "pre-political, flaring forth episodically only to relapse in a sullen and torpid accommodation."[62] Resistant entities even came, in the ultimate indignity, to be seen as the creations of colonialism, part of its processes of production and rule. Take the facility with which the resistant peasant community fitted the political and economic modes of colonialism. The reputedly backward, small-scale, kin-based and inert peasant community, outside history and ancestrally oppressed, was itself an object of the colonial project. This "natural community" became an adjunct of the fragmentation and suppression of precolonial institutions of an enormous scale, organizational complexity, and purposiveness.[63]

This all-encompassing extraversion of the Occident can be countered in another, quite distinct literature in which resistance becomes transgression. Here the resistant force of savages and peasants is ostensibly appropriated and pitted against the very order that, as we have just seen, marginalizes and contains their resistances. Academic engagements with transgression of this kind are diverse. A surrealist ethnography and a surreal sociology make large contributions, as do literary criticism and psychoanalysis.[64] In the absence of the noble savage, or nobility in general, as a transcendent origin, the literature plunges into the alternative resort to an ignoble savagery. This savagery can provide a negative origin insomuch as identity can succumb to it and disintegrate and thus has to be continually maintained against it. In another variant, identity can be lost yet affirmed in the recourse through transgression to a primal, undifferentiated whole beyond mundane experience. Oceanic as it may sound, this strategy is impelled only by some ranges of human activity, the erotic and the violent performed with savage excess.[65] One must transgress in order to be redeemed, be lost to oneself in order to find oneself—hardly novel scenarios. These realms of the transgressive, "the space of a savage exteriority" (the phrase is Foucault's), encompass those entities that they endow with "limited being."[66] "No simple infraction can exhaust" transgression, which operates as a "spiral" always moving beyond any particular containment by limited being.[67] In the absence of a positively containing noble exteriority, transgression extends infinitely to all that may ever be, and through its plasticity the labile limits of "order" are set yet constantly adjusted. As this perverse normality of transgression indicates, it is held in a responsive relation to order or limited being. It is thus in a sense encompassed by and sustains them, like the contained resistance described earlier. This account of resistance, then, ends with an incommensurability similar to that extracted from Diderot. In their mutual encompassing, order and transgression cannot relate in any achieved or resolved way, but that ultimate impossibility of relating is what sets the relation between them. For all its radical separation of transgression and order, savagery and civilization, incommensurability subsists within this structuring, if not structure, of power.

The imperative still to see monsters thus remains intense. Fantastic as monsters may be, "we do not" or cannot, as Pagden reminds us, "fabricate . . . our counter-image out of nothing;" the very use of the other as a counterimage makes its actuality "a matter of real concern," and so it becomes "equipped with a dense and particular cultural identity.[68] In that immense and dire process of fabrication, occidental knowledge was extended to incorporate a savage that itself was mute and mysterious, unable to countermand the terms of its own making. Whether those upon whom savagery is thrust may speak and thus provide "another knowledge" or whether "dominant structures of representation" remain impermeable is a matter of fraught debate in postcolonial theory.[69] My argument in this chapter has come from in between these positions, and I will now, finally, use it to illustrate resistances observed from "remote recesses" in "dominant structures of representation."[70]

This is to seek something like another knowledge in its suppression—an exercise in which, to emulate Rushdie's large-nosed hero, we have to "sniff absences through walls."[71] The first example is a study of an unremarked revolution in Papua New Guinea when resistance to the system of indentured labor transformed not only the colonial labor relation but the entire legal system, rendering both in liberal terms.[72] Law, and, eventually, liberalism are things that, of course, can come only from the civilizing colonist. They are, furthermore, things intrinsically contrary to the colonized savages and their ways. Yet it was the resistances of the colonized and not imperial importation that initiated a liberal legal and economic order. This was done in part negatively through resistance against the authoritarian system of indentured labor. The resistance, through the cumulation of its "everyday" forms *and* through extensive organization, created conditions in which that system could no longer operate. Positively, resistance involved, against great odds, sustained and effective demands on colonial law for it to honor its attenuated promise of liberal legality. No part of this resistance, no trace of such "native" origins of liberal legality mark its postcolonial presence in Papua New Guinea.

Another no less "hidden history" is provided by colonial Sri Lanka.[73] Although often advanced as a model of quiescent colonialism, Sri Lanka was riddled with resistances to colonial rule. Here, as elsewhere, colonialists were incapable of seeing extensively organized resistances to a rule premised on the inability of an inadequate and fragmented populace to engage in such activity. Nowhere was this resistance more dramatic than in its effect on the colonial courts. These courts had little efficacy in their own terms, yet they were popular precisely because of this. In their very failure, the courts operated in conformity with indigenous expectations and designs. This outcome was achieved through litigants' skillfully adapting and subverting the courts' processes. There was, in short, something of a popular takeover—a takeover from within that hollowed out the substance of colonial law but that left it looking impeccably and occidentally civilized. Justice was seen to be done.

Conclusion

We could conclude by relating all this to the large and revelatory concern nowadays with the construction of occidental identity in exclusion. This construction involves that which is acceptable or within the identity being created in its difference to that which is unfit and excluded. Looked at in reverse, if the excluded were to reenter, as it were, then the identity would disintegrate. All of which, so the story continues, is a somewhat figurative way of discerning processes that remain internal to the identity. There is no "without" because the supposedly excluded is a fantastic projection of what is "within," although it is repressed there. This projection, however, has palpability, as we have observed. In ascribing what is excluded to the colonized, peasants, and other incommensurables, not only must their difference to what emerges within be fabricated and asserted but also their similarity to what is within must be denied. The resistances of the colonized, which have just been described, succeeded because they adroitly used organizational and juridical modes that were the putative preserve of the Occident. Such a sameness of what should be different locates a "remote recess" in a globalized occidental identity, from which it can be seen as partial and precarious.

NOTES

1. István Rév, "The Advantages of Being Atomized," *Dissent* 34, no. 3 (1987): 349.

2. Eva Hunt and Robert Hunt, "The Role of Courts in Rural Mexico," in *Peasants in the Modern World,* ed. Philip K. Bock (Albuquerque: University of New Mexico Press, 1969), 109–39. See also the important account of a case involving, and not involving, the Haida Indians in Peter Goodrich, *Languages of Law: From Logics of Memory to Nomadic Masks* (London: Weidenfeld and Nicolson, 1990), chap. 6.

3. This is hardly an unusual point: see, e.g., Anthony Giddens, *A Contemporary Critique of Historical Materialism,* vol. 1: *Power, Property, and the State* (London: Macmillan, 1981), 36, 131.

4. Anthony Pagden, *European Encounters with the New World* (New Haven: Yale University Press, 1993).

5. Ibid., 74.

6. Hayden White, *Tropics of Discourse: Essays in Cultural Criticism* (Baltimore: Johns Hopkins University Press, 1978), 193–94.

7. Peter Mason, *Deconstructing America: Representations of the Other* (London: Routledge, 1990), contains an abundance of examples: see, e.g., 78–79.

8. See, e.g., Immanuel Wallerstein, *Historical Capitalism* (London: Verso, 1983), 75–93. Far from simply countering a fantastic alterity, proximity becomes intrinsic to its operation, as we shall see.

9. Pagden, *European Encounters*, 174, 179, 183.

10. Ibid., chap. 5.

11. Ibid., 158–59.

12. Denis Diderot, *Supplément au Voyage de Bougainville, Pensées Philosophiques, Lettre sur les Aveugles* (Paris: Garnier Flammarion, 1972), 155, 176–77.

13. Ibid., 158–59, 178. For Montaigne the state of "men fresh from the hands of the gods" (borrowing from Seneca) "surpasses . . . the ideas and the very aspirations of philosophers": "Of Cannibals," in *Essays*, trans. J. M. Cohen (Harmondsworth: Penguin, 1958), 110.

14. Diderot, *Supplément*, 150, 175.

15. Pagden, *European Encounters*, 156.

16. Diderot, *Supplément*, 147, 175, 178. The savage was to become typically recessed by being set in a particular place, by being intrinsically attached to "the land," so much so (and this became a pervasive theme in the Pacific) that savage people would decline or "die out" if this connection were broken.

17. Ibid., 148.

18. L. Okon, *Nature et Civilisation dans le Supplément au voyage de Bougainville de Denis Diderot* (Frankfurt am Main: Peter Lang, 1980), 75. Such inconsistency was, however, characteristic of the genre. Montesquieu's infinitely perceptive Persians, for example, once fine and surpassing critics of the French, were eventually demoted in a murderous and erotic delirium: *Persian Letters* (Harmondsworth: Penguin, 1973), letter 145 onward—and for the explicit authorial motivation see 284–86.

19. Denis Diderot, *Rameau's Nephew and D'Alembert's Dream*, trans. Leonard Tancock (London: Penguin, 1966); G. W. F. Hegel, *Phenomenology of Spirit*, trans. A. V. Miller (Oxford: Clarendon Press, 1977). Here, as so often before, I am greatly indebted to Richard Norman for making his richly annotated Hegel library my own.

20. Diderot, *Rameau's Nephew*, 102. See Hegel, *Phenomenology of Spirit*, 317–18.

21. See Maire Jaanus, "'A Civilization of Hatred': The Other in the Imaginary," in *Reading Seminars I and II: Lacan's Return to Freud*, ed. Richard Felstein et al. (Albany: SUNY Press, 1996), 326.

22. Diderot, *Rameau's Nephew*, 96.

23. Hegel, *Phenomenology of Spirit*, 305–6, 321–23, 312.

24. Ibid., 317.

25. Diderot, *Rameau's Nephew*, 103.

26. Ibid., 34. Perhaps Wilde said it best in "The Critic as Artist" (where we may substitute "sincerity" for "nobility"—see Lionel Trilling, *Sincerity and Authenticity* [Cambridge: Harvard University Press, 1972], 26–47):

> The true critic . . . will realise himself in many forms, and by a thousand different ways, and will ever be curious of new sensations and fresh points of view.

And so there is a problem when the critic is enjoined to the sincere:

> A little sincerity is a dangerous thing, and a great deal of it is absolutely fatal. . . . What people call insincerity is simply a method by which we can multiply our personalities.

Complete Works of Oscar Wilde (London: Collins, 1966), 1048.

27. White, "The Noble Savage Theme as Fetish," in *Tropics of Discourse,* 191.

28. Ibid., 192.

29. Ibid., 172–74; Diderot, *Supplément,* 172–73.

30. The following analysis could be contrasted with Derrida's wonderful denaturing of Rousseau's "nature": Jacques Derrida, *Of Grammatology,* trans. Gayatri Chakravorty Spivak (Baltimore: Johns Hopkins University Press, 1976). Here I could be preserving more of nature and of the tension between it and writing/law than Derrida would allow. There may well be no "outside of the text" (ibid., 158) so that nature can only be nature in and of a text. But we cannot be contained "inside" the text, for we seem, naturally, able to move beyond and deconstruct it.

31. Diderot, *Supplément,* 148, 157–59.

32. See Pagden, *European Encounters,* 150.

33. Diderot, *Supplément,* 178, 185.

34. Ibid., 180.

35. Ibid., 184–85.

36. Diderot, *Rameau's Nephew,* 113.

37. Diderot, *Supplément,* 178.

38. Ibid., 186; and see Patrick Riley, *The General Will before Rousseau: The Transformation of the Divine into the Civic* (Princeton: Princeton University Press, 1986), 203.

39. Pagden, *European Encounters,* 150.

40. I have tried to show how occidental passions can be attached to or come out of a place and yet still be universal in Peter Fitzpatrick, "'We Know What It Is When You Do Not Ask Us': Nationalism as Racism," *in Nationalism, Racism, and the Rule of Law,* ed. Fitzpatrick (Aldershot: Dartmouth, 1995), 3–26.

41. Diderot, *Supplément,* 178, 184, 186. For a placing of Freud in this scenario see Peter Fitzpatrick, "'In the Exigency of His Longing': Freud's Discovery of Law and Fiction in *Totem and Taboo,*" *New Formations,* 32 (1997): 143.

42. Pagden, *European Encounters,* 183.

43. "Waiting for the Barbarians," in *The Poems of C. P. Cavafy,* trans. John Mavrogordato (London: Hogarth Press, 1951), 28–29.

44. Cf. Michel Foucault, "Preface to Transgression," in *Language, Counter-Memory, Practice,* trans. Donald F. Bouchard and Sherry Simon (Ithaca: Cornell University Press, 1977), 29–52.

45. Pagden, *European Encounters*, 150, 155.

46. Diderot, *Supplément*, 147, and the Conradian "stage direction" at 151.

47. The repetition is necessary because the supposed resolution never resolves, yet a fractured civilization and its legality must persist in their productive demand for resolution: cf. Homi Bhabha, *The Location of Culture* (London: Routledge, 1994) chap. 3.

48. Jaanus, "Civilization of Hatred," 346.

49. See Roger Cotterrell, "Law as Object of Attachment: From Durkheim to the Simpson Trials," Queen Mary and Westfield College, typescript.

50. Ranajit Guha, "Chandra's Death," in *Subaltern Studies V: Writings on South Asian History and Society*, ed. Guha (Delhi: Oxford University Press, 1987), 141.

51. The designation comes from Peter Dews, "Power and Subjectivity in Foucault," *New Left Review* 144 (1984): 72, 90. The question whether resistance can be theoretically elaborated could be seen as a pervasive one in Foucault's work: see Roy Boyne, *Foucault and Derrida: The Other Side of Reason* (London: Unwin Hymon, 1990), chap. 3. The point enters shortly in the setting of transgression.

52. E.g. Peter Dews, "The Nouvelle Philosophie and Foucault," *Economy and Society* 8, no. 2 (1979): 127. I do not directly confront the issue of how, with power being all-pervasive (including its constituting our very subjectivity), we can stand apart from it and recognize it as such.

53. Michel Foucault, *Power/Knowledge: Selected Interviews and Other Writings, 1972–1977*, trans. Colin Gordon, Leo Marshall, John Mepham, and Kate Soper (Brighton: Harvester Press, 1980), 142.

54. Michel Foucault, *The History of Sexuality*, vol. 1: *An Introduction*, trans. Robert Hurley (Harmondsworth: Penguin, 1981), 95.

55. Foucault, *Power/Knowledge*, 81; Foucault, "Afterword: The Subject and Power," in *Michel Foucault: Beyond Structuralism and Hermeneutics*, ed. Hubert L. Dreyfus and Paul Rabinow (London: Harvester Wheatsheaf, 1982).

56. Foucault, *The History of Sexuality*, 96.

57. Foucault, *Power/Knowledge*, 138, 142.

58. For a notable instance see Jean Comaroff, *Body of Power, Spirit of Resistance: The Culture and History of a South African People* (Chicago: University of Chicago Press, 1985), 10, 119.

59. An abundance of such vocabulary can be found in Michel de Certeau, *The Practice of Everyday Life*, trans. Steven Rendall (Berkeley and Los Angeles: University of California Press, 1984); and for perhaps the most cited application of such perspectives to the third world see J. C. Scott, *Weapons of the Weak: Everyday Forms of Peasant Resistance* (New Haven: Yale University Press, 1985).

60. Cf. Mike Featherstone, "Global Culture: An Introduction," in *Global Culture: Nationalism, Globalization, and Modernity*, ed. Featherstone (London: Sage, 1990), 10.

61. J. C. Scott, "Everyday Forms of Peasant Resistance," *Journal of Peasant Studies* 13, no. 2 (1986): 5, 6.

62. See Donald Crummey, "Introduction: 'The Great Beast,'" in *Banditry, Rebellion, and Social Protest in Africa,* ed. Crummey (London: James Currey, 1986), 1–29; Eric Hobsbawm, *Primitive Rebels: Studies in Archaic Forms of Social Movement in the 19th and 20th Centuries* (Manchester: Manchester University Press, 1959), 2; Scott, *Weapons of the Weak,* 35; Scott, "Everyday Forms," 6–7. Scott does deal with concerted action also.

63. Peter Fitzpatrick, "Custom as Imperialism," *in Law, Society, and National Identity,* ed. J. M. Abun-Nasr, U. Spellenberg, and U. Wanitzek (Hamburg: Helmut Buske Verlag, 1990).

64. For an irreverent and engaging survey see Marianna Torgovnick, *Gone Primitive: Savage Intellects, Modern Lives* (Chicago: University of Chicago Press, 1990). The insidiousness of the primitivism that she excoriates is confirmed in her ultimately identifying with it: see David Goldberg, *Racist Culture: Philosophy and the Politics of Meaning* (Oxford: Blackwell, 1993), 157–59.

65. As with Diderot, the laws can be characteristically inhibiting. Bataille arranged "a human sacrifice in Paris as a way of 'loosing the sacred' and paving the way for a revolution which would flood the streets of the city with blood." However, "the victim was to sign a presacrificial agreement absolving his murderers of legal responsibility. The legal considerations finally thwarted the plan"—presumably because such an agreement would not have been legally effective because of the "public policy" of the very order to be swept away in the sanguinary deluge: Torgovnick, *Gone Primitive,* 108.

66. Michel Foucault, *L'Ordre du Discours* (Paris: Gallimard, 1971), 37; Foucault, "Preface to Transgression," 34–35.

67. Foucault, "Preface to Transgression," 35.

68. Pagden, *European Encounters,* 184–85.

69. Benita Parry, "Problems in Current Theories of Colonial Discourse," *Oxford Literary Review* 9 (1987): 27, 45. In this piece Parry advocates recognition of "another knowledge"—very much a minority view. For a noted argument on the other side see Gayatri Spivak, "Can the Subaltern Speak?" in *Marxism and the Interpretation of Culture,* ed. Cary Nelson and Lawrence Grossberg (Urbana: University of Illinois Press, 1988).

70. "Remote recesses" here refers to Diderot's description of the incipiently enveloped Tahitians: see n. 16, and the accompanying text.

71. Salman Rushdie, *Midnight's Children* (London: Pan Books, 1982), 435.

72. Peter Fitzpatrick, "Transformations of Law and Labour in Papua New Guinea," in *Labour, Law, and Crime: An Historical Perspective,* ed. Francis Snyder and Douglas Hay (London: Tavistock, 1987).

73. See Peter Fitzpatrick, "Crime as Resistance: The Colonial Situation," *Howard Journal* 28, no. 4 (1989): 272, 275–76, analyzing, against the grain, John D. Rogers, *Crime, Justice, and Society in Colonial Sri Lanka* (London: Curzon Press, 1987).

A Moral Geography of Liberty: John Stuart Mill and American Free Speech Discourse

Paul A. Passavant

The American Constitution establishes rights on the authority of the sovereign of the national community—the American people whose will the Constitution represents. The Bill of Rights protects the liberties of Americans. Therefore, the practice of claiming constitutional rights, like freedom of speech, brings into play assumptions, counterassumptions, and struggles over the substance of the American people. These struggles help constitute the regulatory norms of this imagined community and the nature of its boundaries. If the background assumption of an *American* rights-bearing community is necessary to establish the possibility for protecting American constitutional rights in an international context in the first place, this assumption also establishes the limits of these rights in the boundaries that distinguish America from other possible peoples and places.

In this essay, I explore the American constitutional right of freedom of speech and press by way of the conventional construction of the time and space coordinates associated with the emergence of a right to free speech. The narrative that locates America as a place where one legitimately claims rights to free speech is the American appropriation of the "Millian paradigm," which refers to J. S. Mill's work on free

---

An earlier version of this essay appeared in a Special Issue on Law and Postcolonialism, edited by Eve Darian-Smith and Peter Fitzpatrick in *Social and Legal Studies* 5, no. 3 (1996). Reprinted by permission of Sage Publications.

speech. When Americans assert a right of free speech, they often inhabit this discourse to produce sensible claims. The Millian paradigm offers a frame of inclusion and exclusion for identifying a people for whom freedom of speech is appropriate and those for whom it is not. Mill's system of enabled and disenabled identities functions as a symbolic politics of speech to produce a "West" and the "Rest." This moral geography[1] structures the claims to free speech rights, and is, in turn, constituted by the process of invoking a right to free speech.

Mill and American Free Speech Protections

I define the Millian paradigm as a predominant, if not the dominant, discourse of freedom of speech in the United States. This discourse defines the system of speech to be a marketplace of competing ideas. Persons enter this system as reasoning subjects who, in exercising these capacities, distinguish good ideas from bad and make progress toward truth. The familiar statement "the best response to bad speech is more speech" is given its meaning by being situated within this discourse. It tells individualists that this clash and conflict helps to develop individual capacities. It tells absolutists why they should value freedom of speech as a right. For liberals who use the absolutist position as a pole to situate their understanding of speech rights, this paradigm becomes a principle that can stand above the fray of bias or politics in order to aid in the adjudication of controversies. In other words, this discourse provides a vocabulary that allows one to talk about issues involving freedom of speech, allows one to value it as a right, and constrains the sorts of utterances that can be made about this right. It creates a problematic.[2]

Mill's free speech scheme, however, is double-edged. The Millian paradigm emphasizes progress toward truth as the main purpose of free speech and places responsibility on the reasoning capacities of its subjects. On these grounds, speech that is unlikely to contribute toward truth, and persons unlikely to be able to push forward this progress, have no claim on speech rights. *Chaplinsky v. New Hampshire* (1942) trades on the Millian paradigm's exclusionary aspects. In this case, Justice Murphy argues that certain categories of speech may be excluded from First Amendment protection. These "utterances are no essential part of any exposition of ideas, and are of such slight social value as a step to truth that any benefit that may be derived from them is clearly outweighed by the social interest in order and morality."[3]

The First Amendment's importance has increased substantially since World War I—especially since the late 1930s with the establishment of the "preferred position" doctrine. This legal doctrine defines certain provisions of the Bill of Rights to be more fundamental than others. During the middle of the twentieth century, legal intellectuals defended and interpreted this doctrine. America was represented as the "land of liberty," and a few rights were seen as fundamental to this liberty—so fundamental that they occupied a "preferred position" in constitutional adjudication—with the First Amendment coming to be the predominant right within this small subset of fundamental rights. Thus American liberty became closely associated with the First Amendment, and specifically with freedom of speech. Footnote 4 of Justice Stone's opinion in *United States v. Carolene Products,* (304 U.S. 144 [1938]) is taken to be the constitutional origin of the preferred position doctrine.[4]

After World War II, many legal intellectuals made claims that America was a nation that particularly enjoyed and respected liberty, and that the First Amendment was fundamental to its greatness.[5] For instance, Robert McKay argued that it "is not too strong to say that without freedom of speech and thought, all other provisions in the Constitution would lack foundation and might well not survive."[6] The preferred position doctrine creates for McKay a "mood" that "recalls to mind the simple but majestic fact that here is a society in which the important freedoms count for something." For McKay, "freedom of speech and conscience" is something particular to the Euro-American population that has existed in America since its beginning—the First Amendment and *United States v. Carolene Products,* note 4, are merely landmarks along a constant evolution. This "preference for freedom" can be traced to England, and it "le[ads] unmistakably toward the first amendment" and Justice Stone's famous footnote. Therefore, the preferred position is just a recent codification of this essential preference for freedom, rather than its creation. Indeed, McKay argues that Justice Stone can claim credit for its "expression" but cannot claim "authorship" for the "idea that lies behind."[7] Thus, for McKay, "the first amendment has been accorded a preferred position in this larger sense at least since 1791." Freedom of speech is something integral to America, and America is defined as the embodiment of this principle. As such, America acts as a norm others may strive toward if they seek to practice freedom of speech, and as a standard to measure their efforts.

The work of McKay illustrates the way in which much of the intellectual production pertaining to the preferred position doctrine reflects Mill's "On Liberty," in that free speech is taken to be the foundation for all other liberties. Mill took the West in general, and England in particular, as the standard of liberty and "progress," while legal theorists like McKay do the same, only they insert America into the narrative as the nation with the special "preference for freedom."

When John Adams discusses "freedom of thinking, speaking and writing," which is opposed to power, or when Mill presents his argument about liberty by starting with "Liberty of Thought: from which it is impossible to separate the cognate liberty of speaking and writing," one can see how freedom of speech is organized around what Derrida has described as the metaphysics of presence.[8] This means that the self and its consciousness are made prior to social interactions, such as speech, as if something of the self's consciousness could elude social intercourse. Speech and writing, rather than being themselves constitutive of meaning, are presented as representatives of consciousness which, in applying its reason to brute data, is the creator of meaning. The proximity of one's voice to one's self allows one to convince oneself that one originates and controls the meaning of one's speech, according to this myth.[9]

In contrast to these "logocentric" models of the self, I take a genealogical approach that stresses the ways in which different social formations demand different identities or relations of the self.[10] On this understanding, the model of free speech organized around the metaphysics of presence becomes a rather transparent justification of a particular present produced by a particular social formation. It points to a determined result of this formation—the normative self and related self-consciousness—as its legitimizing foundational condition.

On the genealogist's account, different discursive formations produce different preconditions and commitments that constrain the direction inquiries may take through their regulation of the significant and the insignificant. What one recognizes as reasonable can only emerge in relation to preconditions and preexisting rules for distinguishing the meaningful from the meaningless. To privilege practices of speech that appear reasonable, make progress toward truth, or deepen intelligibility, therefore, is to privilege speech practices that further entrench this discursive formation. Speech that refused to play by the rules of this formation would not further any of the goals conceivable from within this formation, hence it could not be identified as "progressive." And speech that refused to recognize the grammar of this formation would be, by definition, insignificant.

For example, First Amendment jurisprudence has taken for granted an American self-inscription within the Millian paradigm that puts forth this nation as reflecting the historical progress of reason. Against this background, it has created the category of obscenity as being the opposite of reason or the intellect (*Paris Adult Theatre I v. Slaton,* 413 U.S. 49 [1973] [upholding state efforts to bar distribution of obscenity to consenting adults]), and as lacking *social* value (*Roth v. U.S.,* 352 U.S. 964 [1957]; *Miller v. California,* 413 U.S. 15 [1973] [cases defining obscenity standards]). Properly speaking, it is not *speech.*[11] Therefore, practices of nudity that society values, such as the ballet, fall within First Amendment protection, while those that society does not, such as "nude dancing," have been found to be open to regulation (*Barnes v. Glen Theatre,* 501 U.S. 560 [1991]). In this way we can understand one of the senses in which the recognition of "writing" has been determined by ethnocentrism.[12]

The genealogist rearranges the research problematic. Instead of pursuing a greater understanding of the Western practice of free speech and then hypothesizing the interventions necessary to impart this practice to the underdeveloped non-West, the genealogist pursues a different question. The genealogist investigates the array of subjectivities and regimes of knowledge constitutive of "Western modernity" and "non-Western stagnation" by using the dominant free speech discourse as both a reflection of, and a practice that has helped to produce, this particular world. If we understand the production of these identities, familiar discussions about "freedom of speech" appear in a new light. To this end, I turn my attention to Mill because his work on liberty of speech is still an important landmark that continues to orient debate about freedom of speech in America.

Mill's Multidimensional Moral Geography

In this section I probe Mill's use of speech-related terms such as *reading, literature, press,* and *discussion.* The use and meaning that he makes of these concepts are constituted in the context of a Eurocentric geography, a spatial imaginary that is created by the invocation of these loaded terms. This reciprocal relationship between the terminology and the geography creates an economy of meaning that is put into play the moment any particular aspect of it is invoked. Mill's frequent use of speech-related terms reflects his understandings about the West in general, and England in particular. In turn, his use of this terminology creates these identities by marking their borders. One might argue that Mill is concerned with stabilizing two entities, an "internal" frontier and an "external" border. This essay focuses on the external border and the seepage into the West's presence that it fails to prevent.

Though rarely acknowledged in an explicit way by the political or legal literature, this economy of meaning is reinvoked and structures the arguments Mill makes throughout "On Liberty." We can therefore understand "On Liberty" to be performing a map of liberty. It inscribes a moral geography of civilization and barbarism that describes and delimits who merits liberty. This distinction, as we shall discover through an investigation of Mill's other essays, is constituted through speech-related terminology like *discussion.* In turn, Mill's speech-related terms acquire their meaning only in the context of his Eurocentric moral geography.

Edward Said notes that an Orientalist politics requires a place to be identified as the "Orient." This process necessitates a large-scale intervention by Western social science that constitutes a certain "type" of being and articulates it to a specific geographic locale.[13] Thus, a form of culture creates a map organizing the world.[14] Analogous to Said's tracking of a form of knowledge that creates both a justified colonizer and a place to be colonized, I want to demonstrate that a right of freedom of speech as a distinguishing characteristic of the West (or England or America as representatives of the West) depends upon a mapping of places of speech, and of nonspeech, which creates the foundations for the valorized speech rights (foundations that will, in turn, justify a lack of speech rights elsewhere).

These issues are important for legal studies because law and social space are interwoven. Not only is law produced in specific spaces, but "those spaces, in turn, are partly constituted by legal norms. Either way, law cannot be detached from the particular places in which it acquires meaning and saliency."[15] To talk about law's determinacy, and therefore the stability of free speech practices and the First Amendment, is not only to make a claim about the stability of history (as

McKay and others do by describing free speech as essential to American identity over time), but also about the stability and naturalness of social space. To this end, I examine the temporal *and* spatial imaginaries that underwrite speech rights in the place of America as it takes itself to be the exemplar of Western civilization.

The Time and Place of Speech

Legal or political theorists who approach freedom of speech through the Millian paradigm, whether explicitly or implicitly, pay little attention to what Mill said about the non-West. Perhaps his remarks are considered unfortunate but irrelevant to the principles that he enunciates for the practice of liberty within the West. But Mill the imperialist and colonial administrator is linked to Mill the theorist of Western freedom. One of the points of intersection is what he had to say about speech-related phenomena.

In "Representative Government" Mill describes the age in which he lived as "days of discussion": "in these days of discussion, and generally awakened interest in improvement, what formerly was the work of centuries, often only requires years."[16] In "Civilization," his present is a "reading age."[17] In "The Spirit of the Age," Mill writes,

> The progress which we have made, is precisely that sort of progress which increase of discussion suffices to produce. . . . When all opinions are questioned, it is in time found out what are those that will not bear a close examination. Ancient doctrines are then put upon their proofs; and those which were originally errors, or have become so by change of circumstances, are thrown aside. Discussion does this. It is by discussion, also, that true opinions are discovered and diffused.[18]

Discussion and reading, for Mill, mark the boundary between one historical age and another and are a cause in this historical progression.

In summarizing Tocqueville's conclusions in a favorable review essay, Mill performs a series of substitutions that give substance to the "present" defined by reading, discussion, and literature. He first identifies the object of Tocqueville's books as "the modern world," which is then exchanged for "tendencies of a progressive civilization," which is then exchanged for "the nations of civilized Europe."[19] Thus, by the end of two pages, a temporal sequence also becomes a geographic and ethical one. To reinforce this exchange and displacement, Mill states that certain forms of particularly bad government belong to "past ages, and can no more exist out of the pale of Asiatic barbarism."[20] In this way he also associates the past with a geographic place which is also synonymous with a people, articulating time, place, and people. He replicates this relationship in "On Liberty" by associating non-Europeans with an age of nonmaturity. The identity Mill creates for non-Europeans justifies a refusal to engage with "different" peoples and cultures dialogically or as equals, and legitimates a practice of authority—the sort that a rational parent exercises over an irrational or prerational child—as opposed to the right of speech.

Mill's boundaries around "progressive civilization" are explained when he argues that China is a homogeneous and stationary community, while—giving a slight rebuke to Tocqueville for his use of the term "*law* of progress"—"the European family of nations is the only one which has ever shown any capability of spontaneous improvement, beyond a certain low level."[21] He then shifts from a geographical to a temporal and ethical boundary, emphasizing that to the "spirit of commerce and industry or to its consequences [i.e., "acquirements of the mind,"] we owe nearly all that *advantageously* distinguishes the present period from the middle ages."[22] Historical progress, as we can see here, is not just a brute fact, but a regulatory norm with ethical significance.

Mill uses the word *civilization* with some frequency, and he recognizes its instability as a category through his struggles to maintain civilization's connection with its object—Europe. Mill concedes that *civilization* sometimes refers to human improvement in general, but he appropriates a more narrow sense of the word. Specifically, civilization stands for "that kind of improvement only which distinguishes a wealthy and populous nation from savages or barbarians." Civilization, on this understanding, "is the direct converse or contrary of rudeness or barbarism," or the life of a savage tribe. In its narrow sense, it refers to the ontology of a place—Europe generally, and Great Britain in particular. "All these elements exist in modern Europe, and especially Great Britain, in a more eminent degree, and state of more rapid progression, than in any other place or time."[23]

Civilization is a precondition of Mill's defense, in "On Liberty," of freedom of speech. As such, it doubles as a useful definition of the present that he also describes as "days of discussion" or a "reading age." Spatially, it constitutes an exclusionary boundary in Mill's moral geography by inscribing the place of a "civilized community,"[24] and other places of rudeness and barbarians. Temporally, the discourse of "civilization" not only denies to non-Europeans the ethical standing of an interlocutor, but also begins to signify the otherness inescapably within the place of Europe.

Identifying the Civilized Self and Protecting Its Consciousness

Savages are not only outside of the capitalist economy, but they are the other of civilization because they also illustrate the opposite of the "powers and acquirements of the mind," and this helps explain why "rude nations, or semi-civilized and enslaved nations" have made such a poor showing in war against the civilized. "Discipline, that is, perfect cooperation, is an attribute of civilization."[25] This form of knowledge is the power that the savage lacks. "Look at the savage," Mill tells us, "he has bodily strength," but it is "only civilized beings who can combine." The problem of the savage is that his "impulses cannot bend to his calculations." The savage and the slave both lack the self-control necessary for discipline or cooperation. Their selves are not properly constituted.

If civilization distinguishes its self by its abilities of self-control, bending impulses to calculation, its power of knowledge or the mind, then these qualities are all understood as the inverse of the body (and the mind) of the savage. The civilized mind recognizes itself because it is not the body of the savage. Superior to the savage body is the self demanded by and trained to fit into farming, manufacturing, and commercial and military practices. Mill wonders what could teach a savage to cooperate? One answer is the division of labor in manufacturing, "the great school of co-operation."[26] If manufacturing produces the appropriately disciplined self, then these habits of discipline, he thinks, can be transferred to other areas where they may be needed.

Not only is the Western metaphysics of presence preserved along an external boundary through the control or military defeat, and thus the negation, of the savage body, but Mill also understands it to be threatened by the body that suffers or is in pain. In this case, mere spatial imaginaries fail Mill, and he must supplement their geography with a temporal axis in order to address the otherness within the place of Europe.

> There is another circumstance to which we may trace much of the good and of the bad qualities which distinguish our civilization from the rudeness of former times. One of the effects of civilization . . . is, that the spectacle, and even the very idea of pain, is kept more and more out of sight of those classes who enjoy in their fullness the benefits of civilization. . . . The state of perpetual personal conflict . . . from which it was hardly possible for any person, in whatever rank of society, to be exempt, necessarily habituated every one to the spectacle of harshness, rudeness, and violence, to the struggle of one indomitable will against another, and to the alternate suffering and infliction of pain. . . . [But now, a]ll those necessary portions of the business of society which oblige any person to be the immediate agent or ocular witness of the infliction of pain, are delegated by common consent to peculiar and narrow classes: to the judge, the soldier, the surgeon, the butcher, and the executioner.[27]

In this remarkable passage, we have the issue of the maintenance of the civilized or "refined classes." The metaphysics of presence, in addition to the self-present subject, can also imply certainty through proximity by referring to either the "fact" of "experience," or "seeing it" with one's "own eyes," so to speak, both of which imply direct and unmediated knowledge. In this passage, Mill describes a past age of "perpetual conflict." This is not an age of reason, but of its opposite—an age of force and its associated indecent body ("rudeness," "suffering," "pain") uncontrolled by middle-class norms of behavior. These things need to be kept at a distance in order to prevent the corruption of Europe's pure consciousness of reason associated with its civilized or refined body. This, as Mill explains in referring to violence, "is rather a thing *known of* than actually experienced" (emphasis added). This is a distant knowledge, for "even the very *idea* of pain" is kept from the most civilized classes. Mill thus protects the purity of the civilized self's consciousness.

Interestingly, Mill concedes that such violence cannot be confined to Europe's past, but this violence also occupies its present (though it is "almost at an end"). Therefore, in order to preserve its "present," which partakes of the metaphysics of presence rather than violence, a boundary must be created within Europe's present to guard its purity. The "judge, the soldier, the surgeon, the butcher, and the executioner" constitute an anomalous category to mediate between civilization and barbarism; to protect civilization from its own barbarity. They are the ones who are the "immediate agent[s] or ocular witness[es] of the infliction of pain," so that the practice does not "degrade" the "minds" of the community by intervening as a direct experience or even as an idea. The civilized community maintains its presence of mind by maintaining its distance, making violence and pain only something "known of."

Civilization, therefore, is constituted against both the savage of bodily strength but no self-control and the violence of Europe's past. In this way Mill makes doubly sure to maintain a strict boundary around the West's identity not only through geographic measures, but by denying cotemporality to its other through its association with the past. European identity, civilized and described by discussion and reading, permeated by literature, is thus predicated upon the absolute negation of the savage (an identity and negation, however, that is deferred through the reappearance of violence within the present of Europe). The Western body is amenable to discussion because it is civilized or disciplined, and the West's institutions produce selves amenable to discussion's benefits or pushing knowledge forward. This capacity of discussion, however, is integrally linked with its juxtaposition to the savage body. All of these dimensions of Mill's argument—geography, time, the Western mind and body—labor to give a basis to the West as fundamentally a place of discussion.

The Presence and Absence of Bodies of Speech

The contradiction between speech-related phenomena and barbarians or savages can be illustrated by Mill's statements with regard to India. For Mill, "publicity"—public scrutiny—is "ample power, and security enough for the liberty of the nation." For Mill, "publicity and discussion . . . are a natural accompaniment of any, even nominal, representation." The "triumph of democracy . . . [depends] upon the natural laws of the progress of wealth, upon the diffusion of reading, and the increase of the facilities of human intercourse."[28]

Of course, discussion and its concomitant publicity makes an assumption: "A certain amount of conscience, and of disinterested public spirit, may fairly be calculated on in the citizens of any community ripe for representative government."[29] Some people, however, may be "more or less unfit for liberty."

> A rude people . . . may be unable to practice the forbearances which it demands: their passions may be too violent, or their personal pride too exacting, to forgo private conflict. . . . In such a case, a civilized government, to be really advantageous to them, will require to be in a considerable degree despotic: to be one over which they do not themselves exercise control, and which imposes a great amount of forcible restraint upon their actions. (149)

For Mill, institutions need to relate to the "stage of advancement" of the people (173), and a "despotism" is necessary to "tame the savage" (175), because the "first lesson of civilization [is] that of obedience" (202). Therefore, "subjection to a foreign government . . . is often of the greatest advantage to a people, carrying them rapidly through several stages of progress, and clearing away the obstacles to improvement which might have lasted indefinitely if the subject population had been left unassisted to its native tendencies and chances" (207). The "mind" needs to "be disciplined into the habits required by civilized society" (174); otherwise the basis for discussion properly understood does not exist.

India, according to Mill, is a "peculiar country," and in certain respects, "totally different" from England, which, as we have learned, is a leading example of civility. What is "totally different" from civilization exists in a different place and time, justifying a refusal to engage with it dialogically on a basis of equality. Perhaps their empirical voices make noise, but they fail to achieve "speech" and therefore receive no authorization for a right of discussion. Thus, rather than engaging in dialogue with India, Mill states that India must be studied, and "the study of India must be as much a profession in itself as law or medicine." India must be studied and ruled, not engaged as a speaking subject. Mill asserts that "the great security for good government—public discussion—does not exist for India, as it exists for this country [i.e., England] and its other dependencies." Thus, "the public of India afford no assistance in their own government. They are not ripe for doing so by means of representative government." The dividing line between England and India, again, is also expressed in terms of civilization: "I do not think that India has yet attained such a degree of civilization and improvement as to be ripe for anything like a representative system."[30]

Some of England's other "dependencies" are not in the same position as that of India. For, as Mill argues, some dependencies "are composed of people of similar civilization to the ruling country; capable of, and ripe for, representative government: such as the British possessions in America and Australia. Others, like India, are still at a great distance from that state."[31] While this passage does much work toward the creation of India as a place, geography cannot totalize Mill's field of explanation of why India is not yet ripe for discussion or representative government; or rather, he needs to amend a strictly Eurocentric map, with a more differentiated one. The principal distinction, finally stated, is this: "It is now a fixed principle of the policy of Great Britain, professed in theory and faithfully adhered to in practice, that her colonies of European race, equally with the parent country, possess the fullest measure of internal self-government."[32] Thus, as he testifies before the House of Lords, in "Canada and Australia there are local representative bodies perfectly competent to exercise that antagonistic discussion, which seems to me an essential element of good government everywhere; but for India you cannot have any local body which shall produce that result." Therefore, the "only means of ensuring the necessary discussion and collision of opinions is provided within the governing body itself," that is, by those who have made India an object of knowledge and have "studied India as it were professionally."[33]

In this way, we can see how the capacity for discussion is grafted to the civilized, English body. Because the very concept of discussion is constitutive of Western identity and is created through the rejection of the savage body, discussion simply makes no sense in the East, unless carried out by the English (or other civilized people). Indeed, as Mill states forcefully in "On Liberty," discussion is meant to prevent England and the West from degenerating and becoming like the East. As Mill puts it, "We have a warning example in China."[34] One could also say that the speech practices of the English national body will be oriented toward maintaining its distinction from China as long as China, for instance, continues to be a warning example in this way.

The Moral Geography of "On Liberty"

The moral geography practiced by Mill in "On Liberty" is hardly marginal to his central concerns about speech-related phenomena and their fundamental relation to liberty in general. Rather, just as the boundary between the civilized West and the savage or barbarian is the condition of possibility for discussion, so his remarks to begin "On Liberty" which inscribe this map and its boundaries cannot be taken as peripheral to what he has to say in the rest of the essay. They must be understood as the very condition of possibility for his main argument.

In his "Introductory" to "On Liberty," Mill's main argument is that "the sole end for which mankind are warranted . . . in interfering with the liberty of action of any of their number is self-protection. That the only purpose for which power can be rightfully exercised over any member of a civilized community, against his will, is to prevent harm to others."[35] For the genealogist, of course, such a principle only defers the ultimate question, which now becomes: what identity formation and its privileged self ought to be protected? Mill responds to the genealogist's question with a crucial clarification. This clarification was already hinted at through his use of the qualification "civilized" to define the community to which his argument applies.

> It is, perhaps, hardly necessary to say that this doctrine is meant to apply only to human beings in the maturity of their faculties. We are not speaking of children, or of young persons below the age which the law may fix as that of manhood or womanhood. . . . *For the same reason, we may leave out of consideration those backward states of society in which the race itself may be considered as in its nonage. . . . Despotism is a legitimate mode of government in dealing with barbarians,* provided the end be their improvement. . . . *Liberty, as a principle, has no application to any state of things anterior to the time when mankind have become capable of being improved by free and equal discussion* . . . (a period long since reached in all nations with whom we need here concern ourselves).[36]

In this way, Mill has mapped the civilized community for whom liberty pertains onto Europe and England, which is then determined as a place through its juxtaposition to the East through the "warning example" provided by China.[37] It is also determined temporally and racially through the reference to other races as "backward." These backward states of society are mapped as regions where despotism is appropriate, thereby creating a multidimensional moral geography articulating people, place, and time. Rather than understand this moral geography as peripheral to the main concerns of "On Liberty," I have argued that a proper understanding of the conditions of possibility for "discussion" renders this map critical to the subject position that authorizes a particular voice to assume the protection of "freedom of speech." Furthermore, the reciprocal semiotic power of "discussion" acts as a marker of a specific identity formation. In this formation, "discussion" and other speech-related phenomena attempt to stabilize the "West" as especially self-present and its position as a measure of true accomplishment, and therefore of justified value rather than "accidental" force.

The Hinge between Mill's Orientalist and Domestic Politics

In "On Liberty," Mill states:

> The greater part of the world has, properly speaking, *no history*, because the despotism of Custom is complete. *This is the case over the whole East*. . . . Those nations must once have had originality; they did not start out of the ground populous, *lettered*, and versed in many of the arts of life; they made themselves all this, and were then the greatest and most powerful *nations* of the world. What are they now? *The subjects or dependents of tribes*. . . . A people, it appears, may be *progressive* for a certain length of time, and then stop: when does it stop? When it ceases to possess individuality.[38]

In this passage Mill once again argues that speech-related phenomena, this time "letters," are a sign of progress. He concedes that this was once part of the East's past, when these nations were "progressive." Writing about the present, however, "On Liberty" attempts to ensure the contemporary protection of discussion in the West as the means of maintaining its difference from the East. As we have seen in Mill's remarks to the House of Lords, India is unfit for discussion, and the only discussion that occurs there is through the English ruling body. I have already argued that discussion, which leads to progress, for Mill, marks the boundary between civilization and the savage or barbarian.

Here, Mill takes the next step by arguing that today the East has, properly speaking, no history.

Speech-related phenomena guarantee presence and access to reason. The West, defined by its association with discussion, indeed, constituted by it, has become the standard of historical progress, while the East, lacking discussion, is without history. Now, the West exemplifies history. Its confidence of this fact is guaranteed by discussion, just as there is certainty that the East lacks history because it lacks discussion. The only way, therefore, for the East to join history is under the auspices of the West—if it will ever become Westernized. This is a standard with miragelike qualities because there can be no "West" without an "East"; this is a development the East will never achieve. For such a development to be conceivable, however, it could only occur at the hands of the West.

Once again, Mill's honesty is disarming. Referring to the Chinese, he argues that "if they are to be farther improved, it must be by foreigners."[39] Similarly, good government in India is associated with English presence and is something England *gives to* the people of India and then *persuades* them that this has been done.[40] India has no moral agency in the matter due to its inscription within the East. Similarly, in Mill's "Non-Intervention," barbarians, that is, the peoples of the non-West, are excluded from the argument, but the problem is that this "fundamental distinction" between civilized nations and barbarians is not apprehended by those who "write in strains of indignant morality on the subject."[41]

According to Mill, to "suppose that the . . . same rules of international morality, can obtain between one civilized nation and another, and between civilized nations and barbarians, is a grave error." The reason for this fundamental difference relates to the difference in the presence of mind between the civilized and the barbarian.

> In the first place, the rules of ordinary international morality imply reciprocity. But barbarians will not reciprocate. They cannot be depended on for observing any rules. *Their minds are not capable of so great an effort, nor their will sufficiently under the influence of distant motives.* In the next place, nations which are still barbarous have not got beyond that period during which it is likely to be for their benefit that they should be conquered and held in subjection by foreigners. Independence and nationality, so essential to the due

> growth and development of a people further advanced in improvement, are generally impediments to theirs. The sacred duties which civilized nations owe to the independence and nationality of each other, are not binding towards those to whom nationality and independence are either a certain evil, or at best a questionable good.[42]

At root, the problem is this: just as in "On Liberty," where the East once was a collection of "nations," but degenerated to tribes or subjects or dependents of tribes, inter*national* morality cannot apply to barbarians who are not *nations,* because they have no rights as *nations.* Thus, Mill argues:

> To characterize any conduct whatever towards a barbarous people as a violation of the law of nations, only shows that he who so speaks has never considered the subject. A violation of great principles of morality it may easily be; but barbarians have no rights as a *nation,* except a right to such treatment as may, at the earliest possible period, fit them for becoming one.[43]

The treatment in question for barbarians, he tells us in "On Liberty" and "Representative Government," is "despotism."

What contributes to the conditions of modern nationalism, thus entry into community that can claim a right to international morality? Discussion. As he argues in "Representative Government":

> It is by political discussion that the manual labourer . . . is taught that remote causes and events which take place far off, have a sensible effect even on his personal interests; and it is from political discussion, and collective political action, that one whose daily occupations concentrate his interests in a small circle round himself, learns to feel for and with his fellow-citizens, and becomes consciously a member of a great community.[44]

In "Representative Government" Mill's treatment of the manual laborer, whose vote he takes great care to dilute if not exclude, becomes linked with his treatment of the barbarian through the importance that he gives to discussion, with each narrative informing the other. The barbarian could not be part of international morality because the barbarian lacks speech-related phenomena to guarantee presence of mind. This is signified by an inability to allow the will to be guided by "distant motives," suggesting that the savage is ruled by immediate appetites—functions of an uncontrolled body rather than the guidance of regulatory reason. In "Representative Government," the manual laborer will begin to perceive and understand "remote causes and events" through discussion. The manual laborer is thereby brought within the fold of national consciousness. The manual laborer is also being brought within the fold of history.[45] Both of these moves are linked with the normalizing effects of discussion, and both are denied barbarians. Just as Mill excludes from the vote those who cannot read, write, or do arithmetic—such persons could have no "real political opinion;" this is a suffrage accessible (and thus limited) to "all who are in the *normal* condition of a human being"—the barbarian is excluded as "not ripe" for representative government.[46] Discussion marks an ethical division, as illustrated by the barbarian's lack of a claim on international justice or self-government and the grant of moral standing through citizenship, with its associated voice and vote, to the English manual laborer. We might also note that discussion becomes a distributive and regulatory process through Mill's scheme for weighting the vote according to increases in education.

Conclusion

Mill's very use of the term *discussion* is born out of the distinction between civilization and barbarism. Thus, I have treated Mill's use of this concept and other metaphors for speech-related phenomena as a hinge for joining his two sides—Mill the great theorist of Western liberty and Mill the Orientalist, imperialist, and colonial administrator. Mill answered the question "To whom do rights refer?" with an argument about civilization. This argument served as an important precondition—one that established the basis for a justified claim of right, and was itself mapped according to a multidimensional moral geography in which the "West" and the "Rest" were bounded according to racialized axes. Thus, Mill's Orientalist politics, rather than being an issue of peripheral importance for his arguments pertaining to liberty in the West, in fact established the conditions of their possibility as a vehicle for defining the identity formation of the West and the preconditions for justified claims of right.

As a perceptive analyst, however, Mill recognized that practices he took to be symbolic of barbarism could not be kept at the distance his spatial imaginary strove to keep them. These practices existed in the place of Europe, and Mill attempted to protect Europe's presence of mind by limiting these practices to its past. But this, too, was unsuccessful. The final success of attempts to control and project outward such impurities in order to save a privileged identity must always be deferred, as it was for Mill. This is what Geoffrey Bennington means when he argues that the other always maintains a haunting presence.[47]

For Mill, the English working class achieved the ethical status of national citizens to the extent that they could be distinguished from barbarians. But insofar as they resembled barbarians in their lack of speech-related capital, they were either excluded from rights or their voices were reduced in value through Mill's weighted voting scheme. Any basis that is used to justify rights can be used in the next instant as the basis that is used to deny them.

Michael Shapiro has argued that conversations always occur within a "preconstituted meaning system"—a "protoconversation"—that provides a spatiotemporal location for the conversation; an economy of meaning for the said and the unsaid.[48] In light of these remarks, we can regard the Millian paradigm as a "protoconversation" that has been appropriated by Americans to inscribe the place of America within a universe of social possibilities. Locating America in this way as a precondition for specific conversations about free speech *(a)* enables the possibility of protecting free speech; *(b)* regulates its practice, including the subjectivity one must assume as a matter of practice; and *(c)* limits the recognition of potentially legitimate claims of right. At the same time, practices of speech help locate the place of America.

I would not claim that the narrative exemplified here by Mill has maintained a constant significance throughout America's history, though one can find many examples of its tendencies. The abolitionist Wendell Phillips pronounced the right to petition, a species of the First Amendment guarantees, to be "as firmly fixed in the soil of America as the Saxon race which brought it here." One hundred years later, Zechariah Chafee defended free speech rights as the "traditions of our race."[49]

The values of this moral geography inform the very process of creating American subjects who can produce socially valued speech, and whose speech is therefore protected under the Constitution. These values allow Chief Justice Burger to judge that penalties imposed by a high school upon a boy who gave a speech laden with "sexual metaphor" did not violate the First Amendment, for the purpose of the public school is to prepare pupils for "citizenship in the Republic" (*Bethel School District v. Fraser,* 106 S.Ct. 3159 [1986] at 3163). This process involves the inculcation of "fundamental values of habits and manners of civility" (3163). Thus, schools must teach by example the shared values of a civilized social order. . . . The schools, as instruments of the state, may determine that the essential lessons of civil, mature conduct cannot be conveyed in a school that tolerates lewd, indecent, or offensive speech and conduct such as that indulged in by this confused boy" (3164). Here, the narrative Burger draws upon to justify punishment of the boy is the same narrative that underwrote the colonial project. If we recall Mill's association of the savage with the lack of maturity that describes European children, as well as the history of associating excessive or deviant sexuality with the savage,[50] then it becomes apparent that the identity of an American national subject is constituted in a relation of difference from the savage. Thus, Burger describes the school as legitimately disciplining a student, rather than illegitimately violating speech rights.

Dissenting from Burger's opinion in *Paris Adult Theatre I v. Slaton* (1973), which happens to cite Mill's "On Liberty" in passing, Justice Douglas argues:

> When man was first in the jungle he took care of himself. When he entered a societal group, controls were necessarily imposed. But our society—unlike most in the world—presupposes that freedom and liberty are in a frame of reference that makes the individual, not government, the keeper of his tastes, beliefs, and ideas. That is the philosophy of the First Amendment, and it is the article of faith that sets us apart from most nations in the world. (413 U.S. 49, Douglas dissenting at 73)

In addition to Burger's use of the metaphor "civilized," or Douglas's geotemporal "frame of reference," many other discussions of free speech also use metaphors that refer to Mill's multidimensional geography and derive their meaning from it. Metaphors like "inert" (*Whitney v. California* [1927], [Brandeis concurring]), "traditionalist," and "underdeveloped" are used to inscribe non-Western peoples.[51] Correspondingly, references are made to the West as "rational," "progressive," "modern."[52] Together, they produce an image of "vigorous enlightenment . . . triumph[ing] over slothful ignorance" (Black, *Martin v. Struthers* [1943]). All of these metaphors impose temporal and normative dimensions on their geographic referents (and normative referents on their geotemporal dimensions).

Although some of the most important political thinkers in late-nineteenth- and early-twentieth-century America used a rights paradigm even more severely racialized than Mill's arguments about liberty,[53] such narratives became less significant to the extent that America located its identity in opposition to Soviet communism. More recently, however, with the waning of the Cold War mapping of geopolitical identities, Mill's global imaginary has become newly significant for understanding America's place in the world. Indeed, the foreign policy analyst Samuel Huntington's infamous *Foreign Affairs* article encourages readers to look at the world through the prism of, in his own words, "The West versus the Rest."[54]

This identity formation surfaces in recent thinking about freedom of speech. Judge Posner has found it persuasive to evoke images of the "Saudi" and "Islamic clergy" as negative points of reference to win American support for his conception of what is entailed by freedom of speech (*Miller v. Civil City of South Bend,* [1990] [Posner concurring]). The constitutional scholar Samuel Beer has defended American "government by discussion," which is defined as embodying the rational modern spirit as opposed to the particularist practices of Eastern, traditionalist societies.[55]

Finally, the polemicist Jonathan Rauch has evoked the moral geography I have used Mill to exemplify. Rauch uses this moral geography as the lens through which he views the American controversy over hate speech codes and multicultural curricula. He describes the calls for these policies as the most far-reaching challenge to the "modern West" and Western liberal science since the days of the great battles between religion and science.[56] Rauch also associates the advocacy of these policies with the sort of fundamentalism that he finds exemplified in the death sentence Ayatollah Khomeini pronounced on Salman Rushdie (22 and passim). Thus this controversy over questions of knowledge, culture, and free speech has surfaced anxieties about the location of America and its boundaries—haunting anxieties that Rauch attempts to manage through the spatial and temporal controls provided by

Mill's moral geography. The year 1989 bears the weight of the crumbling of the Iron Curtain and the Rushdie affair. Rauch calls February 1989 a "defining moment" for *Western* intellectuals (20–21). And so perhaps it was.

NOTES

The author would like to thank Lisa Bower for her comments on an earlier version of this paper presented before the Law and Society Association, June 1995. The author would also like to thank Tina Mai Chen, Peter Fitzpatrick, Richard Merelman, Alan Norrie, Patrick Riley, and Michael Shapiro for their comments on earlier drafts of this essay. This essay is dedicated to the memory of Charles O. Passavant, a true intellectual.

1. Michael Shapiro, "Moral Geographies and the Ethics of Post-Sovereignty," *Public Culture* 6 (1994): 479–502.

2. Mill's position, that it is through the "collision of adverse opinions that the remainder of the truth has any chance of being supplied," has an echo in American First Amendment doctrine through Justice Holmes's dissent in *Abrams,* in which he states that "the best test of truth is the power of the thought to get itself accepted in the competition of the market" (*Abrams v. United States* 250 U.S. 616 [1919]). Another moment in the First Amendment canon that exemplifies the Millian paradigm is Justice Brandeis's famous concurring opinion in *Whitney v. California,* 274 U.S. 357 (1927).

3. *Chaplinsky v. New Hampshire,* 315 U.S. 568 (1942) (defining "fighting words" to be outside First Amendment protection). For a more recent use of Mill to lend a more principled constraint to First Amendment jurisprudence, emphasizing Mill's exclusive aspects, see R. George Wright, "A Rationale from J. S. Mill for the Free Speech Clause," *Supreme Court Review* 1985:149–78. Some important First Amendment cases have been more explicit about their reliance on Mill by citing him directly; cf. *New York Times v. Sullivan,* 376 U.S. 254 (1964) at nn. 13, 19. Various commentators on constitutional law also use Mill to grasp the Supreme Court's First Amendment case law; cf. Harry Kalven Jr., in *A Worthy Tradition,* ed. J. Kalven (New York: Harper and Row, 1988); Murray Dry, "Free Speech in Political Philosophy and Its Relation to American Constitutional Law: A Consideration of Mill, Meiklejohn, and Plato," *Constitutional Commentary* 11 (1994): 81–100; Thomas Scanlon, "A Theory of Freedom of Expression," *Philosophy and Public Affairs* 1 (1972): 204–26.

4. Cf. C. Herman Pritchett, *The American Constitution,* 3d ed. (New York: McGraw Hill, 1977), 305–8 for a discussion in the context of the First Amendment.

5. The legal intellectuals who defended and defined the preferred position doctrine were preceded by the trailblazing efforts of Zechariah Chafee, who theorized and, according to David Rabban, essentially *created* modern free speech constitutional protections through creative reinterpretations of restric-

tive precedents. Chafee directly cited Mill as the justification for constitutional protection of free speech. See Zechariah Chafee Jr., *Free Speech in the United States* (Cambridge, MA: Harvard University Press, 1954), 30, 31, 138; David Rabban, "The Emergence of Modern First Amendment Doctrine," *University of Chicago Law Review* 50 (1983): 1207–1355.

6. Robert McKay, "The Preference for Freedom," *New York University Law Review* 34 (1959): 1188.

7. Ibid., 1185–88.

8. John Adams, "Dissertation on the Canon and the Feudal Law," in *The Works of John Adams*, ed. C. F. Adams (Boston: Little and Brown, 1851), 3:447–64; J. S. Mill, "On Liberty," in *Three Essays*, ed. R. Wollheim (New York: Oxford University Press, 1975), 28; Jacques Derrida, *Of Grammatology*, trans. Gayatri Chakravorty Spivak (Baltimore: Johns Hopkins University Press, 1976).

9. The logic of censorship is usually based upon this model of consciousness as well. Censorship makes sense if one is attempting to prevent consciousness or reason from becoming contaminated by some biasing force. For an example of this, see Herbert Marcuse, "Repressive Tolerance," in *A Critique of Pure Tolerance* (Boston: Beacon, 1970), 81–123, who explicitly embraces Mill's initiating assumptions but argues that in face of massifying effects and false consciousness, the assumption of the subject who can discern truth from falsehood by using reason no longer holds.

10. Cf. Michael Shapiro, *Reading the Postmodern Polity: Political Theory as Textual Practice* (Minneapolis: University of Minnesota Press, 1992).

11. Frederick Schauer, "Speech and 'Speech'—Obscenity and 'Obscenity': An Exercise in the Interpretation of Constitutional Language," *Georgetown Law Review* 67 (1979): 899–933.

12. Cf. Derrida, *Of Grammatology*. *Barnes v. Glen Theatre* 501 U.S. 560 (1991).

13. Edward Said, *Orientalism* (New York: Vintage, 1979), 211, 216.

14. See also Edward Said, *Culture and Imperialism* (New York: Alfred A. Knopf, 1993).

15. Nicholas K. Blomley, *Law, Space, and the Geographies of Power* (New York: Guilford Press, 1994).

16. J. S. Mill, "Considerations on Representative Government," in *Three Essays*, 266, 144–423.

17. J. S. Mill, "Civilization," in *Essays on Politics and Culture*, ed. Gertrude Himmelfarb (New York: Doubleday, 1962), 69.

18. J. S. Mill, "The Spirit of the Age," in *Essays on Politics and Culture*, 10.

19. J. S. Mill, "Tocqueville on Democracy in America, vol. II," in *Essays on Politics and Culture*, 234–35.

20. "Tocqueville," 258.

21. "Tocqueville," 282–83. Mill's use of "spontaneous" suggests that European nations were able to independently progress, while non-Europe has needed to be stimulated by the presence of Europeans. Support for this comes from "On Liberty," which argues that if China is to progress, it will have to be at the hands of foreigners.

22. See "Civilization," 53; "Tocqueville," 283, emphasis added.

23. "Civilization," 51, 52, 53.

24. Cf. "On Liberty," 15.

25. "Civilization," 55

26. Ibid., 56.

27. Ibid., 64–65.

28. "Representative Government," 226, 201; "Civilization," 60. There is "no danger," Mill adds, "of the prevalence of democracy in Syria or Timbuctoo" ("Civilization," 60).

29. "Representative Government," 243–44.

30. "The East India Company's Charter," testimony before the Select Committee of the House of Lords, June 21–22, 1852, in *Writings on India,* ed. J. M. Robson, M. Moir, and Z. Moir (Toronto: University of Toronto Press, 1990), 49, 51.

31. "Representative Government," 402.

32. Ibid., 403

33. "East India Company's Charter," 45, 49.

34. "On Liberty," 88.

35. Ibid., 15.

36. Ibid., 15–16, emphasis added.

37. Ibid., 87–88.

38. Ibid., 87–88, emphasis added.

39. Ibid., 89.

40. "East India Company's Charter," 39.

41. J. S. Mill, "A Few Words on Non-Intervention," in *Essays on Politics and Culture,* 406.

42. Ibid.; emphasis added.

43. Ibid.

44. "Representative Government," 276.

45. This is due to the position that a sense of history is an attitude of the openness of social phenomena to rational comprehension. This presents phenomena as open to study of cause and effect, and once this knowledge is mastered, events then become amenable to human intervention and control. Cf. J. G. A. Pocock, *The Machiavellian Moment* (Princeton: Princeton University Press, 1975).

46. "Representative Government," 279, 281, emphasis added; "East India Company's Charter," 49, 51.

47. Geoffrey Bennington, *Legislations: The Politics of Deconstruction* (New York: Verso, 1994).

48. Shapiro, *Reading the Postmodern Polity.*

49. Wendell Phillips, "The Right of Petition," in *Wendell Phillips on Civil Rights and Freedom,* ed. Louis Filler (New York: Hill and Wang, 1965), 24; Chafee, *Free Speech in the United States,* 107.

50. Anne McClintock, *Imperial Leather: Race, Gender, and Sexuality in the Colonial Contest* (New York: Routledge, 1995).

51. Thomas Spragens, *The Irony of Liberal Reason* (Chicago: University of Chicago Press, 1981), chap. 9.

52. Ibid.

53. Paul A. Passavant, "Racism, National Identity, and Civil Liberties in the Thought of John Burgess and Woodrow Wilson," paper presented at the meeting of American Political Science Association, 1995.

54. Samuel P. Huntington, "The Clash of Civilizations?" *Foreign Affairs* 72 (1993): 22–49.

55. Samuel Beer, *To Make a Nation* (Cambridge: Harvard University Press, 1993), 66, 401–2.

56. Jonathan Rauch, *Kindly Inquisitors: The New Attacks on Free Thought* (Chicago: University of Chicago Press, 1993), 12, 26–27.

Part 2

The Persistence of the Colonial

Francisco de Vitoria and the Colonial Origins of International Law

Antony Anghie

While Hugo Grotius is generally regarded as the principal forerunner of modern international law, historians of the discipline trace its primitive origins to the works of Francisco de Vitoria, a sixteenth-century Spanish theologian and jurist.[1] Consequently, it is entirely appropriate that the Carnegie Endowment commenced its renowned series Classics of International Law with Vitoria's two famous lectures, *De Indis Noviter Inventis* and *De Jure Bellis Hispanorum in Barbaros*.[2] Vitoria's contributions to the discipline are various, and scholars examining the issue have pointed, among other things, to Grotius's indebtedness to him,[3] and to Vitoria's identification of certain fundamental theoretical issues confronting international law. Scholars still refer to the enduring significance of Vitoria's thinking on the law of war and on the rights of dependent peoples.[4]

Vitoria's two lectures, as their titles suggest, concern relations between the Spanish and the Indians. Colonialism is the central theme of these two founding texts of international law. It is hardly possible to ignore the fact that Vitoria is preoccupied with a colonial relationship. While traditional approaches to Vitoria duly acknowledge this fact, they fail to appreciate the extent to which Vitoria's jurisprudence is constructed around his attempts to resolve the unique legal problems arising from the discovery of the Indians. Instead, these traditional

---

An earlier version of this essay appeared in a Special Issue on Law and Postcolonialism, edited by Eve Darian-Smith and Peter Fitzpatrick in *Social and Legal Studies* 5, no. 3 (1996). Reprinted by permission of Sage Publications.

approaches essentially characterize Vitoria as extending juridical doctrines already developed in Europe to determine the legal status of the Indians.[5]

My argument, in contrast, is that while Vitoria's jurisprudence relies in many respects on existing doctrines, he reconceptualizes these existing doctrines or else invents new ones to deal with a novel problem. The essential point is that international law, such as it existed in Vitoria's time, did not *precede* and thereby effortlessly resolve the problem of Spanish-Indian relations; rather, international law was created out of the unique issues generated by the encounter between cultures. It is in this context that the question arises: what is the relationship between the origins of international law and the colonial encounter in these, the first teachings on international law?

The classical problem confronting the discipline of international law is the problem of how order is created among sovereign states.[6] The identification of this problem as the defining dilemma of the discipline has encouraged scholars to explore Vitoria's work in terms of his understanding and treatment of it.[7] My argument is that Vitoria does not interpret the problem of Spanish-Indian relations as a problem of creating order among sovereign states, of deciding how the competing claims of the sovereign Spanish and the sovereign Indians are to be resolved. Rather, Vitoria's work addresses a prior set of questions. Who is sovereign? What are the powers of a sovereign? Are the Indians sovereign? How are the respective rights and duties of the Indians and the Spaniards to be decided?

In dealing with these issues, Vitoria focuses on the social and cultural practices of the two parties. He assesses and formulates the rights and duties of the Indians, for example, by examining their rituals, customs, and ways of life. Vitoria confronts, then, not the problem of order among sovereign states, but the problem of creating a system of law that could be used to account for relations between societies that he understood to belong to two very different cultural orders, each with its own ideas of propriety and governance. Sovereignty doctrine—by which I broadly refer to the complex of rules deciding what entities are sovereign, and the powers and limits of sovereignty—was not already formulated and then simply applied by Vitoria to resolve the problem of creating order between different societies. Rather, sovereignty doctrine emerges through his attempts to address the problem of cultural difference.[8]

I explore the relationship between colonialism and international law, cultural difference and sovereignty doctrine, by focusing on four broad issues. First, I focus on Vitoria's repudiation of traditional techniques of accounting for relations between the Spanish and the Indians. Having dismissed the old medieval jurisprudence based on the notion that the pope exercised universal authority, Vitoria clears the way for his own version of secular international law. Second, I discuss techniques by which Vitoria creates a universally binding system of law by evoking a system of natural law, which creates a common framework binding Spanish and Indian alike. Third, I consider the rules and norms prescribed by this system, and the effect of their application to Spanish-Indian relations. Finally, I examine the question of enforcement and the sanctions applied once the norms prescribed by natural law have been violated. In each of these areas, I delineate how Vitoria's understanding of cultural difference and the identity of the Indian shapes his jurisprudence, and how in turn this jurisprudence determines the legal status of the Indians.

I conclude by suggesting that this reinterpretation of Vitoria's work is a means of rethinking the relationship between colonialism and international law.

Vitoria and the Problem of Universal Law

Spanish title over the Indies was conventionally accounted for by applying the jurisprudence developed by the Church out of the several centuries of interaction between the Christian and heathen worlds. Within this framework, the Indians could be characterized as Saracens, as heathens, and their rights and duties determined accordingly. The traditional framework relied basically on two premises. First, of the three types of law that the medieval Western world identified—divine, human, and natural[9]—human relations were governed by divine law, which was asserted to be primary by many scholars and theologians of the fifteenth century. Second, the pope exercised universal jurisdiction by virtue of his divine mission to spread Christianity. Consequently, sovereigns, the rulers of Europe, relied upon the pope's authority to legitimize their invasions of heathen territory; in expanding the Christian world by military conquest, these rulers were making real the jurisdiction that the pope possessed in theory.[10] Pope Alexander VI's papal bull dividing the world into Spanish and Portuguese spheres exemplified this set of doctrines: the rule of the sovereign was legitimate only if sanctioned by religious authority.

Vitoria vehemently denies each of these assertions, and in the course of refuting the conventional basis for Spanish title, creates a new system that essentially displaces divine law and its administrator, the pope, with natural law administered by a secular sovereign. Thus, the emergence of a secular natural law—the natural law that was proclaimed to be the basis of the new international law—is coeval with his resolution of the problem of the legal status of the Indian, for it is this problem that initiates Vitoria's inquiry.

Vitoria commences his construction of a new jurisprudence by considering whether "the aborigines in question were true owners in both private and public law before the arrival of the Spaniards" (par. 315, p. 120). Could the Indians, the unbelievers, own property? The traditional answer was no. In the absence of a temporal administration of divine law, the Indians had no property rights. But Vitoria reformulates the relationship between divine, natural, and human law. Having examined numerous theological authorities and incidents in the Bible, he concludes that whatever the punishments awaiting them in their afterlife, unbelievers such as the Indians were not deprived of property in the mundane realm merely by virtue of their status.

> Unbelief does not destroy either natural law or human law; but ownership and dominion are based either on natural law or human law; therefore they are not destroyed by want of faith. (Par. 322, p. 123)

Crucially, then, Vitoria places questions of ownership and property in the sphere of natural or human law, rather than divine law. Because divine law is inapplicable to questions of ownership, the Indians cannot be deprived of their lands merely by virtue of their status as unbelievers or heretics.[11] Vitoria's argument that vital issues of property and title are decided by secular systems of law—whether natural or human—inevitably diminishes the power of the pope, for these secular systems are administered by the sovereign.

Vitoria further undermines the position of the Church by refuting another justification for Spanish conquest of the Indies: the proposition that "the Emperor is lord of the whole world and therefore of these barbarians also" (par. 340, p. 130). Vitoria denies that the emperor could have acquired universal temporal authority through the universal spiritual authority of Christ and the pope. He questions whether divine law could provide the basis for temporal authority, methodically denies a number of assertions of papal authority, and concludes, "The Pope is not civil or temporal lord of the whole world in the proper sense of the words 'lordship' and 'civil power'" (par. 351, p. 153). Vitoria goes even further to assert that even in the spiritual realm, the pope lacks jurisdiction over the unbelievers (par. 353, p. 136). The pope's authority is partial, limited to the spiritual dimension of the Christian world.

Vitoria's rejection of the pope's universal authority, which had empowered sovereigns to pursue military action against heathens and infidels, results in a novel problem.

> Now, in point of human law, it is manifest that the Emperor is not lord of the world, because either this would be by the sole authority of some law, and there is none such; or if there were, it would be void of effect, inasmuch as law presupposes jurisdiction. If, then, the Emperor had no jurisdiction over the world before the law, the law could not bind someone who was not previously subject to it. (Par. 348, p. 134)

The Spanish and the Indians are not bound by a universal, overarching system; instead, they belong to two different orders, and Vitoria interprets the gap between them in terms of the juridical problem of jurisdiction. The resolution of this problem is crucial both for Vitoria's new jurisprudence and his construction of a common legal framework that would resolve the status of the Indians. The two techniques by which Vitoria addresses jurisdiction comprise two related parts: first, his complex characterization of the personality of the Indians, and second, his elaboration of a novel system of universal natural law.

Vitoria first focuses on the issue of Indian personality. As his own work suggests, the writers of the period characterized the Indians as being, among other things, slaves, sinners, heathens, barbarians, minors, lunatics, and animals. Vitoria repudiated these claims, humanely asserting that

> the true state of the case is that they are not of unsound mind, but have, according to their kind, the use of reason. This is clear, because there is a certain method in their affairs, for they have poli-

> ties which are orderly arranged and they have definite marriage and magistrates, overlords, laws and workshops, and a system of exchange, all of which call for the use of reason; they also have a kind of religion. Further, they make no error in matters which are self-evident to others; this is witness to their use of reason. (Par. 333, p. 127)

For Vitoria, then, the Indians established their own versions of many of the institutions found in Vitoria's world, in Europe itself.[12] They are governed by a political system that has its own coherence and possess the reason necessary, not only to create institutions, but to determine moral questions that are "self-evident" to others.

Vitoria's characterization of the Indians as human and possessing reason is crucial to his resolution of the problem of jurisdiction. He argues, "What natural reason has established among all nations is called *jus gentium*" (par. 386. p. 151). The universal system of divine law administered by the pope is replaced by the universal natural-law system of *jus gentium,* the rules of which may be ascertained by the use of reason. As a result, it is precisely *because* the Indians possess reason that they are bound by *jus gentium.* Vitoria hardly mentions the concept of *jus gentium* in his earlier discussion. Nevertheless, the problem of jurisdiction is resolved by his simple enunciation of this concept, which he elaborates primarily by demonstrating that it creates doctrines that govern Spanish-Indian relations. Natural law administered by sovereigns rather than divine law articulated by the pope becomes the source of international law governing Spanish-Indian relations.

The character of this natural law is illuminated in Vitoria's argument that the Spanish have a right under *jus gentium* to travel and sojourn in the land of the Indians; and that, providing the Spanish do not harm the Indians, "the natives may not prevent them."

> [I]t was permissible from the beginning of the world (when everything was in common) for any one to set forth and travel wheresoever he would. Now this was not to be taken away by the division of property, for it was never the intention of peoples to destroy by that division the reciprocity and common user which prevailed among men, and indeed, in the days of Noah, it would have been inhuman to do so. (Par. 386, p. 151)

The natural law that solves the problem of jurisdiction is based on something akin to a secular state of nature existing at "the beginning of the world." As this passage suggests, *jus gentium* naturalizes and legitimates a system of commerce and Spanish penetration. Spanish forms of economic and political life are all-encompassing because supported by doctrines prescribed by Vitoria's system of universal law. The gap between the two cultures now ceases to exist, in that a common framework is established by which both Spanish and Indian behavior may be assessed. Equally important, the particular cultural practices of the Spanish assume the guise of universality because they derive from the sphere of natural law.

The Indians seem to participate in this system as equals. The Spanish trade with the Indians "by importing thither wares which the natives lack and by exporting thence either gold or silver or other wares of which the natives have abundance" (par. 389, p. 152). Each side enters knowingly into these transactions, meeting the other's material lack and possessing, implicitly, the autonomy to decide what is of value to them. The Indian who enters the universal realm of commerce has all the acumen and independence of market man—not the timid, ignorant, childlike creature Vitoria presents earlier. The fairness of the system and the equal status of the parties is further suggested by Vitoria's argument that the Indians are subject to the same limitations imposed on Christian nations: "it is certain that the aborigines can no more keep off the Spaniards from trade than Christians can keep off other Christians" (par. 390, p. 153). Reciprocity, it seems, would permit the Indians to trade freely in Spain.

While appearing to promote notions of equality and reciprocity, Vitoria's scheme finally legitimizes endless Spanish incursions into Indian society. Vitoria's innocuous enunciation of a right to "travel" and "sojourn" extends to the creation of a comprehensive, indeed inescapable, system of norms that are inevitably violated by the Indians. For example, Vitoria asserts that "to keep certain people out of the city or province as being enemies, or to expel them when already there, are acts of war" (par. 382, p. 151). Thus any Indian attempt to resist penetration amounts to an act of war that justifies retaliation. Each encounter between the Spanish and the Indians therefore entitles the Spanish to "defend" themselves against Indian aggression and, in so doing, expand Spanish territory.

Vitoria endorses the imposition of Spanish rule by another argument that relies explicitly on cultural differences. In establishing his system of *jus gentium,* Vitoria characterizes the Indians as having the same ontological character as the Spanish. This is a crucial prerequisite for his elaboration of a system of norms that he presents as neutral and founded upon qualities possessed by all people. According to Vitoria, Indian personality has two characteristics. First, Indians belong to the universal realm they share with all other human beings because they have the facility of reason and hence a means of ascertaining *jus gentium,* which is universally binding. Second, however, they differ from the Spanish because the Indians' specific social and cultural practices are at variance from those required by the universal norms, which in effect reflect Spanish practices. Thus the Indian is schizophrenic, both alike and unlike the Spaniard. The gap between the Indian and the Spaniard, described primarily in cultural terms by detailed references to their different social practices, is now internalized; the ideal, universal Indian possesses the capacity of reason and therefore the potential to achieve perfection. This potential can only be realized, however, by the adoption or the imposition of the universally applicable practices of the Spanish. The discrepancy between the ontologically "universal" Indian and the socially, historically, "particular" Indian must be remedied by the imposition of sanctions that effect the necessary transformation. Indian will regarding the desirability of such a transformation is irrelevant: the universal norms Vitoria enunciates regulate behavior, not merely between the Spanish and the Indians, but among the Indians themselves; thus the Spanish acquire an extraordinarily powerful right of intervention and may act on behalf of the people seen as victims of Indian rituals: "it is immaterial that all the Indians assent to rules and sacrifices of this kind and do not wish the Spaniards to champion them" (par. 403, p. 159).[13] Thus Spanish identity is projected as universal in two different but connected dimensions; it is externalized, acting as the basis for the norms of *jus gentium,* and internalized, representing the authentic identity of the Indian.

War, Sovereignty, and the Transformation of the Indian

Vitoria's argument that the Indians are human but lacking in proper understanding led him to suggest that they should be treated as children in need of education that could be provided by the Spanish. The relationship between the Indians and the Spanish was that of trusteeship; Spanish governance of the Indians was to be "for the welfare and in the interests of the Indians and not merely for the profit of the Spaniards" (par. 408, p. 161). Within this context, Vitoria's writings were used to defend against Spanish excesses in the New World.[14]

In his second lecture, however, Vitoria presents a very different set of arguments regarding the acquisition of Spanish title over the Indies.

War, the central theme of Vitoria's second lecture, is vitally important to an understanding of his jurisprudence first, because the transformation of the Indian is to be achieved by the waging of war, and second, because Vitoria's concept of sovereignty is developed primarily in terms of the sovereign's right to wage war.

War is the means by which Indians and their territory are converted into Spaniards and Spanish territory, the agency by which the Indians thus achieve their full human potential. Vitoria, I have argued, displaces the realm of divine law and thereby diminishes the power of the pope. Nevertheless, once Vitoria outlines and consolidates the authority of a secular *jus gentium* that is administered by the sovereign, he reintroduces Christian norms within this secular system; proselytizing is authorized now, not by divine law, but the law of nations, and may be likened now to the secular activities of traveling and trading. Vitoria elegantly presents the crucial transition:

> [A]mbassadors are by the law of nations inviolable and the Spaniards are the ambassadors of the Christian peoples. Therefore, the native Indians are bound to give them, at least, a friendly hearing and not to repel them. (Par. 396, p. 156)

Thus all the Christian practices that Vitoria dismissed earlier as being religiously based, as limited in their scope to the Christian world and therefore inapplicable to the Indians, are now reintroduced into his system as universal rules. This astonishing metamorphosis of rules that are condemned by Vitoria himself as particular and relevant only to Christian peoples into universal rules endorsed by *jus gentium* is achieved simply by recharacterizing these rules as originating in the realm of the universal *jus gentium*. Now, Indian resistance to conversion is a cause for war, not because it violates divine law, but the *jus gentium* administered by the sovereign.

Vitoria elaborates on the many situations in which war is now justified.

> If after the Spaniards have used all diligence, both in deed and in word, to show that nothing will come from them to interfere with the peace and well-being of the aborigines, the latter nevertheless persist in their hostility and do their best to destroy the Spaniards, they can make war on the Indians, no longer as on innocent folk, but as against forsworn enemies and may enforce against them all the rights of war, despoiling them of their goods, reducing them to captivity, deposing their former lords and setting up new ones, yet withalwith observance of proportion as regards the nature of the circumstances and of the wrongs done to them. (Par. 395, p. 155)[15]

Given that any Indian resistance to Spanish presence is a violation of the law of nations that would justify sanctions, Spanish war against the Indians is inevitable and endless. The Indian is ascribed with membership within an overarching system of *jus gentium,* with intention and volition; as a consequence of this, violence originates within Vitoria's system through the deviance of the Indian.

Vitoria's exploration of the law of war raises many of the traditional questions that still occupy international lawyers. Who may wage war? When can it be waged? What limits must be observed? What constitutes a just war? War is a special phenomenon, furthermore, because it is the ultimate prerogative of the sovereign.[16] Thus Vitoria's most sustained and explicit exploration of sovereignty doctrine occurs in the context of his examination of the law of war.

Vitoria understands sovereignty, in part, as a relationship—the sovereign has a duty toward his people and the state; and as certain prerogatives—the right to wage war and to acquire title being among the most prominent. The sovereign, the prince, is the instrumentality of the state, posited almost as the metaphysical embodiment of the people.[17] The prince expands the state, as the successful waging of war brings people outside the state within its scope.[18]

While Vitoria thus defined the powers of the sovereign, he had greater difficulty in identifying the sovereign himself. "Now the whole difficulty is in the questions: What is a State and who can properly be called a sovereign prince?" Sovereigns cannot be defined independently of states. The state, claims Vitoria, "is properly called a perfect community." But then "the essence of the difficulty is in saying what a perfect community is" (par. 425, p. 169). Vitoria's answer is tautologous: "By way of solution be it noted that a thing is called perfect when it is completed whole, for that is imperfect in which there is something wanting, and, on the other hand, that is perfect from which nothing is wanting" (par. 426, p. 169). Neither does it help to define the sovereign as the ultimate authority within the community, for even this proposition is subject to complex qualifications; the complicated hierarchies of the time defy Vitoria, and he acknowledges that a

> doubt may well arise whether, when a number of States of this kind or a number of princes have one common lord or prince they can make war of themselves without the authorization of their superior lord. (Par. 426, p. 169)

Amidst this confusion, Vitoria finally resorts to empiricism, citing as examples of sovereignty the kingdoms of Castile and Aragon, communities that have their own laws and councils.

The foregoing suggests that the power of the state has not been consolidated in any significant way. Authority is too dispersed, and hierarchies, while established theoretically, are too uncertain to convincingly structure sovereignty doctrine. Vitoria's discussion of sovereignty is at its most detailed, however, in his analysis of the laws of war, because it is the sovereign who declares war and exercises all the rights of war.

Just-war doctrine is a crucial aspect of the whole complex of issues relating to the law of war, as the sovereign is entitled to go to war only in certain circumstances. Hence Vitoria poses the question: does the sovereign's subjective belief in the justice of the war ensure that the war is indeed just (par. 434, p. 173)?

Vitoria denies that subjective belief would suffice to render a war truly just, because "were it otherwise, even Turks and Saracens might wage just wars against Christians, for they think they are thus rendering God service" (par. 435, p. 173). Instead of examining the issues of subjective belief and just-war doctrine and then deciding whether or not they applied to the Saracens, Vitoria arrives at his conclusion by first establishing the proposition, the fundamental premise of his argument, that *the Saracens are inherently incapable of waging a just war.* The initial exclusion of the Saracens—and, in this case, by extension, the

Indians—then, is fundamental to Vitoria's argument. In essence, only the Christians may engage in a just war; and, given Vitoria's argument that the power to wage war is the most important prerogative of sovereigns, it follows that the Saracens can never be truly sovereign.

Earlier, in his first lecture, Vitoria had argued that the Indians too possess their own form of rulership, that they "have polities which are orderly arranged and they have definite marriage and magistrates, overlords, laws and workshops" (par. 333, p. 127). Such a passage may suggest that Indian communities are governed by sovereigns; but Vitoria's insistence, in his analysis on just war, that only Christian subjectivity is recognized by the laws of war, ensures that the Indians are excluded from the realm of sovereignty and exist only as the objects against which Christian sovereignty may exercise its power to wage war.

The task of identifying sovereign authority and defining the powers wielded by such an authority, in the complex political systems of Renaissance Europe, proved extraordinarily difficult, and the techniques and conceptual distinctions used by Vitoria for this purpose were problematic and ambiguous. The distinction between the Indians and the Spanish, however, was emphatic and well developed. Indeed, in the final analysis, the most unequivocal proposition Vitoria advances as to the character of the sovereign is that the sovereign, the entity empowered to wage a just war, cannot, by definition, be an Indian.

Since the Indians are by definition incapable of waging a just war, they exist within the Vitorian framework only as violators of the law. The normal principles of just war, which would prohibit the enslaving of women and children, do not apply in the case of the pagan Indians.

> And so when a war is at that pass that the indiscriminate spoliation of all enemy-subjects alike and the seizure of all their goods are justifiable, then it is also justifiable to carry all enemy-subjects off into captivity, whether they be guilty or guiltless. And inasmuch as war with pagans is of this type, seeing that it is perpetual and that they can never make amends for the wrongs and damages they have wrought, it is indubitably lawful to carry off both the children and women of the Saracens into captivity and slavery. (Par. 453, p. 181)[19]

Once fault is established, as the above passage suggests, the war waged against the Indian is, in Vitoria's phraseology, "perpetual." Similarly, in his discussion of whether it is lawful and expedient to kill all the "guilty" in the course of a war, Vitoria suggests that this may be necessary because of the unique case of the unredeemable Indian.

> [A]nd this is especially the case against the unbeliever, from whom it is useless ever to hope for a just peace on any terms. And as the only remedy is to destroy all of them who can bear arms against us, provided they have already been in fault. (Par. 457, p. 183)

As the previous discussion suggests, it is not difficult in Vitoria's system to establish that the Indians are guilty or "in fault." A certain respect is extended to sovereignty in the case of wars between European powers, as the "overthrow of the enemy's sovereignty and the deposition of lawful and natural princes" are "utterly savage and inhumane measures" (par. 465, p. 186). In the case of the Indians, however, such a deposition is not merely permitted but necessary to save the Indians from themselves. These conclusions stand in curious opposition to other parts of Vitoria's work, where he emphasizes the humanity of the Indians. Simply, war waged against the Indians acquires a metalegal status.[20] Many of the legal doctrines of consent, limits, and proportion that Vitoria outlines earlier cease to apply to the Indian once the all-encompassing and inescapable obligations of *jus gentium* are breached.

In summary, then, there are two essential ways in which sovereignty relates to the Indian: in the first place, the Indian is excluded from the sphere of sovereignty; in the second place, it is the Indian who acts as the object against which the powers of sovereignty may be exercised in the most extreme ways. The most characteristic and unique powers of the sovereign, to wage war and acquire title over territory and over alien peoples, are defined in their fullest form by their application on the nonsovereign Indian.

Conclusion

Vitoria continuously alludes to the theme of the novelty of the discovery of the Indians: thus his work addresses the controversy generated by "the aborigines of the New World, commonly called the Indians, who came forty years ago into the power of the Spaniards, not having been previously known to our world" (par. 306, p. 116). He argues that "at the time of the Spaniards' first voyages to America they took with them no right to occupy the lands of the indigenous population." In these different ways, Vitoria seizes upon the discovery of the Indians to claim that traditional understandings of law were inadequate to deal with such a novel situation; in so doing Vitoria clears the way for his own elaboration of a new, secular, international law.

My argument, then, is that Vitoria is concerned, not so much with the problem of order among sovereign states but the problem of order among societies belonging to two different cultural systems. Vitoria resolves this problem by focusing on the cultural practices of each society and assessing them in terms of the universal law of *jus gentium.* Once this framework is established, he demonstrates that the Indians are in violation of universal natural law. Indians are included within the system only to be disciplined.

The problem of cultural difference plays a crucial role in structuring Vitoria's work—his notions of personality, *jus gentium,* and, indeed, sovereignty itself. Vitoria's jurisprudence can be seen to consist of three primary elements connected with this problem. First, a difference is postulated between the Indians and the Spanish, rendered primarily in terms of the different social practices and customs of each society. Second, Vitoria formulates a means of bridging this difference, through his system of *jus gentium* and his characterization of the Indian as possessing universal reason and therefore capable of comprehending and being bound by the universal law of *jus gentium.* Third, the Indian, possessing universal reason and yet backward, barbaric, uncivilized, is subject to sanctions because of his failure to comply with universal standards. It is precisely whatever denotes the Indian as different—customs, practices, rituals—that justifies the disciplinary measures of war, directed toward effacing Indian identity and replacing it with the universal identity of the Spanish. These sanctions are administered by the sovereign Spanish on the nonsovereign Indians.

Cultural difference is also crucial to Vitoria's version of sovereignty doctrine. Vitoria's attempts to outline a coherent vision of sovereignty doctrine in the shifting political conditions of Renaissance Europe encountered a number of difficulties that he tried to resolve by proposing various distinctions—between, for example, the public and the private, the municipal and international spheres. Each of these attempts fails,[21] however, and ultimately, the one distinction that Vitoria insists upon and that he elaborates in considerable detail is the distinction between the sovereign Spanish and the nonsovereign Indians. Vitoria bases his conclusions that the Indians are not sovereign on the simple assertion that they are pagans. In so doing he resorts to exactly the same crude reasoning that he had previously refuted when denying the validity of the Church's claim that the Indians lack rights under divine law because they are heathens. Despite this apparent contradiction, Vitoria's overall scheme is nevertheless consistent: the Indians who inevitably and invariably violate *jus gentium* are denied the status of the all-powerful sovereign who administers this law.

Clearly, then, Vitoria's work suggests that the conventional view that sovereignty doctrine was developed in the West and then transferred to the non-European world is, in important respects, misleading. Sovereignty doctrine acquired its character through the colonial encounter. This is the darker history of sovereignty, which cannot be understood by any account of the doctrine that assumes the existence of sovereign states.

Vitoria is an extremely complex figure; a brave champion of Indian rights in his own time,[22] he may also be seen as an apologist for imperialism whose works are all the more insidious precisely because they justify conquest in terms of humanity and liberality.[23] My argument, however, is that Vitoria's real importance lies in his developing a set of concepts and constructing a set of arguments that have been continuously used by Western powers in their suppression of the non-Western world, and that are still regularly employed in contemporary international relations in the supposedly postimperial world. In particular, we see in Vitoria's work the enactment of a formidable series of maneuvers by which European practices are posited as universally applicable norms with which the colonial peoples must conform if they are to avoid sanctions and achieve full membership. Vitoria's jurisprudence demonstrates, furthermore, that the construction of the barbarian as both within the reach of the law and yet outside its protection creates an object against which sovereignty may express its fullest powers by engaging in an unmediated and unqualified violence, justified as leading to conversion, salvation, civilization. Non-European peoples have been continuously characterized as the barbarians compelling the further extension of international law's ambit.

The classic question of how order is created among sovereign states and the framework of inquiry it suggests lends itself to a peculiarly imperialist version of the discipline, as it prevents any searching examination of the history of the colonial world that was explicitly excluded from the realm of sovereignty. The interactions Vitoria examines occur, not between sovereign states, but the sovereign Spanish and non-sovereign Indians. The crucial issue, then, is how it was decided that the Indians were not sovereign in the first place.

Once the initial determination had been made and accepted that the colonial world was not sovereign, the discipline could then create for itself, and present as inevitable and natural, the grand redeeming project of bringing the marginalized into the realm of sovereignty, civilizing the uncivilized, and developing the juridical techniques and institutions necessary for this great mission. Within this framework, the history of the colonial world would comprise simply of the history of the civilizing mission.

Vitoria's account of the inaugural colonial encounter suggests that an alternative history of the colonial world may be written by adopting a different framework and posing a different set of questions. How was it determined that the colonial world was nonsovereign in the first place? How were the ideas of universality and particularity used for this purpose? How did a limited set of ideas that originated in Europe present themselves as universally applicable? How, armed with these concepts, did European empires proceed to conquer and dominate non-European territories? Furthermore, if sovereignty is so intimately connected with the problem of cultural difference, and if it is explicitly shaped in such a manner as to empower certain cultures while suppressing others, vital questions must arise as to whether and how sovereignty may be utilized by these suppressed cultures for their own purposes. The vocabulary of international law, far from being neutral, or abstract, is mired in this history of subordinating and extinguishing alien cultures. By examining these issues as they arise in Vitoria's work we may finally write a different history of the relationship between colonialism and international law and, thereby, of international law itself.

NOTES

My thanks to the Summer Stipend Program, College of Law, University of Utah; to Eve Darian-Smith, Peter Fitzpatrick, and Thomas Franck; to Karen Engle, Daniel Greenwood, Ileana Porras, Uta Roth, Lee Teitelbaum, and other colleagues at the University of Utah; and, in particular, to David Kennedy for patiently and painstakingly reading and commenting on numerous versions of this work.

1. On Grotius, see David Kennedy, "Primitive Legal Scholarship," *Harvard International Law Journal* 27 (1986): 1. For accounts of Vitoria's place in the discipline of international law, and his relationship to Grotius, see James Brown Scott, *The Spanish Origin of International Law* (Oxford: Clarendon Press; London: H. Milford, 1934); Arthur Nussbaum, *A Concise History of the Law of Nations,* (New York: MacMillan, rev. ed. 1954). I am also generally indebted to Edward W. Said, *Orientalism* (New York: Vintage Books, 1979) and Edward W. Said, *Culture and Imperialism* (New York: Alfred A. Knopf, 1993).

2. The titles of the two lectures may be translated as "On the Indians Lately Discovered" and "On the Law of War Made by the Spaniards on the Barbarians." The two lectures are collected together in *Franciscus de Victoria De Indis et de ivre Belli Relectiones* 116, ed. Ernest Nys, trans. John Pawley Bate, Classics of International Law, no. 1 (1557; rpt. Washington, D.C.: Carnegie, 1917). "Victoria" is more commonly referred to in the literature as "Vitoria," and I have accordingly adopted the latter version. Citations to paragraph and page numbers are hereafter given in the text.

3. Scott, *Spanish Origin.*

4. Thomas M. Franck, *Fairness in International Law and Institutions* (New York: Oxford University Press, 1995), 248; Quincy Wright, *Mandates under the League of Nations* (Chicago: University of Chicago Press, 1930); Christopher Weeramantry, *Nauru: Environmental Damage under International Trusteeship* (Melbourne: Oxford University Press, 1992), 78.

5. Thus Kooijmans, for example, asserts that the doctrines that applied to relations between European states were simply extended to relations between Spain and the Indies. Kooijmans claims that

> the dealings of the Spaniards with the Indians were subject to the rules that apply to intercourse between states. Vitoria introduced an essentially new element in relentlessly drawing the consequences from the theories that applied in Europe to those territories which until then had remained outside the European horizon. . . . [T]he rules that apply to European interstate intercourse also apply to the intercourse with the American-Indian political communities, because there is no intrinsic difference. The small Indian states are legal persons, they enjoy the same rights as European states.

Koojimans does make it clear, however, that for Vitoria, the Indians would acquire the rights of states once "these communities correspond to the requirements laid down by him for the state." Pieter Hendrik Kooijmans, *The Doctrine of the Legal Equality of States: An Inquiry into the Foundation of Inter-national Law* (Leyden: A. W. Sythoff, 1954), 59.

6. Louis Henkin, Richard C. Pugh, Oscar Schachter and Hans Smit, *International Law: Cases and Materials* 2d Ed. (St. Paul, Minn.: West Publishing, 1987).

7. See, for example, Kooijmans, *Doctrine of Legal Equality.* Kennedy discusses this point at some length.

> Most historians who treat primitive texts do so in a way which both presupposes and proves the continuity of the discipline of international law-reaffirming in the process that the project for international law scholars is and always was to construct a social order among autonomous sovereigns. ("Primitive Legal Scholarship," 11)

8. I use the unsatisfactory term *cultural difference* to denote, broadly, Vitoria's characterization of the Indians as different on the basis of their different social practices, rituals and ways of life. I have also explored the question of the relationship between international law and cultural difference in Antony Anghie, "The Heart of My Home: Colonialism, Environmental Damage, and the Nauru Case," *Harvard International Law Journal* 34 (1993): 445.

9. Alfred Rubin, "International Law in the Age of Columbus," *Netherlands International Law Review* 39 (1992): 10–11.

10. Ibid.; Robert Williams, *The American Indian in Western Legal Thought* (New York: Oxford University Press, 1990), 45.

11. "From all this the conclusion follows that the barbarians in question cannot be barred from being true owners, alike in public and private law, by reason of the sin of unbelief or any other mortal sin, nor does such sin entitle Christians to seize their goods and land" (Vitoria, *De Indis,* par. 328, p. 125).

12. Anthony Pagden, *The Fall of Natural Man: The American Indian and the Origins of Comparative Ethnology* (Cambridge: Cambridge University Press, 1986).

13. Indeed, for Vitoria, it would suffice for these purposes if the Spaniards were obstructed in their attempts to convert the Indians. This affects the "welfare of the Indians themselves," in which event the Spanish may intervene "in favor of those who are oppressed and suffer wrong" (par. 398, p. 157).

14. Pagden, *The Fall of Natural Man,* 1986.

15. Vitoria implies that this is how the Indians may achieve salvation; they must be destroyed in order to be saved. Donne in Holy Sonnet X captures the theme of violence and salvation powerfully:

> Batter my heart, three-personed God; for you
> As yet but knock, breathe, shine and seek to mend;
> That I may rise, and stand, o'erthrow me, and bend
> Your force to break, blow, burn, and make me new.

I, like an usurped town, to another due,
Labour to admit you, but oh, to no end,
Reason, your viceroy in me, should defend,
But is captived, and proves weak or untrue.

Thus, the argument that a people or a city must be destroyed in order to be saved is a very old one.

16. Vitoria asserts, "Any one, even a private person, can accept and wage a defensive war. This is shown by the fact that force may be repelled by force" (par. 422, p. 167). Thus, while the individual, in exceptional circumstances, exercises rights comparable to the right to wage war, only the state properly enjoys all the rights both to declare war and wage war to its fullest extent.

17. The prince is the entity in whom all power is vested, "for the prince only holds his position by the election of the State. Therefore he is its representative and wields its authority; aye, and where there are already lawful princes in a State, all authority is in their hands and without them nothing of a public nature can be done either in war or in peace" (par. 425, p. 169).

18. "It is, therefore, certain that princes can punish enemies who have done a wrong to their State and that after a war has been duly and justly undertaken the enemy are just as much within the jurisdiction of the prince who undertakes it as if he were their proper judge" (par. 433, p. 172).

19. It is notable that Vitoria refused to characterize the Indians as slaves in his first relectio. Now, however, with respect to war and the new scheme of natural law he outlines, he achieves much the same result: the enslavement of the whole Indian population, including women and children.

20. Yasuaki Onuma, *A Normative Approach to War: Peace, War, and Justice in Hugo Grotius* (New York: Oxford University Press, 1993).

21. In the final analysis, as Kennedy argues, Vitoria "does not locate the sovereign between a distinct municipal and international legal order, nor does he distinguish internal and external or private and public sovereign identities" (Kennedy, "Primitive Legal Scholarship," 35).

22. Scott, *Spanish Origin.*

23. Williams, *American Indian.*

Islamic Law and English Texts

John Strawson

English texts do not merely present Islamic law, they construct it. For over two hundred years a body of knowledge about Islamic law has been built not only in the English language but within the Orientalist discourse. Edward Said points out that

> everyone who writes about the Orient must locate himself vis-à-vis the Orient; translated into his text, this location includes the kind of narrative he builds, the kinds of images, themes, motifs that circulate in his text—all of which add up to deliberate ways of addressing the reader, containing the Orient, and finally representing it or speaking on its behalf.[1]

In this essay I will explore some of the English texts that have represented Islamic law and so spoken on its behalf.

The persistence of legal Orientalism is a result of complex ingredients; European power, intellectual credibility and subtlety, as well as racism. It does not merely assert power, but it also uses the superior location that power provides to motivate an intellectual system that necessarily subjects Islam to European evaluation. Law, however, is a very sensitive part of any culture, as it is intimately bound up with legitimacy and rule. It is for this reason that there has been some resistance to the idea that law can be subject to the Orientalist critique. Mayer, for example, claims that "Said's Orientalism is not a concept

An earlier version of this essay appeared in a Special Issue on Law and Postcolonialism, edited by Eve Darian-Smith and Peter Fitzpatrick in *Law and Critique* 6, no. 1 (1995). Reprinted by permission of Deborah Charles Publications.

developed for application to the field of law."[2] She argues that it is only applicable to literature, philosophy, and anthropology. Said himself does not deal with law, but in passing says of Sir William Jones that "his official work was the law, an occupation with symbolic significance for the history of Orientalism."[3] By turning to the eighteenth century and the work of Jones and his associates, I think that the symbolic significance of their work will become apparent.

The development of legal Orientalism has taken a path different from those in other cultural fields because of the role law played in colonial rule. In introducing his translation of *Al Sirajiyyah,* Jones makes this clear: "[P]ractical utility being my ultimate object in this work, it has nothing to do with literary curiosities. However agreeable soever, they might have been in their proper places."[4] This motivation has undoubtedly had an impact on the texts themselves. However, it is the way in which these texts have been chosen for translation, compiled and introduced that we find the Orientalist methodology. In explaining the elements of Orientalism, Mitchell writes that by means of "three features—essentialism, otherness and absence—the colonial world can be mastered and the colonial mastery will in turn reinscribe and reinforce these defining features."[5] The need to regulate Islamic law in the interests of colonialism often produces very terse introductions to selected areas of law in an effort to capture it. These texts were mobilized to train a cadre of colonial officials and seduce the Indian Muslims into the orbit of British legitimacy. The overriding aim, however, was to make Islamic law understandable to the English lawyer or official. One nineteenth-century author's explanation of the need for English texts was that "the English student is entirely at sea when he first attempts to master the native text books."[6]

This close connection between colonialism, the practical requirements of government, and the presentation of Islamic law continues to have an impact on current literature. The leading text that continues to influence Western scholars is Joseph Schacht's *Introduction to Islamic Law,*[7] which contains both an overview and a detailed exposition on certain topics. The book is a significant construction of Islamic law in both presentation and definition. In setting the scene Schacht tells us,

> The Arabs were and are bound by traditions and precedent. Whatever was customary as right and proper, whatever the forefathers had done deserved to be imitated. This was the golden rule for

> Arabs, whose existence on a narrow margin and in an unpropitious environment did not leave much room for experiments and innovations which might upset the precarious balance of their lives.[8]

The Arabs are thus presented in an essentialist way; they are conservative, tied by tradition and precedent. They have been so historically and remain so today. Schacht does not blame the Arabs but explains their culture in mechanistic relation to the hot desert environment. Before he has explained anything about Islamic law, he has insisted that Arabs, from whose culture Islamic law derives, are not like Schacht's readers; Arabs are the Other, not merely distinct, but by their nature resistant to modernism. In this manner he enframes our expectations about Islamic law. So clear is the conservative nature of the Arabs that he claims the sunna, one of the two principal sources of Islamic law, is in fact the hallmark, not of Islam, but of Arab society.[9] "In this idea of precedent or *sunna* the whole conservatism of the Arabs found expression."[10]

The sunna becomes a technical device that prevents an adaptation or development of Arab or Islamic societies, in which "the idea of the *sunna* presented a formidable obstacle to every innovation, and in order to discredit anything, it was and still is enough to call anything an innovation."[11] It is noteworthy that Schacht emphasizes the timelessness of Arab society.

Schacht's representations of Arab society contain a contradiction, as the emergence of Islam constituted a revolution within Arab society. Islam was not only a new religion but was also a new political system that rapidly grew into an empire stretching from the Atlantic to the Gulf. Addressing this historical fact, Schacht clings to his notion of inherent conservatism, observing, "Islam the greatest innovation that Arabia saw, had to overcome this obstacle, and a hard fight that was." He rationalizes away the revolutionary transformation by arguing that "the old conservatism reasserted itself; what had shortly before been an innovation now became the thing to do, a thing hallowed by precedent and tradition, a *sunna*."[12] In this way Schacht keeps the Arabs in the cultural order that he has assigned for them, and so he sees that the "ancient Arab concept of the *sunna*" becomes "one of the core concepts of Islamic law." Islamic law, like Arab society, becomes essentially fixed in time. Schacht creates a framework in which Islamic law is fixed, impervious even to revolutionary changes. Unlike Western legal systems, which also base themselves on tradition and precedent but appear responsive to change, Islamic law is frozen. Schacht does not reflect on the paradox that in the United States, where he was a professor, common law is a source of law, and its legal methodology is entirely reliant on precedent.

Schacht also defines Islamic law very strictly, using the concept "in the narrow meaning of the term." While he fails to say what he means, he does explain the scope of his subject:

> [W]orship and ritual, and other purely religious duties, as well as constitutional, administrative and international law have been omitted, the first because they developed under different conditions and in close connection with dogma, the second on account of its essentially theoretical and fictitious character and intimate connection with the relevant institutions with the political history of the Islamic states rather than with the history of Islamic law.[13]

This means that apart from "general obligations" and procedure, Islamic law becomes contracts, inheritance, family, and penal law. It is significant that Schacht dismisses any area where Islamic law might regulate political power, whether national or international. Schacht thus reinforces the notion that Islam is deficient in such areas and Islamic law therefore incomplete and primitive. His reasoning, that these areas are "essentially theoretical and fictitious" and too connected to political history, implies a rather narrow grasp of Western legal systems and evinces no acquaintance with the much-talked-about British constitution.

Schacht has support for this approach from a contemporary, Noel Coulson, who analyzes the legal basis of the Ummayyid and Abbasid states by reference to the constitutional doctrines of the European Enlightenment and found them wanting. On the Ummayyid state (which ceased to exist in 750 C.E.) he comments that it "was not based upon any separation of the executive and judicial functions." Of the Abbasid dynasty, which survived until 1252 C.E. we are told, "the shari'ah courts never attained that position of supreme judicial authority independent of political control, which would have provided the only sure foundation and real guarantee to the ideal of Civitas Dei."[14] Both Schacht and Coulson find Islamic notions of public law lacking in the essentials of legitimacy, and they establish this deficit by reference to European criteria taken almost as facts. In this they remain true to the legal Orientalist tradition of which they are a part.

Legal Orientalists had not always regarded these municipal and international areas of Islamic law as beyond the worth of study. In the eighteenth century, when the British colonialists in India began their systematic translations of Islamic legal texts, they included these elements of public law as a matter of course. Furthermore, the historians of pre-British India spent considerable effort in attempting to understand the structures of government and constitution in the Moghul Empire. The contributions of these eighteenth-century Orientalists, however, were transformed by the requirements of colonial rule, and in the process Islamic public law was literally deleted from the texts. Schacht's theory of the "theoretical and fictitious" character of Islamic law should be placed in the context of this political practice—an example of what Azim calls "the collusion between the literary text and the process of western political domination."[15]

During the eighteenth century the colonial authorities in India decided that Islamic law would continue to be applied to its Muslim subjects. Under the direction of Sir William Jones the huge task of the translation of Islamic legal texts was undertaken. The most systematic work was Charles Hamilton's translation of *al-hidaya al-marghinani,*[16] the earliest complete Islamic legal text in English. The original dates from the late twelfth century and takes the form of a commentary on Islamic law complied by Ali ibn Abu Bakr Al-Marginani. It has been described as "easily the most popular reference for the Hanafi school."[17] As is the case with such classical works, legal principles and doctrine are developed with intertextual references to the Qur'an and the sunna, as well as to cases argued before courts and to authoritative pronouncements by leading scholars. As the author was such a scholar *(mujtahid),* he occasionally made authoritative statements himself. The text gives the lie to the idea that Islamic law is particularly rigid or fixed in time. Each topic is discussed through the presentation of the appropriate sources (Qur'an and sunna) and various ways of interpreting and applying them, followed by a discussion of particular cases, a variety of possible solutions to difficult problems, and a general commentary.[18] The work does deal with public law, including international law. Hamilton's explanation of the import of these passages is significant.

> This book contains a chief part of what may be properly termed the political ordinances of Mohammed, and is useful both in a historical and a legal view,—in the former, it serves to explain the principles upon which the Arabians proceeded in their first conquests, (and in which they have been imitated by all successive generations of Mussulmans,) and in the latter, as many of the rules here laid down, with respect to subjugated countries, continue to prevail in all of that description at the present day.[19]

This section of the work (book 9, "*Al-Seyar*—the Institutes") has ten subheadings dealing with a variety of topics that Western lawyers would recognize as international and constitutional law. The topics include the law of treaties, of armed conflict, of occupation, of taxation and elements of government, and of political and religious rebels. Hamilton's argument is that this section reveals something of the core methodology of Islamic jurisprudence.

In 1870 the second edition of the book appeared, edited by Standish Grove Grady. The book has a new purpose; Grady explains that "this work has been made a text book by the Council of Legal Education for the examination of students of the Inns of Court, who are qualifying for the call to the English Bar, with a view to practicing in India." The text also differs from the 1791 edition, for the chapter on public law and international law has been removed: "A large portion of the work having become obsolete, in consequence of the abolition of slavery, and from other causes, I have expunged the books containing these portions from the present edition."[20] In this manner *al-hidaya* appears without the public-law section, and in this form the English edition remains today in circulation as a reference book in South and Southeast Asia.[21]

In the 1791 edition Hamilton is at great pains to introduce his subject to the European reader. He urges that "to enter fully into the spirit of the text, it is required that we keep in mind the state of society in Arabia at the time when Mohammed and his companions began to introduce something like a system of jurisprudence."[22] A full introduction is beyond the capacity of a translator, he remarks, yet his eighty-nine pages constitute, even today, a readable and informed introduction to Islamic law. His scholarly care is indicated by the inclusion of an index of Arabic terms in Arabic script. This index is removed from Grady's edition. Eighty years of colonialism had transformed a classical work of Islamic law into a positive instrument for colonial rule. Despite the changes to the text, we must not lose sight of the methodology that Hamilton creates in his introduction. Hamilton too is a colonialist, and the purpose of translation is not purely scholarly.

Hamilton's preliminary discourse to the *Hedaya* is groundbreaking in the Western construction of Islamic law. It creates the framework that continues to influence legal Orientalism. Among its elegant phrases and lofty ideals the contours of the Orientalist discourse emerge. Indeed, the text's sophistication perhaps explains the persistence of this critique. Orientalism is not necessarily a crude science. Hamilton's translation is aimed at providing the colonial administration and in particular its judicial branch with an authoritative English version of Islamic law. The practical purpose, though, is not the first issue that he addresses.

> The diffusion of useful knowledge; and the eradication of prejudice, though not among the most brilliant consequences of extended empire and commerce, are certainly not the least important—To open and to clear the road to science; to provide for its reception in whatever form it may appear, in whatever language it may be conveyed:—these are advantages which in part atone for the guilt of conquest, and in many cases compensate for the evils which the acquisition of domination too often inflicts.[23]

These seductive sentiments appear sensitive to the consequences of colonialism, but they are the foundation of the transformation of an encounter between two cultures into an encounter on the colonial terrain itself. Hamilton puts it that "the preservation of what we have obtained depends upon the proper use of power: and the right application of those means which Providence has placed in our hands for continuing, and perhaps increasing, the happiness of a large portion of the human race." Hamilton does not challenge the legitimacy of colonial power, but rather raises the question of how that power will be used, fully aware that the success of the colonial project rests on more than naked force. He comments that "the permanency of any foreign domination (and indeed the justification of holding such domination) requires that a strict attention be paid to the ease and advantage, not only of the governors, but of the governed."[24] In this manner the Orientalist discourse establishes the superiority of European values. The use of knowledge, the happiness of the population, and the interests of the governed will be judged by colonial interests. It is not necessarily a question of disparaging the culture or values of the Other. It is a question of subjecting them to a particular standpoint.

In this context Hamilton sets out to explore the character of Islamic law. Whereas Schacht sees conservatism and backwardness, presenting it as static, Hamilton understands its dynamism and often indeterminate character. Hamilton's concern is not the conservative nature of Islam, but its falsity. He calls the Prophet Muhammad "the impostor of Mecca" and refers to his "pretended mission." This religious element of Orientalism is pronounced throughout the eighteenth and nineteenth centuries, when Christian missionaries went hand in hand with colonial administrators and were often scholars themselves. In the twentieth century religious concerns have been replaced by an obsession with proving that Islam is backward in inevitably opposing human rights.[25]

Hamilton's judgment is acute, and he is open to presenting Islamic law in a favorable light, even compared to English law. One example is the position of women. "To the political and speculative enquirer," he writes, "the most curious features of this book are . . . the passages which particularly concern women," from which "it appears, that the female sex are, among the Mussulmans, invested with many personal rights and independent privileges." He points to the rights in the Hanafi school that women have with regard to choice in marriage, and their rights to property in marriage "as her exclusive property."[26] This commentary is particularly ironic given the West's current representation of the oppression of women under Islamic law.[27] It is interesting that when Hamilton turns to that other modern image of Islamic law, the mutilations associated with some punishments instituted under the *hudud*,[28] he criticizes them on humanitarian grounds. However, Hamilton has the honesty to admit that "we have nothing better to offer by way of substitute."[29] He is undoubtedly referring to the harsh punishments imposed by contemporary English criminal law, including the death penalty for such crimes as theft. Mutilation may be cruel, but all the colonial power can offer in exchange is public execution.

This approach to the subject demonstrates the strength of the Orientalist method. Its subtlety and sensitivity to the topic lend a degree of intellectual credibility to its contributions. Orientalism does not have to condemn or always find the subject under study inadequate when compared to its Western counterpart. In his fine introduction, Hamilton pays strict attention to historical and linguistic detail. He is painstaking in his explanations of the disputes among Muslims during the time of the first four caliphs (successors to Muhammad) and the emergence of the split between Sunni and Shi'a. His glossary of Arabic terms is testimony to his assumption that the judges who will use the text will want to see key words in their original. While Hamilton is able to make favorable comments about Islamic law, he seizes what Said calls the "superior location" of Europe. Hamilton judges Islamic law and opens an entire process of judging it. This is not the violence that stamped much of the literature during the great rivalry between Islam and Europe from the seventh century onward. While Orientalism was nourished by these images, such as the crusades, its approach was informed by the power of colonial possession. Hamilton's *Hedaya* is the logical result of the violence of territorial occupation. The kernel of Orientalism is its insistence on the right to subject the Orient and its culture to European judgment, a judgment that during the years of colonial rule the Orient could not ignore. The Orientalist discourse increasingly becomes one of pillars of colonialism itself. It is on this basis that *al-hidaya al-marghinani* becomes Hamilton's *Hedaya* and so is transformed into a tool through which British judges and administrators supervise Islamic law. In this way the British define the scope and purpose of Islamic law.

Hamilton understands that his translation will serve imperial interests wider than the good government of India.

> The advantages to be derived from a development of the institutes of Mohammed are, however, not confined to the administration of justice in our Asiatic territories. The commerce of Great Britain extends to almost every region where his religion is professed, and as this work is a commentary upon the judicial code of the Ottoman as well as the Mogul empire, and is applicable to the customs and judicial regulations of Cairo, Aleppo or Constantinople, as well as of Delhi or Moorshebad,—it can scarcely fail to open a source of desirable knowledge to the merchant and the traveler.[30]

Hamilton presents a refreshingly honest view of Britain's role in the world. He sees his work as both scholarly and practical, assisting in securing his country's imperial role. Hamilton is conscious that a significant ideological task has fallen to him. In his last paragraphs he addresses this issue.

> At the present eventful period, when we have seen new empires springing into birth, and the old indignantly throwing off the long-riveted chains of despotism, the grandest remain fabric of Islamism seems to be hastening to its fall. In expecting this mighty ruin, we are naturally led to inquire upon what principles the fabric was founded, and to what causes we are to attribute its decay. Some parts of the following treatise are particularly calculated to assist us in such an investigation.[31]

Hamilton's text is thus not presented as merely scholarly work, serving as a practical guide for government in India, nor useful in extending British commerce to the Muslim world, but is also evidence of the decayed character of Islam. Hamilton's confidence in the complete collapse of Islam (no doubt reflecting a common view) is, to us, startling. He sees his work as an important historical record of a decaying empire. The paramouncy of Europe is unquestioned.

> We may there observe that, however, sagaciously it might be formed for the sudden extension of dominion, during an age when mankind were involved in the darkest gloom of superstition and ignorance, the Mussulman system, civil and religious, is but wretchedly adapted to the purposes of public security or private virtue. We may observe, with some degree of laudable exultation, its obvious inferiority, in every useful view, to that excellent system that we posses, and which is so admirably calculated to promote the temporal good of mankind, as well as their eternal happiness![32]

In these passages all the main concepts of Orientalism appear: despotism, darkness, superstition, ignorance, inability of the Orient to help humanity to progress, the obvious superiority of Europe and the equally obvious decay of the East. These positions Hamilton does not appear to be under obligation to argue, as he believes that these assumptions will be shared by his readers, more than he believes that the *Hedaya* itself is evidence of backwardness. This is all the more intriguing given his treatment of Islamic law in much of his introduction. His methodological dualism involves presenting Islamic law alongside the theoretical framework of Europe, but Hamilton rarely deploys the latter to pronounce directly on the former. This indicates a high level of confidence at the birth of legal Orientalism. The reader is already on Hamilton's side, and allusions to falsity are enough. Whatever the value of a particular norm of Islamic law, the whole system is invalid. Hamilton's inclusion of the public-law elements does not threaten the legitimacy of colonialism. Rather, their inclusion is part of the process of making Islamic law understandable to the eighteenth-century official. Grady removes them, thinking that the nineteenth-century student would find them unnecessary, possibly confusing. It is also the case that the nineteenth-century administrators would not need to deal with the theoretical issues that they raise, as the right to colonial rule is so firmly established. By removing them, Grady presents an authentic Islamic legal text shorn of an important area of law and its methodology, and so Islamic law appears incomplete. In the hands of the Orientalists the scope of Islamic law is thus subject to constant review. The power of translation merges with colonial power, producing not merely an appropriated text, but an ongoing cultural occupation.

The eighteenth-century Orientalists arrived in India with the European Enlightenment as their intellectual inspiration. This prepared them for the East, armed especially with theory of Oriental despotism. Whereas Christianity stood for gentleness and moderate government, Montesquieu opined, Islam was subject to the "despotic fury of the prince."

> Whereas Mohammedan princes constantly kill or are killed, among Christians religion makes princes less timid and consequently less cruel. The prince counts on his subjects, and the subjects on the prince. Remarkably, the Christian religion, which seems to have no other object than the felicity of the other life, is also our happiness in this one![33]

While civil society exists in Christian Europe, therefore, it is absent in the Islamic East. This theory is explored by the eighteenth-century scholar Alexander Dow in *The History of Hindustan,* which begins with a "dissertation on the origin and nature of despotism in Hindustan," in which Dow reveals a European essentialism. "The faith of Mohommed," he writes, "is peculiarly calculated for despotism; and is one of the greatest causes that must fix for ever the duration of that species of government in the East."

> Governors, magistrates and inferior offices, invested with powers of the principal despot, whose will is law to the empire, exercise their authority with rigour. The idea of passive obedience is carried though every vein of the state. The machine is connected in all its parts, by arbitrary sway, and is moved by the active spirit of the Prince; and levity or oppressiveness of government in all its departments depends on the nature [*sic*] despotism of his mind.[34]

Dow presents a clear picture of society dominated by the state, itself the whim of the prince. Dow explains that "the simplicity of despotism recommends it to an indolent and ignorant race of men." However, he is ready to admit that it "is not so terrible, as men born in free countries are apt to imagine." Indeed, Dow has some difficulty in demonstrating how despotism sits naturally with Islam. He does, however, produce four factors to sustain his argument. The first is the general environment, particularly a hot climate. He claims that Islam gives "unlimited power" to every man over his own family, that the father is "the absolute despoiler of life and death," and that this pattern is reproduced in society a whole—though a strong family system would appear to undermine the state's direct power over individuals, Dow adds two factors that illustrate the lengths to which he will go for evidence: too much bathing and the prohibition on alcohol. "The frequent bathing inculcated by the Coran, has by debilitating the body a great effect on the mind . . . of a bewitching kind." Continuing in this vein, he notes that "the prohibition of wine is also favourable to despotism. It prevents that free communication of sentiment that awakens mankind from a torpid indifference to their natural rights."[35] A dirty, drunken European is the prototype of a free person.

In Dow's text, Islamic facts and European theory jostle each other. In portraying the political system of the Moghul Empire, he has the honesty to picture something rather different than the theory of Oriental despotism would suggest. Rather than law as subject to the whim of the prince, he discusses the "strict impartiality" of the courts established during the reign of Shah Jahan (1627–56). Under the rule of Aurangzeb (1656–1707) a free legal service for the poor was established, whereby the monarch "commanded that men versed in the usages of the several courts, in the precepts of the Coran, and in the regulations established by edicts, should attend at public expense and give their opinion to the poor in matters of litigation." Aurangzeb, we are told, punished judges severely for "corruption and particularity." Indeed, in the end Dow has to admit that "the courts of justice ran though the same gradations which the general reason of mankind seems to have established in all countries subject to regular government."[36] The main difficulty for Dow and his contemporaries in the colonial administration was their encounter with a sophisticated system of government and law that included principles that the Enlightenment regarded as its own.

> The Mohammedans carried into their conquest a code of laws [that] circumscribed the will of the Prince. The principles and precepts of the Coran, with the commentaries on that book, form an ample body of laws, which the House of Timur always observed; and the practice of ages had rendered some ancient usages and edicts so sacred in the eyes of the people that no prudent monarch would chose to violate either by a wanton act of power.[37]

Dow's commentary indicates that Islamic jurisprudence contained principles for limiting government by law. Painful though it might be for the colonialists to admit, a century before Montesquieu an Islamic society practiced the rule of law.[38] The conquest of Muslim India threw perplexing theoretical and cultural problems to the victors. The Orientalist discourse of this period reflects this quandary, juxtaposing the theory of Oriental despotism with the realities of Islamic rule, side by side. As we saw in Hamilton, this dualism, although inherently contradictory, had the great strength of maintaining historical accuracy while retaining the right to pass judgment. Through this process colonialism legitimized the occupation of territories, peoples, and cultures. It is clear from this brief foray into the literature that Islamic public law was well known in the eighteenth century. Hamilton would have shared Dow's theoretical framework as he set about the translation of the *Hedaya*. Islamic public law was not to be denied; it had to be explained through European values, subjected to its judgment, and thus enframed.

The eighteenth-century Orientalists thus deftly made sense of the world of which they had taken possession. Their statements about Oriental despotism and a reasonably factual record of the Moghul Empire inform one another. The unity of the text brings the Islamic constitutional system into the orbit of despotism, a form of guilt by association.

This process can be seen whether exploring the political and constitutional system or Islamic law in general.

Islamic law had to become explicable and put to use, and understanding Islamic law has to be seen as a process in itself. Reading both Hamilton's and Dow's work, we become aware of the struggle to make sense of Islamic law. A few years before the publication of Hamilton's *Hedaya,* Gladwin explains the purpose of his brief text as conveying "a general idea of Mahammedan law, of which we are little informed."[39] These writers are not conspiring to misrepresent Islamic law but rather are trying to grasp its essence using familiar cultural and legal references. This can also be seen in Jones's introduction to *Al Sirajiyyah,* in which he explains how the Islamic courts used leading authoritative works.

> [T]heir compositions have equal authority in all Mohammedan courts, which follow the system of Abu Hanifah, with those of Littleton and Coke in the Courts at Westminister; and there is a wonderful analogy between the works of the Arabian and English lawyers, and between those and their several commentators; with this difference in favour of own country that Littleton is always too clear to need a gloss, and with this difference in favour of the Arabs, that sole object of Sharif was to explain and illustrate his test, without any display of his own erudition.[40]

In this manner Jones orders the way of looking at Islamic law through English legal idioms. In so doing he establishes a method that was to be followed, not merely by the British, but also by many Indian Muslims in the century and a half that followed, so that Islamic law became encapsulated within an English framework.[41] Drawn onto English cultural territory, Islamic law can be understood and rescued from the alleged chaos and despotism of the Orient. This is of course more than just creating familiarity for British officials or indeed the general public. At the initial stages of colonial occupation Islamic law is enframed in English law through the identification and translation of key texts. Jones explains that as a practical manner "if we give judgements only from native lawyers and scholars, we can never be sure that we have not been deceived by them."[42] The colonial representation of Islamic law becomes not merely an inevitability but a necessity. The colonial practice interacts with legal theory and so shapes its object of study. It is from this source that legal Orientalism merges with Western jurisprudential lineages and seems so naturally a part of them.

The rise of Islamist militant politics in much of the Muslim world during the past two decades has created the basis for new encounters between Islam and Europe. This has particularly important implications for the field of law, where as Mallat remarks, "the concerns of the Islamist advocates has primarily taken legal form."[43] The creation of Islamic states in Iran and Sudan, Islamic upsurges in Algeria and Egypt, and discussions on the role of *shari'a* in most Muslim countries raise critical questions about the relationship between Islam and world order and between Islamic law and international law. At the present time this encounter remains trapped within the postcoloniality of international society. Mayer reflects this problem quite clearly when she says that "the principle of the supremacy of international law is a given in world order," and that international law rests on "Western traditions of individualism, humanism and rationalism."[44] Mayer's arguments are not merely theoretical but inform current practice in this area. In the dispute between the United Nations Human Rights Commission and Sudan, Professor Gaspar Biro (author of the Report on Sudan) responds to his Sudanese critics by commenting that "in terms of human rights, the only question is whether or not national legislation is compatible with existing international instruments."[45] Mayer's and Biro's comments represent both the violence of positivism and postcolonialism, neither of which serves the victims of abuses in Sudan or other parts of the Islamic world. Their assumptions of the natural superiority of the West in human-rights matters not only defies historical record but is built on the colonial constructions of Islamic law. In portraying human rights as essentially Western they and their Islamist opponents enter in a tragic collusion that sustains the parochialism of law. In reaching beyond our postcolonial world, both sides of the former imperial divide have every interest in constructing a new jurisprudential discourse on an inclusivist basis. In challenging legal Orientalism we are not only able to rethink our images of Islamic law but to discover rich lineages for a universal jurisprudence. Rereading Islamic legal history outside of the walls of Orientalism can be a significant contribution to this process. In reflecting on these issues Springborg's comment on life in an Islamic community in the early Middle Ages is refreshing.

> Far from being victims of Oriental despotism, the average citizen in these communities enjoyed a degree of legal and economic freedom, personal and corporate rights and immunities which compares favourably with those of the citizen in the modern "democratic" state.[46]

NOTES

1. Edward W. Said, *Orientalism* (Harmondsworth: Penguin Books, 1978), 20.

2. Anne Elizabeth Mayer, *Islam and Human Rights: Tradition and Politics* (Boulder Colo.: Westview Press, 1991), 10.

3. Said, *Orientalism*, 78.

4. Sir William Jones, *Al Sirajiyyah* (Calcutta: Joseph Cooper, 1792), iv. This is a classical work on the Islamic law of inheritance according to the Hanafi School, and was one of Jones's great achievements. The work itself comprises a preface by the translator, his translation of the commentary on the law, and the original Arabic text. The Hanafi School is one of the four schools of Islamic jurisprudence of the Sunni branch of Islam, named after Abu Hanifa (700–767 C.E.) ,whose school was based in Baghdad.

5. Timothy Mitchell, "Orientalism and Exhibitionary Order," in *Colonialism and Culture,* ed. Nicholas B. Dirks (Ann Arbor: University of Michigan Press, 1992), 289.

6. Standish Grove Grady, *A Manual of the Mohammedan Law* (London: W. H. Allen, 1869), xxx.

7. Joseph Schacht, *Introduction of Islamic Law* (Oxford: Clarendon Press, 1964). His influence can be seen in many current works. For example, it is relied upon by Leila Ahmed, *Women and Gender in Islam: Historical Roots of a Modern Debate* (Cairo: American University in Cairo Press, 1993), 88–93.

8. Schacht, *Introduction of Islamic Law,* 17.

9. Islamic law *(al-shari'a)* derives from two main sources, the Qur'an, believed by Muslims to have been revealed to the prophet Muhammad (between 610 and 632 C.E.) and *al-sunna,* which are the traditions of the Prophet and his companions. Both sources were originally oral, but after the death of Muhammad, the Qur'an was committed to writing. *Al-sunna,* which comprises thousands of reports, were collected together in six authoritative written versions in the ninth century C.E. Schacht's theoretical framework implies that he is examining "Arab" rather than Islamic law, and indeed he approaches his topic like the legal anthropologists (e.g. Hoebel, Gluckman, Bohannan, Cory).

10. Schacht, *Introduction of Islamic Law,* 17.

11. Ibid.

12. Ibid.

13. Ibid., 112.

14. Noel Coulson, *History of Islamic Law* (Edinburgh: University of Edinburgh Press, 1964), 120, 121.

15. F. Azim, *The Colonial Rise of the Novel* (London: Routledge, 1993), 5.

16. Published under the title *The Hedaya*, 4 vols. (London: T. Bensley, 1791). Its original title is *al-hidaya fil forou*, which means "guide on particular points." Hamilton's translation is from a specially prepared Persian version of the Arabic.

17. Sobhi Mahmassani, *Falasafat Al-Tishri Fi Islam* [The Philosophy of Law in Islam], trans. Farhat J. Ziadeh (Leiden: E. J. Brill, 1961), 49.

18. Islamic law is developed through a series of discourses that resulted in the formation of various schools of law, each with their distinctive approach to particular issues. The major texts therefore contain aspects of this discourse. It is because of the diffuse character of the *shari'a* that it has proved very difficult to codify. While modern Islamists call for the straight path of Islamic law—*al sirat al mustaqim*—any research into classical Islamic law finds a pluralism within the jurisprudence that makes any straight path improbable. It is significant that colonialists and many subsequent Western commentators have, however, found it politically convenient to adopt an approach that has much in common with today's Islamists,

19. *The Hedaya,* 1:lxxi–lxxii.

20. Charles Hamilton, *The Hedaya: A Commentary on the Mussulman Law,* 2d ed., with a preface and index by Standish Grove Grady (London: Wm. H. Allen, 1870), iv. Grady used this edition to teach his course in Islamic law at the Council of Legal Education during the 1870s.

21. At least two editions reproduce the 1870 version of *The Hedaya.* One is Charles Hamilton, *The Hedaya or Guide* (Lahore: Premier Book House, n.d.), the other, Charles Hamilton, *The Hedaya: Commentary on Islamic Law* (New Delhi: Kitab Bhavan, 1985). Part of the section dealing with public law in the introduction is retained, and a note explains that "this book has been omitted, as it has hardly any practical effect" (Hamilton, *The Hedaya: A Commentary on the Mussulman Law,* xviii).

22. *The Hedaya,* 1:xxxix.

23. Ibid., 1:iii.

24. Ibid., 1:iv.

25. See John Strawson, "A Western Question to the Middle East: Is There a Human Rights Discourse in Islam?" *Arab Studies Quarterly* 19, no. 1 (1997): 31–58.

26. *The Hedaya,* 1:lxiv, lxv.

27. This can be seen in the way in which the Western media portray the discriminatory policies of the Taliban in Afghanistan as the inevitable result of the application of Islamic law to women, despite the opposition from many Islamic societies, including Iran. This serves the purpose of claiming that the West is the defender of women's rights. For an alternative reading on Islam and women, see Fatima Mernissi, *Islam and Democracy: Fear of the Modern World,* trans. Mary Jo Lakeland (London: Virago Press, 1993), 149–71.

28. This is one of the three categories of crime in Islamic law that comprises six offenses: *sariqa* (theft), *haraba* (rebellion or highway robbery), *zina* (fornication), *qadhf* (unproven accusations of fornication), *sukr* (intoxication), and *ridda* (apostasy). Once the offenses have been proved, fixed penalties must be applied; these include mutilation, corporal punishment, and death.

29. *The Hedaya,* 1:lxxi.

30. Ibid., 1:lxxxvii.

31. Ibid.

32. Ibid.

33. Montesquieu, *The Spirit of Laws,* trans. Anne M. Cohler, Basia Carolyn Miller, and Harold Samuel Stone (Cambridge: Cambridge University Press, 1989), 461.

34. Alexander Dow, *The History of Hindustan,* 3 vols. (London: T. Becket and P. A. De Hondt, 1772), 1:xiii, xv.

35. Ibid., 1:xxi, xxii, xiv, xvi.

36. Ibid., 1:xxvi, xxvii, xxix.

37. The essay entitled "An Enquiry into the State of Bengal," ibid., 1:lii.

38. For a contemporary and exciting study of the theory of Oriental despotism and the reality of the East, see Patricia Springborg, *Western Republicanism and the Oriental Prince* (Cambridge: Polity Press, 1992).

39. F. Gladwin, *An Epitome of Mohammedan Law* (Calcutta: William Mackay, 1786), v.

40. Jones, *Al Sirajiyyah,* iii. By "test" he seems to mean investigating the logic of the argument. Sayyid Sharif was one of the authors of *Al Sirajiyyah.*

41. There are many texts that, although quite scholarly and replete with Arabic references, are essentially within this mold; see for example, Seyed Ali Ameer, *Mohammedan Law* (Calcutta: Thacher, Sprink, 1892); Abdur Rahim, *The Principles of Mohammedan Jurisprudence* (Calcutta: Baptist Mission Press, 1905); and Badruddin F. Tayabji, *A Handbook of Muhammadan Law* (Mylapore: Madras Weekly Notes, 1914). There could be readings of these texts that see them as subversive of colonial rule in that they usually begin with excellent introductions to Islamic law and then change track into a positivist exposition that seems unrelated to the former.

42. *The Letters of Sir William Jones,* ed. G. Cannon (Oxford: Clarendon Press, 1970), 2:795.

43. Chibli Mallat, *The Renewal of Islamic Law* (Cambridge: Cambridge University Press, 1993), 1.

44. Mayer, *Islam and Human Rights,* 209, 44.

45. Quoted by Paul Lewis, *International Herald Tribune,* March 9, 1994. This does not imply any support for Sudan's interpretations of Islamic law. For an alternative but Islamic view of Sudan see Abdullahi Ahmed An-Na'im, *Towards an Islamic Reformation: Civil Liberties, Human Rights, and International Law* (Cairo: American University in Cairo Press, 1992), 125–36.

46. Patricia Springborg, "The Contractual State: Reflections of Orientalism and Despotism," *History of Political Thought 8* (1987): 399.

The View from the International Plane: Perspective and Scale in the Architecture of Colonial International Law

Annelise Riles

> *When I first became acquainted with the country the natives thought their country the biggest in the world. When new-comers differed from them on this point, they roundly called them liars. That was fifty years ago, and in the meantime the slow but steady pressure of education afforded by the Mission Schools has taught them otherwise.*
>
> A. B. Brewster, *The Hill Tribes of Fiji*

> *The countryside, the immense geographic countryside, seems to be a deserted body whose expanse and dimensions appear arbitrary (and which is boring to cross even if one leaves the main highways), as soon as all events are epitomized in the towns, themselves undergoing reduction to a few miniaturized highlights.*
>
> Jean Baudrillard, "The Ecstasy of Communication"

The representational gaze has by now become a ubiquitous motif of scholarship about colonial law and administration. Following the insights of Michel Foucault and recent trends in feminist theory, numerous writers have turned their attention to the perspective that often animated colonial rule.[1] In the pages below, I wish to contribute to this line of inquiry by considering the sense of dimension or scale that characterized the international legal project of the colonial era.[2] An implicit notion of scale—of the difference between large and small—is

An earlier version of this essay appeared in a Special Issue on Law and Postcolonialism, edited by Eve Darian-Smith and Peter Fitzpatrick in *Law and Critique* 6, no. 1 (1995). Reprinted by permission of Deborah Charles Publications.

a crucial foundation for the effect of perspective, colonial or otherwise. As such, the turn in contemporary criticism toward the study of colonial perspective might also be a study of colonial notions of scale.

When we turn to the nineteenth-century international lawyer's worldview, we find that scale is a fundamental, if unremarked, aspect of the disciplinary project. The international lawyer's task, I argue, was to transform "local" disputes into matters of global importance, into stepping stones in the trajectory toward global peace. What differentiated the local and the global for the nineteenth-century international lawyer was precisely a notion of size or scale. What was international and global, in other words, was understood as larger than what was local or national. From the vantage point of the international lawyer's globalizing gaze, distant events "on the ground" were "spotted" as international issues, and the adjudication of international disputes was understood to take place on an "international plane" different in scale from these events themselves. This globalizing perspective, I believe, was central in giving effect to the discipline's normative project of cosmopolitanism.[3]

What does it mean, then, for "local" events to become international by becoming "larger" as they become global? It is difficult to talk about this notion of scale in international legal culture because it is an implicit, naturalized starting point, a base taken for granted by all sides upon which the more important, contested issues are played out. Perhaps it is this ubiquitous notion of scale that makes such normative debate possible in the first place.

This question addresses itself as much to the state of contemporary critical theory as it does to nineteenth-century international law. Notions of scale, perspective, and place surface everywhere in contemporary theory. If we take international law, as nineteenth- and twentieth-century international lawyers have, to be an institutional elaboration of modern and liberal philosophical themes, a consideration of how these themes operate for international lawyers may hold important implications for the way the same notions are deployed in "critiques" of modernist thought.

In order to consider this question, however, we lawyers must manufacture a rhetorical situation that will allow us to apprehend our taken-for-granted notion of scale. I suggest, therefore, that we treat a routine move of international legal strategy, chosen from one ordinary controversy of the colonial period, as if it presented a puzzle for us.

Why do the lawyers in the case below make the move that they make? How do the lines of argument work for them?

The case I have in mind dates to late-nineteenth-century colonial Fiji. The claimants were Americans whose lands in Fiji had been confiscated by the Land Claims Commission of Fiji's first governor, Sir Arthur Gordon, who arrived in the British colony in 1875.[4] An amateur ethnologist, Gordon envisaged his primary task to be the preservation of native culture from the harm of civilization.[5] The commission's task, therefore, was to investigate every European title to ensure that the property had been alienated according to what Gordon lovingly called "ancient custom."[6] Among those denied title were a group of Americans who shared none of Gordon's nostalgia for cultural difference.

The conflict catapulted to the international plane when, on July 1, 1887, after ten years of frustration at pressing the issue through administrative appeal, the claimants wrote to the president of the United States, Grover Cleveland.[7] Cleverly spotting an issue of international law, Cleveland forwarded the letter to the State Department,[8] which appointed a special agent to travel to Fiji to investigate the claims.[9] Over the next thirty-five years, the affair languished on the desks of British Foreign Office and State Department lawyers, who exchanged endless diplomatic correspondence on the subject.[10] By 1896, State Department documents relating to one claimant's case amounted to 1,717 pages of written material, 163 pages of printed material, and another 852 pages of British government documents.[11]

This affair now found itself caught in the trajectory of a new narrative. The late nineteenth century saw a flurry of activity aimed at the expansion of the rule of law in the international sphere. Theorists during this classical period of international legal doctrine treated international law as a project of elaborating the rules for a new and higher order of society,[12] a society of states.[13] The first steps toward true world government would be to convince the "civilized states" to submit disputes to voluntary arbitration in hopes that this process eventually would lead to the establishment of a binding world court.[14] As enthusiastic supporters of the judicial settlement of international disputes, the United States and Britain established in 1910 a Pecuniary Claims Arbitration procedure under the auspices of the Hague Convention of 1907.[15] Among the outstanding claims between the two countries listed in a schedule appended to the agreement were the Fiji claims. The propriety of Gordon's colonial policies had now become "Class I—claims based on an alleged denial in whole or in part of real property rights," grouped together with events in New Zealand, the Malay Peninsula, South Africa, Quebec, New Mexico, and New York.[16]

The puzzle I wish to unravel concerns the correspondence between the British and American lawyers at two junctures. First, during negotiations between the parties over whether to submit the dispute to arbitration, the Americans write to the British Foreign Office and present a classic international legal perspective on the events. They take note, first, of the deed of cession, and second, of the lack of the kind of judicial procedures on the part of the Land Claims Commission that they claim are mandated by international law, and they conclude by suggesting the appointment of a mixed commission to resolve the claims.[17] At this point, they have presented the events from a perspective that looks as effortlessly on a conflict in Fiji as on a series of facts located in any other part of the world, and that finds in the Fijian case a matter of interest to the cosmopolitan center.

The conflict now appears to be a conversation between sovereigns in the cosmopolis. Yet the British respond in a quite different way. There simply is no issue of international law to discuss, they contend, because the Land Claims Commission was fully impartial.[18] A focus that cuts to a fact, a change to a different level of analysis, wrecks the architecture that sustains an international conversation.

Later in the negotiation process, in response to the State Department's detailed arguments about the illegality of British actions, the British drop to the local level with a surprise challenge to the identity of the American claimants. "Lord Salisbury may be aware," the colonial office writes to the foreign office, "that among the American claims advanced in Fiji some, it is understood, were put forward by . . . the American Consul on behalf of the bastard offspring of Native women who, of course, are not American citizens."[19] Without citizenship, there can be no contest, for access to international law must depend on the transformation of rightful citizens' claims into those of the representative state. The surprise proves effective: On this basis, the Department of State reduces the number of claims from fifty-three to only ten.[20]

We might note at the outset the notion of scale at work here. The tribunal's schedule of claims assumes a position equidistant from New York and New Zealand. The conversation between British and American lawyers, for their part, is meaningful because they are understood to be near to one another. Fiji, in contrast, is distant, and small for both parties. What contributed, then, to this sense of distance between an "international plane" and national activity?[21] One central element was the way international lawyers treated certain events that "close up" might have loomed large, as receding from view. Culture and race, for example, become explicitly distant subjects, understood in the metaphor of territory, and recede into the background of a cosmopolitan conversation like fragments of context for a foregrounded text. The character of Fijian culture now appears as a memorandum of evidence in the appendix to the British memorial,[22] behind other foregrounded concerns. The crucial issue, the British argue, is not the factual question of the nature of Fijian culture but the legal question of how to handle such custom.

> [A]ll the authorities are in agreement that until a comparatively short time before the cession the idea of such alienation was entirely unknown to the natives of Fiji, and that it was only by a gradual process of education that the character of such a transaction became understood at all.
>
> The point upon which a divergence of opinion may be detected is the question whether such alienation, being unknown as part of ancient custom, could ever become "legal."[23]

The topic of culture is by no means "effaced" from the conversation because it is backgrounded, however. On the contrary, the sense of dimension is maintained precisely by the understanding that if one were to look closer, if one were to alter the scale, one would find it. It is the experience of effecting this change in scale, moreover, the transformation of perspective that relegates culture to the appendix, that makes the distance of dimension real.

Plucked into the global arena by lawyers who "spot" legal issues, facts become building blocks of law, issues of legal significance. The friendship between Gordon and the members of the Land Claims Commission becomes a matter of inadequate procedure, for example. The expectations of Europeans and Americans about access to the spoils of colonialism become "land," and land becomes an element and fact of a new global arena. Certain elements of local scale are fished out—land, a deed of cession the British once enticed a Fijian chief to sign, the personal relations between members of the Land Claims Commission—so that it is not the entire landscape that is viewed from a distance. This local knowledge can be divorced from any particular argument "on the ground" to become simply phrases or appendices so that when one focuses again on local scale, when one turns to the appendix of the memoranda, for example, these facts now loom large against other elements of local context. It is as though this local arena itself already contains the difference of scale that separates global and local. Nevertheless, what relates the global arena in perspectival terms to a local realm below is the feeling that behind such terms as *land* and *cession* lie other phrases, other conflicts, other facts, and other perspectives. Every lawyer knows that on close examination, law dissolves into fact.[24]

This sense of scale is elaborated much more through practice than through debate. The conversation of thirty-five years between British and American diplomats is an exchange of hundreds of short letters marked by their strict adherence to diplomatic form that speak far more frequently of the relationship among diplomats than they do of distant events in Fiji. A typical letter reads,

> Foreign Office, March 18, 1897
> SIR: I have had the honour to receive Mr. Bayard's note of the 8th instant, respecting the land claims of the United States citizens in the Fiji Islands, and I have not failed to communicate a copy to Her Majesty's secretary of state for the colonies.
> I have, etc.,
> (For the Marquess of Salisbury:)
> F. H. VILLIERS[25]

Yet who, we might ask, is F. H. Villiers? It is from his vantage point that the national environment and the details of the dispute look small and distant. And yet a global perspective must, by definition, overcome the subjectivity of any particular viewer. The metaphorical relationship between the society of states and a society of individuals that creates a distance of scale between persons and states[26] mandates that the individual and state are not literally identical. The international lawyer cannot occupy both positions at once. If he is a global viewer, he is not a local one.

The international lawyer, then, transforms himself into something greater and more universal than the subjectivity he shares with Gordon, the American claimants, or the Fijians whose lands have been alienated,[27] just as the claims themselves must be transformed from those of persons into those of states. The lawyer becomes the state's representative[28] and even communicates with the state as entities of the same scale: In countless letters, the lawyer notes, "I am instructed by my Government to represent to Her Majesty's Government . . ."[29] And this transformation emphasizes the distance between the local and global, for in order to get from one to another, a change must take place, a work must be done.[30] The lawyer, then, is located in space—in the space of the international plane and in the space he understands himself to occupy in the locality of daily life—and yet looks down from a vantage point that is greater than any particular space and captures in its gaze all space. And what is important is that contrary to the very notion of a difference between the state and the individual, and between the global and the local that animates the project of international law, the diplomat or lawyer understands himself to stand in both vantage points at once.

The observations above make evident, I think, that this difference of scale between an international plane and local events carries with it a notion of perspective. Perspective, of course, itself is both scale or dimension and the particularity of a point of view. Both notions work together here: For the international lawyer, to be situated "above," and to loom larger than local events, was also to view the world below and to understand his view as a unique vantage point. The unique aspect of this global perspective that made of the world a subject of viewing, however, was precisely the fact that it was a perspective from no point in particular. From Hugo Grotius, the mythical founder of the discipline, to the Enlightenment theorists of international law, to the institutional internationalism of today, one finds a hope for world order through reason that is effectuated in this detached view from above.[31]

Yet if it is a view from nowhere, the global perspective is also a view from an international plane.[32] The global is both a *way of looking* that eclipses all others, and a *space* or place. The nation is a way of imagining identity that grafts itself onto a notion of territory. The local, as "location," is also an ideology. The cosmopolis is a utopian space as well as a set of scientific and moral values,[33] and the international lawyer's task is not simply to view the world in global or local terms but also to contribute to the architecture of this global space. The problem of enforcement of international law, for example, concerns the fact that violations of international law take place *simultaneously* in local, domestic spheres, within the purview of another legal system. International lawyers must train citizens and governments who see only local events, therefore, to conceptualize them as events occurring also on an international plane. The lawyer's task becomes both to view the world in a way that makes possible a difference of dimension, and to maintain a boundary that delineates and defines the cosmopolitan space. The perspectives that animate the case are not simply different orders of seeing built together into one constant sense of scale, one way of reflecting on "place," therefore. Behind each fact or space is not just another fact but also another perspective. To change orders of knowledge is to change *ways* of seeing.

In this light, we can return to the legal arguments presented above as strategic shifts from one scale to another. The representation of a globalizing perspective, and the allusion to an international plane of activity, is as much a part of the American strategy, of course, as is the precise American argument about judicial procedure, for the American objective is to transform the conflict into a matter of diplomatic importance. Likewise, the British argument involves a shift of perspective that refuses the global. The shift to a different scale that is also a different order of knowledge—from law to fact, for example—entails an element of surprise. The appeal to the exoticism of the fact thus provides a means of refusing the international plane by suddenly dissipating the sense of physical closeness between American and British lawyers, and by moving to a different notion of what is close and what is far. The shift in perspective produces a confusion of categories—including literal miscegenation in the case of the British turn to citizenship arguments—which topples the possibility of conflict on a global scale. The perspectival trick here is to produce an element of the local that collapses the architecture of scale that differentiates local and global in the first place. The difference of scale between global and local gives the international plane its sense of "realness." When scale is collapsed, the difference between global and local is made to look unnatural, synthetic, two-dimensional rather than three.

In several recent works, Marilyn Strathern has described the scale that animates modern Euro-American knowledge, and the relationship of scale to perspective, as an experience of partiality. In considering what it means to Euro-Americans to know things, Strathern relates notions of scale to an understanding of a *diversity* of ideas, facts, or forms. Dimension is created by the "constantly receding horizon of what there was to know" such that every fact is grounded in other facts:

> That modern dimension of grounding or context in turn yielded a sense of perspective, the "point of view" from which an entity was seen. One could always gain a new perspective by providing a new context for what was being observed. . . . *This plurality was a given,* and complex society awarded itself the ability to superimpose perspectives (self-conscious "constructions") upon a plurality inherent in the nature of things.[34]

At any level of scale, phenomena seem equally complex, Strathern argues. Switch from macroanalysis to microanalysis, and the subject is no simpler. The result is a "relativizing effect," for our awareness that at another order of scale we would encounter a new and equally complex set of phenomena "gives the observer a sense that any one approach is only ever partial, that phenomena could be infinitely multiplied." We experience "information 'loss'" as we switch from one order of magnitude to another, and this creates the sense that our accounts are never sufficient. "An answer is another question, a connection a gap, a similarity a difference, and vice versa."[35]

Yet in Strathern's account of modern knowledge, while perspectives change, scale itself is held constant. The difference between macroanalysis and microanalysis, for example, is not at issue for those Euro-Americans she describes, no matter how partial each level is understood to be. What are we to make, therefore, of the quintessentially liberal international lawyers' strategic movement between levels of scale that itself sometimes collapses scale and sometimes reconstructs it again? It is perhaps tempting to understand it as a kind of internal critique of the universalizing project of law and colonialism in which the coherence of global perspective is foiled by inner contradiction or the encroachment of "difference."[36] Yet to do so, I think, would be to fail to consider how the experience of what we interpret as powerful tools of critique was mediated for the nineteenth-century Euro-American. In a study of distance, scale, and space in late-nineteenth- and early-twentieth-century Europe and America, for example, Stephen Kern finds that this period was marked precisely by a heterogeneity of perspective.[37] Contrary to the "schizophrenia" that many postmodern theorists now read into notions of mutation or heterogeneity of perspective,[38] Kern paints a picture of the apprehension of the irreconcilable partiality of perspectives as a source of creativity, innovation, and hope.[39] In international legal conversation as well, we might conclude, strategic invocation of different orders of seeing, the distortion of scale, and the transformation of the subject from one scale to another were routine and comfortable parts of the practice of international law, giving effect to the very notion of scale they flattened.

One implication of this collapse of scale at the heart of modern liberalism's institutional project surely is to point out that much more is shared on a symbolic level between institutional elaborations of modernity on the one hand and contemporary critiques of that project on the other. The normative debate between postcolonial legal scholars and their subjects is made possible, it seems, by the way in which perspective is held constant. Whatever else they may not agree upon, late-nineteenth- and late-twentieth-century international lawyers, colonial administrators, and postcolonial critics alike generally understand a difference of scale to separate the local from the global. Whether we choose to "think globally, and act locally,"[40] to defend and elaborate a new global space,[41] to protect the local against the encroachment of global relations,[42] or to marvel at its strangeness,[43] we share a notion of scale that makes a normative critique intelligible. Often, moreover, this opposition induces precisely the normative debate about the elaboration of a cosmopolitan space of communication in which particularism can be reorganized into a universal whole that graced the pages of the international legal document a century ago.[44]

This is important, I believe, because there is a trend in contemporary scholarship that finds critical bite in making the point that the representations of "hegemonic" institutions such as international law are "partial," in emphasizing what is small, or local (and these two are often equated in this scholarship), or in the confusion of categories that is taken to "warp" perspective. Yet as we rush to dismantle the architecture that sustains this international plane, to critique the pretensions of the globalizing gaze, and to expose its partiality and the political interests it serves, caution seems in order. A look at the international lawyer's view indicates that this dismantling of the architecture that sustains the universalizing gaze is as central to the perspectival effect that delineates global and local as were the technologies that emphasized the distance between spheres. In perspectival terms, tearing down the scaffolding is quite the same as putting it back together again. Both share the same sense of scale—and as I have argued, this sense of scale was by no means marginal to the enterprise.

Likewise, the collapse of scale implicit in the flattening of perspective has been taken as indicative of a postmodern moment,[45] one outside and beyond a modern past. The poststructuralist strategy of "fishing"[46] knowledge out of context into a new pastiche, too, recalls the issue-spotting of the international lawyer. And indeed, recent poststructuralist writings seem to echo this international legal project when they advocate the deconstruction of nationhood through a method of reading out of context in the service of a new global space, understood, again, in terms of an opposition of unity to difference.[47] Even the overlay of topographical and perspectival ways of apprehending knowledge that characterized the world of the international lawyer now finds considerable currency.[48] However, as we have seen, the distortion of perspective, the deconstruction of orders of knowledge and their recombination into new and unnatural vistas is as much a part of the effect of liberalism as it is a part of postmodern critique and imagination.

Finally, the alternation between incommensurable perspectives associated with contemporary feminist theory claims for itself a vantage point set apart from liberalism that provides a possibility for critique. Yet as we saw, the international lawyer's distance between global and local was effected in part by the occupation of seemingly incongruous positions. This realization demands, I think, that we question the power of perspectivism as a tool for imagining a new and truly postcolonial law or politics.

I do not intend these observations as yet another layer of critique. The realization that our contemporary perspectival moves against scale were anticipated a century ago is devastating only if one assumes that what productive academics do is critique, and that critique involves transforming or otherwise making something of perspective. Perspective, from this position, is always assumed to be perspective *on* something, something that itself is not a perspective but rather a kind of raw material for observation. The object of perspective, for these critics, is the fact upon which the scholar or lawyer works her theory.

Yet if we turn back to the international legal arguments above, we find that the global is *both* perspective and place. Perspective is also its own subject matter, and the act of viewing and the material that is viewed are one and the same. Behind perspective is not just the thing that is viewed (space), but also another perspective.

To take a cue from the scale of the international plane, in which the incommensurables of perspective and space were already one, therefore, we might turn our attention to this contemporary notion of perspective as an "outside" and therefore productive critical move. We can begin with the recognition that a critique or view that comes "after" is always also the territory that comes before.

NOTES

I owe special thanks to Peter Fitzpatrick, Angelia Means, Adam Reed, and Marilyn Strathern for conversation and detailed comments. I am also indebted for useful criticism to the Law and Social Theory seminar group at the University of Canterbury and to the "Anthropological Methods in the Realm of the International" discussion at the 1994 Law and Society Annual Meeting, as well as to the Ford Foundation for financial support.

1. See, e.g., P. Rabinow, *French Modern* (Cambridge: MIT Press, 1989) (interpreting French urban planning policies in colonial Algeria as "an urban parallel to Bentham's *Panopticon*"); F. Cooper and A. L. Stoler, "Tensions of Empire: Colonial Control and Visions of Rule," *American Ethnologist* 16 (1989): 609; T. Mitchell, "Orientalism and the Exhibitionary Order," in *Colonialism and Culture*, ed. N. Dirks (Ann Arbor: University of Michigan Press, 1992), 289–317. So pervasive is the theme of colonial perspective that one recent work, again citing Foucault's image of the Panopticon, identifies the colonial interest in surveillance as one of twelve basic "rhetorical modes" which are said to form a "repertoire for colonial discourse." D. Spurr, *The Rhetoric of Empire* (Durham, N.C.: Duke University Press, 1993).

2. For further elaboration of international law's implication in colonial expansion, see Antony Anghie, "'The Heart of My Home': Colonialism, Environmental Damage, and the Nauru Case," *Harvard International Law Journal* 34, no. 2 (1993): 445–506.

3. In this sense, the international lawyer's globalizing view mirrors the powerful globalism of a variety of rhetorics now critiqued by many contemporary writers. Elspeth Probyn speaks for many critics, for example, when she notes the "ways in which women's practices and experiences have been historically dismissed as local" and the way in which the epistemology of location works to "fix the subaltern outside the sanctified boundaries of knowledge, determining the knowledge of the subaltern as peripheral and inconsequential." E. Probyn, "Travels in the Postmodern: Making Sense of the Local," in *Feminism/Postmodernism*, ed. L. J. Nicholson (New York: Routledge, 1990), 178.

4. See "Report of Mssrs. Williamson and Carew, Land Commissioners, on

'Emuri,' together with the Testimony and Proceedings on the Hearing before Them," *American and British Claims Arbitration, Fiji Land Claims of George Rodney Burt, Benson Robert Henry, John B. Williams, Isaac M. Brower, Memorial of the United States in Support of the Claims* (1914), Exhibit 26, at 199–204 (hereinafter *U.S. Memorial*).

5. See J. D. Legge, *Britain in Fiji, 1858–1880* (London: Macmillan, 1958).

6. "Report of the Lands Commission," quoted in *Pecuniary Claims Arbitration, George Rodney Burt, Answer of His Majesty's Government*, Annex 4, at 46 (July 9, 1923) (hereinafter *British Memorial, Rodney Burt*).

7. See Mis. Doc. No. 173, 51st Cong., 1st Sess. (1890).

8. *U.S. Memorial*, 15.

9. Ibid., 16–17. The special agent, George H. Scidmore, was appointed in 1891 and filed his report with the Dept. of State on July 3, 1893, after a year of research in Fiji. See "Report of Mr. George H. Scidmore, special agent of the Department of State to investigate claims of American citizens to lands in Fiji," S. Doc. No. 126, 54th Cong., 1st Sess. 2 (1896).

10. See generally, correspondence reprinted in S. Doc. No. 140, 56th Cong., 2d Sess. (1901).

11. See *Message from the President of the United States*, S. Doc. No. 126, 54th Cong., 1st Sess. 2 (1896).

12. The views of the publicist Thomas Lawrence exemplified the enthusiasm of the time:

> I have indicated my belief that the period of rapid development through which we are now passing may end, if those who stand for righteousness among the nations are at once sane in their aims and earnest in their endeavors, in the establishment of an organized international society, with legislative, executive, and judicial organs. Were this once done, war would in time become as abnormal and infrequent as rebellion.

T. J. Lawrence, *The Principles of International Law*, 4th ed. (Boston: D. C. Heath, 1910), v.

13. See W. E. Hall, *International Law* (Oxford: Clarendon Press, 1880), 5.

14. During this period, for example, the American Society for the Judicial Settlement of International Disputes was founded for the "promotion of the project to establish a judicial tribunal which will do for the civilized world what the ordinary courts of justice do for the individual and to encourage recourse to it when established." "The American Society for Judicial Settlement of International Disputes," *Judicial Settlement of International Disputes*, 1910–12 (1910): 25.

15. See Agreement between Great Britain and the United States for the Settlement of Pecuniary Claims, Aug. 18, 1910, 211 CTS 408.

16. Ibid.

17. Letter from E. J. Phelps to the Marquis of Salisbury, Head of the Foreign Office, November 12, 1887. On file at the Public Records Office, London.

18. Letter from J. Pauncefote to Colonial Office, appending a draft letter to the United States Minister, December 28, 1887. On file at the Public Records Office, London.

19. Letter from John Bramston, Colonial Office, to Lord Salisbury, Foreign Office, December 9, 1887, Collection of the National Archives of Fiji.

20. Letter from John Sherman, U.S. Dept. of State, to John Hay, American Embassy, London, November 16, 1897, printed in S. Doc. No. 140, 56th Cong., 2d Sess. 10 (1901).

21. One of the characteristics of the sense of scale and perspective I consider below is that it never becomes the subject of explicit conversation. This creates a problem for this piece, for the lack of nicely worded quotations in the documents renders it difficult to communicate in a very short number of words the sense of scale that emerges from them. I have settled for presenting my conclusions about this perspective in essay form in hopes that skeptical readers will look for more detailed evidence in the wider project of which this is a part.

22. *British Memorial, Rodney Burt,* Annex 4.

23. *British Memorial, Rodney Burt,* Annex 4, at 41.

24. Cf. T. J. Lawrence, *The Principles of International Law* (Boston: D. C. Heath, 1895), vii (noting that he has endeavored to include the facts of each international controversy in his description of the rules of international law "so that the points of law may be seen in relation to the actual circumstances which were before the courts").

25. Letter from F. H. Villiers, British Foreign Office, to Mr. Carter, American Embassy, March 18, 1897, reprinted in Claims of B. R. Henry and Others, S. Doc. No. 140, 56th Cong., 2d Sess. 5 (1901).

26. See, e.g., T. J. Lawrence, *Essays on Some Disputed Questions in Modern International Law* (Cambridge: Deighton, Bell, 1884), 57:

> The lawyers on the whole regard Sovereignty as the Sovereignty exercised by individuals, and the result was extremely important to international law, for the assumed individuality of sovereigns enabled its founders to regard states as moral beings bound by moral rules.

27. The British lawyers act out this subjectivity, this shared sense of scale with the persons "on the ground," for example, as they correspond with and request advice from Gordon's successors in the Fijian colonial administration. See, e.g., letter from J. B. Thurston to Lord Knutsford, December 21, 1888, Collection of the National Archives of Fiji.

28. The affinity between person and state, and the transformation it engenders, is the subject of much discussion by the publicists of the time. For example, William Hall writes, "States have a moral nature identical with that of individuals, and that with respect to one another they are in the same relation as that in which individuals stand to each other who are subject to law." W. E. Hall, *International Law* (Oxford: Clarendon Press, 1880), 13.

29. See, e.g., Phelps, letter to Marquis of Salisbury.

30. "Probably it is best to say with Oppenheim that persons, like territory, are objects of International Law, and reserve the term subjects for those artificial persons who are either sovereign states, or communities closely akin to them through the possession of some of the distinguishing marks of statehood." Lawrence, *Principles of International Law,* 4th ed., 73.

31. Craig Owens quotes Heidegger's observation that "the fact that the world becomes a picture at all is what distinguishes the essence of the modern age." Craig Owens, "The Discourse of Others: Feminists and Postmodernism," in *The Anti-Aesthetic: Essays on Postmodern Culture,* ed. H. Foster (Seattle: Bay Press, 1983), 66. Note that whether this "transcendental perspective" represents an accurate reflection of the philosophical position found in the canonical Enlightenment texts is not at issue here. What I describe is a popular or institutional view of the Enlightenment project from the vantage point of the nineteenth-century international lawyer that, whether well founded in the writings of Kant and others or not, provided the moral zeal for the international lawyer's task.

32. Cf. D. Kennedy, "A New Stream of International Law Scholarship," *Wisconsin International Law Journal* 7, no. 1 (1989): 8: "Law purports to be *both* above, removed, or neutral with respect to political life *and* the procedural rules, the instrumental expression, the forum and historical embodiment of political culture."

33. Cf. S. Toulmin, *Cosmopolis: The Hidden Agenda of Modernity* (Chicago: University of Chicago Press, 1990), 128.

34. M. Strathern, *After Nature: English Kinship in the Late Twentieth Century* (Cambridge: Cambridge University Press, 1992), 7, 8.

35. M. Strathern, *Partial Connections* (Savage, Md.: Rowman and Littlefield, 1991), xiv, xv, xxiv.

36. Following Foucault, for example, Paul Rabinow argues that the administrative discourses he documents in *French Modern* coalesce only momentarily before they dissolve into contradiction.

37. From Albert Einstein's theory of relativity to Mauss and Durkheim's relativization of systems of classification and Nietzsche's "perspectivism," the intellectual climate was replete with the notion that space and distance was a matter of perspective, that no inherent spatial reality existed outside of the many heterogeneous perspectives of the viewer. Stephen Kern, *The Culture of Time and Space, 1880–1918* (Cambridge: Harvard University Press, 1983), 132–38. Kern follows the trend into the arts, where he notes the innovations of painters such as Cézanne in introducing "truly heterogeneous space in a single canvas with multiple perspectives of the same subject" (141), and the cinema, where directors experimented with camera angles juxtaposed in rapid succession in a way that violated the singular transcendental perspective of past cinematography.

38. See, e.g., J. Baudrillard, *America,* trans. C. Turner (London: Verso, 1988); F. Jameson, *Signatures of the Visible* (New York: Routledge, 1990).

39. Kern notes, for example, the critic Remy de Gourmont's celebration of the capacity to "tour the world" in a single film, and Hugo Münsterberg's observation that, in cinema, "[e]vents which are far distant from one another so that we could not be physically present at all of them at the same time are fusing in our field of vision, just as they are brought together in our own consciousness. . . . Our mind is split and can be here and there apparently in one mental act" (*Culture of Time,* 219).

40. I have in mind the popular slogan of the international environmental movement.

41. See, e.g., D. Kennedy, "Autumn Weekends: An Essay on Law and Everyday Life," in *Law and Everyday Life*, ed. A. Sarat and T. R. Kearns (Ann Arbor: University of Michigan Press, 1993), 191–235.

42. See, e.g., C. Geertz, *Local Knowledge* (New York: Basic Books, 1983).

43. Guattari, for example, celebrates the "paradox" of the global that evidences "a multiplication of anthropological approaches, a planetary intermixing of cultures, paradoxically accompanied by a rising tide of particularisms, racisms, and nationalisms." F. Guattari, "Regimes, Pathways, Subjects," in *Incorporations*, ed. J. Crary and S. Kwinter (New York, Zone, 1992), 16.

44. William Connolly, for example, begins with the normative problem of how to bridge subjectivity—how to take seriously the difference of the other—and surprisingly ends on the topic of "global politics." See W. Connolly, "Identity and Difference in Global Politics," in *International/Intertextual Relations*, ed. J. Der Darien and M. J. Shapiro (Lexington, Mass.: D.C. Heath, 1989), 333.

45. See J. Baudrillard, "The Ecstasy of Communication," in Foster, *The Anti-Aesthetic*, 128.

46. I borrow the term from Vincente Rafael's recent study of the translation of Christian idioms into Tagalog. Rafael notes that "Listening-as-fishing and remembering-as-haunting both entail the appropriation of what comes before oneself (in both temporal and spatial senses). They are ways, therefore, of localizing what is outside of one." Vincente L. Rafael, *Contracting Colonialism: Translation and Christian Conversion in Tagalog Society under Early Spanish Rule* (Durham, N.C.: Duke University Press, 1992), 12.

47. See, e.g., H. K. Bhabha, "Introduction: Narrating the Nation," in *Nation and Narration* (London: Routledge, 1990), 5 (describing a new global space as "this *inter*national dimension both within the margins of the nation-space and in the boundaries *in-between* nations and peoples . . . the problematic unity of the nation to the articulation of cultural difference in the construction of an *inter*national perspective").

48. I am thinking here of the affinity between theories that focus on *categories* and the *boundaries* that delineate them, theories that map out *networks* of relationships, and theories that emphasize the relationship between *perspectives* on a subject. In the domain of critical international law, for example, Ashley and Walker's study of sovereignty integrates a "suspicion of all assertions of sovereign privilege . . . a voice beyond politics and beyond doubt, a voice of interpretation and judgment from which truth and power are thought to emanate as one" with a critique of attempts to delineate and defend disciplinary and territorial boundaries. See R. K. Ashley and R. B. J. Walker, "Reading Dissidence/Writing the Discipline: Crisis and the Question of Sovereignty in International Studies, *International Studies Quarterly* 34 (1990): 367.

Part 3

The Postcolonial Without

Subalternity and International Law: The Problems of Global Community and the Incommensurability of Difference

Dianne Otto

A recurring feature of post–Cold War *new world order* narratives is the assertion that a democratic reshaping of the international community is under way.[1] However, a largely uncontested silence surrounds the implications of expanding democratization for international lawmaking processes.[2] The global production of the new democratic imperative has focused attention on issues of governmental legitimacy within states, effectively circumventing questions of representation, participation, and legitimacy in the global polity.[3] The validity of this maneuver relies on continuing acceptance of the United Nations model wherein democratic pretensions always already capitulate to the de facto balance of global power.

Successful management of this treacherous terrain, so as to prevent democratic demands from spilling over into the international arena, relies on a classical liberal conception of the international community as a citizenry of formally equal nation-states that limits the access of nonstate groupings, individuals, and humanity to interna-

---

An earlier version of this essay appeared in a Special Issue on Law and Postcolonialism, edited by Eve Darian-Smith and Peter Fitzpatrick in *Social and Legal Studies* 5, no. 3 (1996).

tional democratic and legal subjecthood. In this chapter I explore the productive tensions between emancipatory ideas of democracy and the current state-based structure of the international community. From these tensions emerge possibilities for reshaping the processes by which international law is formulated. In particular, I am concerned to ask whether it is possible to imagine processes whereby nondominant, nonelite, *subaltern* individuals and groupings could participate as subjects of international law.[4] To address this question I draw on some of the theoretical perspectives developed by members of the Indian Subaltern Studies Collective.[5]

Of critical importance is how the multiplicity of global difference is treated: whether *difference* is perceived as a threat to international *order* or, alternatively, as part of the dynamic of a transformative vision of international community. Members of the Subaltern Studies group, in tracing the colonial techniques and strategies that led to the formation of the nation-state of India, suggest that modern European knowledge (modernity) is the standard and foundation against which difference is understood in the postcolonial, and now post–Cold War, world. As a result, difference in the modern frame is recognizable only if it is commensurate or coextensive with the European imagination. All other difference is relegated to a *clamor,* a shadow world of superstition, randomness, or criminality because it cannot be articulated on its own terms within the European frame.[6] This silencing and marginalization of incommensurability is the focus of the Subaltern Studies project. The project suggests various strategies that could assist in challenging the exclusionary devices of modernity in ordering the global community.

The following discussion of these issues is divided into four sections. First, in order to provide a context for consideration of Subaltern Studies possibilities, I examine the foundations of the international order that was revitalized by the establishment of the UN in 1945. This examination reveals its European history and commitment to an imperialist-designed state-based conception of the international community. The attendant lawmaking processes authorize and perpetuate its Eurocentric foundation, frustrating the participation, and limiting the power, of non-European states.

Second, I explore the most significant challenge to European domination of the international polity during the Cold War years: a challenge precipitated by the last reshaping of the international community with the recognition of decolonized states. From the early 1970s a united and determined lobby of third world states,[7] calling themselves the Group of 77 (G77), challenged Europe's continuing global economic domination by promoting more egalitarian and democratic lawmaking processes through the UN General Assembly (GA).

Third, I critique the strategy of the G77, drawing on Subaltern Studies perspectives that suggest that the postcolonial modern state remains steadfastly a European construction, albeit with various indigenous interpretations, replete with strategies making it impervious to the voices of the subaltern.[8] Through their uncritical commitment to modernity, postcolonial states are complicit in the silencing of subalternity.

In the fourth section, I outline the problem, identified by Subaltern Studies scholars, of the incommensurability of the difference of subalternity within the European frame. I ask how Subaltern Studies knowledges might inform the current discussions of the reshaping of the international community and animate its democratic, emancipatory potential. In particular I focus on identifying transformative possibilities for addressing questions of *difference,* without assimilation, in the international community and conclude that the disciplinary assumption that multiplicity and order are themselves incommensurable must be unlearned.

The European Foundation of the United Nations Community of States and International Law

The primary purpose of the UN, negotiated during the final months of World War II, was to promote a global *order* that would maintain international peace and security by striking a new balance between protecting state autonomy and facilitating cooperation between states. One feature of this new regime was a commitment to ending colonial forms of domination, evidenced by the promotion of respect for the right of peoples to equal rights and self-determination as one of the fundamental purposes of the UN.

The UN Charter, and these new ideals, reflected the European history of the evolution of the international community, despite the claims to universal application. During the eighteenth and nineteenth centuries, modern Europe, as a product of Enlightenment rationalist thinking, had increasingly understood itself as the center of world history. European states shared cultural, religious, and economic histories that were strong unifying forces. This, coupled with the idea of European *superiority*, set the scene for global European expansionism following the Peace of Westphalia, an endeavor supported by the *order* of international law.[9] As Mohammed Bedjaoui, former president of the International Court of Justice, observed in 1985,

> This classic international law thus consisted of a set of rules with a geographical bias (it was a European law), a religious-ethical inspiration (it was a Christian law), an economic motivation (it was a mercantilist law) and political aims (it was an imperialist law).[10]

It was law that was founded on the violence of European imperialism, not law based on global consent.

By 1945, European domination of world affairs had taken the form of supremacy of the Great Powers: the United States, United Kingdom, France, Soviet Union, and China (although it should be noted that China, after 1949, usually identified itself as a third world nation). These states assumed permanent membership of the most powerful organ of the UN, the Security Council, and held the individual power to veto any Security Council decision. By acquiescing to the dominance of the post–World War II powers, the UN structure promoted deference to de facto power arrangements between states, understood from a European viewpoint, as the primary means of advancing world peace and stability. One result was that the Cold War polarization between the West and Eastern Europe was able to divide the entire globe into two antagonistic camps, both with their origins in, and loyalties to, Europe. As many third world commentators have observed, the shift from European domination to the control of the Great Powers, which quickly became bipolar, had simply changed the form of European hegemony, not its substance.[11]

The powerful adversarial motif and language of the bipolar world helped to disguise the fundamental commonalities of the two primary camps. Both Western and Eastern European states emerged from, and were made possible by, an Enlightenment history that conceived of the world's multiplicities in universally applied Eurocentric narratives. Both viewed history as a worldwide evolutionary movement, the West toward global capitalism and the East toward international socialism, with Europe at the most advanced stage of each development. Their conduct in international relations was guided by the need for both camps to have a stable international system that would defer to their dominance and allow their different conceptions of global progression to unfold.[12]

The common ground between the East and West was extensive, notwithstanding oppositional motivations and rhetoric. While the future of the system of modern states was theorized differently, both traditions were wedded, for that moment at least, to the state-based structure of the international community. As a result, capitalist and Communist states shared a strong commitment to international law's protection of state sovereignty and territorial integrity, and to the positivist view that states' consent must form the basis of international law. Both groupings of states supported the principles that led to the implementation of the decolonization agenda through the UN. Most significantly, for present purposes, both took an occidental view of the third world as *other,* a sensibility that Edward Said describes in his seminal work, *Orientalism,* as

> an *elaboration* not only of a basic geographical distinction (the world is made up of two unequal halves, Orient and Occident) but also of a whole series of "interests" which . . . it not only creates but also maintains; it *is,* rather than expresses, a certain *will* or *intention* to understand, in some cases to control, manipulate, even to incorporate, what is a manifestly different (or alternative and novel) world.[13]

The occidental view was a powerful signifier of European unity and superiority, even across the Cold War barricades.

To become a member of the UN community, and to obtain full international citizenship and sovereign legal personality, an entity must generally qualify as a state. Although the legal criteria for statehood are contestable and unstable, a starting point is provided by the 1933 Montevideo Convention on the Rights and Duties of States, which reflects customary international law on this point. The convention mandates four more or less objective criteria: a permanent population, a defined territory, a government, and *independence* in the form of the capacity to enter into legal relations with other states (article 1). It is widely agreed that these criteria are necessary, but probably not sufficient, for statehood. For instance, there is continuing debate about whether statehood is determined solely by the operation of international law or whether, more importantly, it depends on the political act of recognition by other states.[14] Further, post–Cold War guidelines issued by the European Community on the recognition of new states in the former Eastern bloc suggest additional *objective* requirements of statehood such as a democratic constitution and certain human-rights guarantees.[15] Although my discussion is confined to the classic customary requirements set out by the Montevideo Convention, the argument I am about to make, that European forms are enforced through conceptions of statehood, can also be applied to the mooted additional criteria and to recognition policies.[16]

The experience of postcolonial states in realizing their right to self-determination illustrates how the four customary requirements of statehood are measured against European standards and viewpoints. The first two requisites, of defined population and territory, were satisfied by maintaining the colonially determined subdivisions of entire continents, irrespective of precolonial identities and organization. This was mandated by the legal principle of *uti possidetis juris* (unalterability of colonial frontiers), which enforced imperialist-designed unities of territory and peoples in the form of the nation-state. Self-determination was denied to peoples who lived in areas within or straddling colonial borders.[17] The brutality and lack of consent involved in such total disregard for what existed prior to European conquest continues to reverberate in the many *civil* conflicts that are being waged today in record numbers.

The second two customary requirements of statehood, of government and independence, were also understood in the European sense as based on centrally organized systems and institutions backing up the ultimate authority of the state and achieving a shift in citizens' primary loyalty from family, religious, or community association to the imagined nation-state.[18] The superiority of the modern nation-state was thus juxtapositioned with the *traditional* social formations that predated the *civilizing mission* of the European colonists around the globe.

In effect, the requirements of statehood repeat the founding violence of colonialism by inscribing it in a new legal narrative that relegitimates its imperialist outcomes. Jacques Derrida refers to this as the "mystical foundation of authority," by which the violence of the foundations and the maintenance of law is justified and silenced retrospectively.[19] By enforcing nation-statehood upon diverse communities and multiplicitous identities, international citizenship requires becoming *civilized* according to European standards that involve succumbing to what Michel Foucault describes as the modern techniques of "governmentality,"[20] something that I will return to in the third section.

States, when joining the UN's community of states, formally *consent* to being bound by international law in their adoption of the UN Charter and the International Court of Justice Statute appended to it. The fictional dimensions of this consent are readily apparent, belying social contractarian theories which originated in European liberal philosophy and rely on consent to legitimate international law's authority. However, despite its fictional dimensions, social-contract theory has dominated the way that states' interrelationships are postulated and the legal conceptualization of states' rights and duties.[21] Member states are understood as autonomous, self-interested, sovereign units in a relationship of formal equality with each other. As subjects and creators of international law, states are assumed to be independent, to operate according to their own free wills, and to be able to pursue their self-interest, irrespective of any social or economic imbalance. One problem, as critical legal theorist Nigel Purvis explains, is that "[l]iberalism itself makes no room for a theory of justice in the world because it imagines the pursuit of liberty as the only legitimate substantive objective."[22]

The tension between social contractarian/positivist positions and notions of justice is reflected in debates about the sources of international law. The classic sources are formally spelled out in article 38 of the ICJ Statute, which recognizes three primary sources and is, arguably, not an exhaustive list. The first primary source referred to by the statute is law made by way of specific agreement between states in the form of treaties or other binding compacts. The second is customary law, which is traditionally understood as established by the long-term and virtually consistent practice of states accompanied by the belief that they are legally bound to so act. The third source is found in general principles of law that, in the statute's infamous words, are "recognized by civilised nations." The statute also recognizes two subsidiary means of determining international law: the teachings of highly qualified legal experts and judicial decisions, although the principle of *stare decisis* does not operate in international law.

While positivists would argue that these sources are strongly consent based, falling into the category of "hard" international law, natural lawyers would emphasize the extraconsensual "soft" law quality of justness, particularly present in custom and general legal principles. In contrast to hard law, soft legal principles and instruments are understood as arising from authoritative agreement between states that is not necessarily legally binding in a formal sense at the time the agreement is made. Examples may include GA resolutions and declarations, "framework" conventions that establish mechanisms for cooperation between states, and nonbinding codes of conduct. "Soft" law may also refer to newly emerging international law, apparent from state practice and belief. David Kennedy, highlighting the links between soft law and extraconsensual notions of justice, argues that the hard and soft narratives of international-law sources are interrelated and essential to the precarious balancing of autonomy and community in the global system of states: "Without a sense of *both* the distinctiveness of consent and justice *and* of their inseparability, sources discourse could not reflect both sovereign autonomy and equality."[23]

However, Kennedy's scheme, wherein justice and self-interest are balanced in the contestation of the authority of the sources of international law, was not the experience of the emerging lobby of postcolonial states. In their view, law arising from *civilized* legal principles and from long-standing custom offered very little scope as a vehicle for substantial change. From this perspective, the former involves an outright rejection of non-European legal principles leaving no room for maneuver. The latter, customary law, is based on the activities of states during the colonial era and, in Bedjaoui's eloquent view, remains

> [b]ackward looking, conservative because static, iniquitous in its content, ponderous in its formation . . . [and] cannot be of real use in the development of new rules and could actually be an obstacle to any attempt at change.[24]

This left formal interstate agreement as the main vehicle for challenging the European foundations of international law: hardly a promising option. The apparent imperviousness of international law to non-European intervention helped create the impetus for the G77's contestation of global European hegemony during the 1970s and 1980s, which will be examined in the next section.

Alternatively, it can be argued that the UN commitment to decolonization was a positive indication of the gradual erosion of European dominion. But this misunderstands the context and terms of this commitment. Imperialism, which had earlier justified European occupation of territories through conquest, was no longer legitimate in the ascendant liberal view, which led to the emergence of new principles of equal rights and self-determination. These new principles provided both the moral and legal foundations for decolonization, although this commitment was undoubtedly bolstered by the coincidence of clear economic reasons to pursue such a policy.[25] But, as I have argued, decolonization was only available, on narrow terms, to entities that resembled the modern European nation-state. The effect was that decolonization repeated imperialism, but with a new legal and moral appearance.

Paradoxically, it is also true that the same liberal ideas that buttress the power of Europe contain the seeds of resistance. As the number of non-European states increased during the 1950s and 1960s, the Eurocentric orientation of the UN framework became increasingly unacceptable within its own terms. The liberal rhetoric of sovereign equality and universal standards exposed the reality that third world states were only partial members of the society of states. Colonial domination was obviously continuing, albeit in a different guise, not only mandating the adoption of European laws and values but also, significantly, leaving global economic control with the Western-dominated Bretton Woods system of financial institutions, established in 1944, which operate independently from the UN.[26]

In result, it was clear that third world difference was silenced by its relegation to the spheres of *tradition* or *underdevelopment*. In addition to requiring homogeneity in the form of modernity, gross economic disparities were completely ignored. The complicity of the international legal system in these developments became the focus of a major third world strategy to challenge European hegemony by developing new lawmaking processes that would be inclusive of their concerns. In Europe's own terms, it was argued that the existing state of affairs was undemocratic, discriminatory, and inequitable.

Third World Challenges

In the years between 1945 and 1989 a significant change occurred in the makeup of the UN with the trebling of its membership as a result of decolonization. As a consequence, developed states were no longer in the numerical majority. This led to a number of attempts by third world states to counter Eurocentric domination by promoting more egalitarian procedures and substantive economic justice within the international community of states. A central platform in these attempts was the challenge to international lawmaking processes launched by the G77 through its promotion of the New International Economic Order (NIEO). The agenda was to assert the autonomy, and protect the wealth, of third world states from European control.

Luis Echeverria Alvarez, the president of Mexico, summarized the aspirations of the G77.[27] The general aims were to promote justice in the distribution of the resources of the world and equity in participation in economic decision-making. The more specific goal was to establish a firm legal footing for the NIEO that would base the rights and duties of states on new legal principles, including

> freedom to dispose of natural resources; the right of every nation to adopt the economic structure it considered most suitable and to treat private property as the public interest required; renunciation of the use of economic pressures; subjection of foreign capital to domestic laws; prohibition of interference by supranational corporations in the internal affairs of states; abolition of trade practices that discriminated against the exports of non-industrial nations; economic advantages proportionate to levels of development; treaties guaranteeing stable and fair prices for basic products; transfer of technology; and greater economic resources for long-term untied aid.

The aim was to dismantle the international legal order that had legitimated colonialism and imperialism and thereby end Western domination of the world economy that continued despite the attainment of political independence by almost all formerly colonized peoples.

The strategy was to utilize the recently acquired majority of the third world in the GA where every member state has one vote. While GA resolutions do not formally have legislative force, in certain circumstances they may be considered to have the authority of conventions or to be an expression of custom.[28] The G77 hoped to upgrade the legal status of GA resolutions through asserting their sui generis legislative character. In this way they planned to counter third world marginalization and carve out a role for the UN in promoting economic justice.

While the UN Charter clearly locates responsibility for economic matters within the UN (articles 1[3], 55, and 56), Western commitment to the Bretton Woods institutions had prevented this from eventuating. In fact, the establishment of the World Bank, International Monetary Fund, and General Agreement on Tariffs and Trade had been a conscious policy of the West to keep economic questions out of GA control.[29] Many third world commentators argued that this separation of power was directly oppositional to the principles of the UN Charter.[30] The G77 strategy was to bring the international economic system within the control of the UN by reshaping it through the soft-law processes of GA resolutions, which are made on the basis of the juridical equality of all states. The unity with which the diverse third world lobby operated was a reflection of the strength of their sense of exploitation and subjugation by the West.[31] Many observers noted the optimism and newfound confidence that accompanied the promotion of the NIEO. Wang Tieya, for example, writes of the "eagerness" of states representatives to participate in activities that will ensure that "international law be gradually rewritten to reflect the revolutionary changes that have taken place since the end of the Second World War."[32]

The resort to soft law, based on principles of democracy, justice, and substantive equality, was necessitated by the impediments inherent in the imperialist foundations of traditional sources of hard law or, as in Kennedy's view referred to above, the traditional interrelatedness of hard and soft law. European control was deeply embedded in treaty processes, custom, and general principles of law. In contrast to the "iniquitous" traditional lawmaking processes, the egalitarian character of GA resolutions presented an appropriate alternative site for the NIEO to launch itself.[33]

Soft law, like that created by many GA resolutions, has been identified by some legal theorists as the principle means of developing international law.[34] They have questioned whether it is always desirable to attain the legal status of hard (consent-based) law because of its slow process of formation and inflexibility. Such views are vigorously contested by positivist, social contractarian legal theorists.[35] They charge that soft law introduces ambiguity, bias, and conceptual weakness to international law, which will lead to "mediocrity" and the "dilution" of normativity. Yet it is instructive to remember that the precarious legislative powers of the GA did not stop the West from adopting a strategy similar to the G77's, in the 1950s, when GA resolutions were used to authorize UN action in the Korean War while the Security Council was deadlocked on the issue.[36]

The 1974 Charter of Economic Rights and Duties of States (CERDS) (GA Res 3281 [XXIX]), one of the founding instruments of the NIEO, endorsed many of the established principles of international law in relation to economic matters. Significantly, the CERDS strongly reiterated the principle of territorial sovereignty, despite the previous failure of decolonized states to realize this principle in practice. It also reaffirmed the sovereign equality of states, in spite of this having worked against third world states in the past.

In addition, the CERDS promoted many equitable legal principles in the areas of trade and economic cooperation, which attracted considerable hostility from Western states. The innovations included affirmative action in relation to developing states; nondiscrimination on the basis of political, economic, and social differences between states; noncoercion in the form of colonialism, neocolonialism, and all forms of foreign domination; and collective economic security including conducting economic affairs in a way that respects the interests of other states. In forefronting equitable principles, the CERDS included the new concept of "the common heritage of mankind [*sic*]" (article 29), something that third world states had been promoting in earlier negotiations concerning the law of the sea. The idea was that any benefits gained from exploiting the resources of areas outside the national jurisdiction of states, like the deep sea-bed, be shared equitably between states rather than belong to those (developed) states with the technological capabilities to exploit them.

As their proposals indicate, the G77 states were attempting to introduce a substantive notion of justice to international law, in addition to developing more democratic legal processes. This was a response to liberal positivism's ability to ignore global imbalances of power by claiming a position of neutrality and objectivity that, in reality, operated as a code for European privilege. The G77 was keen to replace the self-interested individualism of liberal positivism with legal principles that were consistent with the third world ideals of "solidarity" or "collective legitimacy."[37] Wil Verwey describes it as follows:

> The effort to (partially) replace the principle of freedom by that of protection, the principle of equality by that of inequality, the prin-

> ciple of reciprocity by non-reciprocity, comes in its essence to the introduction of the principle of *solidarity* in international economic law.[38]

Prompting this reimagining of the international community was the idea that the third world was reasserting an ethical framework, which had been stifled by colonialism, and thereby rejecting the European dualism that separates legalism from morality.

In this way the G77's legal strategy was fundamentally linked to the philosophy of the broader liberation struggles of colonized peoples. Leopold Sedar Senghor, the first president of an independent Senegal, describes the African ontology as follows:

> [T]he African has always and everywhere presented a concept of the world which is diametrically opposed to the traditional philosophy of Europe. The latter is essentially *static, objective, dichotomic;* it is, in fact, dualistic, in that it makes an absolute distinction between body and soul, matter and spirit. It is founded on separation and opposition: on analysis and conflict. The African, on the other hand, conceives the world, beyond the diversity of its forms, as a fundamentally mobile, yet unique, reality that seeks synthesis.[39]

While there are many who then, and now, reject the homogenizing effects of nativist philosophy,[40] reclaiming an affirmative precolonial identity was a powerful unifying force. It was productive of a great deal of third world activism and could perhaps be regarded as an example of what Gayatri Chakravorty Spivak would read as "a *strategic* use of positivist essentialism in a scrupulously visible political interest."[41] By which I take her to mean that essentialism may be defended for its strategic benefits in certain contingent and continually contested circumstances. But the nativist position does fail to recognize the heterogeneity of non-Western peoples, an issue that will reemerge in the Subaltern Studies perspectives in the next section.

Many commentators now argue that the NIEO ultimately failed.[42] This view is supported by the consensus adoption of a new blueprint for global economic cooperation by the GA in 1990 that made no reference to the NIEO.[43] But the result is not so clear-cut. The framework and principles established by the early resolutions of the NIEO have undoubtedly influenced a diverse range of subsequent policy and program instruments. These include initiatives dealing with the transfer of technology, health, the control of transnational corporations, environmental protection, disarmament, energy, the resources of the sea, and food production.[44] Acceptance of the flexibility and usefulness of soft-law instruments in dealing with contentious issues is now widely acknowledged, notably in relation to the environment and the rights of indigenous peoples.[45] The International Court of Justice has recognized NIEO soft-law principles of equity in disputes about distribution of resources and the determination of boundaries.[46] Perhaps most significantly, it is generally agreed that the concept of a "common heritage" legal regime has attained the status of customary international law with regard to the deep sea-bed and to the moon.[47]

On the other hand, it must be conceded that the major aims of the NIEO were frustrated. The goals of reshaping the international economic environment and transferring economic benefits from developed to developing states are a long way from being realized. The two central disputes of the CERDS were never resolved—first, the issue of expropriation or nationalization of property owned by foreigners in decolonized states and the associated questions of compensation and, second, the justification of commodity cartels.[48] Also, very little impact on the Bretton Woods financial institutions was achieved.[49] Finally, the approach of the NIEO precipitated, or perhaps exacerbated, a deeply entrenched polarization between the West and the third world (with the Eastern bloc prevaricating) that, in some views, was counterproductive.[50] This antipathy continues today in the North-South divide of the post–Cold War period.

The attempt at a transformation of the ethical underpinning of international law also has continuing disruptive effects. The critique of liberal positivism, particularly its claims to neutrality and universality, was effectively made, and, as a result, new dimensions have been added to the thinking of critical legal scholars and natural lawyers.[51] In the mainstreaming of the "common heritage" idea, the whole of humanity has become a juridical subject that is a conception of international community that extends across the boundaries imposed by the atomized system of nation-states. That law can and should be fundamentally informed by a paradigm of substantive equality remains in contention and productive of transformative possibilities.

Despite its oppositional stance to Western domination, the G77 strategy relied on an arsenal of liberal legal concepts to support its case including self-determination, democracy, equity, participation, nondiscrimination, equality, and state sovereignty. In so doing, the strategy remained uncritical of modernity itself. A Subaltern Studies perspective would suggest that the G77 challenge was both made possible, and also prevented from substantial success, by the uncritical embracing of a European framework. The paradox that this brings to light is explored in the work of the Subaltern Studies Collective. In the next section, a Subaltern Studies analysis of the G77 strategy is developed.

A Subaltern Studies Analysis

The initial question at the center of the work of the Subaltern Studies scholars in the early 1980s was how, in the formation of the independent Indian nation-state, the nationalists came to represent an Indian elite, closely allied to the British colonialists, rather than the mass of the Indian people.[52] As critical historians, the impetus for their investigations was the imperialist fiction narrated by mainstream Indian history that, in Ranajit Guha's words,

> fails to acknowledge, far less interpret, the contribution made by the people *on their own*, that is, *independently of the elite* to the making and development of this [Indian] nationalism. . . . the poverty of this historiography is demonstrated beyond doubt by its failure to understand and assess the mass articulation of this nationalism except, negatively, as a law and order problem, and positively, if at all, either as a response to the charisma of certain elite leaders or in . . . terms of vertical mobilization by the manipulation of factions. The involvement of the Indian people in vast numbers, sometimes in hundreds of thousands or even millions, in nationalist activities and ideas is thus represented as a diversion from a supposedly "real" political process.[53]

Through the work of Subaltern Studies scholars seeking to fill the gaps and silences in dominant historical narratives, many important events in Indian history have been meticulously reworked. The role of popular participatory democratic politics, in incidents characterized by colonial histories as random, unlawful insurgencies or the result of manipulation due to religious fanaticism or charismatic leaders, is gradually being exposed.[54]

What commenced as an essentially empirical task, seeking to write into Indian history accounts of popular nationalism, quickly became multidimensional, producing critiques of modernity and nationalism and addressing complex issues associated with the epistemological question of who could speak for whom, and beyond.[55] Guha identifies two dominant "elite" streams of historical narrative vying to represent the process of Indian decolonization.[56] Both streams privilege the interests and perspectives of ruling groups and credit the achievement of Indian nationalism to the activities of those groups. Guha associates one stream with "colonialist elitism," which understands Indian nationalism as the inevitable outcome of a process of European governance and institution building. He describes the second stream as "bourgeois-nationalist elitism," which credits the indigenous elite with serving the cause of the people in leading them from colonial domination to freedom in the form of the independent nation-state.

The colonial and nationalist historical narratives of India, identified by Guha, correspond with the dominant narratives of the UN community, outlined in the previous two sections: the first produced by the UN Charter framework with its imperialist foundations and modern expressions of European liberalism, and the second produced by the G77 in the process of seeking full membership in the UN community through promotion of the NIEO. The remainder of this section discusses these two narratives from a Subaltern Studies perspective before turning, in the last section, to the question of re-presenting incommensurable difference within the global community and its laws.

The UN Charter sets about the task of promoting and maintaining international peace and security by establishing a modern institutional framework for ordering the international community of states. In this endeavor it is allied with the colonialist historiography of India that narrates the *civilizing mission* of the colonial power as the establishment of institutions of modern government. In this view, the Indian nation goes through a kind of reeducation that enables a nationalist elite to come to desire the introduced systems and eventually take responsibility for maintaining and perpetuating them in the indigenous setting.[57]

Subaltern Studies scholars understand modern government as a means of systematizing, categorizing and ordering diverse social experience and consciousness so that it becomes commensurable with the dominant European knowledge frame—that of Enlightenment rationalism. In order to explain how this works in the colonial situation, Dipesh Chakrabarty draws on Foucault's analysis of "governmentality," which highlights the reliance of modern governments on the techniques of measurement.[58] Foucault's point is that without statistics, rational institutions and representative systems of government cannot be built.[59]

Chakrabarty observes that one of the first tasks in the British colonization of India was to produce modern archives of knowledge that had not previously been systematized or documented. This colonial project relied on the social sciences to devise methods and categories for information gathering. Ultimately, people came to largely fit the categories constructed by European systems of knowledge, although incommensurable knowledges are never completely erased and remain potentially disruptive. To the extent that non-European difference is made *knowable* in the European imagination, it becomes ordered into the modern state and thereby *controllable.*

Social science contributes the method of "causality" to deal with dissidence and insurgency.[60] In the social-science view, such disorder is understood as a kind of reflex response to discrete "causes" like poverty and unemployment, or as connected with criminality or religious fanaticism. These causes, once identified, can be policed and managed by the art of government.[61] In this paradigm, popular insurgency is understood as external to the subaltern consciousness, as a reaction to a precise cause that can be rationally addressed, rather than acknowledged as a contestation of the subjugation that the modern state apparatus enforces and maintains. As Guha explains, "To know the cause of a phenomenon is already a step taken in the direction of controlling it."[62]

Chakrabarty uses the examples of the categories of religion and caste to illustrate this point. Both schemas were central to the British project of making the Indian people the objects of colonial knowledge. Both were key categories in the regular census that the British undertook in India despite, as Chakrabarty points out, the absence of these categories from statistical data that the British collected about its domestic population. The "caste" and "religion" systems of the British sorted people into absolute and hierarchical divisions, placing limits on identities that had previously been experienced as multilayered, negotiable, and contingent. Chakrabarty suggests that the eventual identification with precise dualistic categories has led to the playing out of the modern problems of race and ethnicity in India, evidenced in the 1949 partition of India and Pakistan and in the religious and caste conflicts prevalent in India today. In his view, "the very structure of modern governmentality carries with it the seeds of ethnic bloodbath."[63]

The legal system, introduced by the British, played an important role in institutionalizing the European frame and eradicating the subject effects of noncommensurable difference. Gayatri Chakravorty Spivak notes that

> in the constitution of that Other of Europe, great care was taken to obliterate the textual ingredients with which such a subject could cathect, could occupy (invest?) its itinerary—not only by ideological and scientific production, but also by the institution of the law.[64]

Legal argument is a powerful forum in which dominant narratives of social reality are produced and reproduced as normative, and alternative discourses are silenced.[65] In this way, law plays a constitutive role, alongside the social sciences, in defining the colonial subject and, given the connection between knowledge and power, in legitimating dominant distributions of power.[66] In codifying Hindu law, for example, the colonizers reduced a "polymorphous structure of legal performance" to a disciplined, modern "binary vision."[67]

The connection between the processes that colonized India and the ordering techniques of the international community of states is made succinctly by Chakrabarty.

> My point is that the social assumptions on which the classification and organization of census figures rested were fundamentally modern: they showed India to be a collection of "communities" whose "progress" or "backwardness" could be measured by the application of some supposedly "universal" indices. This is exactly how the modern world of nation states is structured—it is a united but internally hierarchized world where some countries are described as measurably—or should I say immeasurably—more "advanced" than others. . . .The word "civilization" has long since fallen out of favour; we preferred to talk about "progress" in the

> nineteenth century and "development" in the twentieth, but the idea of a united world with an internally articulated hierarchy, measurable by some universally-agreed indices, has remained with us.[68]

The discourse of the UN Charter is revealed, from this perspective, as highly coded. It reproduces the patterns of European domination that operate within the now decolonized states at the global level.

The UN Charter fosters a system of universal "governmentality" by establishing institutions able to collect vast amounts of information about its members. The Economic and Social Council enjoys the broad brief to study and report on (read *sociologize and supervise*) international economic, social, cultural, educational, health, and related matters (article 62[1]). Member states are able to set up global specialized agencies (read *centralize expert knowledge*) covering a similar range of fields (article 57[1]). The UN Charter provides for the "administration" (read *governmentalization*) of non-self-governing and trust territories by member states (articles 73 and 75). Article 73(e) specifically requires the collection of "statistical and other information of a technical nature relating to economic, social, and economic conditions" as a responsibility of administering authorities. Article 88 envisages that the Trusteeship Council will formulate a "questionnaire" to form the basis of annual reports by the states responsible. In other words, the UN Charter itself equates progress toward eventual statehood with the establishment of systems that record and monitor (read *control and discipline*) the indigenous population.

All of this information and assessment eventually takes the form of recommendations to member states, the GA and the Security Council, providing rationalizations and justifications (read *finding causes*) for the activities (read *police and surveillance work*) of the most powerful global institutions. What claims, on the surface, to be the neutral application of social-science techniques aimed at the progressive economic and social development of all peoples has the effect of deepening global European domination. As a result, the diversity of knowledges emanating from different epistemological and ontological frameworks is violently repressed and disciplined in the operation of the UN's international community of states.

The complicity of the international legal system in globally normalizing and instituting the knowledges of modern disciplinary

Europe has already been canvassed. Legal claims to rationality, objectivity, and neutrality are reinforced by the categories of the social sciences, and law's place as a "prominent conversation" in international relations[69] reinscribes normativity into new elite knowledges. But simultaneously, because legal argument cannot produce the neutral outcomes it lays claim to, it emerges as a site for contesting "objective" social realities,[70] as the G77 set out to do.

But the massive effort of the G77 to change the Eurocentric international order through the platform and program of the NIEO was, from a Subaltern Studies view, analogous to the claims of the Indian nationalists who purported to be leading the subaltern classes to emancipation and freedom. The interests represented by the postcolonial states, no matter how well intentioned, were those of the nationalist elites who had more or less uncritically assumed the governmental mantle that was the bequest of the colonizers. In this way, the strategy of the NIEO was shaped by the European imagination and not, as was often claimed, by an autonomous third world sensibility and vision that was inclusive of subaltern interests.

As we have seen, the work of the Subaltern Studies scholars in the Indian context showed that nationalist history was nowhere concerned to document the independent aspirations and activities of subaltern peoples. The participation of the Indian people in the anticolonial struggle was represented as an effect or reflection of the leadership of the indigenous elite. Activities that challenged this "fine" leadership were depicted as the "terrible" binary opposite of anticolonialism by elite discourses, a technique that Guha calls the "prose of counter-insurgency."[71]

Attempts to write the subaltern experience into Indian history led to a critique of nationalism itself as a European ideology. The task of unifying the nation, where there was no sense of unity before, was very important for the emergence of the modern state of India. In effect, nationalism, secularism, and self-determination became the modernizing or *civilizing* ideologies par excellence. The nationalist struggle relied on the mobilizing power of the claim that the colonial government was not accountable to the local people. Actualizing the deliverance of the state from colonial control involved reclaiming the state as an expression of the *true* Indian nation, which meant bringing the Indian identity into a relationship of commensurability with modernity. To this end, peasant struggles were interpreted and harnessed as support for the nationalist cause that involved engaging the subaltern imagination within an elite nationalist, but still European, frame.[72]

The Subaltern Studies view roundly rejects the nativist narratives that were successfully promoted by the nationalists in the independence struggle. The critical question from a subaltern view was, as Said describes it, "which India for which Indians?'[73] The nativist call to unity utilized the European tactic of essentializing and dualizing difference. This technique helped to silence narratives that were inconsistent with or oppositional to the nativist view. It forced a homogeneity on the diversity of, what became, the Indian nation enabling the elite to claim that they spoke for all and leaving incommensurable subaltern experience silenced. The point is, in Chakrabarty's view,

> that the question of Indian unity has never been settled beyond all doubt and disputation. . . . The British cobbled a political India together for reasons of administrative convenience [and t]he nationality question was muddied from the beginning.[74]

The strategy of the G77 in advancing the NIEO may be critiqued in a similar manner. The first point to be made is that the third world "revolution" in the international community did not involve a critique of the modern nation-state. Quite the reverse. Like the Indian nationalist movement before it, the agenda set out by the G77 in the CERDS was to claim the fullest rights of statehood as represented in the ideal model of the European state. The NIEO strategy sought to erect and strengthen the postcolonial nation-state as a bulwark against European intervention, failing to see that the nation-state itself necessitated operating within a disciplinary European framework.

The nativist strategy of claiming to represent a coherent international third world viewpoint and ethic repeated the nationalist strategy of unifying the nation by promoting a single Indian identity at the expense of the diversity of subaltern peoples. In the global context, the championing of third world difference made powerful claims to advocating a nonhegemonic, socially just, cooperative world community. In reality, the assertion of a univocal non-European identity relegated incommensurable third world voices to the position of alien. This reproduced the modernizing effects of nationalism in the silencing of subalternity in the international community.

Certain Indian intellectuals, who fear that critiquing modernity is playing into the hands of Indian Hinduvta fundamentalists, have charged the Subaltern Studies project with promoting a new indigenism in the subject of the subaltern.[75] In addition, Spivak remarks that Guha's mapping of the colonial stratification of the Indian peoples "could hardly be more essentialist and taxonomical." But she attempts a defense on the grounds that "because of the imperialist epistemic, social and disciplinary inscription, a project [i.e., Subaltern Studies] understood in essentialist terms must traffic in a radical textual practice of differences."[76] That is, since the object of the project's interest is the impossible task of excavating a presence that European thought has rendered impossible, it is necessarily involved in difference by attempting to give voice to a social absence, which is difference itself. She endorses the Foucauldian suggestion that making the unseen visible can have important disruptive effects, but that "it is the slippage from rendering visible the mechanism to rendering vocal the individual . . . that is consistently troublesome."[77]

Returning, then, to the G77 strategy: it failed to make visible the mechanisms of hierarchy and exclusion that made third world identification possible. The apparent paradox of its reliance on liberal ideals to promote its alternative vision is, in the Subaltern Studies view, entirely consistent. As in the case of the nationalist Indian elite, the claim to a new world order of solidarity and equality reflected the transition from the imperialist to the liberal worldview of Europe, not the dawning of an emancipatory alternative. Principles of self-determination and the equality of nation-states emphasized by the G77 are, in fact, key techniques aimed at disciplining global difference and nurturing the third world desire for modernity that is essential to the internationalization of Europe in the postcolonial world.

Despite the many progressive goals of the NIEO, and the continuing disruptive effects of its achievements, the G77 strategy failed to develop a critique of modernity itself and in so doing helped to entrench European hegemony. Whether this was inevitable, or whether there are ways to contest a dominant form of power that challenge its hegemony, is the question addressed in the next section.

The Problem of Incommensurability and the Future of the International Community

In searching for the voice of the Indian peasant in the process of formation of the Indian nation, Subaltern Studies scholars found that, first, Indian modernity was impossible to think about except in relation to

European modernity and, second, that it wasn't possible to theorize the Indian peasant except by way of the European thought apparatus. In other words, experience that was noncommensurable and therefore *outside* the European experience was not representable within the language of modern knowledge. This does not mean that the subaltern are unable to talk but rather, that they are not admissible on their own terms. Their presence is marked by moments of disruption and discontinuity that are discernible at the periphery of mainstream historiography. Chakrabarty likens this to a Derridean "trace" of something that cannot be completely erased by modernity's assertions of universality.[78]

Indian elite historiographies variously describe the moments of disruption by subaltern speech as a "clamor," the spread of "rumor," the noise of "the mindless rabble," the disorganization of "the traditional community," and the impulse of "religious fanaticism." The effect is that historiography collaborates with governmentality in regulating subaltern activity, which calls the whole system into question, to a mode of speech that is not admissible in the modern frame. Legal processes, introduced by the British, played an important role in adjudicating the boundaries of acceptable speech. At the limits, Anglo-Indian law enforced "the myth of unreadability"[79] in order to produce a verdict that was consistent with colonial superiority and dominance.

A central issue for Subaltern Studies is whether it is possible to give voice, without assimilation, to the difference that appears at the intersection of the modern and its *other.* At this juncture, the relationship of domination and subordination between the Indian or colonial elite and the peasant is contested. This raises the important methodological question of whether it is possible to break the "code of counterinsurgency," which renders the peasants' activities unreadable, and represent the insurgent's point of view in a way that does not result in the epistemic violence of forcing its commensurability.

In Spivak's view, the consciousness of the subaltern "can be no more than a theoretical fiction to entitle the project of reading."[80] Her response to the tendency apparent within Subaltern Studies to excavate a peasant consciousness from the archives of the elite is to read this, instead, as the retrieval of the subaltern "subject effect." The effect of an operating subaltern subject is produced by the conjunction of networks of ideological, political, economic, historical, legal, and other kinds of power. These texts intersect and interweave to construct the appearance of subaltern consciousness that, in Spivak's view, is better understood as an expression of the relationships of domination/resistance experienced by the peasant.

Homi Bhabha uses the term *hybridization* to explain how the discourse of colonial power enables a productive rereading that makes possible the articulation of alternate narratives. He suggests that the colonial discourse expresses an ambivalence between, on the one hand, its claim to authority and truth and, on the other hand, its displacement of difference that questions its authority, which nevertheless is always present as a trace, a "hybrid." In this view, not unlike Foucault's, domination is productive rather than repressive because

> [t]he place of difference and otherness, or the space of the adversarial . . . is never entirely on the outside or implacably adversarial. It is a pressure, and a presence, that acts constantly, if unevenly, along the entire boundary of authorization. . . . Resistance . . . is the effect of an ambivalence produced within the rules of recognition of dominating discourses as they articulate the signs of cultural difference and reimplicate them within the deferential relations of colonial power—hierarchy, normalization, marginalization, and so forth.[81]

The Subaltern Studies collective is concerned to map this productivity and thereby come closer to the relationship of power experienced by the peasant and the possibilities of resistance to domination that it contains.

Edward Said considers it a "crucial point" to recognize that the relationship of domination and subordination is one of interdependence, and therefore that the uncovering of subaltern history is not a "separatist enterprise."[82] He notes that "no matter how one tried to extricate the subaltern from elite histories, they are different but overlapping and curiously interdependent territories." The power of the peasant to resist her or his oppressor comes from interaction with the dominant mode of power, and, as in the Gramscian view, history unfolds in the resulting movement against and away from relations of domination.

This recognition of interdependence means that the central question for the Subaltern Studies collective is how to push at the boundaries of modernity rather than how to give voice to what is outside it.

The goal is to understand what modernity means, and develop strategies to deal with it, not to take a countermodern position. Collective members admit that global European production includes themselves and their project and that, in their excavations of the subaltern, they are working within European hegemony.[83] But their focus is on the transformative possibilities at the limits of Western philosophy where the potential for bringing the subaltern into Indian modernity lies. It is, in many ways, a deeply democratic project.

The European production of the desire for democracy is also within the dominant discourse of the international community, in the norms of self-determination and sovereign equality. To date, these norms have been narrowly and unevenly applied to a community theorized as a society of nation-states. In the tensions between the rhetoric and reality of these democratic norms are the seeds of resistance. One response to the tensions, illustrated by the G77 platform, is to insist that European standards apply universally in practice. But the desire to become commensurable with the European experience is a central dynamic of European hegemony, not the foundation of a new world order, as claimed by the G77.

The Subaltern Studies perspective, in contrast, pushes the question of democracy beyond the goal of expanding the polity to be more inclusive and representative of difference. As Chakrabarty explains,

> [S]ubaltern histories written with an eye to difference cannot constitute yet another attempt . . . to help erect the subaltern as the subject of modern democracies, that is, to expand the history of the modern in such a way as to make it more representative of society as a whole. This is a laudable objective in its own terms, and has undoubted global relevance. But thought does not have to stop at political democracy or the concept of egalitarian distribution of wealth. Though the aim of achieving these ends will legitimately fuel many immediate political struggles, this kind of thought is fundamentally insensitive to philosophical questions of difference, and can acknowledge difference only as a practical problem.[84]

The response of representative politics and democratic pluralism continues to adopt Europe as the universal benchmark, falling well short of the subaltern challenge.

So, how can the Subaltern Studies framework inform the current discussions of the reshaping of the international community and its democratic potential? I will outline three ways in which a subaltern analysis can contribute to these discussions: first, in unmasking the European nature of the form of modern thought; second, in theorizing a different epistemological point of knowing from which alternatives may be imagined; and third, in raising the possibility of a political philosophy that can speak in noncommensurability.

First, the deconstructive approaches of the Subaltern Studies project, in searching for presences that European thought has made impossible, enable the European genealogy of the dominant international discourses on community and democracy to become transparent. This makes it possible to, at least, identify and "denaturalize"[85] the parametric distortions of European hegemony. It makes visible questions of difference that can lead in directions alternative to that of liberal pluralism, which embraces difference only to the point that the supremacy of European modernity is not threatened.

Applying this approach, first, to the idea of *community* in the European frame, it becomes apparent that community is largely understood as oppositional to *individualism.* The result of this dualization is that both alternatives are defined by each other, thereby foreclosing additional possibilities. As Iris Marion Young explains:

> Each entails a denial of difference and desire to bring multiplicity and heterogeneity into unity, although in opposing ways. Liberal individualism denies difference by positing the self as a solid, self-sufficient unity, not defined by or in need of anything or anyone other than itself. . . . Community, on the other hand, denies difference by positing fusion rather than separation as the social ideal.[86]

Young argues that the idea of community is too encoded with hegemonic dualisms to be able to express a radical politics of difference. Yet *community* is a concept that has often been used to imagine other collectivities besides the nation-state, not only by Subaltern Studies scholars but also by indigenous peoples, feminists, gays and lesbians, and environmentalists. The deconstructive approaches of Subaltern Studies, and Young, indicate that an emancipatory strategy needs to reimagine *community* as networks of multiplicitous, contradictory, and dynamic social processes always enabling change for the better rather than as a vision of an ideal authentic society, which relies on the erasure of difference, as inherent in the idea of the modern nation-state.

Similarly, the dominant idea of *democracy* is shaped by its dualization with *tyranny* that neatly forecloses what Chantal Mouffe describes as "the composite, heterogeneous, open and ultimately indeterminate character of the democratic tradition."[87] This maneuver is evidenced in the post–Cold War narratives of international democratization that interpret democratic practice formally, as coextensive with periodic elections and representative politics, and restrictively, as contained within the domestic jurisdiction of states. The alternative project of radical democracy must, as Mouffe describes it, develop

> a hegemony of democratic values, and this requires a multiplication of democratic practices, institutionalizing them into ever more diverse social relations, so that a multiplicity of subject-positions can be formed through a democratic matrix.[88]

Once the distortions of European hegemony are exposed, it becomes possible to recognize alternative democratic discourses at the edges of modernity and to imagine options for radical resistance within modernity. Indigenous discourses of sovereignty and international legal personality, for example, directly contest the continuing efficacy of the nation-state and reveal dominant representational categories as ordered by imperialist European terrains of meaning.[89]

This leads into the second way in which a Subaltern Studies perspective can contribute to emancipatory transnational understandings of community and democracy: by conversing with the *clamor,* currently contained at the peripheries of modernism, and repositioning its effects at the forefront of history and politics. As Spivak observes, the subaltern is a category that makes us think about the question of the limits of what is possible in relation to all knowledge.[90] This suggests the possibility of imagining other ways of being, from within European traditions of thought, that do not fix identities in precise, dualistic, and unidimensional categories.

Breaking the "code of counterinsurgency" and retrieving the position of *other* from the dualisms of European thought is a critical project. The "ferocious standardizing benevolence of most US and Western European human-scientific radicalism" must be resisted.[91] Difference needs to be written into the narratives of international community and democracy, and into the post–Cold War problematic of the North and the South. This involves replacing the dominant elite position of knowing with the multifarious and disruptive positions of subaltern knowledges.

This is not simply a task of letting the oppressed speak for themselves or of expanding the pluralist democratic polity. Spivak, using Derrida's words, describes the process as "rendering *delirious* that interior voice that is the voice of the other in us."[92] This returns us to Said's "crucial point" that the relationship of domination and subordination is "curiously interdependent" and Guha's Gramscian observation that "subordination cannot be understood except as one of the constitutive terms of a binary relationship of which the other is dominance."

Repositioning the *other* of Europe means interrogating our individual participation in its construction. Frantz Fanon's final rhetorical question in *Black Skin, White Masks* puts it thus: "Was my freedom not given to me then in order to build the world of *You?*"[93] In developing conversations and coalitions in the spaces between the *self* and the *other,* which is always present in its standards, between the center and the peripheries of modernism, an emancipatory democratic community begins to form. These transformative spaces are within us all as we occupy variously, partially and contingently, multiple positions containing aspects of oppressor and oppressed.[94] From a rereading of the hybrid narratives that rationalize domination can emerge productive expressions of difference able to resist neocolonization.

The third transformative contribution of Subaltern Studies to international conversations about community and democracy is its promotion of the possibility that noncommensurability can be a positive dynamic of social relations rather than something that requires disciplining and silencing. Other ways of being have always coexisted in the modern world, as subaltern scholars have revealed through their examination of Indian society, but are appropriated, subordinated, and silenced by modern institutions and discourses. The imperialist urge to *improve* the world by standardization must be dislodged. Instead we need to develop ways of being that would enable us to live with the inconsistency and instability of human multiplicities, and the accompanying discomfort and uncertainty.

Taking the conversational image a little further, this will involve a change in language in order to have conversations across different epistemologies and temporalities.[95] Spivak emphasizes that it requires the "unlearning" of the urge to represent the subaltern and the drive to find ways for the subaltern to speak. She says, with reference to First World feminist projects,

> In seeking to learn to speak to (rather than listen to or speak for) the historically muted subject of the subaltern woman, the postcolonial intellectual *systematically* "unlearns" female privilege. This involves learning to critique postcolonial discourse with the best tools it can provide and not simply just substituting the lost figure of the colonized.[96]

International lawyers and scholars need to confront the question of whether "genuinely 'non-violative' relations between the Self (the West) and its Other" are possible.[97]

The international legal system is a powerful site for contestation of the limits of the readability of ideas about community and democracy. Because law has the constitutive power to universalize certain knowledges and to disqualify others, the ability to speak to and influence lawmaking processes is a critical determinant of access to power. But international law, like all European institutions, is founded on the violence of imperialism and, more recently, governmentality. The question of justice demands the possibility of transformation, of "the recasting or refounding of law and politics."[98]

As a start to the crucial task of creating conditions for an international community that is founded on something other than violence and discipline, the strategies suggested by Subaltern Studies of disrupting European hegemony, of developing conversations between Europe and its *other,* and of learning to live with incommensurability, must be taken up in a practical way by international legal scholars and practitioners. Possibilities for alternative practices of collectivity and alliance are present in the limits of the liberal ideas of democracy, community, and justice and in the contestation of the interests served by the modern architecture of the nation-state. International lawyers need to develop the tools that will enable us to speak to these possibilities and unlearn European systems of privilege.

Conclusion

The apparently inclusive gesture of the opening lines of the UN Charter, "we, the peoples of the world" is deeply exclusionary in practice. Experience that is incommensurable with, and disruptive of, European hegemony is marginalized and disciplined by the processes of government of the postcolonial modern nation-state. The same technologies of power are instituted globally by the UN community of states.

The post–Cold War narratives of global interdependence and expanding democratization herald a reshaping of the international community of states. However, just as nationalism unified the postcolonial nation-states in the image of Europe, so too could the discourse of a new world order unify the global polity in the mirror of the West. The transformative possibilities presented by the ending of the Cold War may be subverted to the cause of European expansionism in its most recent guise of global free-market "development."

But, as members of the Subaltern Studies collective show, within the modern discourse of a new world order are the seeds of resistance and change. The liberal European constructs of democracy, equality, and self-determination, while reinforcing Enlightenment rationalism, simultaneously open the way to recognizing disruptive knowledges at the edges of modernity, not outside the European frame but also not fully within it. Of critical importance to an alternative, antidisciplinary strategy is the question of how the multiplicity of global difference is treated. Diversity must be recognized as more than a practical problem of representative processes in pluralist democracies. The hope of truly nonviolative relationships begins with the interrogation of our own individual participation in the construction of *self* (the West) and its *other*.

International law, as a "prominent conversation" in international relations, could play a powerful role in this transformation. Although law is one of the disciplinary techniques of global governmentality, it is a site where the limits of the readability of narratives of difference, community, and democracy are constantly contested. It provides one forum for representing the incommensurability of difference within the global polity.

The strategy of the G77 to promote principles designed to achieve substantive justice remains an important productive strand of a transformative dynamic. As Derrida aptly observes, "Nothing seems to me less outdated than the classical emancipatory ideal."[99] In addition, while modernity must be unmasked as a European production, methods must be developed to give voice, without assimilation, to knowledges at the limits of Enlightenment epistemologies. There is no doubt that the international community could be imagined as a collectivity that is vastly more participatory than the existing society of nation-states, that international democracy could foster heterogeneous, contingent, and situated networks of interconnections in contrast to the static elitism of representative politics, and that international law could be refounded on something other than imperialism and governmentality. To achieve these shifts, the understanding that multiplicity is incommensurable with order, and that order depends on force and discipline, must be unlearned.

NOTES

I would like to thank Dipesh Chakrabarty for his support of this project, and also Rosemary Hunter and the anonymous referees for their helpful and enthusiastic comments.

1. Other common themes associated with the post–Cold War *new world order* are the development of global free-market ideology, increased opportunities for promotion and protection of universal human rights, and expanded scope for collective action in response to unlawful aggression within and between states. These themes interact with, and help to shape and contest, the discussions of international community and democracy but are not discussed here in any depth.

2. James Crawford, *Democracy in International Law* (Inaugural lecture) (Cambridge: Cambridge University Press, 1993).

3. Thomas Franck, "The Emerging Right to Democratic Governance," *American Journal of International Law* 86 (1992): 46–91; Ferdinand R. Teson, "The Kantian Theory of International Law," *Columbia Law Review* 92 (1992): 53–102.

4. Edward W. Said, in his foreword to *Selected Subaltern Studies,* ed. Ranajit Guha and Gayatri Chakravorty Spivak (New York: Oxford University Press, 1988), i–x, traces the term *subaltern* to Antonio Gramsci's *Prison Notebooks* (1971). In Gramsci's usage, subalternity is the opposite to a *dominant, elite,* or *hegemonic* position of power, and the interaction between dominant and subaltern groupings is the essence of history. Subaltern Studies scholars use the notion broadly, as inclusive of all those subordinated in South Asian society, whether according to class, gender, caste, religion, age, office, or any other system of hierarchizing difference into relations of domination and subordination.

5. Guha and Spivak, *Selected Subaltern Studies.*

6. Ranajit Guha, "The Prose of Counter-Insurgency," in Guha and Spivak, *Selected Subaltern Studies,* 45–88.

7. I use the term *third world* advisedly because it highlights the hierarchical ordering of the UN member states that is important to acknowledge for two reasons: first, the term reflects the self-assumed superiority of the first and second Worlds of Europe, and, second, it became the symbol of unity and solidarity for postcolonial states in their struggle to resist European dominance.

8. I do not want to suggest that there is a single, unified Subaltern Studies

view. The view that I am representing here is drawn from, and limited by, my own perspective and experience. It has been developed with the assistance of one member of the Subaltern Studies Collective, Dipesh Chakrabarty.

9. William Blackstone, *Commentaries on the Laws of England, Book 1* (1765; New York: Garland, 1978); Annelise Riles, "Aspiration and Control: International Legal Rhetoric and the Essentialization of Culture," *Harvard Law Review* 106 (1993): 723–40.

10. Mohammed Bedjaoui, "Poverty of the International Order," in *International Law: A Contemporary Perspective,* ed. Richard Falk, F. Kratochwil, and S. H. Mendlovitz (Boulder, Colo.: Westview Press, 1985), 153.

11. Mohammed Bedjaoui, *Towards a New International Economic Order* (New York: Holmes and Meier, 1979); Surakiart Sathirathai, "An Understanding of the Relationship between International Legal Discourse and Third World Countries," *Harvard International Law Journal* 25 (1984): 395–419.

12. Antonio Cassese, *International Law in a Divided World* (Oxford: Clarendon Press 1986), 105–10.

13. Edward W. Said, *Orientalism* (1978; rpt. Middlesex: Penguin, 1995), 12.

14. James Crawford, *The Creation of States in International Law* (Oxford: Clarendon Press, 1979).

15. Roland Rich, "Recognition of States: The Collapse of Yugoslavia and the Soviet Union," *European Journal of International Law* 4 (1993): 36–65.

16. Adamantia Pollis and Peter Schwab, "Human Rights: A Western Construct with Limited Applicability," in *Human Rights: Cultural and Ideological Perspectives,* ed. Pollis and Schwab (New York: Praeger, 1979), 4–34; Raimundo Pannikar, "Is the Notion of Human Rights a Western Concept?" *Diogenes* 120 (1982): 76–95; Russel L. Barsh, "Democratization and Development," *Human Rights Quarterly* 14 (1992): 120–34.

17. M. G. Keladharan Nayar, "Self-Determination beyond the Colonial Context: Biafra in Retrospect," *Texas International Law Journal* 10 (1975): 321–45; Ved P. Nanda, "Self-Determination under International Law: Validity of Claims to Secede," *Case Western Reserve Journal of International Law* 13 (1981): 257–80.

18. Benedict Anderson, *Imagined Communities* (1983; rpt. London: Verso, 1991).

19. Jacques Derrida, "Force of Law: The 'Mystical Foundation of Authority,'" *Cardozo Law Review* 11 (1990): 921–1045.

20. Michel Foucault, "Governmentality," in *The Foucault Effect: Studies in Governmentality,* ed. G. Burchell, C. Gordon, and P. Miller (London: Harvester Wheatsheaf, 1991), 87–104.

21. Jonathan I. Charney, "Universal International Law," *American Journal of International Law* 87 (1993): 529–51.

22. Nigel Purvis, "Critical Legal Studies in Public International Law," *Harvard International Law Journal* 32 (1991): 98.

23. David Kennedy, "The Sources of International Law," *American University Journal of International Law and Politics* 2 (1987): 28.

24. Bedjaoui, *New International Economic Order,* 137.

25. Cassese, *Divided World.*

26. Clarence C. Ferguson, "Redressing Global Injustices: The Role of Law," in *Third World Attitudes toward International Law: An Introduction,* ed. F. E. Snyder and S. Sathirathai (Boston: Martinus Nijhoff, 1987), 369–77; Peter J. Opitz, "The United Nations and the Emancipation of the Third World," *Law and State* 35 (1987): 7–21.

27. Luis Echeverria Alvarez, *Summary of Address,* UN Conference on Trade and Development Proceedings, Third Session, UN Doc T.D./180, vol. 1A, part 1. The quote is from p. 186.

28. Richard Falk, "On the Quasi-Legislative Competence of the General Assembly," *American Journal of International Law* 60 (1966): 782–91; Rosslyn Higgins, *The Development of International Law through the Political Organs of the United Nations* (London: Oxford University Press, 1963).

29. Ferguson, "Redressing Global Injustices."

30. Bedjaoui, *New International Economic Order.*

31. Ram Prakash Anand, *International Law and the Developing Countries: Confrontation or Cooperation?* (Boston: Martinus Nijhoff, 1987).

32. Wang Tieya, "The Third World and International Law," in *The Structure and Process of International Law: Essays in Legal Philosophy, Doctrine, and Theory,* ed. R. St. John MacDonald and D. M. Johnston (Boston: Martinus Nijhoff, 1983), 955 at 963.

33. Bedjaoui, *New International Economic Order.*

34. Tadeusz Gruchalla-Wesierski, "A Framework for Understanding 'Soft Law,'" *McGill Law Journal* 30 (1984): 37–88; Christine M. Chinkin, "The Challenge of Soft Law," *International and Comparative Law Quarterly* 38 (1989): 850–66.

35. Charles N. Brower and John B. Tepe, "The Charter of Economic Rights and Duties of States: A Reflection or Rejection of International Law?" *International Lawyer* 9 (1975): 295–318; Prosper Weil, "Towards Relative Normativity in International Law," *American Journal of International Law* 77 (1983): 413–42.

36. Anand, *Law and Developing Countries.*

37. Ibid.

38. Wil D. Verwey, "The New International Order and the Realization of the Right to Development—a Legal Survey," in Snyder and Sathirathai, *Third World Attitudes,* 826.

39. Leopold Sedar Senghor, "Negritude: A Humanism of the Twentieth Century," in *Colonial Discourse and Postcolonial Theory: A Reader,* ed. Patrick Williams and Laura Chrisman (New York: Columbia University Press, 1994), 30.

40. Franz Fanon "On National Culture," in *The Wretched of the Earth* (Middlesex: Penguin 1961/1967), 166–89; Radhika Coomaraswamy, "To Bellow Like a Cow: Women, Ethnicity, and the Discourse of Rights," in *Human Rights of Women: National and International Perspectives,* ed. Rebecca Cook (Philadelphia: University of Pennsylvania Press, 1994), 39–57.

41. Gayatri Chakravorty Spivak, "Subaltern Studies: Deconstructing Historiography," in Guha and Spivak, *Selected Subaltern Studies*, 3–34 at 13.

42. Thomas Franck, "Lessons of the Failure of the NIEO," paper presented to the annual conference of the Canadian Confederation of International Law, October 17, 1986, contra S. K. Chatterjee, "The Charter of Economic Rights and Duties of States: An Evaluation after 15 years," *International and Comparative Law Quarterly* 40 (1991): 669–84.

43. Russel L. Barsh, "A Special Session of the UN General Assembly Rethinks the Economic Rights and Duties of States," *American Journal of International Law* 85 (1991): 192–200.

44. Kenneth R. Simmonds, "International Law and the New International Economic Order," in *International Law: Teaching and Practice*, ed. Bin Cheng (London: Stevens, 1982), 67–76; Chinkin, "Challenge of Soft Law."

45. Pierre-Marie Dupuy, "Soft Law and International Environmental Law," *Michigan Journal of International Law* 12 (1991): 420–33; Russel L. Barsh, "Indigenous Peoples: An Emerging Object of International Law," *American Journal of International Law* 80 (1986): 369–85; Marcia Langton, "The United Nations and Indigenous Minorities: A Report on the United Nations Working Group on Indigenous Populations," in *International Law and Aboriginal Human Rights*, ed. Barbara Hocking (Australia: Law Book Co., 1988), 83–92.

46. Chinkin, "Challenge of Soft Law."

47. Christopher C. Joyner, "Legal Implications of the Concept of the Common Heritage of Mankind," *International and Comparative Law Quarterly* 35 (1986): 190–99; Alexandre Kiss, "Conserving the Common Heritage of Mankind," *Revista Juridica de la Universidad de Puerto Rico* 59 (1990): 773–77.

48. Chatterjee, "Charter of Economic Rights."

49. Barsh, "Special Session."

50. Franck, "Lessons of the Failure."

51. Richard Falk, *Explorations at the Edge of Time: The Prospects for World Order* (Philadelphia: Temple University Press, 1992).

52. Said, foreword.

53. Ranajit Guha, "On Some Aspects of the Historiography of Colonial India," in Guha and Spivak, *Selected Subaltern Studies*, 43.

54. Shahid Amin, "Gandhi as Mahatma," in Guha and Spivak, *Selected Subaltern Studies*, 288–349; Gautum Bhadra, "Four Rebels of Eighteen-Fifty-Seven," in Guha and Spivak, *Selected Subaltern Studies*, 129–77.

55. Gayatri Chakravorty Spivak, "Can the Subaltern Speak?" in *Marxism and the Interpretation of Culture*, ed. Cary Nelson and Lawrence Grossberg (Urbana: University of Illinois Press, 1988), 271–313.

56. Guha, "Some Aspects of Historiography." Guha uses the term *elite* to refer to dominant groupings in India whether they be constituted by Indians or foreigners. Among the dominant indigenous groups he includes classes and interests that operate locally or regionally, as well as those that operate at the all-India level, which serve the interests of large feudal, industrial, commercial, and bureaucratic interests. The dominant foreign groups include the British, industrialists, merchants, missionaries, landlords, planters, and financiers.

57. Ibid.

58. Dipesh Chakrabarty, "Modernity and Ethnicity in India," forthcoming in *Multicultural States: Rethinking Difference and Identity*, ed. David Bennett (London: Routledge, forthcoming 1998).

59. Foucault, "Governmentality."

60. Guha, "Prose of Counter-Insurgency."

61. Foucault, "Governmentality."

62. Guha, "Prose of Counter-Insurgency," 74.

63. Chakrabarty, "Modernity and Ethnicity," 19.

64. Spivak, "Can the Subaltern Speak?" 280.

65. Carol Smart, *Feminism and the Power of Law* (London: Routledge, 1989).

66. I agree with Carol Smart's contention that the disciplinary role of social sciences is not displacing the role of law, as is Foucault's view, but rather reinforcing its power.

67. Spivak, "Can the Subaltern Speak?" 281.

68. Chakrabarty, "Modernity and Ethnicity," 15.

69. Purvis, "Critical Legal Studies."

70. Martti Koskenniemi, *From Apology to Utopia* (Helsinki: Finnish Lawyers' Publishing, 1989).

71. Guha, "Prose of Counter-Insurgency."

72. Ibid.

73. Said, foreword, ix.

74. Chakrabarty, "Modernity and Ethnicity," 17.

75. Chakrabarty, "Modernity and Ethnicity."

76. Spivak, "Can the Subaltern Speak?" 284–85

77. Ibid., 285.

78. Dipesh Chakrabarty, "Marx after Marxism," *Meanjin* 52 (1993): 426.

79. "Interpreting Oriental Cases: The Law of Alternity in the Colonial Courtroom," *Harvard Law Review* 107 (1994): 1711–28.

80. Spivak, "Subaltern Studies," 12.

81. Homi K. Bhabha, "Signs Taken for Wonders: Questions of Ambivalence and Authority under a Tree Outside Delhi, May 1817," in *The Location of Culture* (London: Routledge, 1994), 171–72.

82. Said, foreword, viii.

83. Chakrabarty, "Marx after Marxism."

84. Ibid., 427–28.

85. Chakrabarty, "Marx after Marxism."

86. Iris Marion Young, "The Ideal of Community and the Politics of Difference," in *Feminism/Postmodernism*, ed. L. J. Nicholson (New York: Routledge, 1990), 307.

87. Chantal Mouffe, "Radical Democracy: Modern or Postmodern?" in *Universal Abandon? The Politics of Postmodernism*, ed. Andrew Ross (Minneapolis: University of Minnesota Press, 1988), 41.

88. Ibid.

89. Robert A. Williams, "Encounters on the Frontiers of International Human Rights Law: Redefining the Terms of Indigenous Peoples' Survival in

the World," *Duke Law Journal* (1990): 660–704; Dianne Otto, "A Question of Law or Politics? Indigenous Claims to Sovereignty in Australia," *Syracuse Journal of International Law and Commerce* 21 (1995): 65–103.

90. Spivak, "Can the Subaltern Speak?" 283.

91. Ibid., 294.

92. Ibid.

93. Frantz Fanon, *Black Skin, White Masks* (1952; London: Paladin, 1970), 165.

94. Angela P. Harris, "Race and Essentialism in Feminist Legal Theory," *Stanford Law Review* 42 (1990): 581–616.

95. Chakrabarty, "Marx after Marxism."

96. Spivak, "Can the Subaltern Speak?" 295.

97. Chakrabarty, "Marx after Marxism," 423.

98. Derrida, "Force of Law," 971.

99. Ibid.

An Ontological Approach to Constitutionalism in Sri Lanka: Contingency and the Failure of Exclusion

Roshan de Silva

Sri Lanka (or Ceylon until 1972) gained independence from Britain in 1948 under a Whitehall-drafted constitution. Prior to the British arriving in Ceylon in 1796, the island had been subject to Portuguese (1505–1656) and Dutch (1656–1796) colonial rule. Each left their distinctive mark, be it Christianity, Roman-Dutch law, or settler European communities. As far as the current "ethnic" composition of the island is concerned, the Sinhalese (mainly Buddhist) comprise 74 percent of the population, the Tamils (mainly Hindu) comprise 18 percent, the Muslims who are descendants of both Arab traders and Hindu and possibly Buddhist converts to Islam comprise 7.1 percent, the Burghers (descendants of Portuguese and Dutch settler communities) and Eurasians comprise 0.3 percent, the Malays (descendants of Malay soldiers from the Dutch East Indies), comprise 0.3 percent, while the Veddhas (the indigenous people of the island), and other "ethnic" groups comprise about 0.3 percent.[1] In 1972 a new internally produced constitution came into operation, and in 1978 this was replaced by a constitution with a highly centralized executive presidency modeled on the French system that coexists alongside a Westminster parliamentary model. Since the late 1970s the Liberation Tigers of Tamil Eelam (LTTE) have been pursuing the establishment of a separate ethnic Tamil state in the North and East of Sri Lanka.

An earlier version of this essay appeared in a Special Issue on Law and Postcolonialism, edited by Eve Darian-Smith and Peter Fitzpatrick in *Social and Legal Studies* 5, no. 3 (1996).

The foundations of the postcolonial conflict between Sinhalese and Tamils and other minority groups in Sri Lanka were established in the period of British colonial rule between 1796 and 1948.[2] With colonialism came the claimed rationalism of the West, which intellectually made its presence felt in the form of an Orientalist colonial historiography. It was a historiography that not only appropriated Sri Lanka for the purposes of a Western narrative of progress, but also projected two dominant assumptions: that there had been a great Sinhala civilization that had gone into decline due to "invasions" from a predominantly Tamil South India and that antagonistic "racial" groups had long existed.[3]

Far from questioning the classificatory categories of colonial historiography, an emerging Sinhalese historiography from the middle of the nineteenth century assumed the past social and political centrality of "race" and Buddhism.[4] Sinhalese nationalists drew upon the social and political capital that associated the Indo-Aryan origins of the Sinhalese language with membership in the mythical "Aryan race."[5] Such exclusivist claims became the foundation for the Sinhalese Buddhist revivalist movement at the end of the nineteenth century, and through the proliferation of print technology the revivalist movement was able to extend its influence among an emerging Sinhalese bourgeoisie.[6]

The result of such exclusivist claims was to project the predominantly Hindu Tamil as an "invader" from South India. In doing so, the Sinhalese, like the amnesiac who suffers a loss of memory, forgot their own past as "invaders" from north India.[7] In the period after colonial rule, and particularly after 1956 when the forces of Sinhalese nationalism came to power, an increasingly Sinhalese Buddhist–dominated state began the process of "restoring" the Sinhalese and Buddhism to the "idealized" status they had both enjoyed prior to European colonial rule. In attempting to construct a coherent Sinhalese Buddhist identity both Buddhism and Sinhalese mythology began to increasingly serve as fetish objects, the sacred markers of special ethnic entitlement.[8] These markers were then activated in the project of postcolonial nation building. Intrinsic to this task of nation building were the narratives of constitutionalism. At a normative level these narratives partly incorporated the fetishized[9] tropes of Sinhalese Buddhist culture.

While it would be possible to analyze the debates surrounding the 1972 constitution in terms of the dynamics of conflict established in the late colonial and more recent postcolonial period, the approach I pursue here stresses a phenomenological method. It seeks to restore legal discourse in Sri Lanka to the hierarchical ontology that constitutes the cosmology of Sinhalese Buddhism.[10] The point I wish to emphasize, therefore, is that when the law speaks, it discloses the memory of Buddhist cosmos. The memory of this cosmos has been "there from the beginning" but as Lungstrom notes has "withdrawn from the clearing light."[11]

For Bruce Kapferer,[12] whose phenomenological anthropology I extend to an analysis of the 1972 constitutionalism of Sri Lanka, the domain of phenomenology following Heidegger is that which remains hidden or concealed.[13] In the argument that follows, I return the language of law in Sri Lanka to its "origin" in the silent and invisible echo of the cosmology of Buddhism. Furthermore it is not only this cosmology that is inscribed in this constitutional order, but, as will be evident, the mythical narratives of Sinhalese Buddism are also identified as maintaining a hidden presence within the text of the 1972 constitution. The point I wish to make is that the 1972 constitution reflects as a contingent historical moment the experiential world of the cosmology of Sinhalese Buddhism.

The story I expand upon here is one of a failed exclusion, and one that paradoxically marks its success. I shall trace this failed exclusion of the Tamil other in a reading of the opening three chapters of the 1972 constitution of Sri Lanka, which enunciate the structure of the state, the status of Buddhism, and the status of the Sinhala and Tamil languages. The failure of exclusion manifests itself in the principle of "hierarchical encompassment" developed by Kapferer.[14] Through hierarchical encompassment the irresolvable and ambivalent relation between Sinhalese and Tamil is played out. The constitution, in acknowledging the presence of the Tamil other, neither fully excludes nor fully includes the other. Instead it encompasses the other in a hierarchical relation that locates the other on the margins of the text. The marginalized presence of the Tamil other within the constitution operates as an "excess" that prevents the constitution from achieving a coherent self-identity. Excess here alludes to something that is always more or surplus to that which can actually be identified.[15]

I shall elaborate upon this principle of hierarchical encompassment in a reading of the Sinhalese Buddhist cosmos that Kapferer persuasively contends operates as an ontological scheme that orientates Sinhalese Buddhists toward their world of experience.[16] The irresolvable ambivalence present in the constitution is, I believe, reflected in the Sinhalese Buddhist cosmos in which the demonic as the other of the

Buddha is never fully excluded but never included either. These cosmological relations of flux that utilize the central metaphors of unity, fragmentation, and reordering are, as Kapferer suggests (50–65), present in the mythology of Sinhalese Buddhism. I shall argue that the failure of exclusion in the constitution is evidenced in the cosmology of Sinhalese Buddhism, and the world of Sinhalese mythology.

More importantly, the marginalized presence of the other within the constitution reflects the ontological scheme of the Sinhalese Buddhist cosmos in which the demonic stands in a marginalized relation of encompassment to the Buddha. My argument here extends Kapferer's thesis that the ontological scheme of the Sinhalese Buddhist cosmos is present in both the practices of Sinhalese nationalism and exorcism rituals in which the demons of individual possession stand encompassed by the forces of the Buddha and in the practices of Sinhalese nationalism that seek to incorporate the Tamil other in a marginalized relation.[17] The failure of the constitution to achieve an identity in itself is, I shall maintain, not unique to the foundational text of the Republic of Sri Lanka (Ceylon between 1948–72 was a constitutional monarchy with the governor-general as the British monarch's representative, its head of state). The irresolution of identity within the constitution is reflected in the dynamics of flux that structure the cosmology of Sinhalese Buddhism. The undecidable movement of exclusion and inclusion present in the constitution is further exemplified in the stories of Sinhalese Buddhist mythology in which the demonic stands encompassed in a hierarchical relation. That which is outside is simultaneously inside as well.

I want to stress briefly at this point that the cosmology of Sinhalese Buddhism, far from being a transcendental signifier, manifests its orientational potency only in the flesh-and-blood world of the social. In a sense, therefore, the meaning of ontology awaits its moment of arrival in the social world of lived experience. The 1972 constitution is one such lived experience.

The 1972 Constitution and the Buddhist Cosmos

The three provisions of the constitution I have chosen for consideration best reveal the ontological scheme of the Buddhist cosmos with its central metaphors of unity, fragmentation, and reordering.[18] The articles on the structure of the state, the place of Buddhism, and the status of the Sinhala and Tamil languages encompass the other in a hierarchical relation of marginalization.

Unitary or Federal State?

During March 1971 the Constituent Assembly debated whether Sri Lanka should be a unitary state. Central to this debate was whether Sri Lanka should continue with the centralized colonial state that it had inherited on independence in 1948, or attempt a more devolved and decentralized future. While the left-wing coalition government led by the Sri Lanka Freedom Party and the conservative opposition United National Party supported the maintenance of the unitary structure, the Federal Party, which represented the majority of Tamil opinion in the island, proposed a decentralization of legislative and administrative power through a federal model.[19]

For the Federal Party, devolution was projected as inclusive of the pluralistic ethnocultural diversity of Sri Lanka. However, the combined forces of Sinhalese parliamentary nationalism publicly campaigned against federalism, maintaining it would fragment the territorial integrity of Sri Lanka and by implication the Sinhalese Buddhist social order. Such a fear of federalism was given voice to by a prominent Sinhalese nationalist MP, Prins Gunasekera, who in the Constituency Assembly observed,

> For over 2000 years the Sinhala people have lived in Ceylon. To them Ceylon is their motherland. This motherland was frequently invaded from South India. . . . The history of Ceylon tells us that the Sinhala people fought incessantly against Indian invaders to keep this country for themselves . . . [and] the Sinhala people look upon the Tamil people now inhabiting the Northern and Eastern provinces as descendants of the invading forces whom they have been fighting to keep this country for themselves. This explains . . . why the Sinhala people fight against all proposals to grant concessions [such as federalism] to the Tamil people.[20]

On the other hand a Tamil MP from the Federal Party observed that "the question of federalism is the question of respect [for] the dignity of groups and individuals, however weak, however small and however insignificant they may be."[21] Invariably the combined forces of Government and Opposition united against the Federal Party, and Article 2 of the constitution declared, "The Republic of Sri Lanka is a Unitary State."

While in the Tamil invocation of federalism is seen the possibility of respecting the alterity of the ethnic other in a nonappropriative relation, for the Sinhalese such an invocation is seen as standing in a fragmenting relation to the hierarchical order of the Sinhalese-dominated state. This hierarchical order is classically represented in the model of the unitary state. In Gunasekera's historical projection, the Tamils invade the Sinhalese nation from the outside, initiating the entry of an antagonistic social relation. The Tamil as the cause of an antagonistic social relation must therefore stand outside, and yet simultaneously inside, the Sinhalese nation in a hierarchical relation. Like the demons of individual possession that similarly attack the body of the Sinhalese victim from the margins of the Buddhist cosmos, constant watch must be maintained against the fragmenting claim of federalism.[22] The Tamil other therefore stands in a relation of hierarchical encompassment within the order of the unitary state.

Protecting Buddhism

During the debates on the status of Buddhism, the Government proposed, "The Republic of Sri Lanka shall give to Buddhism the foremost place and accordingly it shall be the duty of the State to protect and foster Buddhism while assuring to all religions the rights granted by Section 18 (1) (d)," which guaranteed "freedom of thought, conscience and religion." The Federal Party proposed a more inclusive form of words that placed a burden upon the state to "protect and foster" all religions. It failed to win support, and the Government's proposal was incorporated as Article 6.

Buddhism stands in an encompassing relation to other religions. The potentially fragmenting relation of other religions is incorporated in a hierarchical relation. More importantly the burden placed upon the state has echoes from the world of Sinhalese Buddhist myth.

The duty of the state to "foster" Buddhism has its mythic parallel in the postconquest building program of King Dutugemunu (circa 200 B.C.E.), the heroic Sinhalese king who reestablishes the Sinhalese polity in the north central part of Sri Lanka. Following his defeat of the

(Hindu) Tamil king Elara, he initiates the building of Buddhist monuments. His actions are designed to stabilize the Buddhist cosmos from its fragmenting potential. Furthermore, they signify his atonement for the violence of his conquest over Elara, and in doing so Dutugemunu seeks to reestablish stability within the Buddhist cosmos.[23]

More importantly, in Dutugemunu's actions is inscribed the cosmological account of history presented in Buddhism. As Kapferer notes, for Buddhism "history constitutes an interwoven stream of events in which the results of actions at one moment are manifest in beneficence or suffering at another."[24] The indecisive movement between these two poles is the principle of karma. Through karma historical events are interconnected.

Karma is the acquisition of merit through the pursuance of meritorious acts, the object of which is an escape from the endless cycle of rebirth (samsara) that Buddhism posits.[25] It is this release from rebirth that constitutes renunciation of the world and an experience of nibbana (liberation).[26] The actions of Dutugemunu reflect karmic principles. The building of monuments to the Buddha is karmic in that it is integral to Dutugemunu's own renunciation of the world.

I am not suggesting that the state is engaged in a movement toward nibbana, but I am suggesting that the state in enunciating a duty to "foster Buddhism" is implicitly engaged in karmic principles. The karmic principles of birth, death, and rebirth are, as I will go on to show, present in the overall scheme of the Buddhist cosmos with its central metaphors of unity, fragmentation, and reunification in hierarchy. The state, like the Dutugemunu of mythic history, seeks to engage itself in acts of cosmic stabilization against the fragmenting capacity of the potentially demonic. The potentially demonic is in the terms of Article 6 of the constitution implicitly figured as the fragmenting possibility of other religions that must stand in a relation of hierarchical encompassment. The irresolvable and ambivalent relation between Buddhism and other religions is played out in the form of an encompassment that successfully evades the possibility of a determinate exclusion.

Hierarchy and Language

The failure of exclusion is also manifest in the constitutional provisions that enunciate the status of the Sinhala and Tamil languages. Chapter 3 of the constitution contains five articles (7–11) under the respective headings of "Official Language," "Language of Legislation," and "Language of the Courts." Here I shall restrict myself to a consideration of the first two. The provisions on language that were invariably passed in the face of opposition from the Federal Party enunciated the following:

> Article 7. The Official Language of Sri Lanka shall be Sinhala as provided by the Official Language Act . . . of 1956.
>
> Article 8(1). The use of the Tamil language shall be in accordance with the Tamil Language (Special Provisions) Act . . . of 1958.
>
> (2). Any regulation for the use of the Tamil language made under the Tamil Language (Special Provisions) Act . . . and in force immediately before the commencement of the Constitution shall not in any manner be interpreted as being a provision of the Constitution but shall be deemed to be subordinate legislation. . . .
>
> Article 9(1). All laws shall be enacted or made in Sinhala.
>
> (2). There shall be a Tamil translation of every law so enacted or made.
>
> Article 10(1). All written laws, including subordinate legislation in force immediately prior to the commencement of the Constitution, shall be published . . . in Sinhala and in Tamil translation as expeditiously as possible. . . .
>
> (3). Unless the National State Assembly otherwise provides, the law published in Sinhala under the provisions of subsection (1) of this section, shall, as from the date of such publication, be deemed to be the law and supersede the corresponding law in English.

The Official Language Act of 1956 elevated Sinhala to the status of an official language. In doing so it had the simultaneous effect of relegating the Tamil language to a secondary status. While this demotion was implicit in the act, it was explicit in the executive regulations made under the act by which prospective employees in the public service had to acquire an examinable knowledge of Sinhala. This requirement immediately placed Tamil speakers in the North and the East at a disadvantage because, unlike Tamils in the predominantly Sinhalese parts of Sri Lanka, they had a very limited knowledge of Sinhala.[27]

The Tamil Language (Special Provisions) Act of 1958 placed the use of Tamil on a statutory basis. Its primary objective was to alleviate the immediate difficulties faced by Tamil speakers (which included the Muslim inhabitants of eastern Sri Lanka), as a result of the Official Language Act. Briefly, the act provided for the use of Tamil for educational purposes, for examination for the purpose of entry into the public service, for prescribed administrative purposes in the Northern and Eastern Provinces and for the use of Tamil between persons and public officials in the Northern and Eastern Provinces. However the Sinhalese-dominated Parliament only approved the regulations for the implementation of the act in 1966.[28] Due to the delay in implementing the act, any beneficial effects were limited, and by the late 1960s a generation of disaffected Tamil youth was coming of age.

The 1972 constitution incorporated both the Official Language Act and the Tamil Language (Special Provisions) Act. However, the logic of its incorporation was hierarchical and the regulations for the use of Tamil are attributed the status of subordinate legislation. In a paradoxical move Article 8(2) deems regulations made under the Tamil Language (Special Provisions) Act, outside of the constitution, but also gives space to the Tamil other in a marginalized relation. The other insists upon being present in the constitution. In a simultaneous move the other is both outside and inside at the same time, even if the space of the inside is marginalized.

The provisions of Article 9(1) and (2) also manifest the principle of hierarchical encompassment. Sinhala as the language of legislation stands in a hierarchical relation to Tamil as the language of translation. Article 10(1) and (3) operate to similar effect. Article 10(1) proposes that all existing legislation (prior to the commencement of the constitution) be published in Sinhala and then in Tamil translation. Article 10(3) not only explicitly displaces the validity of legislation in English, in favor of the Sinhala translation, but implicitly relegates the Tamil translation to a subordinate status.

The impact of these provisions is to establish Sinhala in a hierarchical relation to the Tamil language. The fragmenting potential of Tamil stands encompassed by the Sinhala language. The metaphor of fragmentation was deployed by the Government when the Federal Party introduced amendments designed to establish parity of status between the Sinhala and Tamil languages.[29] Any attempt at parity of status was projected as threatening to the unitary structure of the state, a move that would set in motion the forces of fragmentation, fragmenting not only the state, but the Sinhalese Buddhist nation itself.

Like the demons of the Buddhist cosmos that are encompassed by the Buddha, the fragmenting potential of the Tamil language stands encompassed by the Sinhala language in a hierarchical relation. Just as the Buddhist cosmos, which I shall elaborate upon below, is structured by an ambivalence that precludes the demonic from a determinate exclusion, the Tamil other is incorporated in a hierarchical relation of marginalization within the constitution. It is neither fully excluded nor fully included.[30] It fails to do both. As an excess, the Tamil other succeeds in breaching the boundary and distorting the outline[31] of the constitution's claimed self-identity as a projection of the desires of the majority Sinhalese people. The boundary (i.e., its external limit) of the constitution's self-identity confronts its limit, what it can never fully be, as it finds itself tethered to the excess that is the Tamil other. This internal limit prevents the constitution from achieving a full identity with itself.[32] Simultaneous to the failure of a full identity, is the ultimate failure of exclusion. Its identity fails through the undecidable relation between Sinhalese and Tamil in which the Tamil insists upon being present. The other is ever present even if in a marginalized space that is never quite outside but never quite inside either.

I shall elaborate upon this failure of exclusion within the 1972 constitution through a consideration of the dynamics of flux that characterize the Sinhalese Buddhist cosmos. What I want to suggest here is that the fundamental failure of exclusion within the 1972 constitution manifests itself at a much more profound level within the ontological scheme of the Sinhalese Buddhist cosmos. Ambivalence is central to the experiential world of the Sinhalese Buddhist cosmos, in which any move toward coherence fails as the Buddha and the demonic find themselves tethered to each other, neither succeeding in establishing a determinate exclusion.

The Ontological Scheme of the Sinhalese Buddhist Cosmos

Here I elaborate upon the ontological dynamic of Sinhalese Buddhism that I shall argue is reflected in the constitutional provisions considered above. More importantly, the dynamic of ambivalence identified above is evidenced in the dynamics of flux present in the cosmos.

By *ontology* I refer, following Kapferer, to those constitutive forces of being that position and orient human beings within their existential realities.[33] Ontological meaning is not prior to the experience of daily reality, but is simultaneous with it. Ontology as the condition of existence provides the motivational frame in which human beings reach out toward the world of experience. The meaning of such experience is ontologically derived, but meaning achieves its force through the engagement of ontology in a contingent historical event, through which the possibilities of the "logic"[34] or dynamic of ontology achieve motivational potency. Ontology, while separated from the world of conscious reflection,[35] is yet integral to consciousness through its "logic," which is ingrained in the everyday sociocultural practices of human beings.

Ontology is therefore prereflective, beneath consciousness, but "exists in reflective consciousness as a moment of ideology [or what I shall call discourse] and always as only a possibility or as a limited realisation of ontological potential."[36] My concern here, then, is the extent to which the discursive construction of the unitary state and the privileging of both Buddhism and the Sinhala language reflect the ontological dynamic of the Sinhalese Buddhist cosmos. Importantly, therefore, I maintain that the potency of the ontological dynamic of the Buddhist cosmos is realized in the contingency of historical experience. The opening three chapters of the 1972 constitution are here posited as reflecting one such historical experience.

I shall first trace the nature of hierarchy within the Sinhalese Buddhist cosmos. While the idea of hierarchy in the West is associated with fixity, or the division of the social into rigid boundaries, hierarchy within the cosmology of Buddhism is associated with flux, and the failure of coherence. While the governing principles of hierarchy within Sinhalese Buddhism determine both the nature of the parts of the social and their interconnection, it is within the space of the interconnection that the play of ambivalence manifests itself.

The cosmology of Sinhalese Buddhism places knowledge of the *dhamma* (the Cosmic Law) in an encompassing relation to political power (or *artha*), the ideal Buddhist king being the one who gives up the pursuit of *artha* in favor of asserting the encompassing principles of the *dhamma*. Knowledge of the *dhamma* can therefore be seen as standing in diametrical opposition to that which is other to the Buddha, the demonic. The Buddha is pure and the demonic polluting. The relation between the Buddha and the demonic defines the boundaries of existence and nonexistence. While the relation of human beings to this boundary is determined by the degree of their orientation to the Buddha or to the demonic, the cosmology of the Buddha is seen as ultimately encompassing of the demonic[37] but not destroying of the demonic.

The logic of Sinhalese Buddhist hierarchy is described by Kapferer as one of "progressive encompassment and transformation."[38] The demonic as a lower form of existence can through incorporation by the unifying principles of the Buddhist cosmos be transformed and move upward in hierarchy. The demonic can thus be progressively encompassed within this Buddhist hierarchy. This hierarchical ontological scheme, for example, informs Sinhalese rituals of healing and group protection.[39] However that which is unified can at another moment break down into a fragmented form "but can be re-constituted once again into a higher encompassing possibility."[40] However, the dynamic of flux between the Buddha and the demonic ensures that the boundary between an encompassing unity (associated with purity) and a fragmented state of being (associated with pollution) is open and subject to fluctuation. The dominant relation is one of ambivalence in which the movement toward an exclusion of the demonic fails, the demonic instead being encompassed within the Buddhist cosmos.

The central metaphors of the Sinhalese Buddhist cosmos, of unity, fragmentation, and reordering, are reflected in the opening three chapters of the constitution and the political debates that surrounded their coming into being. Both Tamils and other religions, who by implication represent the demonic potential of the Sinhalese Buddhist–dominated state, stand encompassed within the hierarchical order of the unitary state, of Buddhism—which it is the state's duty to "protect and foster"—and of the Sinhala language. The attempts by the Federal Party to introduce a federal state structure and parity of status for all religions and languages was projected as fragmenting of the Sinhalese-dominated state. Instead, the opening three chapters of the constitution encompass the fragmenting potential of Tamils and other religions in a hierarchical relation of marginalization. Just as the presence of the

Tamil other prevents the constitution from achieving a full identity with itself, the presence of the demonic similarly prevents the cosmos from achieving a coherent or replete identity. Both the Tamil other and the demonic other of the Buddha exist on the borders, the former on the border of the text and the latter on the border of the cosmos. Any determinate exclusion fails by virtue of the ambivalent relation between Sinhalese and Tamil and the Buddha and the demonic. More importantly, the ontological scheme of the Sinhalese Buddhist cosmos with its dominant metaphors of unity, fragmentation, and reordering is reflected in the discursive structure of the opening three chapters of the 1972 constitution.

Having elucidated upon the failure of exclusion in the 1972 constitution through a reading of the Sinhalese Buddhist cosmos, I would further suggest that this is not where the story of ambivalence ends. The world of Sinhalese Buddhist mythology provides further evidence of an ambivalent relation between the forces of the demonic and the Buddha. Below I give further consideration to the mythic account of King Dutugemunu, the logic of which, I have already suggested, is present in Article 6 of the constitution, which placed a burden on the state to "foster" Buddhism, the king, like the state, engaged in the pursuit of karma.

Ambivalence in Buddhist Mythology

The Pali chronicles, *Dipavamsa* and *Mahavamsa,* "the chronicles of the great dynasty" that record the rule of the ancient kings of Sri Lanka up to the thirteenth century, were compiled by Buddhist monks in the fourth and sixth centuries, respectively.[41] The *Mahavamsa* was updated at various points up to the thirteenth century.[42]

Both the *Dipavamsa* and *Mahavamsa* begin by enunciating the cosmology of Sinhalese Buddhism. The Buddha is glorified and then follows an account of the Buddha's mastery of Mara (the anti-Buddha as the personification of death). This is followed by an account of the Buddha's three visits to the island (although he probably never traveled outside of his native north India), and his domestication of demonic beings, preparing the island for human habitation. Finally there follows an account of the coming of King Mahasammata (the Great Elect), who as a former incarnation of the Buddha is the first Buddhist king that restores order to a fragmenting Buddhist cosmos. Out of disorder is born order. The Buddha and his embodiment, the king, are the source of order.

This account of the Buddhist cosmos is more than just a prelude to the stories that recall the cosmogenesis of the Sinhalese people, the birth of the Sinhalese polity, its fragmentation, and its heroic rebirth under King Dutugemunu. Rather it constitutes the paradigm for the historical narrative of the Pali chronicles. In its unfolding of historical events the chronicles reflect the ontological scheme of the Buddhist cosmos (with its metaphors of unity, fragmentation, and reordering) that informs Sinhalese Buddhist history.[43]

The story of Dutugemunu represents the movement through unity, fragmentation, and reordering.[44] Dutugemunu's movement into the demonic is occasioned by his refusal to listen to his father, King Kakavanna of Magama, who implores him not to make war against the Tamil king Elara of Anuradhapura. His refusal to obey his father initiates the process of fragmentation.[45] He flees into the forest, the margins of the social order. Like the demons of the cosmos and the Tamil other within the constitution, Dutugemunu occupies a space of marginality.

It is only from the margins of the polity that the process of a transformative encompassment of the demonic can begin. As with the demons of the cosmos whose journey from the margins toward the center of the Buddha initiates the process of their own encompassment, Dutugemunu's own transformation from a demonic being can only begin from the margins.

Once his father dies, Dutugemunu has himself consecrated the new king of Magama. From being on the margins of the social order, he moves back inside it. By encompassing his own disordering potential he moves from being demonic to being benevolent and correspondingly moves upward in hierarchy. Higher encompassment awaits in his encounter with Elara. The analogy that can be drawn from this process with the constitutional provisions considered here is striking. The unitary state (Article 2), the duty of the state to "protect and foster" Buddhism (Article 6), the elevation of Sinhala to the status of both an official language and the language of legislative enactment, and the simultaneous relegation of Tamil to a subordinate status of legislative translation (Articles 7, 8, 9, and 10), encompass, but never exclude, the disordering potential of the Tamil other. This process of encompassment accords the Tamil other a marginalized presence within the text.

Like the demons of the Buddhist cosmos, the Tamil occupies a marginal space within the text.

The movement of Dutugemunu toward Elara's kingdom represents the vertical movement of Dutugemunu through the Buddhist cosmos. His movement is analogous to the march of the demons who attack from the margins of the cosmos. In his defeat and slaying of Elara is manifest Dutugemunu's final transformative encompassment of the remnants of his demonic being, and the corresponding movement through hierarchy. He transcends his demonic being. In according honor to Elara in the celebration of funeral rites (which in Buddhism and Hinduism contains symbolic reference to sacrifice and rebirth), Dutugemunu not only incorporates Elara's social order, but also signifies his own "transformation from the demonic to compassionate beneficence."[46] In transcending his demonic being he simultaneously reestablishes the hierarchy of the Buddhist cosmos. But constant watch must be maintained against the forces of demonic fragmentation that still inhabit the margins of the polity centered around Anuradhapura. The inherently fragmenting possibility of the new social order is recognized by Dutugemunu in his decision to build Buddhist monuments, the object of which, I have already observed, is to stabilize the Buddhist cosmos. The demonic, however, still maintains a presence on the margins. The inherently ambivalent relation between Dutugemunu and the demonic margins remains unresolved. Of equal significance, the structure of the myth reflects the ontological scheme of the hierarchical Sinhalese Buddhist cosmos, as represented in Dutugemunu's journey through unity, fragmentation, and reordering.

It is this dynamic of inherent fragmentation that implicitly justifies the unitary state (Article 2), whose structure shall maintain a watchful eye over the hinterland of the state, the space inhabited by the fragmenting claims of the Tamil other who demands both federalism and a parity of status for the Tamil language. In maintaining a watchful eye rather than moving out to destroy, it can never definitively exclude these claims, for they are destined to remain on the margins of the Sinhalese-dominated state. The duty of the state to "protect and foster" Buddhism (Article 6) further arms the unitary state as it confronts the fragmenting potential of not only other religions, but the Tamil "invaders" of Gunasekera's historical projection, who attack from the margins of the state. Unlike Dutugemunu, who only in death (and on becoming a divine god) transcends the ambivalence of the polity of which he is king, the constitution as a living text cannot free itself of the ambivalent relation between Sinhalese and Tamil that pervades its opening three chapters.

So far I have elucidated the impossibility of the constitution achieving an identity in itself by suggesting that ambivalence is much more fundamentally ingrained in the ontological scheme of the Buddhist cosmos, and the discursive structure of the mythic account of Dutugemunu and the rebirth of the Sinhalese polity. More importantly the ambivalence that informs the ontological scheme of the Buddhist cosmos is reflected in two distinct historical events, the mythic story of Dutugemunu and the 1972 constitution. As contingent historical moments they both reveal that "the terms and relations of an ontological scheme receive valuation, a valuation laden with import in a historically lived reality."[47]

I want to conclude by shifting my focus from ambivalence to contingency and identify the contingency of the demonic. Most specifically I want to argue that the Tamil emerges as potentially "demonic" within the contingency of historical experience, and not as the transcendental other of the Sinhalese Buddhist cosmos.

Contingency and the Demonic

I have already suggested that the Tamil other represents the demonic potential of the Sinhalese Buddhist state, against which its unitary form keeps its watchful eye. The Tamil other, however, does not stand in a relation of demonic excess to the hierarchical logic of the Sinhalese Buddhist cosmos. But in the engagement of this ontological scheme in distinctive historical moments, the Tamil other is projected as an excess that prevents the Sinhalese polity/state from achieving a full identity with itself.

It is possible to identify a discursive shift in the recording of the story of Dutugemunu in the *Mahavamsa* to the recording of the same events in the thirteenth-century text, the *Pujavaliya*. The *Pujavaliya* (History of Offerings), written by the monk Mayurapada, is primarily a commentary on the *dhamma* but does contain a literary trope projecting the presence of a Tamil menace. In both the *Dipavamsa* and the *Mahavamsa*, Elara, although a Hindu, is accorded the status of a righteous king who ruled justly and wisely,[48] but in the *Pujavaliya* he has descended to the status of an unrighteous king who destroyed Buddhist monasteries. The monk Mayurapada was a contemporary of King Magha of Kalinga in south India, who in 1235 C.E. launched an invasion of Sri Lanka.[49] In the Pali literature, Magha is memorialized for the destruction he caused and is projected as a Mara-type figure. It is this historical experience of Magha that almost certainly accounts for Elara's descent to unrighteousness.[50]

A more profound descent in Elara's status is recorded in the seventeenth-century text, the *Rajavaliya,* a discourse on the history of Sinhalese Buddhist kingship up to the arrival of the Portuguese. In the *Rajavaliya* (Lineage of Kings) Elara and his followers are equated with the rampaging hordes of Mara. This descent of Elara to the status of the absolutely demonic must be seen in the light of the social trauma initiated with the coming of the European powers and the Dutch expulsion of the Portuguese by 1656. The increasing projection of Tamils as agents of demonic fragmentation may stand as a metaphor for the traumatic rupture of colonial penetration.[51]

This discursive shift in the projection of Tamils in both the period just prior to the entry of the West and the early colonial period does reveal a certain dynamic. The rise of Dutugemunu, "given the logic of transformation through hierarchy and the principle of encompassment, should be coincident with a decline of Elara into fragmented subordination, a move to the demonic."[52]

These later texts thus reveal interpretational possibilities latent in the ontological scheme of the Sinhalese Buddhist cosmos, but which are activated in a contingent historical experience, such as during the "invasion" from south India, European colonialism, or the 1972 constitution. The ontological scheme of the Buddhist cosmos is therefore significant in the increasing projection of Elara and Tamils in general as potentially "demonic."

Tamils are therefore seen as increasingly occupying a space on the margins of the Sinhalese social order. They can never be absolutely outside the social order, for the demonic is ultimately encompassed within hierarchy. But as Kapferer suggests, "ontologically . . . the alignment of Tamils with the demonic can have dreadful consequences,"[53] as they come to occupy a potentially fragmenting relation to the heart of Sinhalese Buddhist identity and existence, therefore challenging at an ontological depth a Sinhalese Buddhist being in the world.[54]

Conclusion

The story I have presented here is one of ambivalence and contingency. The failure of the first three chapters of the 1972 constitution to establish a closure through a determinate exclusion of the Tamil other is revealed to be a process mirrored in the world of Sinhalese Buddhist mythology. Both, I have argued, reflect the hierarchical ontological scheme of the Sinhalese Buddhist cosmos, which itself is structured through an ambivalent relation between the Buddha and the demonic. The ontological scheme of the Buddhist cosmos hence receives its motivational or temporal force within the contingency of historically discursive moments. The cosmology of Sinhalese Buddhism is therefore not historically transcendent, but historically contingent. The reflection of this ontological scheme in the mythology of Sinhalese Buddhism and the discursive form of those provisions in the 1972 constitution is such as to make the Tamil other a powerful metaphor of both "state and personal destruction."[55]

As the mark of an excessive projection, the Tamil other prevents the Sinhalese Buddhist state from achieving a full identity with itself. Indeed, if the Tamil other could ever be absolutely excluded, the Sinhalese-dominated state would cease to exist. By extension the fragmentation of the Sinhalese Buddhist cosmos would be complete. While the Buddha stands in an encompassing relation to the demonic, the demonic can never absolutely be excluded. To conclude, the unsayable echo of the law speaks in the ghostly figure of the Buddha, who although absent, maintains an invisible and hidden presence.

NOTES

For Sam, for being herself.

Thanks to Peter Fitzpatrick and Bruce Kapferer for encouragement and support, to Colin Perrin for comments on an earlier first draft, and to Stuart Mann.

1. K. M. de Silva, *Managing Ethnic Tensions in Multi-Ethnic Societies: Sri Lanka, 1880–1985* (London: University Press of America, 1986), 417.

2. Bruce Kapferer, *Legends of People, Myths of State: Violence, Intolerance, and Political Culture in Sri Lanka and Australia* (London: Smithsonian Institution Press, 1988), 90–93.

3. John D. Rogers, "Historical Images in the British Period," in *Sri Lanka: Roots of a Conflict,* ed. J. Spencer (London: Routledge, 1990), 90–92.

4. Ibid., 93–94.

5. Steven Kemper, *The Presence of the Past: Chronicles, Politics, and Culture in Sinhala Life* (London: Cornell University Press, 1991), 199–200; Stanley J. Tambiah, *Buddhism Betrayed? Religion, Politics, and Violence in Sri Lanka* (London: University of Chicago Press, 1992), 131.

6. Richard Gombrich, *Theravada Buddhism: A Social History from Ancient Benares to Modern Colombo* (London: Routledge, 1988), 185–88, 174; Kemper, *Presence of the Past*, xii.

7. Kemper, *Presence of the Past*, 54–60.

8. Tambiah, *Buddhism Betrayed?* 59–60; Kapferer, *Legends of People*, 93–99.

9. Slavoj Žižek, *Tarrying with the Negative: Kant, Hegel, and the Critique of Ideology* (Durham: Duke University Press, 1993), 161; Homi K. Bhabha, *The Location of Culture* (London: Routledge, 1994), 74–75.

10. It emphasizes the temporalization of this cosmos in the contingent event of the law. In a different context that emphasizes the relation between Heidegger's thought of Being and legal discourse, see Alexander Carnera Ljungstrom, "The Silent Voice of Law: Legal Philosophy as Legal Thinking," *Law and Critique* 8, no. 1 (1997): 76; Panu Minkkinen, "Right Things: On the Question of Being and Law," *Law and Critique* 7, no. 1 (1996): 82.

11. Ljungstrom, "Silent Voice of Law," 88–89.

12. Bruce Kapferer, *A Celebration of Demons: Exorcism and the Aesthetics of Healing in Sri Lanka* (Bloomington: Indiana University Press, 1983), and *Legends of People.*

13. While it does not show itself, it is at the same time according to Heidegger "something that belongs to what shows itself and it belongs to it so essentially as to constitute its meaning and its ground (*Being and Time*, trans. John Macquarrie and Edward Robinson [Oxford: Blackwell, 1962], 59). Heidegger goes on to locate this meaning in "those primordial experiences in which we achieved our first ways of determining the nature of Being" (44). In the context of Sri Lanka Kapferer *(Legends of People)* locates this "primordial experience" in the cosmology of Sinhalese Buddhism.

14. This principle of "hierarchical encompassment" has been developed by Kapferer in *Legends of People*, 11. Here, Kapferer analyzes the relation between the ontological dynamic of the cosmology of Sinhalese Buddhism and the practices of Sinhalese Buddhist nationalism.

15. Bhabha, *The Location of Culture*, 66–84.

16. Kapferer, *Legends of People.*

17. Kapferer, *Legends of People*, 99–103; and *A Celebration of Demons.*

18. Kapferer, *Legends of People*, 11–12. The 1972 constitution is broadly occidental in form and content and therefore does not in its entirety lend itself to an analysis from within the dynamics of the Buddhist cosmos. However, in its discursive production in the Constituent Assembly between 1970 and 1972, themes that have their "origins" within the Buddhist cosmos were elaborated upon. It is these themes that concern me here. Constitution of the Republic of Sri Lanka (Colombo: Government Publications Bureau, 1972) (available in the library of the School of Oriental and African Studies, University of London).

19. Constituency Assembly Debates: Vol. 1, No. 12; Col. 385–440 (Colombo: Government Publications Bureau, 1972) (available in the library of the School of Oriental and African Studies, University of London).

20. Constituency Assembly Debates: Vol. 1, No. 13; Col. 473.

21. Constituency Assembly Debates: Vol. 1, No. 12; Col. 397.

22. Kapferer, *Legends of People,* 86.

23. Kemper, *Presence of the Past,* 63–64; Kapferer, *Legends of People,* 57–58.

24. Kapferer, *Legends of People,* 8.

25. Gombrich, *Theravada Buddhism,* 46–49.

26. Through understanding and practicing the *dhamma* (the Buddhist doctrine/Cosmic Law) it is possible to have an experience of nibbana (*nirvana* in Sanskrit) a state of liberation/salvation from "greed," "hatred," and "delusion" (Gombrich, *Theravada Buddhism,* 24). Nibbana is the realization of *things as they are,* freed of a perceptive order structured through greed and hatred (metaphors for desire or *thirst* as the Buddha described it) and delusion (a metaphor for ignorance). Nibbana, which means "blown out," is the blowing out of a perceptive order structured through "thirst." For a summary presentation of Buddhist doctrine see Gombrich, *Theravada Buddhism,* 60–65.

27. Stanley J. Tambiah, *Sri Lanka: Ethnic Fratricide and the Dismantling of Democracy* (London: I. B. Tauris, 1986), 78–79.

28. de Silva, *Managing Ethnic Tensions,* 182.

29. Constituency Assembly Debates: Vol. 1, No. 27; Col. 1986.

30. In a different context see Colin Perrin, "Approaching Anxiety: The Insistence of the Postcolonial in the Declaration on the Rights of Indigenous Peoples," *Law and Critique* 6, no. 1 (1995): 67–68.

31. In a different context see ibid., 69.

32. In the context of a blocked individual identity see Slavoj Žižek, *For They Know Not What They Do: Enjoyment as Political Factor* (London: Verso, 1991), 109–12.

33. Kapferer, *Legends of People,* 79–84.

34. Kapferer, *Legends of People,* 220 n. 5.

35. Jürgen Habermas, "The Undermining of Western Rationalism through the Critique of Metaphysics: Martin Heidegger," in *The Philosophical Discourse of Modernity,* trans. Frederick G. Lawrence (Cambridge: Polity Press, 1987), 143–44.

36. Kapferer, *Legends of People,* 84. Kapferer describes ideology as a "selective cultural construction whereby certain significances relevant to experience are systematically organised into a relatively coherent scheme" (80). Because Kapferer does not collapse ideology into an explicit or implicit reference to "truth" or "falsity," an ideological process being the engagement of the logic of ontology within the contingency of the social, it seems that ideology for Kapferer bears a similarity to Foucault's concept of discourse. Foucault observed that "in every society the production of discourse is at once controlled, selected, organised and redistributed" ("The Discourse on Language," in *Untying the Text: A Post-Structuralist Reader,* ed. R. Young [London: Rout-

ledge, 1981], 52). Discourses, far from being systems of reference in which a relation of transparency between language and the object of representation is established, are "rather practices which systematically form the objects of which they speak" (Michel Foucault, *The Archaeology of Knowledge,* trans. A. M. Sheridan Smith [London: Tavistock, 1972], 49). From discourse it is but a step to the conception of a "discursive formation" (Foucault, *Power/Knowledge: Selected Interviews and Other Writings, 1972–1977,* trans. Colin Gordon, Leo Marshall, John Mepham, and Kate Soper [London: Harvester Wheatsheaf, 1980], 109–25), the means by which the mediated effects of power and knowledge are produced. Discursive formations are historically contingent and reflect a dominant episteme that establishes a relational network in which meaning is constituted. By extension, then, the construction of culture into an organized scheme depends on the organization of cultural objects through discourse into a discursive formation that establishes the discursively produced objects of culture into relational network.

37. Kapferer, *Legends of People,* 11.

38. Ibid.

39. Kapferer, *A Celebration of Demons.*

40. Kapferer, *Legends of People,* 12.

41. Pali, a classical Indian language derived from Sanskrit, is the sacred script of Theravada Buddhism. *Theravada* means "Doctrine of the Elders," a reference to the senior monks who preserve tradition. It thus implies a certain doctrinal conservatism (Gombrich, *Theravada Buddhism*). *Theravada* came to Sri Lanka in approximately 250 B.C.E. from North India, where the Buddha had preached the *dhamma* (Kemper, *Presence of the Past,* 32–33), the Buddhist doctrine that, because it both describes and prescribes, is both "Truth" and "Law" (Gombrich, *Theravada Buddhism,* 1–3).

42. Kemper, *Presence of the Past,* 34–38.

43. Kapferer, *Legends of People,* 50–65.

44. Kemper, *Presence of the Past,* 59–65.

45. The failure of the son to obey the father and the Oedipal slaying of the father is a dominant trope in Sinhalese Buddhist mythology (Gananath Obeyesekere, *The Work of Culture: Symbolic Transformation in Psychoanalysis and Anthropology* [Chicago: University of Chicago Press, 1990], 143–56).

46. Kapferer, *Legends of People,* 63.

47. Ibid., 80.

48. Kemper, *Presence of the Past,* 61.

49. Tambiah, *Buddhism Betrayed?* 140–42, 145–47.

50. W. I. Siriweera, "The Dutthagamani-Elara Episode: A Reassessment," in *Ethnicity and Social Change in Sri Lanka,* ed. Social Scientists Association (Colombo: Karunaratne, 1984), 54–73; Tambiah, *Buddhism Betrayed?* 139–42.

51. Kapferer, *Legends of People,* 81; Renata Salecl, *The Spoils of Freedom: Psychoanalysis and Feminism after the Fall of Socialism* (London: Routledge, 1994), 86–87.

52. Kapferer, *Legends of People,* 81.

53. Ibid., 82.

54. These dreadful consequences are manifest in the hierarchical structure of Sinhalese violence against Tamils, which in articulating the metaphors of a Sinhalese Buddhist exorcism ritual (Tambiah, *Buddhism Betrayed?* 46–57; Kapferer, *Legends of People,* 111) seek to reencompass the Tamil other at the base of hierarchy.

55. Kapferer, *Legends of People,* 116.

Postcolonialism: The Emperor's New Clothes?

Jeannine Purdy

More than thirty years ago, Jean-Paul Sartre wrote in his preface to Frantz Fanon's *The Wretched of the Earth*, "In the colonies the truth stood naked, but the citizens of the mother country preferred it with clothes on: the native had to love them, something in the way mothers are loved."[1] The naked truth of colonialism was exposed in Fanon's powerful evocation of "a world cut in two," a world divided between the colonizers and the wretched of the earth—the colonized. And according to Fanon, in such a world, "The dividing line, the frontiers are shown by barracks and police stations."[2]

Police stations, as sites of legal violence, were regarded as crucial to the maintenance of the divided world of a colonial regime. Fanon's project, however, cannot be simply assimilated with more recent critiques of law, such as Austin Sarat and Thomas Kearns's "A Journey through Forgetting: Toward a Jurisprudence of Violence." Unlike the "ubiquity of law's violence" posited by Sarat and Kearns, Fanon was concerned to show that the function of, and the attitudes toward, law and its violence varied according to which side of the colonial divide one stood on.[3] If one stood on the side of the colonizers,

> the educational system, whether lay or clerical, the structure of moral reflexes passed down from father to son, the exemplary honesty of workers who are given a medal after fifty years of good and loyal service, and the affection which springs from harmonious

An earlier version of this essay appeared in a Special Issue on Law and Postcolonialism, edited by Eve Darian-Smith and Peter Fitzpatrick in *Social and Legal Studies* 5, no. 3 (1996). Reprinted by permission of Sage Publications.

> relations and good behavior—all these *aesthetic expressions of respect for the established order* serve to create around the exploited person an atmosphere of submission and of inhibition *which lightens the task of policing considerably.*[4]

More than thirty years ago Fanon showed us that the violent law known to the colonized was not the law known to others.

But what if, even after the work of Fanon and others like him, the colonizers wanted, no less than they did in the past, to be loved? Whatever the variations between the theorists of "postcoloniality," because postcolonialism facilitates a view of the world as fundamentally altered, it enables the colonizers once more to demand the love of "the native" as they proclaim their progress beyond the colonial.[5] While it is undoubtedly true that "postcolonial" studies is a far from unified field, it is my contention that within the play of colonial discourse analysis, psychoanalysis, deconstruction, feminism, and "other forms of Marxism" that constitute the postcolonial terrain,[6] what may have been intended to do no more than give recognition to the changing circumstances of colonialism (alluded to later) has perhaps proved far more "dangerous" than intended.[7] Writing as a member of the Tangankald peoples, who are the traditional owners of South Australia, Irene Watson states,

> A myth was created, that is, colonialism ended when the UN outlawed its existence. This myth has become an effective genocidal tool of the state and has left the door open for the rhetoric of "postcolonialism" to spread throughout the states' academic institutions.[8]

As indicated by the word itself, *post*colonial analyses often in effect go far beyond being supplementary to analyses of colonialism, such as Fanon's. Issues of class and violence, crucial to Fanon's analysis, now often receive only cursory acknowledgment, if any.[9]

After Colonialism?

Francis Snyder and Douglas Hay indicate something of the academic proclivity to divide and categorize on the basis of what they describe as the "main fault lines" of time and space. They note the entrenched divisions found in academic reasoning "between past and present, on the one hand, and between First World and Third World, on the other."[10] Peter Fitzpatrick elaborates upon something of the constitutive nature of such posited divisions, with reference to notions of "us" and "them," and how these are integral to our legal systems and sense of "civilization." Edward Said also trenchantly comments upon the divisions colonizers made between themselves and their rivals. He notes, "The pattern is, alas, always the same: critics of colonialism . . . attack abuses in places and by powers that do not greatly touch them." When European nations dominated, "European intellectuals were prone to attack the abuses of rival empires, while either mitigating or excusing the practices of their own. . . . Doctrines of cultural exceptionalism are altogether too abundant."[11]

We find the tendency in our reasoning to create divisions between us and them, the civilized and the savage, now and then. Snyder and Hay indicate how such reasoning can limit our understanding. Fitzpatrick and Said sound more dire warnings: Fitzpatrick indicates its connection with racism; Said with imperialism. It is my contention that the categories that divide the world into colonial and postcolonial reinforce such constitutive—and self-exculpatory—reasoning.[12] Although the conceptual movement from the colonial to the postcolonial has been widely adopted within academic circles, it has not proved equally persuasive to others. In particular those who are *most* marginalized because of their race/ethnicity and economic position seem *most* recalcitrant in the face of claims that we now occupy a postcolonial world. For example, Abdullah Omowale, one of the Muslimeen involved in the attempted coup in Trinidad and Tobago of 1990, writes of the actions of the prime minister of the Republic that

> he opened the pages of the IMF [International Monetary Fund] Doomsday Book putting the entire country into social, political, economic and moral reverse gear.
>
> Twenty-eight years of national independence was swept aside as the cast-off garment of colonialism was rebuttoned tightly around us.[13]

With particular reference to Northern Ireland, Liam O'Dowd states that the failure to acknowledge and confront the resilience of colonialism into the late twentieth century "promotes facile assertions of global interdependence and mutual interests in what is misleadingly termed a post-colonial and post-nationalist world."[14] The Caribbean author W. Richard Jacobs describes another aspect of this resilient colonialism, the "neo-colony":

> Independent by name, flying its own flag, promulgating laws from its own Parliament, but dependent in all material and metaphysical ways on the umbilical cord which ties it to the metropolitan centre. The neo-colonial status, while it might in the short-run satisfy the ruling class, is a most debilitating, humiliating and ultimately dehumanising experience, for it facilitates the sucking of the economic blood of the neo-colony and the reciprocal fattening of the metropole in full view of all—the wretched of the earth as well as the metropolitan imperialist interests.[15]

Roger Moody, writing of indigenous peoples, comments that to treat colonialism as a thing of the past is to "ignore militarization, the de-development of the Third World, the spread of corporate capitalism, the continuing seizure of indigenous peoples' lands and the adulteration of their spirituality and culture." Indeed the Aboriginal activist Sam Watson specifically utilizes the language of colonialism to describe the contemporary position of Australian Aboriginal peoples. Others, who do not use that language, write in terms of stasis with the past. For example, Eve Fesl, a Koori academic and activist, describes the position of Aboriginal people of her parents' generation as slavery. Robert Bropho, an elder of the Nyungah peoples of southwest Australia, writes of the history of Western Australia since white occupation as a series of "waves of destruction."[16] At a time when Bropho envisages the ethnocide of his people, assertions of postcolonialism appear neither accurate nor appropriate.

The debates over the colonialist content or otherwise of the contemporary world not only raise issues of definition.[17] In particular, the issue should not be overlooked of *who* it is who has authority to define colonialism and, therefore, who should decide if and when colonialism's unambiguous reference to violence and economic exploitation is no longer adequate to comprehend what is occurring. In the divided world described by Fanon there would be reason to be skeptical of the perceptions of colonialism held by both the colonizers and the colonized middle classes, who had "totally assimilated colonialist thought in its most corrupt form."[18] Reason for skepticism increases if an assessment is made of the terms upon which colonialism has been recognized and condemned. For, like the critics of the past, postcolonial critics of colonialism also often "attack abuses in places and by powers that do not greatly touch them."[19]

Thus, while it may be true that the existence of colonialism *within* the first world is now admitted, we make this admission as citizens of a *post*colonial world. This is evident in Australia, where, in spite of the overtly colonial nature of relations with its indigenous peoples, Mervyn Hartwig wrote that before 1978 only one writer had identified these relations in such terms.[20] More recently there has been a much more widespread acceptance of the colonial nature of *historical* relations between white and Aboriginal peoples in Australia.[21] It is, however, most often in *Aboriginal* interpretations of *contemporary* relations that colonialism and stasis with the past figure.[22] For non-Aboriginal Australians, it would seem that even if the horrors of colonialism can no longer be confined to occurring somewhere else (preferably the third world), it is at least possible now to confine its occurrence to a distant and barbarous time—the past.

Again, while it may be true that the horror of historical European colonialism in the third world is now widely accepted, this acceptance has often been made by those who would not regard their own privilege and that of their nations as being implicated in contemporary colonialism. The absence of any resolute recognition of the contemporary realities of violence and class has enabled us to ignore a great deal, including what Aimé Césaire describes as the rule of the "modern barbarian. The American hour. Violence, excess, waste, mercantilism, bluff, gregariousness, stupidity, vulgarity, disorder."[23] Said notes,

> Yet in general the United States after World War Two considered itself responsible for many parts of the Third World which the British and French had evacuated—Vietnam, of course, is the main instance—and, because of an exceptional history based on the legitimacy of an anti-colonial revolution, largely exempt from the charge that in its own way it began to resemble Britain and France.[24]

Noam Chomsky, Kathy McAfee, and others have clearly documented the mechanics of contemporary U.S. rule, and authors such as Kevin

Watkins have traced its permutations through more recent GATT (General Agreement on Tariffs and Trade) innovations.[25] And while the form of colonial exploitation has changed in many instances,[26] the parallels with earlier, formally colonial times remain evident. For example, the net results of the colonial economic order of the seventeenth through nineteenth centuries described in Eric Williams's *Capitalism and Slavery* and of the early twentieth century described in A. G. Russell's *Colour, Race, and Empire* are starkly mirrored in the economic ramifications of the new world order, exemplified through relations between the United States and the Caribbean.[27]

Colonialism and Economics

According to many colonized peoples' analyses of colonialism, although racism is never merely incidental, it is such economic exploitation that is foundational. Fanon attributes the "inferiority complex" of the colonized *primarily* to economic processes and subsequently to "the internalization—or, better, the epidermalization—of this inferiority"; C. L. R. James states that the "race question is subsidiary to the class question in politics, and to think of imperialism in terms of race is disastrous"; Césaire finds the decisive actors in the colonialist project to have been the

> adventurer, pirate, wholesale grocer and shipowner, gold digger, merchant, appetite and force, and behind them a form of civilisation which at a point in its history finds itself for internal reasons obliged to extend to a world scale the competition of its antagonistic economies.[28]

That is not to ignore that the forms of economic exploitation may have changed since the era of the authors previously cited. Eboe Hutchful, concurring with Wallerstein and others, describes the contemporary era as being characterized by the internationalization of capital in the form of transnational or multinational corporations.[29] In this context, international economic relations no longer involve predominantly the export of commodities and capital by national producers and financiers, but the internationalization of capitalist production, in which the Bretton Woods institutions play a crucial role. Watkins also highlights the increasingly significant role of the control over intellectual property and technology in maintaining first world privilege.[30] Although the forms may have changed, the end remains the same—"the sucking of the economic blood of the neo-colony and the reciprocal fattening of the metropole in full view of all—the wretched of the earth as well as the metropolitan imperialist interests."[31]

Colonialism and Law's Violence

It is not only economic exploitation and marginalization that have remained fundamentally unaltered by the formal political changes of the contemporary era. Hutchful also adopts Marx's analysis of the conditions of exploitation in the "periphery"; that is, as being unrestrained by "natural reason" and hence flagrantly violent,[32] as being valid within the contemporary context. For many colonized peoples, the economic exploitation that characterized colonialism was associated with an equally definitive violence.[33] The similarities between the brutal military incursions described in Russell's (and more recent) studies, therefore, present another aspect of the continuity between the colonial and so-called postcolonial worlds.[34]

As Fanon notes, however, it was not only military force, the barracks, through which the violent divide between the colonizers and the colonized was maintained. The police stations, their functions, and the attitudes toward them were equally integral to this divided world. The issue of postcolonialism is therefore of particular relevance to the role of law in the contemporary world. If Fitzpatrick's thesis of the constitutive nature of our legal systems in defining our civility is accepted,[35] the issue of postcolonialism for law is of even more significance.

The growing acknowledgment of the violence and exploitation perpetrated in what is now known as the colonial era can be reconciled to notions of our own civility through the postulation of a world and a law that have become fundamentally different from that which they were in the past. And it is in the postcolonial that absolution can be found. In the remainder of this chapter, I refer to three broadly grouped interpretations of law that have evolved in tandem with the "postcolonial" world. These interpretations suggest that the significance of law as a penal mechanism has declined as other methods of discipline have increased; that law increasingly has an administrative/discursive character; that "colonial" violence and oppression were somehow aberrant or external to law.

I raise these interpretations in the context of the specific practice of (colonial)[36] law in relation to the colonized peoples of the West Indies and Australia. In particular, my focus is on the practice of law in relation to Trinidadians, predominantly the descendants of the African slaves and Indian indentured laborers transported to Trinidad as part of the colonial labor regime; and the minority indigenous peoples of the colonized state of Western Australia. In the context of what is currently being done to these peoples, it is my contention that the three interpretations of law to which I referred earlier constitute part of the creed of "a multitude of moral teachers, counselors and 'bewilderers' [who] separate the exploited from those in power" and who "hide the domination" in capitalist societies.[37]

My claim that such interpretations are "bewildering" has a specific reference. How law is experienced/viewed *by some* cannot and should not be generalized into a definitive statement of the nature of law *for all.* In particular, such assessments of law will "bewilder" in proportion to the distance between the relative privilege of the proponents of such approaches and the disadvantage of those who, it is often assumed, are being spoken for. Because the distinction between the colonizer and the colonized has become muted through postcolonial theory, a preoccupation with the law as it is known to the colonizers is unrecognized. As a consequence, the continuing role of law's violence in the economic exploitation of colonized peoples goes unheeded.

The Death of the Prison?

Michel Foucault's *Discipline and Punish: The Birth of the Prison* is a key text in modern analyses of law.[38] But somewhat akin to Foucault's Victorians who spoke incessantly about a secret sexuality,[39] Foucault's "birth of the prison" to some degree acts as its tombstone. Although primarily concerned to trace the development of the prison, Foucault's conclusion is that two processes that had "no doubt . . . already begun to a large degree" were "capable of exercising considerable restraint on [prison] use and of transforming its internal functioning." The first was "that which reduces the utility . . . of a delinquency accommodated as a specific illegality, locked up and supervised." The second process was "the growth of all the disciplinary networks, [and] the multiplication of their exchanges with the penal apparatus." With the proliferation of "all these mechanisms of normalisation, which are becoming ever more rigorous in their application, the specificity of the prison and its role as link are losing something of their purpose."[40]

Interpretations subsequent to Foucault's analysis include those that expressly refer to the decline of the prison as an agency of social control and those that simply omit the role of prisons altogether.[41] It is no doubt open to debate whether such interpretations either correctly reflect Foucault's analysis or alternatively can be attributed to his influence. It seems to me, however, that when an author chooses to construct his analysis in terms of the "*birth* of the prison" (*naissance* in the original), it cannot be claimed that its death was not envisaged. This criticism of Foucault is not simply pedantic. Refer, for example, to Foucault's unequivocal assessment of the contemporary significance of the prison.

> If there is an overall political issue around the prison it is not even whether we should have a prison or something other than a prison. At present, the problem lies rather in the steep rise in the use of these mechanisms of normalisation [medicine, psychology, education, public assistance, "social work"] and the wide-ranging powers which, through the proliferation of new disciplines, they bring with them.[42]

I am concerned neither to argue whether an interpretation such as Trotman's is what Foucault intended nor to claim that it is the only possible reading. I would claim, however, that such an interpretation is one that is open on Foucault's text and his account of the normalizing rather than repressive essence of the prison. As I hope to indicate below, however, the decline of the prison is difficult to sustain if one has regard to statistical data documenting the incidence of imprisonment in relation to colonized peoples.

Trinidad and Tobago: Contemporary Imprisonment

In Trinidad and Tobago, prison numbers have varied significantly throughout this century. As can be seen in figure 1, if any overall trend can be discerned, it is one that contradicts the thesis that the use and incidence of imprisonment is in decline.

Moreover, historical data indicate that in 1990 the rate of imprisonment per capita was higher than at any previously documented time.

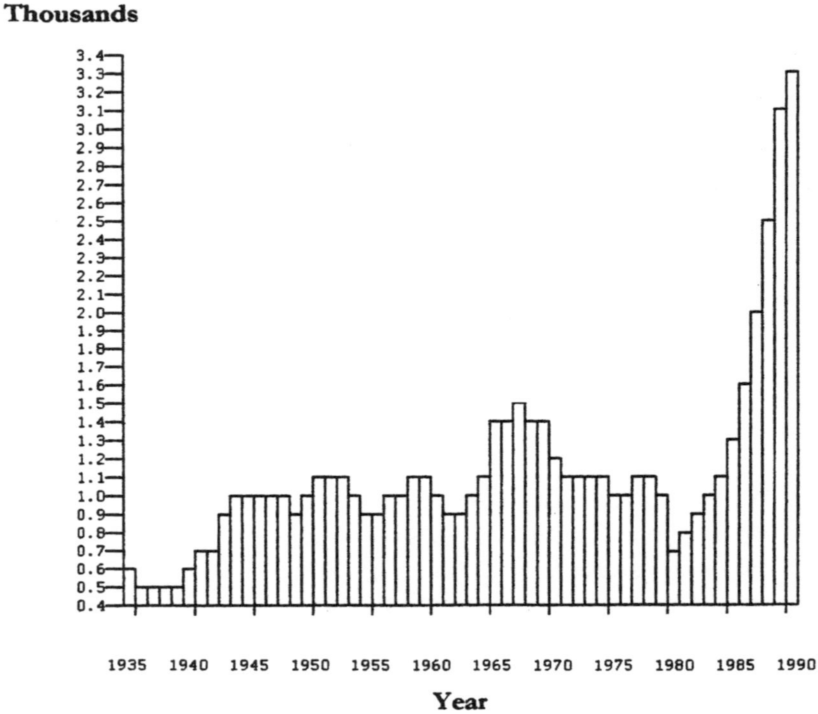

Fig. 1. Daily average prison population, Trinidad and Tobago, 1935–91. (Data from Lystra Hagley, "Crime and Structural Adjustment in Trinidad and Tobago: On the Exercise of Judicial Discretion," *Caribbean Affairs* 6, no. 1 [1974]: 147–54; Trinidad and Tobago Central Statistical Office, *Annual Statistical Digest* [Port of Spain: Ministry of the Economy, 1993].)

That not only refers to per capita rates for this century but includes rates from the latter half of the nineteenth century,[43] an era characterized by the use of criminal law to enforce indentured-"servant" labor regimes and severe cultural repression within a plantation society.[44]

It is of note that in 1990 there had been a coup attempt in Trinidad and Tobago that was followed by extensive rioting, looting, and arson. While the attempted coup and subsequent events no doubt contributed to the high number of imprisonments in that year, the dramatically increasing rate of imprisonment *preceded* the coup attempt and coincided with the intervention of the IMF in Trinidad and Tobago. Therefore, while total committals doubled between 1989 and 1990, they had already tripled from some five thousand to fifteen thousand between 1988 and 1989.[45] Interestingly, perceptions of cause and effect in the relationship between the coup/looting and imprisonment may need to be reversed—conforming to Douglas Hay's suggestion that escalations in law's violence *precede* the wider dissemination of violence throughout society.[46]

It is also clear from the account of Omowale, one of the coup leaders, and the accounts of others who were not involved, that the Muslimeen who led the coup attempt had in fact sought to halt the rioting, looting, and arson.[47] Omowale specifically related the popular uprising to the dissatisfaction of the poor of Trinidad, who suffered most acutely from the "conditionalities" imposed by the IMF. In this he is not alone; Dennis Pantin, a Trinidadian economist, predicted in 1989 that "riots and deaths" would be the consequences of IMF intervention in Trinidad and Tobago.[48]

Therefore, it is difficult to isolate the coup, rioting, and imprisonment rates from the impact of IMF policies in the Republic. Again, it is Hay's association of legal violence with economic conditions and Hutchful's association of violence in the "periphery" with the economic conditions and policies of the metropolitan centers that seems far more pertinent to the recent history of Trinidad and Tobago than any analysis premised on the declining significance of imprisonment in contemporary societies.

Western Australia: Contemporary Aboriginal Imprisonment

Data in relation to the imprisonment of Aboriginal peoples in Western Australia also fail to comply with the "Foucauldian" prediction of the declining use of the prison in modern societies (see fig. 2). It is true that the proportion of Aboriginal imprisonments did decline after peaking at 50 percent of the prison population early this century. However, a sustained decline in Aboriginal prison numbers lasted only until the late 1940s[49] and was principally associated with the implementation of an apartheid system that largely segregated Aboriginal people from the broader society and subjected them to the internal disciplinary regimes of the reserves, settlements, missions, and pastoral stations to which

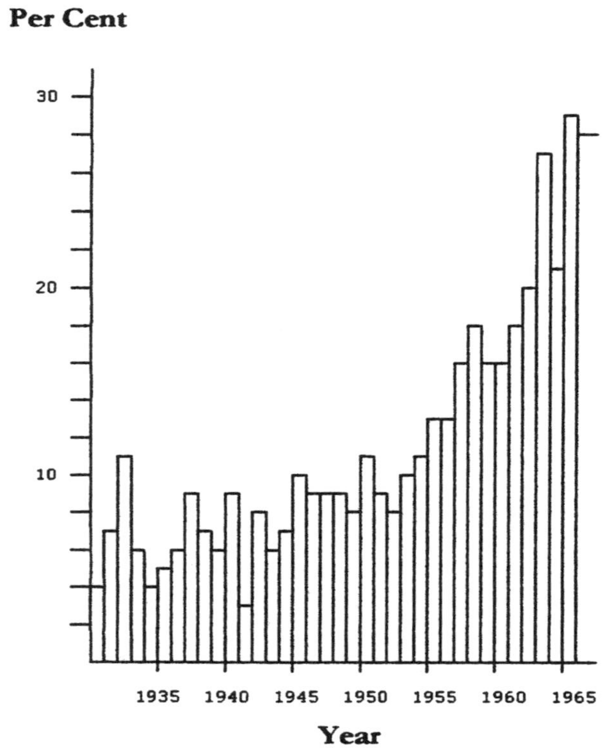

Fig. 2. Aboriginal imprisonment rates in Western Australia as a percentage of total imprisonments, 1930–67. (Data from Western Australia Government Statistician, *Statistical Register of Western Australia* [Perth: Government Printer, 1931, 1942, 1944, 1953, 1963, 1964, 1969].)

they were confined by law.[50] Since the 1950s Aboriginal imprisonment rates have steadily increased, and currently Aboriginal prisoners constitute approximately 30 percent of the prison population.[51]

Although the period since the 1950s is associated with official policies related to the assimilation of Aboriginal peoples, that period also coincided with an exponential increase in mineral exports from Western Australia; an increase that broadly mirrors the increase in the number of Aboriginal prisoners.

It is of note that the growth in mineral exploration and exploitation, as well as agricultural expansion in the southwest,[52] altered the

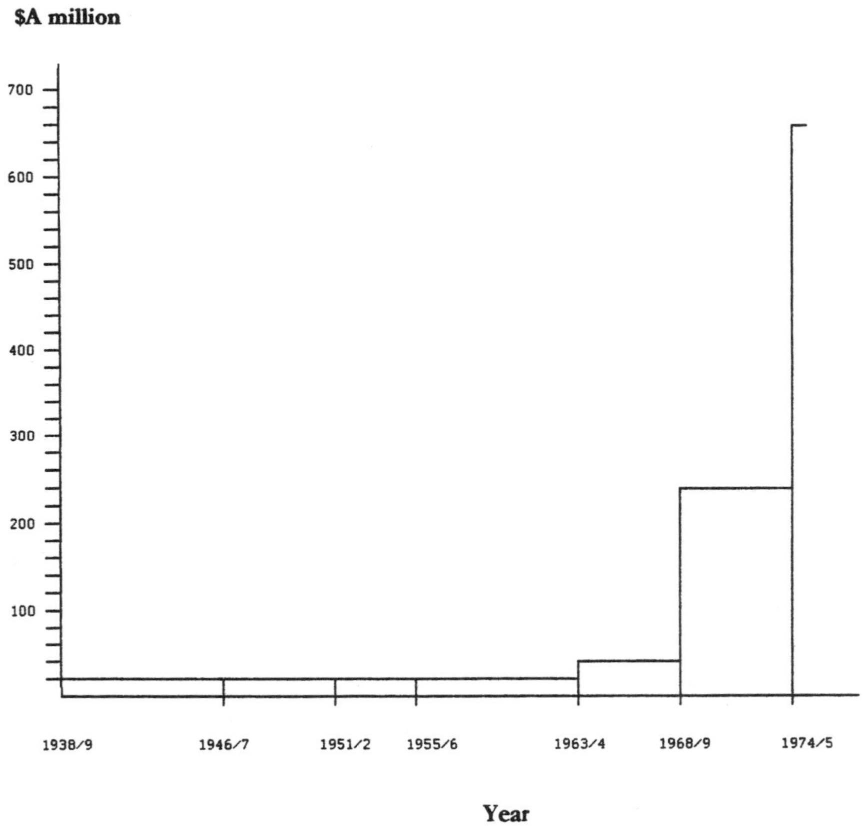

Fig. 3. Net value of mineral production in Western Australia, selected years 1938–39 to 1974–75. (Data from R. N. Ghosh, "Economic Development and Population Growth in Western Australia since 1945," in *A New History of Western Australia*, ed. C. T. Stannage [Nedlands: University of Western Australia Press, 1987], 282.)

economic value of the land on which many of the reserves, settlements, missions, and pastoral stations were established. Therefore, although the closure of these institutions was associated with assimilationist policy, their closure also brought economic benefits to many sectors of the non-Aboriginal society. For many Aboriginal people, however, this era constituted a second wave of dispossession.[53]

Over the period from 1946–47 to 1991–92, rates of Aboriginal imprisonment increased from something of the order of 1.4 to 14 per 1,000. In addition to this, currently Aboriginal people also make up some 50 percent of those incarcerated in the police lockups.[54] It is of note that Aboriginal people in Western Australia constitute something less than 3 percent of the total population. Indeed, Aboriginal people in Australia may now be the most highly imprisoned minority group in the world.[55]

The "Nonspecificity" of Imprisonment

The contemporary imprisonment rates of both Trinidadian and Aboriginal peoples are inconsistent with any thesis that modern disciplinary methods are reducing the incidence of imprisonment in modern society, in particular as it is used against colonized peoples. However, an alternative interpretation of Foucault's thesis may be that it was the specificity, more than the incidence, of imprisonment that was in decline. Even if this is allowed, difficulties remain.

In order to dispute such a thesis one would be required to engage with what must, on the final analysis, remain an imponderable. That is, whether life outside the prison is increasingly resembling life inside.[56] Perhaps from a theoretical perspective, such a thesis is persuasive; but again, much may depend on which side of the prison walls one stands. It would seem to me that both the extremely high incidence of Aboriginal deaths in custody and the graphic horror of imprisonment as described by inmates in the existing prisons of Trinidad should belie this kind of speculation.[57] For many of the present inmates, at least, it would not seem that the "disciplinary techniques" inside the prison particularly resemble those outside.

Beyond this, however, to argue that imprisonment lacks specificity among contemporary disciplinary mechanisms, that it is indeed these mechanisms that are the "overall political issue around the prison,"[58] is to preempt any study of the specific role of imprisonment in contemporary societies. It therefore disables recognition of any particular role that imprisonment plays in the construction of the racially and economically marginalized positions occupied by many colonized peoples. The significance of the violence perpetrated through law is lost if we commence with the thesis that we are all equally subject to effectively analogous "mechanisms of normalization."

Law as Administration/Discourse

The second broad interpretation of law to which I want to refer is related to Foucault's work and is based upon the view of law as an (increasingly) administrative and/or discursive process. For example, Fitzpatrick discusses Foucault's thesis that as law changed in character from a prohibitive to a constitutive form, the judicial institution was incorporated into a continuum of apparatuses "whose function is for the most part regulatory." Alternatively, law has been subject to discourse analysis, and appraisal as literature, on the basis that such analysis and appraisal can comprehend what law is.[59]

The administrative/discursive aspect of law was apparent in the magistrates' courts that I observed in Western Australia, particularly in respect to interactions with non-Aboriginal defendants.[60] Often those summonsed on criminal matters were permitted to plead guilty by way of summons. Their physical presence in court was dispensed with as charges, pleas, and fines were transacted through the medium of discourse and the impersonal agency of the mail. Moreover, even those who were required to be present in the courts tended to plead guilty, and the public spectacle did appear to confirm Fitzpatrick's assertion of the contemporary state's attempts to inculcate "a conformist discipline in its subjects,"[61] which is corollary to the regulative function of law in contemporary societies. For such self-regulating defendants it may well be that law operates as a regulatory, as opposed to punitive, process. Their bodies were not a focal site of the legal process, as were the bodies of those who did not, or who were perceived not to, conform. With respect to the self-regulating defendant, it may also be true therefore to claim that discourse analysis and literary critique provide useful perspectives on the functioning of law.

The same however, does not generally hold true for Aboriginal defendants. Their bodies played a crucial role in the legal processes to which they were subjected. The physical presence of Aboriginal people is overwhelmingly required in the courts—and prisons—of Western Australia. For such people, the language of the law may not only be irrelevant but also incomprehensible.[62] And if Aboriginal people do often plead guilty in the courts, as do other defendants in Western Australia, it is not apparent that this is related to the self-regulating subject discussed by Fitzpatrick. Indeed the fact that most Aboriginal defendants were in custody at the time of their court appearance would indicate just the opposite, that is, the "failure" of these subjects to conform without direct and physical intimidation. (Whereas 17 percent of non-Aboriginal defendants appeared before magistrates while in custody, 60 percent of the Aboriginal defendants I observed were in custody at the time of their court appearance.)[63]

In Trinidad, a country of colonized peoples, the physical and personal, as distinct from the discursive and administrative, processes of law played a significant role. The personal humiliation of defendants was frequently part of the court process. In particular the humiliation of prisoners, as well as the visibility of their "dangerous" (black) bodies, were emphasized through caging and shackling. Moreover, relatively few defendants in that jurisdiction were prepared to plead guilty.[64]

The analysis of law as part of a continuum of disciplinary and regulatory apparatuses failed to provide insight into the highly punitive relations with colonized peoples constituted through the colonizers' law. Moreover, to posit law as discourse in the context of the massive and intervening incarceration of these groups disables our recognition of what is being done to them. It also means that we can dispense with speaking to them. Law's "secrets" may be gleaned from an analysis of legal texts.[65] We, the self-regulating subjects who are likely to know law only as regulatory and discursive, define law in those terms and thereby dispense with the expertise of those who know otherwise. It is also of note that the approach to law as an administrative/discursive practice leads to and consolidates notions of law's equality. The particularity of our positions as white and/or privileged is ignored as our knowledge of law as regulatory and discursive occludes everyone else's.

Law's Violence as History

The third interpretation of law to which I want to refer is one that posits the violence and oppression of the "colonial era" as somehow aberrant or external to law. This interpretation of law both acknowledges the violence of colonialism and diminishes the role of law in its perpetration. My contention is not that such an interpretation is "postcolonial"—except in the broadest sense of implying that the colonial era is now past. Rather it is that our ability to address such analyses, whether they be liberal or just wrong, is diminished if we have no firm grasp of the divide that separates the colonizer's from the colonized's perceptions of law.

The approach to colonial violence as either aberrant or external to law is particularly prominent in Australia, and for that reason I confine my discussion of this interpretation to the Australian context. Its appeal in Australia may well be related to the "internal" character of the colonialism practiced in relation to its indigenous peoples.[66] The concessions that have been made to Aboriginal peoples appear meager even in comparison to the formal political independence that has often been granted in conditions of external colonialism, and that provides legitimacy to the retained colonial legal systems of the "neocolonies."[67]

In Australia, concessions to Aboriginal peoples subsist in such measures as granting them human status for census purposes, the right to vote, and, with the 1992 Mabo decision (*Mabo v. Queensland* [*No.* 2] [1992] 175 CLR 1), the overturning of the *terra nullius* (no one's land) doctrine. With such meager changes to the colonial system, the imperative to locate colonial violence and oppression as external or aberrant to law remains strong if the legitimacy of that retained legal order is to be at all persuasive. An influential proponent of this kind of approach to law in Australia is Henry Reynolds. Reynolds's research has had profound effects upon many (non-Aboriginal) Australians' perceptions of our history and has highlighted the violence, duplicity, and treachery of the early colonists. Coinciding with these themes, however, has been one extolling and vindicating British common law. To quote Reynolds,

> The common law was corrupted in Australia by the nature of the relationship between settlers and Aborigines in the same way it was corrupted in Britain's slave colonies. . . . Forced and uncompensated dispossession was frowned on by the Imperial government but in one way or another the colonists continued to take Aboriginal land and convince themselves it was not theft.[68]

Colonial violence is presented at its highest as being within the purview of the colonial governments, and distinct from the inherited legal system. The imperial policies effecting the appropriation of Aboriginal lands by the British Crown are assumed to have been separable from colonial violence against Aboriginal people; as if the occupation of Aboriginal peoples' lands could have somehow occurred peaceably.

Even beyond such a questionable assumption, Reynolds goes to some length to show the extraneous nature of British laws that *did* allow the uncompensated dispossession of Aboriginal peoples. For example, Reynolds writes of "Land Rights Frustrated" with reference to the colonization of South Australia. It is true, as Reynolds indicates, that the constitution act of that state was drawn up by the company promoting the venture and not by the British government. It is of course the case, however, that the act became effective because it was indeed made law by the British government. Reynolds transforms the apathy of British parliamentarians over the passage of an act that described Aboriginal peoples' lands as "waste and unoccupied," hence making it available for sale by the promoters, into an exoneration of British law in the dispossession of Aboriginal peoples.[69]

As further evidence of the purported concern for Aboriginal people evidenced through British imperial law, Reynolds refers the 1849 Order in Council of the Imperial Government, in which Aboriginal customary rights over land were preserved.[70] While such recognition of Aboriginal rights is not denied, it is important to place it within its broader political and economic context. At the time of this and related imperial legislation evincing concern for Aboriginal land rights, New South Wales had already been granted a partly elected legislative council (Imp.) (5 & 6 Vic. c. 76 [1842]). Therefore, it was after more than fifty years of direct imperial rule and at a time when independence seemed inevitable, that British law for the first time explicitly recognized Aboriginal land rights in Australia. In fact, New South Wales became an independent crown colony just six years after the Order in Council became law in 1849 (Imp.) (18 & 19 Vic. c. 54 [1855]).

Moreover, although colonial governments could not normally override imperial legislation that was specifically enacted to apply to the colony, in 1855 legislation was also enacted by the British Parliament that repealed all imperial legislation relating to the disposal of "waste lands" in New South Wales. That legislation authorized the colonial legislature to repeal any Order in Council made under the imperial legislation, including the Order of 1849 recognizing Aboriginal peoples' rights to land (Imp.) (18 & 19 Vic. c. 56 [1855]).[71] If this is to be taken as evidence of the concern for Aboriginal peoples afforded by the "uncorrupted" form of British law, then the sudden discovery of the value of (limited) democracy for the working people of Hong Kong within a few years of the end of British colonial rule[72] should also be taken as evidence of the strength of the democratic impulse engendered by British common law.

Justice Brennan's Mabo judgment illustrates the significance of this kind of approach to law in Australia, but avoids the difficulties of exonerating the imperial *government* from colonial oppression, while also maintaining the "innocence" of the common law. (Indeed it would seem that far from being concerned to grant Aboriginal peoples land, it was the latter that motivated the judgment; see *Mabo* 175 CLR 1, at 69.) Brennan stated, "Aboriginal rights and interests were not stripped away by operation of the common law on first settlement by British colonists, but by the exercise of a sovereignty over land executed recurrently by Governments" (*Mabo* 175 CLR 1, at 68). While such an approach may address the issue of imperial government complicity in the oppression of Aboriginal peoples, it does so by means of asserting a distinction between the common law and its practice.[73] Such an assurance of a "law" that exists beyond its practice may have been far more persuasive had it not been required to be sustainable over more than two hundred years of Australian legal history.

It is of note that Reynolds draws a parallel between the "corruption" of British common law in Australia and "Britain's slave colonies."[74] Both Reynolds's and Brennan's analyses provide the basis for a quite different parallel to be drawn. Criticizing conventional historical accounts of the British slave trade, Eric Williams noted that such accounts had been written "almost as if Britain had introduced Negro slavery solely for the satisfaction of abolishing it."[75] In contemporary treatments of the history of British common law in Australia, the retreat from the doctrine of *terra nullius* is transformed into a vindication of British common law, rather than an indictment of a system that denied Aboriginal peoples fully human status for more than two hundred years. Paraphrasing Williams, I find that such accounts leave one with the impression that the doctrine of *terra nullius* was introduced into Australian law solely for the satisfaction of abolishing it.

The significance of such accounts however, lies not so much in the issue of their accuracy, but in the implications they hold for our ability to locate sites of oppression and violence against colonized peoples. By exonerating law, it remains unquestionably *within* the capacity of the colonizer's law to "retreat from [such] injustice."[76] Inquiries into the nature of that law, such as those undertaken by Fitzpatrick and Kerruish,[77] are foreclosed, and the issue of whether the colonizers' law can encompass the possibilities of decolonization simply do not arise. Indeed in a "postcolonial" era, even our ability to identify such law as belonging to the colonizer is lost.

Conclusion

It seems that as we have been made to confront the realities of colonialism, we have simply added another maneuver to those relied upon by the colonizers of the past: while they distinguished themselves from their colonial rivals, we distinguish ourselves from our colonial predecessors. Dressing law in the borrowed garb of postcolonialism has made us blind to the ways in which law continues to function as it always has in the colonial context—a context where police use their rifle butts to "speak the language of pure force."[78] For those other than the wretched of the earth, Pierre Bourdieu and Jean-Claude Passeron may well have been right to claim "the emperor is never naked"; as Fanon noted, the "'bewilderers' . . . lighten the oppression," they "hide the domination."[79] And we remain puzzled if "the native" does not love us "something in the way mothers are loved."[80]

NOTES

I would like to thank the University of the West Indies and Professor Maureen Cain for arranging for me to attend the University as a visiting research student throughout 1992, and also to acknowledge the assistance of the La Trobe University School of Social Sciences Research and Travel Grants Committee. I would also like to thank Associate Professor Valerie Kerruish for her insightful comments and assistance in the preparation of this article.

1. Jean-Paul Sartre, preface to Frantz Fanon, *The Wretched of the Earth,* trans. C. Farrington (1963; London: Penguin, 1990), 7.

2. Fanon, *Wretched of the Earth,* 29.

3. Austin Sarat and Thomas R. Kearns, "A Journey through Forgetting: Toward a Jurisprudence of Violence," in *The Fate of Law,* ed. Sarat and Kearns (Ann Arbor: University of Michigan Press, 1991), 211. Since we are not all arrested/imprisoned/flogged/executed, it is clear that the "ubiquitous" violence to which Sarat and Kearns refer is not direct exposure to the physical violence of law. Perhaps theirs is some sort of apprehension of legal violence that, although real, resides at a metaphysical level. My difficulty with such an analysis is that it occludes the position of those whose exposure to law's violence is not confined to the metaphysical. If we accept that law's violence is ubiquitous,

once again it is us—whether we be colonizers, middle class, or anything else—who can claim expertise on this aspect of law; once again, the divisions that Fanon *(Wretched of the Earth)* and others have tried to impress upon us disappear from our consciousness.

4. Fanon, *Wretched of the Earth,* 29; emphasis added.

5. Anne McClintock, "The Angel of Progress: Pitfalls in the Term 'Post-colonialism,'" in *Colonial Discourse and Post-Colonial Theory,* ed. Patrick Williams and Laura Chrisman (New York: Columbia University Press, 1994), 291–304.

6. Patrick Williams and Laura Chrisman, "Colonial Discourse and Post-Colonial Theory: An Introduction," in Williams and Chrisman, *Colonial Discourse,* 5. I am not disputing the significance of feminist perspectives, for example, in the analysis of colonialism. Following the analysis of activists who are, and who work on behalf of, impoverished and colonized women, however, my view is that feminist analysis cannot be isolated from the violence, race, and class in which gender is constituted—and of which it is constitutive, e.g., Cheryl Buchanan, "Sexism and Racism," in *The Indigenous Voice: Visions and Realities,* ed. Roger Moody, 2d ed. (Utrecht: International Books, 1993), 697–702; Mike Cole, "The Aboriginal Struggle: An Interview with Helen Boyle," *Race and Class* 27, no. 4 (1986): 21–43; Karen Moran, *Baryulgil Atrocity* (Melbourne: Radical Women, 1993).

7. Rod Edmond, "Much Ado about Difference," review of *The Location of Culture,* by Homi Bhabha, *Radical Philosophy* 72 (July–August 1995): 38–40; Cedric Robinson, "The Appropriation of Frantz Fanon," *Race and Class* 33, no. 2 (1993): 29–43.

8. Irene Watson, "Indigenous Peoples' Law-Ways: Survival against the Colonial State," *Australian Feminist Law Journal* 8 (1997): 56.

9. Given the diversity of the group of "postcolonial writers," my comments are of necessity generalizations only. For example, my criticisms do not extend to those who use postcolonial periodization, such as Aijaz Ahmad, but who like me "resolve to say things which go against the contemporary trend" (*In Theory: Classes, Nations, Literatures* [London: Verso, 1992], x) and who work in a Marxist/socialist paradigm. There is a large degree of overlap in my own and Ahmad's analyses given the shared emphasis on class, although there are also significant differences given that Ahmad's analysis is constructed through a "postcolonial" category, and my own through the retention of a category of the colonial. Such difference would need to be worked out in terms of the specificities of our enterprises, including location—in India as opposed to Australia and Trinidad; and subject matter—literature as opposed to law. The incommensurability of literature and law, in particular within a class analysis, is emphasized in the criticisms of the "law as literature" genre that follow.

10. Francis Snyder and Douglas Hay, "Comparisons in the Social History of Law: Labour and Crime," in *Labour, Law, and Crime: An Historical Perspective,* ed. Snyder and Hay (London: Tavistock, 1987), 4.

11. Peter Fitzpatrick, *The Mythology of Modern Law* (London: Routledge,

1992); Edward Said, *Culture and Imperialism* (London: Chatto and Windus, 1993), 250, 291.

12. Said's preference for interpreting the contemporary context in terms of imperialism rather than colonialism (*Culture and Imperialism,* 8) runs counter to my own analysis. However, Said's failure to acknowledge the persisting nature of colonial relations in the first world and in particular with reference to the Aboriginal peoples of Australia is of itself a glaring omission that renders his analysis on this point less than persuasive (Jeannine Purdy, "Common Law and Colonised Peoples: Studies in Trinidad and Western Australia," Ph.D. diss., La Trobe University, Victoria, 1995, 23 (Aldershot, England: Dartmouth, 1997), 15. Note that Said is not alone in this omission; see also Williams and Chrisman, *Colonial Discourse,* 4; and Ahmad, *In Theory.*

13. Abdullah Omowale, "Robinson Pulls the Doomsday Coup," *T&T Sunday Mirror,* August 9, 1992; see also Abdullah Omowale, "From Colonialism to Colonialism," *T&T Sunday Mirror,* November 29, 1992.

14. Liam O'Dowd, introduction to Albert Memmi, *The Colonizer and the Colonized* (London: Earthscan, 1990), 31.

15. W. Richard Jacobs, "Societies in Crisis: Introduction," in *Contemporary Caribbean: A Sociological Reader,* ed. S. Craig (Trinidad and Tobago: S. Craig, 1982), 2:277.

16. Moody, *The Indigenous Voice,* xxix; Sam Watson, qtd. in "We Are the Victims of the Legal System," *Green Left Weekly,* March 16, 1994; Eve Mungwa D. Fesl, "White Manoeuvres and Koori Oppression," *Social Justice* 16, no. 3 (1989): 31; Robert Bropho, *Always Was—Always Will Be Our Sacred Land* (Guildford, Western Australia: Fringedwellers of the Swan Valley, 1992).

17. Williams and Chrisman, *Colonial Discourse,* 1–3.

18. Quoted in Robinson, "Appropriation of Frantz Fanon," 82.

19. Said, *Culture and Imperialism,* 250.

20. Mervyn Hartwig, "Capitalism and Aborigines: The Theory of Internal Colonialism and Its Rivals," in *Essays in the Political Economy of Australian Capitalism,* ed. E. Wheelwright and K. Buckley (Sydney: Australia and New Zealand Book Co., 1978), 3:121. It seems there was at least one other work that utilized the colonial hermeneutic in the analysis of Aboriginal/non-Aboriginal relations in Australia, R. H. W. Reece's *Aborigines and Colonists: Aborigines and Colonial Society in New South Wales in the 1830s and 1840s* (Sydney: Sydney University Press, 1974). It is of note that this was a history of colonial society in New South Wales during the 1830s and 1840s.

21. E.g., Tim Rowse, "Aboriginal as Historical Actors: Evidence and Inference," in *Through White Eyes,* ed. S. Janson and S. Macintyre (Sydney: Allen and Unwin/Australian Historical Studies, 1990), 132–54; and Pat O'Malley, "Aboriginal Criminalisation and Colonialism in Australia," *Critical Criminologist* 5, no. 4 (1993): 9–21.

22. E.g., Watson, "Indigenous Peoples' Law-Ways"; Watson, qtd. in "We Are the Victims"; Fesl, "White Manoeuvres"; Bropho, *Always Was.*

23. Aimé Césaire, *Discourse on Colonialism,* trans. J. Pinkham (1955; New York: Monthly Review Press, 1972), 59.

24. Said, *Culture and Imperialism*, 291.

25. Noam Chomsky, *Turning the Tide: The U.S. in Latin America*, 2d ed. (Montreal: Black Rose Books, 1987); Kathy McAfee, *Storm Signals: Structural Adjustment and Development Alternatives in the Caribbean* (Boston: South End Press/Oxfam America, 1991); Kevin Watkins, "GATT and the Third World: Fixing the Rules," *Race and Class* 34, no. 1 (1992): 23–40.

26. European powers and the United States also continue to exercise "old-fashioned" colonial control over a number of territories. For examples, refer to contemporary relations between France and "French" Polynesia, recently highlighted by French nuclear testing; to relations between England and the Malvinas; to the United States and the Panama Canal region and Puerto Rico. Moreover, the "former" European empires continue to reap the benefits of their colonial past and present (Tom Barry, Beth Wood, and Deb Preusch, *The Other Side of Paradise: Foreign Control in the Caribbean* [New York: Resource Center, Grove Press, 1984]; McAfee, *Storm Signals*).

27. Eric Williams, *Capitalism and Slavery* (1944; New York: Russell and Russell, 1961); A. G. Russell, *Colour, Race, and Empire* (London: Victor Gollancz, 1944). On relations between the United States and the Caribbean, see, e.g., Barry, Wood, and Preusch, *Other Side of Paradise;* Chomsky, *Turning the Tide;* and McAfee, *Storm Signals.* Williams sought to reconstruct a historical connection between metropolitan economic interests and colonial (legal) relations, in order to displace official historical accounts of the genesis of slavery in terms of race/racism (*Capitalism and Slavery*, 7) and its decline in terms of philanthropy. I am aware that *Capitalism and Slavery* has been subject to such sustained critique that "it is fashionable nowadays to say that Williams's work is discredited" (Peter Fryer, *Black People in the British Empire: An Introduction* [London: Pluto Press, 1988], 5). While many of Williams's details now require correction, Christopher Fyfe states, "Still one wonders—has the edifice really fallen? Certainly it has not been replaced" (quoted in Fryer, *Black People*, 5). It would not seem to have been displaced from the thinking of many colonized peoples.

28. Frantz Fanon, *Black Skin, White Masks*, trans. C. L. Markmann (1952; London: MacGibbon and Kee, 1968), 13; C. L. R. James, *The Black Jacobins*, 2d ed. (1938; New York: Vintage, 1963), 283; Césaire, *Discourse on Colonialism*, 10, 11. Refer also to the views of Helen Boyle, Karen Moran, Abdullah Omowale, and Bilal Abdullah, all contemporary activists among economically and racially marginalized groups, who strongly emphasize the economic basis of their marginalization (Purdy, *Common Law*, 51, 54, 253, 254).

29. Eboe Hutchful, "The Modern State and Violence: The Peripheral State," *International Journal of the Sociology of Law* 14 (1986): 153–78.

30. Watkins, "GATT and Third World."

31. Jacobs, "Societies in Crisis," 277.

32. Hutchful, "Modern State and Violence," 156, 157.

33. E.g., Césaire, *Discourse on Colonialism;* Fanon, *Wretched of the Earth;* Jack Davis, foreword to D. Graham, *Dying Inside* (Sydney: Allen and Unwin, 1989), vii–x.

34. Russell, *Colour, Race, and Empire;* Barry, Wood, and Preusch, *Other Side of Paradise;* Chomsky, *Turning the Tide;* McAfee, *Storm Signals.*

35. Fitzpatrick, *Mythology of Modern Law.*

36. The legal system of Trinidad and Tobago, like that of Australia, is based on British common law. Although Trinidad and Tobago is a republic, it has retained the Privy Council as its highest court of appeal. In Australia, there is very scarce recognition of the validity of Aboriginal law, and none of Aboriginal sovereignty.

37. Fanon, *Wretched of the Earth,* 29.

38. Michel Foucault, *Discipline and Punish: The Birth of the Prison,* trans. Alan Sheridan (London: Penguin, 1979).

39. Michel Foucault, *The History of Sexuality,* vol. 1: *An Introduction,* trans. Robert Hurley (London: Penguin, 1987).

40. Foucault, *Discipline and Punish,* 306.

41. As examples of these alternatives, see David Vincent Trotman, *Crime in Trinidad: Conflict and Control in a Plantation Society, 1838–1900* (Knoxville: University of Tennessee Press, 1986), 72; and Scott Lash, "Reflexivity and Its Doubles: Structure, Aesthetics, and Communities," in U. Beck, A. Giddens, and Lash, *Reflexive Modernization* (Cambridge: Polity Press, 1994), 110–73, 131, 132. Trotman (72) states that the decline in prison numbers in Trinidad at the end of the nineteenth century was due to the gradual abandoning of the prison as a major agency of social control; his bibliography includes Foucault's *Discipline and Punish.* Lash ignores prisons altogether in his analysis of contemporary society. Of the same population that William J. Chambliss and Edward Sbarbaro ("Creating Moral Panic, Legitimizing Repression, and Institutionalizing Racism through Law," *Socio-Legal Bulletin* 8 [summer 1993]: 4–12) have shown to be subjected to up to 40 percent imprisonment rates, Lash writes that they suffer from a "deficit of regulation," and that they are subject to "neither heteronomous nor self-monitoring but very little monitoring at all" (131, 132) .

42. Foucault, *Discipline and Punish,* 306.

43. Lystra Hagley, "Crime and Structural Adjustment in Trinidad and Tobago: On the Exercise of Judicial Discretion," *Caribbean Affairs* 6, no. 1 (1993): 148, 151; Trotman, *Crime in Trinidad,* 280.

44. Trotman, *Crime in Trinidad;* Bridget Brereton, *Race Relations in Colonial Trinidad, 1870–1900* (Cambridge: Cambridge University Press, 1979); Kelvin Singh, *Bloodstained Tombs: The Muharram Massacre, 1884* (London: Macmillan Caribbean, 1988).

45. Trinidad and Tobago Central Statistical Office, *Annual Statistical Digest* (Port of Spain: Ministry of the Economy, 1992) 53.

46. Douglas Hay, "Time, Inequality, and Law's Violence," in Sarat and Kearns, *Law's Violence,* 141–73.

47. Abdullah Omowale, "The Betrayal of the Truce," *T&T Sunday Mirror,* August 30, 1992; Trinidad Express Newspaper, *Daily Express: Trinidad under Siege: The Muslimeen Uprising: 6 Days of Terror* (Trinidad: Trinidad Express Newspapers, 1990); Chris Searle, "The Muslimeen Insurrection in Trinidad," *Race and Class* 33, no. 2 (1991): 29–43.

48. Dennis Pantin, *Into the Valley of Debt . . . An Alternative Road to the IMF/World Bank Path* (Trinidad and Tobago: Gloria V. Ferguson, 1989), 19.

49. Western Australia Government Statistician, 1912, 1922, 1931, 1942, 1953, 1963.

50. E.g., Anna Haebich, *For Their Own Good: Aborigines and Government in the Southwest of Western Australia, 1900–1940,* 2d ed. (Nedlands: University of Western Australia Press, 1992); Steve Hawke and Michael Gallagher, *Noonkanbah: Whose Land, Whose Law* (Fremantle, Western Australia: Fremantle Arts Centre Press, 1989); Paul Marshall, ed., *Raparapa Kularr Martuwarra . . . Stories from the Fitzroy River Drovers* (Broome: Magabala Books, 1988.)

51. Western Australia Government Statistician, 1963; Western Australia Department of Corrective Services, *Statistical Report of the W.A. Department of Corrective Services, July 1, 1991–June 30, 1992* (n.p., 1992).

52. Haebich, *For Their Own Good;* R. N. Ghosh, "Economic Development and Population Growth in Western Australia since 1945," in *A New History of Western Australia,* ed. C. T. Stannage (Nedlands: University of Western Australia Press, 1987), 267–96.

53. E.g., Robert Bropho, *Fringedweller* (Chippendale, New South Wales: Alternative Publishing Co-operative/Aboriginal Arts Board, Australia Council, 1980, 153.

54. Purdy, *Common Law,* 137; Australian Institute of Criminology, *National Police Custody Survey 1992: Preliminary Report* (Canberra: Australian Institute of Criminology, 1993). Lockups are located at police stations; although they are also sites of incarceration, they are distinct from prisons for statistical purposes.

55. Moody, *The Indigenous Voice,* 435.

56. It seems even this interpretation of Foucault remains contentious. I would refer readers to Foucault's discussion of the incorporation of the juridical institution into a "continuum of apparatuses" (*The History of Sexuality,* 144); the "movement from a schema of exceptional discipline to one of generalized surveillance . . . the gradual extension of the mechanisms of discipline throughout the whole social body, the formation of what might be called in general disciplinary societies" (*Discipline and Punish,* 209); the "great carceral continuum" constituted through the tendency of the "frontiers between confinement, judicial punishment and institutions of discipline" to disappear (297); the transportation of the "penitentiary technique" by the "carceral archipelago from the penal institution to the entire social body" (298); the surveillance and punishment of incarceration as "a principle of relative continuity" (299); the "homogenizing" of the "legal power to punish" and the "technical power to discipline" (303); and as previously cited, that "the specificity of the prison and its role as link are losing something of their purpose" (306).

57. Royal Commission into Aboriginal Deaths in Custody, *Research Paper No. 7. Australian Deaths in Custody 1980–1988: An Analysis of Aboriginal and non-Aboriginal Deaths* (Parkes, A.C.T.: RCIADIC, 1989); Patrick Jagessar, qtd. in "Not Just Prison Anymore: It's Hell behind Bars," *T&T Mirror,* May 22, 1992; Kirklon Paul, "The Prison Sharks: Nothing Escapes his Gaze when he Looks About," *Light,* May 1990.

58. Foucault, *Discipline and Punish,* 306.

59. Fitzpatrick, *Mythology of Modern Law,* 152. For the alternatives, see e.g. Frank Burton and Pat Carlen, *Official Discourse: On Discourse Analysis, Government Publications, Ideology, and the State* (London: Routledge, 1979); and Robert Weisberg, "Private Violence as Moral Action: The Law as Inspiration and Example," in Sarat and Kearns, *Law's Violence,* 175–210.

60. See R. G. Broadhurst, A. M. Ferrante, and N. P. Susilo, *Crime and Justice Statistics for Western Australia: 1991* (Nedlands: Crime Research Centre, University of Western Australia, 1992), 30. I conducted fieldwork in the magistrates' courts of Trinidad and Western Australia while undertaking doctoral research during 1992 and 1993. In total I observed eighteen courts over fifty-five sitting days.

61. Fitzpatrick, *Mythology of Modern Law,* 148.

62. Meredith Wilkie, *Aboriginal Justice Programs in Western Australia* (Nedlands: Crime Research Centre, University of Western Australia, 1991), 13, 14.

63. Jeannine Purdy, fieldnotes, Trinidad Magistrates' Courts, January 29 to June 27, 1992; Western Australia Magistrates' Courts, January 18 to March 2, 1993.

64. Ibid. In the courts that I observed in Trinidad, there was a concentration of phenotypically blacker people among the ranks of those in custody (caged). The nexus between color and class in colonized societies is examined in Purdy, *Common Law.*

65. Burton and Carlen, *Official Discourse,* 20.

66. Harold Wolpe, "The Theory of Internal Colonialism: The South African Case," in *Beyond the Sociology of Development,* ed. I. Oxaal et al. (London: Routledge, 1975), 229–52; Hartwig, "Capitalism and Aborigines."

67. Irene Watson draws a sharp distinction between the position of indigenous peoples and the inhabitants of colonies that were geographically separated from the colonial state. I doubt that formal political independence has brought an equal degree of self-determination to all now independent states, but Watson's point remains a strong one. That is, the position of those whose "lands lie within the colonial state" is even more precarious, in that the logical outcome of the "myth" of postcolonialism for them is the "absorption of Indigenous Peoples into the colonial state" ("Indigenous Peoples' Law-Ways," 56).

68. Henry Reynolds, *The Law of the Land,* 2d ed. (Victoria: Penguin, 1992), 4.

69. Ibid., 103. Reynolds points out that few parliamentarians attended the final reading of the act. I do not doubt that some individual politicians and others were genuinely committed to assisting Aboriginal peoples.

70. Ibid., 125, 146.

71. The strength of this imperial goodwill was tested in the Waanyi case before the Australian National Native Title Tribunal. That case highlighted the attenuated protection afforded Aboriginal people under the Order of 1849 (Re Waanyi Peoples Native Title Application [1995] 129 ALR 118). The decision of the Native Title Tribunal was subsequently overturned by the High Court, but

on different grounds (North Ganalanja Aboriginal Corporation v. Queensland [1996] 135 ALR 225).

More recently the protection of indigenous rights under imperial law was raised in the Wik matter, also before the High Court (Wik Peoples v. Queensland [1996] 141 ALR 129). Although the apparent intentions of the Colonial Office with reference to the subsistence of indigenous rights to land, during the 1840s, were relevant to the outcome of that matter (e.g., Wik 141 ALR 129, at 179, 197), the strength of any actual imperial legal protections was considered so insubstantial that the point was not even argued by counsel for the indigenous appellants before the court (Wik 141 ALR 129, at 192). Note that although concern over the treatment of indigenous peoples by pastoralists was raised by the governor in 1839, the Colonial Office correspondence that evinced the intention to protect indigenous land access was dated some ten years later, after NSW had been granted partial independence.

72. Hong Kong Government Information Services, *A Review of Hong Kong, 1994* (Hong Kong: Government Printer, 1995).

73. Valerie Kerruish, "Reynolds, Thompson, and the Rule of Law: Jurisprudence and Ideology in *Terra Nullius,*" *Law in Context* 7, no. 1 (1989): 120–33.

74. Reynolds, *Law of the Land,* 4.

75. Eric Williams, qtd. in Fryer, *Black People,* 5.

76. Reynolds, *Law of the Land,* quoting Justice Deane of the High Court of Australia, 4.

77. Fitzpatrick, *Mythology of Modern Law;* Valerie Kerruish, *Jurisprudence as Ideology* (London: Routledge, 1991).

78. Fanon, *Wretched of the Earth,* 29.

79. Pierre Bourdieu and Jean-Claude Passeron, *Reproduction in Education, Society, and Culture,* trans. R. Nice (London: Sage Publications, 1977), 36; Fanon, *Wretched of the Earth,* 29.

80. Sartre, preface, 7.

Part 4

The Postcolonial Within

Rites of Passage into the Global Village

Rolando Gaete

The Global Village

The global village is technological. It is crisscrossed by a single but unequal network of highways through which the incessant movement of capital, goods, information, production methods, systems of law, modes of governance, rationalities, and tourism flows. The global technological village achieves the organization of man on a global scale for both the unlimited growth of production and consumption and the "rationalization" of governance and management.[1]

At the vanguard of the total mobilization of humanity in pursuit of the consumption of the earth, the multilateral financial institutions have probably a more important role than the United Nations.[2] Ambitious programs of structural adjustment, imposed during the 1980s,[3] have been followed by political programs after the end of the Cold War. These programs have been pursued mainly by donor countries, which have imposed a political conditionality on aid-receiving third world countries, namely the promotion of good governance and human rights.[4] The threat of a withdrawal of development aid has been used as a sanction against the infringement of human rights.[5]

Human rights have become a banner representing the "civilizing mission" of financial institutions and of the countries that provide most of the funds for these institutions. Human rights provide universal

An earlier version of this essay appeared in a Special Issue on Law and Postcolonialism, edited by Eve Darian-Smith and Peter Fitzpatrick in *Law and Critique* 6, no. 1 (1995). Reprinted by permission of Deborah Charles Publications.

standards of governance and political rationality. After "the conquest of the last ideological frontiers," no other secular ideology is left.[6] Human rights provide the central principle of organization of the modern state.[7]

Building the New Brave World

Respect for human rights is increasingly seen not only as a condition of development but also as an independent goal of development that has to be achieved by means of special strategies. However, there is no single cultural form associated with modernization—no "common culture of modernity."[8] Economic growth and the spread of technology, free markets, and modern systems of law has been shown to coexist with patterns of repressive practices and with various political forms, not all of them democratic.

In Western countries, human rights became universal as a component of the logic of the nation-state that grounds and regulates its power and curbs excesses. The postulate of universality and the overcoming of relativity is a typical modern practice, whether it is expressed by the state as centralizing power that normalizes and destroys local customs and instances or by the Kantian imperative and modern idea of a universal Man. The latter represents the human being who has freed himself from tribal and family attachments and who relates to other human beings in purely secular terms.[9] "Modernity treated all relativity as a nuisance and a challenge."[10] Paradoxically, universal Man appears in the same movement that grounds the state: "the uniformizing ambitions and practices of the modern state, with the war it declared on *les pouvoirs intermédiares,* with its cultural crusades against local customs redefined as superstitions and condemned to death for the crime of resisting centralized management."[11] The ideology of universal Man is a component of the modernizing process of state building in former Western colonies.

Modernization generates resistance. It is a mistake to think that the main opposition to human-rights standards comes from despotic third world governments. Human rights are primarily standards that third world governments are expected to impose against local traditional practices and beliefs—the belief in euthanasia for aged people among the Eskimos, the practice of arranged marriages that is common in many cultures, the application of *hudud* punishments (fixed penalties imposed by the primary sources of Islamic Law, namely the Koran and Sunnah, such as amputations in case of theft) in Islamic countries and the support for the death penalty in many more, female circumcision in various African countries, child labor, and various forms of censorship, to mention just a few.

While the globalization processes continue apace, processes of resistance from the margins and even from the center are also active.

1. Donnelly mentions three on the margins of Western civilization: precolonial African villages, Native American tribes, and traditional Islamic social systems.[12] But perhaps the strongest resistance comes from increasingly confident Confucian systems in Southeast Asia. On the other hand, the large slums around the big cities of the third world are in transition toward urban industrial life and its characteristic rootlessness.
2. Disillusionment with a culture of neo-Darwinian individualism, free markets, and media-driven electoral politics in the very center of planetary imperialism has generated a new interest in communitarianism at the end of the twentieth century. Liberal intellectuals are engaged in a polemics with this emerging concern on many fronts, driven by anxiety that this tendency might weaken the dominant ideological commitment to individual human rights.

It is essential to discriminate between, on the one hand, the universalizing drive of modernity to destroy whatever does not conform and the technological pursuit of more and more efficiency and productivity against which all local resistance is futile, and, on the other hand, certain human rights that are ethical forms of responsibility that can claim with some justification to be truly universal. Two opposite dangers are to be avoided: the absolutism of certain appeals to culture and the absolutism of a humanist secular fundamentalism.

The Danger of Relativism

Cultural relativism asserts that there is no independent method for discovering which moral vision is superior and which cultural practices should be banned from the surface of the earth.[13] At the same time, all cultures are ethnocentric enough to claim that they do provide universal standards. Our gods are always the true gods.

Understandably, a skeptical relativism is commonly the result of this insight. But this relativism suffers from serious flaws.

1. It is self-contradictory since it does support an absolute truth, namely that no culture can be proved to be morally superior. As Howard says, "the concept of cultural relativism is used by both traditionalists and communitarians as a defense of their 'way of life.' . . . But the relativism that is implicit . . . is actually a concept of cultural absolutism."[14] The romantic nostalgia for community is Said's *Orientalism* right-side up.[15]
2. Even worse, this skepticism is defenseless against imperialistic and intolerant cultures since it surrenders any vantage point from where to criticize them.
3. It yields itself to be abused by despotic governments. As Donnelly warns us: "In particular, we must be wary of self-interested denunciations of the excessive individualism of "western" human rights. . . . Arguments of cultural relativism regularly involve urban elites eloquently praising the glories of village life—a life that they or their parents or grandparents struggled hard to escape, and a life to which they have not the slightest intention of returning."[16] And as Afshari writes: many efforts have floundered "on the confusion created by the Islamist activists raising the banner of cultural relativism."[17]

Human-Rights Fundamentalism

In a Kantian fashion and against the claims of cultural absolutism, Howard defines human rights in a Kantian fashion as absolute, "nonderogable claims against the State that we have in our capacity of morally autonomous beings."[18]

This view, which can be called foundationalist, defines human rights as rooted on an ontological basis, independent of, and anterior to, culture and community. In the eighteenth century, the emergence of human rights was also presented as the discovery and consequent "declaration" of irreducible and enduring attributes of the self and the human body.

The Kantian version of this view grounds human rights on the essential autonomy of human beings that allows them to make moral choices. The main objectives of human-rights standards, in this view, are to oppose the regulation of this autonomous sphere—whether it is in the area of intimacy or of market exchanges—and to protect private initiative from the encroachments of power.[19]

Human-rights fundamentalism is found often among those who are immersed in the sometimes heroic struggles against violations of human rights. Those engaged in struggles for human rights within unsympathetic cultures often adopt a robust dogmatic belief in a trans-historical foundation. Some of them have paid with their lives.[20]

Tibi, for example, thinks that "scholarly knowledge is universally valid" and that science provides the model for the knowledge of universally valid standards.[21] In the challenge of Islam, we see "a conflict between a local cultural world view and a standard related to civilizational morality and to the globalized civilizing process."[22] The implication is that a local culture must be sacrificed to the globalization process.

A strong version of this thesis regards universality not as an ontological pregiven but as an end of History, as the necessary historical outcome of the relentless march toward planetary Enlightenment and Freedom. The end of ideologies of total state organization represented dramatically by the fall of the Berlin wall and of ideologies of racial supremacy with the end of apartheid in South Africa led to speculations about the end of history.

This view is skeptical about absolute claims to knowledge on the nature of human beings and offers, instead, a liberal-neo-Hegelian, eschatological view of history as a totalizing planetary process toward a community of free individuals. It assumes optimistically that interpretations of human rights will gradually converge and that a common conception of the good life will eventually prevail once all the world has been successfully colonized by a secular modernizing humanism.

This robust view presents two problems. First, it carries very little conviction in an era struggling also to free itself from metaphysics and unquestionable truths. More important, as Lyotard has shown,[23] the mimetic conformity of justice to ontology silences the victims of justice and produces terror. Burke hit on something when he argued that the Terror of the French Revolution was based on the abstract ideology of "metaphysical rights."

The Relativism of Human Rights in Action

Far from being absolutist, human-rights standards are full of qualifiers that subject the interpretation and implementation of human rights to local conditions. In the West, for all the usual preaching against relativism, human rights navigate in relativistic waters.

This relativism is reflected in the admirable work of the European Commission and Court of Human Rights. One can distinguish a number of characteristics that together produce a strong, and quite justified, relativistic effect.

1. Human rights are minimum standards that apply only to a small number of areas among those where excesses of power are possible. The European Commission of Human Rights declares a great number of applications inadmissible for being "incompatible with the provisions" of the Convention on Human Rights.[24] And so does the Human Rights Committee under the Optional Protocol to the International Covenant of Civil and Political Rights.[25]
2. Human rights are claims against the state, not against instances of private power. At a time of increasing deregulation and privatization, this feature also restricts the scope of application of human-rights standards.
3. Most human rights can be derogated in emergency situations. The idea of human rights grew alongside the consolidation of the modern nation-state and its overriding doctrines of national security and public interest. When the "life" of the state is at risk, governments are entitled to derogate most human rights.
4. Standards are drafted in very abstract terms. A broad formulation has enabled the European human-rights machinery to develop a doctrine of "margin of appreciation" that grants local power holders some latitude to use discretion in their interpretation of these standards, taking local conditions into account.[26]
5. The meaning of the terms used by human-rights standards is elastic. It has been held that while the right not to be tortured is absolute, the notion of torture is relative. As a result, when having to determine whether the use of five techniques of interrogation did in fact constitute torture in *Ireland v. U.K.*,[27] the European Commission and the European Court reached different

conclusions.[28] The same can be said of many crucial words in the discourse of human rights.

6. Judicial decisions on competing claims (rights against rights and rights against communitarian concerns) are not dictated by general principles. Judicial positions on abortion, the death penalty, the prevalence of the right to privacy, the right to publish obscene or blasphemous materials, and so on, and judgments on the weight of policies to prevent disorder or to protect national security or morals, and so forth, are conditioned by local cultural conceptions of the good life and even by contingent political views.[29] Thus the European Court of Human Rights has accepted the cultural contextuality of texts, not only following a common European ideal but also investigating the current common denominator ("evolutionary trends") among European countries.[30]
7. Western countries sometimes make strong reservations to human-rights treaties, subjecting their interpretation to local definitions. For example, the reservation to the Convention on Torture made by the United States stated that the meaning of cruel punishment would be local and defined by American courts implementing American law.[31]

Opinio Juris *as an Aesthetical Universalism*

The workings of human rights are the result of the multiple play between universalistically drafted formulas and cultural difference. It is a play because it is not governed by fixed metaethical criteria.

Metaethical models, capable of presenting the deepest, ultimate ethical truth, can lead to injustice,[32] even when they are *our* models (the models we, liberals, we, *the People,* support).

As Bauman ironically writes: "Truth is, by definition, one—it is the errors that are countless; the same must surely apply to moral propriety."[33] But "the moral is what *resists* codification, formalization, socialization, universalization."[34] The moral can neither be legislated as universal law nor be contractual. The moral action is done even when no equivalent reward is expected to cover the costs: "reciprocity is the vital attribute morality does not possess." [35] Hobbes's foundation of human rights on reciprocity and contract firmly placed them outside the moral sphere, and in a biological sphere that was Darwinist before Darwin.

Acts of justice are singular and must be performed without following a universalizable law grounded on knowledge. It is this feature that Kant regards as the central feature of aesthetics. It is worth exploring whether an aesthetical conception could cut universalism free from its metaphysical or ontological mooring.

An aesthetical universalism is grounded on an unstable sensus communis as defined by Kant in his philosophy of aesthetics. "[W]e allow no one to be of another opinion, without, however, grounding our judgment on concepts. . . . Now this common sense . . . does not say that everyone *will* agree with my judgment, but that he *ought.* And so common sense . . . is a mere ideal norm."[36]

A sensus communis, in Kant's sense, is neither based on an objectively universal law nor produced by an empirically given consensus, but it is a subjectively universal commitment to a contingent normative ideal. In this sense, human rights have become the dominant common sense understood as a common ideal. They are binding because they do not simply express a subjective preference. In Gadamer's words, it is the "truth that is encountered in (aesthetic judgment) and can come to be shared."[37] This contingent sensus communis corresponds to what international law calls *opinio juris,* that is, the shared belief that a particular norm of customary international law is binding on all countries of the world.

This *sensus communis erga omnes* is based on the direct experience of the true and not on an objective, ontologically grounded moral rule, let alone on a utilitarian calculation or on contractual reciprocity. We are not prepared to ask why genocide or torture are wrong or whether they can serve a purpose. We pass judgment before the custodians of human rights have counted the number of corpses or the number of wounds and argue among themselves whether numbers and wounds or other marks constitute the external signs of genocide or torture. Whatever the legal label, we *feel* that the subjection and destruction of bodies are gross denials of what should be called Otherness. This feeling is articulated in what Kant calls *aesthetical ideas,*[38] which are reluctant universalistic claims. The reluctance in making universalistic claims is due to some extent to the decline of the Enlightenment's optimistic belief in a common human foundation or in "our" liberalism as the climax of history, and to an emerging pessimistic and cynical view about the self-justifications of power holders, whether those justifications are based on universalistic assumptions or on excuses based on cultural relativism.

In Search of a Genuine Sensus Communis

Universalists do not deny the wonderful diversity of cultures, conceptions of the good life, and systems of authority in the world. Neither do they question the need to subject universal principles to the local conditions existing within these cultures. These conditions qualify the application of principles but should not override them.

Universalists and relativists seem to agree that either all human rights are universal and indivisible or that none is because they all are rights that all human beings, everywhere and at all times, have or ought to have, simply because they are human and, therefore, they are equally valid.

However, the *opinio juris* of countries varies. Even among those countries that have taken upon themselves the burden of monitoring compliance with human rights in the world today, a distinction is made in practice between serious violations of important human rights and lesser violations. In the United States, the leading country in this respect, the rights under the First and Fourteenth Amendments are regarded as the most relevant rights today. Indeed, virtually all Supreme Court decisions on human rights are taken under either of these two amendments. The latter recognize the right not to have an established Church and the rights to free expression and assembly, to the due process of law, and, by extension, to privacy and the right to the equal protection of the laws. While the due process clause became the soul of a fully free market in the pre-Roosevelt era and the equal protection clause became the basis of assimilationist policies on blacks, the combination of the commitment to secularism and to privacy excluded the religious regulation of private life and led to the recognition of the right to have an abortion in *Roe v. Wade.* Consistent universalists support the right of the United States to impose these principles and practices abroad provided that they are formulated in the language of the Universal Declaration of Human Rights.

Refusal to share an *opinio juris* on some of these practices comes from different quarters.

1. The rights of private autonomy are partly based on the some-

how optimistic Enlightenment assumption that once individual initiative is left alone, the whole community flourishes. The combination of secularism and privacy is at the heart of the Enlightenment and its belief in the unstoppable march of reason. The protection of contractual freedom against the encroachments of the police powers of the state in the early twentieth century in America was based on this assumption. Human rights were regarded by the Supreme Court at the time as both the inner conscience and the fundamental conditions of capitalism.

While countries in the Far East have adopted capitalist methods of organization and production, they are still resisting the logic of the technological drive toward industrialization, with its accompanying forms of atomism, anomie, alienation, and violence. Eastern cultures still emphasize harmony and collaboration over the litigiousness of American society. The Western concept of the autonomous self, engaged in a lonely struggle for survival, is alien to them.[39]

Resistance also comes from within the dominant religions of the West and from Islam. Minimalist-state policies based on a neat separation of the public and the private are not part of the *opinio juris* of many countries.

2. Free speech and free assembly. These rights constitute the identity itself of the West, and in a particular way of the United States, where the case law on these rights is much more sophisticated than European developments. Habermas explained the relationship between this right and the formation of a public space of free discussion in the West.[40]

During the Cold War, the West identified the enemy essentially as the totalitarian denial of this public democratic space, and, at one point, the International Court of Justice had to question the excessive enthusiasm of the United States for the protection of human rights in Nicaragua (under an "enemy" regime) that led to military intervention.[41]

It is too early to say, but it is possible that now that the Cold War has ended there will emerge a new tolerance toward different modes of politics outside the West.

3. Assimilationist policies have been, arguably, effective in the United States, using both the principle of nondiscrimination and programs of affirmative action. However, these policies may not work in countries comprising tribes or peoples with different languages, religions, and customs. There have been times when assimilationist poli-

cies have amounted to cultural genocide. This was the case during the conquest of the American continent. The invasion and forced assimilation of East Timor by Indonesia is one of many contemporary examples.

What human rights norms do rely on a genuine general *opinio juris?* Under international law, there are three factors that strengthen the weight of certain human rights.

1. There are human rights that are regarded *erga omnes,* valid for all human beings. In an often-cited statement, the International Court of Justice held that

> an essential distinction should be drawn between the obligations of a State towards the international community as a whole, and those arising vis-à-vis another State in the field of diplomatic protection. By their very nature the former are the concern of all States. In view of the importance of the rights involved, all States can be held to have a legal interest in their protection; they are obligations *erga omnes.*
>
> Such obligations derive, for example, in contemporary international law, from the outlawing of acts of aggression, and of genocide, as also from the principles and rules concerning the basic rights of the human person, including protection from slavery and racial discrimination.[42]

Usually, aggression and genocide are added to these two examples of "basic rights." However, the dominant opinion is that all human rights fall under this category.

2. Those human rights recognized by that part of customary law called *jus cogens,* which comprises peremptory norms that cannot be changed by treaties, according to the international law on treaties.

While there is no consensus on the identity of these norms, authors agree that they cover at least the rights against genocide, racial discrimination, and slavery.

3. Those human rights that cannot be derogated under any circumstances: rights protecting from genocide and from policies of indiscriminate killings, from slavery and servitude, from racial discrimination, and from torture, and the principles of *nulla poena sine lege* and of freedom of thought and religion.

What seems to be common to these categories of human rights is the call for an openness to the other beyond the individualistic egolatry that grounds human rights in some of the classical writings on rights, and beyond the tribal egolatry that communitarians of all colors support. It is a call for a prescriptive relativism[43] based on an ethos of respect for difference, pluralism, and diversity, which is compatible with weak forms of universalism.

The great revolutions inspired by the rights of man, the American and the French Revolutions, were exercises in nation building. The American Revolution did not change the treatment of American Natives or of Blacks. The French Revolution denied particularity in the name of the general will. Still now, the French Constitution states optimistically that there are no minorities in France.[44]

But the global village will not be built as an enlarged America or France, with a Bill of Rights to keep the component parts of this supranation together. More likely, it will be a forum where various forms of politics and various forms of culture will meet. But it is too soon to say whether globalization will lead to a technototalitarian system governed by the old humanist rhetoric of the West or whether it will open up a new space of cultural dialogue that affirms difference.

NOTES

1. See M. A. Gillespie, *Hegel, Heidegger, and the Ground of History* (Chicago: University of Chicago Press, 1984), 128.

2. Some United Nations agencies depend to some extent on the goodwill and funds of private multinationals. For example, the World Health Organization is careful not to alienate the big pharmaceutical companies.

3. The purpose of these programs has been to get rid of "irrationalities" and distortions such as controls and subsidies on agricultural products to keep prices of basic food low, subsidies for import substitution, an excessive state sector, regulated markets, artificial devaluation policies, and so on.

4. Already in 1975, the Harkin Amendment on clause 116 of the U.S. law on external aid was enacted, denying aid to any country that engages in "consistent pattern of gross violations of internationally recognised human rights."

5. This policy has been applied selectively, being targeted mainly on the sub-Saharan states (with the exception of Nigeria) and not on countries that are more attractive for foreign investment such as China, India, or Indonesia.

6. See R. Gaete, *Human Rights and the Limits of Critical Reason* (Aldershot: Dartmouth, 1993), 1–5.

7. Ibid., at 168ff.

8. R. J. Vincent, *Human Rights and International Relations* (Cambridge: Cambridge University Press, 1986), 50.

9. See B. S. Turner, "Outline of a Theory of Human Rights," *Sociology* 27, no. 3 (1993): 496ff.

10. Z. Bauman, *Postmodern Ethics* (Oxford: Blackwell, 1993), 42.

11. Ibid., 39.

12. J. Donnelly, "Cultural Relativism and Universal Human Rights," *Human Rights Quarterly* 6, no. 4 (1984): 401–19.

13. See P. Hirst and P. Woolley, *Social Relations and Human Attributes* (London: Tavistock, 1982).

14. R. E. Howard, "Cultural Absolutism and the Nostalgia for Community," *Human Rights Quarterly* 15 (1993): 319.

15. Ibid., 327.

16. Donnelly, "Cultural Relativism," 411–12.

17. Reza Afshari, "An Essay on Islamic Cultural Relativism in the Discourse of Human Rights," *Human Rights Quarterly* 16 (1994): 272.

18. Howard, "Cultural Absolutism," 315.

19. As reactivated by Rawls, human rights are the principles of justice that people would select if they were stripped of their identity and culture and ideas about the good and preferences except the aversion to risk-taking, becoming unencumbered selves. Rawls rightly believes that they would play safe and would select principles similar to those that are dominant in his culture since our principles of justice must "accommodate our firmest convictions" (*A Theory of Justice* [Oxford: Clarendon Press, 1972], 20). The ground of justice ceases to be ontological and becomes contingent.

20. For example, Mohammed Mahmoud Taha, executed without trial in Sudan in 1985, as mentioned by B. Tibi, "Islamic Law/Shari'a, Human Rights, Universality, and International Relations," *Human Rights Quarterly* 16 (1994): 286.

21. Ibid., 292.

22. Ibid.

23. J.-F. Lyotard and J. L. Thebaud, *Just Gaming*, trans. Wlad Godzid (Manchester: Manchester University Press, 1985).

24. Article 27 (2).

25. Article 3.

26. This is particularly the case in relation to the requirements of morals: see for example the decision in *Handyside v. U. K.*, Eur. Court of H. R. Series A, No. 20 (1976). For a commentary, see Gaete, *Human Rights*, chap. 6.

27. Publ. ECHR Series A 27 (1978).

28. Article 3 of the European Convention of Human Rights reads:

> No one shall be subjected to torture or to inhuman or degrading treatment or punishment.

In his opinion in *Ireland v. U.K.*, Judge Fitzmaurice stated:

> This wording, perhaps deliberately because of the virtual impossibility of arriving at any completely satisfactory definition of the notions involved, attempts none respecting torture, inhuman treatment or degrading treat-

ment. It is thus left to be determined in the light of the circumstances of each particular case. . . . Such a determination must necessarily be an entirely subjective one, so that differently constituted courts or commissions, functioning at different periods, might, on the basis of similar or analogous facts, reach different conclusions in border-line, or even not so border-line cases." (2 E.H.R.R. 25, at 125).

29. In the United States, an old debate is still going on, on whether the Constitution can be interpreted in the light of general principles and of international human-rights standards, or in the light of principles resting in the American conscience: "so rooted in the traditions and conscience of our people as to be ranked as fundamental" (*Snyder v. Massachusetts,* 291 U.S. 97, 105 (1934). On the other hand, Justice Cardozo, in the same case at 122, invoked "immutable principles of justice, acknowledged *semper ubique et ab omnibus."*

30. The European Court of Human Rights has held that "the Convention is a living instrument which, as the Commission rightly stressed, must be interpreted in the light of present-day conditions. In the case now before it, the Court cannot but be influenced by the developments and commonly accepted standards in the penal policy of the Member States of the Council of Europe." Tyrer Case, par. 31 of the Judgment of the Court, April 25, 1978, A. 26 (1978).

31. This reservation follows the same logic than the declaration of the Saudi minister of foreign affairs stating that for Moslems human rights can only be derived from the Islamic *shari'a* (as cited by Tibi, "Islamic Law/Shari'a," 278).

32. Lyotard and Thebaud, *Just Gaming.*

33. Bauman, *Postmodern Ethics,* 38. Those we accuse share this fundamental insight with us. Women doing anthropological research in some African villages are very reluctant to admit that they have not been circumcised so as not to be considered dirty and morally impure. As Asch comments: "Social conditions not only enforce particular practices; they also inculcate the conviction of their rightness" (qtd. by A. D. Renteln, *International Human Rights: Universalism versus Relativism* [London: Sage, 1990], 65).

There is an old English saying that encapsulates this moral confidence: "All the world's daft save me and thee and thou art a bit queer."

34. Bauman, *Postmodern Ethics,* 54.

35. Ibid., 56.

36. Kant, *Critique of Judgment,* trans. J. H. Bernard (New York: Hafner Press, 1951), section 22.

37. Hans-George Gadamer, *The Relevance of the Beautiful and Other Essays,* trans. Nicholas Walker (Cambridge: Cambridge University Press, 1986), 18.

38. "By an aesthetical idea," writes Kant, "I understand that representation of the imagination which occasions much thought, without however any definite thought, i.e. any concept, being capable of being adequate to it; it consequently cannot be completely compassed and made intelligible by language. We easily see that it is the counterpart (pendant) of a rational idea, which conversely is a concept to which no intuition (or representation of the imagination) can be adequate" (*Critique of Judgment,* section 49).

39. There is no sign for the concept of person in the Chinese language. See on this P. K. Y. Woo, "A Metaphysical Approach to Human Rights from a Chinese Point of View," in *Making Sense of Human Rights,* ed. James W. Nickel (Berkeley and Los Angeles: University of California Press, 1987), 119.

40. Jürgen Habermas, *L'Espace public: Archéologie de la publicité comme dimension constitutive de la société bourgeoise,* trans. Marc B. de Lannay (Paris: Payot, 1978).

41. The United States was implementing a doctrine of intervention on human-rights grounds, as explained by Jeanne J. Kirkpatrick and Allan Gerson, "The Reagan Doctrine, Human Rights, and International Law," in *Right v. Might: International Law and the Use of Force,* ed. L. Henkin (New York: Council on Foreign Relations Press, 1989). The International Court held that "Nicaragua is accused by the 1985 finding of the United States Congress of violating human rights. . . . However, where human rights are protected by international conventions, that protection takes the form of such arrangements for the monitoring or ensuring respect for human rights as are provided for in the conventions themselves" (*Nicaragua v. United States,* 1986 I.C.J. Reports 14).

42. *Barcelona Traction, Light and Power Co. Ltd. (Belgium v. Spain),* 1970 I.C.J. Report 3, at 32.

43. As Redfield argues, skeptical and prescriptive relativism are different. For skeptics, values are relative because "people are brought up to see the value in things that their local experience has suggested." A skeptic does not necessarily respect all systems of value; he "might just as well hate them all." For prescriptive relativism, one ought to respect them (qtd. by Renteln, *International Human Rights,* 73).

44. In *M. K. v. France* (Doc. A/45/40 Apx.) and in *T. K. v. France* (Doc. A/45/40, Apx.), the Human Rights Committee stated that a declaration made by France upon accession to the Covenant stating that there are no minorities in France according to the Constitution was equivalent to a reservation to the Covenant. Therefore, it had the legal effect of exempting France from the application of its Art. 27 that provides for the protection of minorities.

From Law to Popular Justice: Beyond Antinomialism

Alan Norrie

Popular Justice: In Search of a Concept

This paper is prompted by what I see as a long-standing failure to provide an adequate conceptualization of popular justice in the sociology of law. Boaventura de Sousa Santos has written of community (or popular) justice, alongside legal pluralism, as part of the core debate in the sociology of law, but he notes the plasticity and increasing vagueness of these terms such that "the core debate is increasingly a debate about what is being debated."[1] He further notes the relative failure to emphasize the challenge that community justice and legal pluralism make to liberal political and legal theory, and a related tendency to take the state and law, understood as an autonomous process, for granted. My argument will be, somewhat inverting this latter point, that the failure to achieve a more precise conceptualization of popular justice is itself linked to the failure to challenge liberal theory and the idea of law as an autonomous institution. Until we interrogate a certain way of understanding law, we will not understand popular or community justice. The latter terms cover a number of differentiated and specific phenomena in practice, but what governs their possibility in the sociology of law is the conceptual relationship that is established between them and a liberal conception of law as autonomous and formal. If we challenge the concepts of liberal legality, moving in a sense *from* law *to* popular

An earlier version of this essay appeared in a Special Issue on Law and Postcolonialism, edited by Eve Darian-Smith and Peter Fitzpatrick in *Social and Legal Studies* 5, no. 3 (1996).

justice, we will find a more adequate way of talking about the latter. If we do not do so, our comparative understanding of different regulatory systems will remain forever imprecise.

The conceptual failure at the heart of popular justice has different aspects and has a Foucauldian as well as a Weberian form. It is the latter, however, that is the more important in terms of the influence it has had on the popular-justice debate. In general, Weberian perspectives make a major contribution to what Eve Darian-Smith and Peter Fitzpatrick in the introduction to this collection describe as the "plangent irresolution of debates . . . over what law may be." The central problem is a falsely dichotomizing tendency that I term "antinomialism,"[2] which has its main expression in the formal/informal opposition in Weber's sociology of law, but which ramifies into a series of dichotomies that include form and substance, the legal (or bureaucratic) and the popular, the indigenous and the statal, the local and the national, the rational and the irrational, and the individual and the social. My argument will be that antinomialism places Western law on an imperialist pedestal and sets popular justice up to fail. There is a need to cut Western law down to size (which is not the same thing as dismissing it either theoretically or politically) and to give popular justice its due by developing a legal methodology that can explain what Western law and popular justice have in common as differently constituted juridical modes. That methodology, I argue, should be dialectical, in a sense that has not been employed before in legal theory. To do this, I draw on the recent dialectical critical realist philosophy of Roy Bhaskar, which I use as the basis for the development of the idea of *dialectically constituted architectonics of law and justice.* The argument will be that a critical analysis of legal formalism can constitute the basis for constructing such a methodology, which is then applied, albeit briefly, to a particular instance of popular justice. While the bulk of the paper is therefore focused on Western law, its target is a Western conception of such law's "other," as importantly formulated by Weber (and also Foucault mutatis mutandis) as supposedly irrational, informal, popular justice. Its aim is to rescue popular justice as a phenomenon from the morass of false dichotomies that render it theoretically incomprehensible, and also politically unattractive.

I begin by illustrating incomprehensibility. In their book on community mediation in the United States, Merry and Milner write that popular justice is "less inclined to rely on legal forms of discourse and more on the discourse of the world outside the legal system," but they also say that "many of the procedures, symbols, rituals, and forms of language used in popular justice derive from state law." They write that popular justice "provides a stark contrast to the violence and coercion of law," yet also that it "does not necessarily produce a non-violent justice." They claim that popular justice does not "typically challenge the hegemony of state law," but also that it "confronts the legal system with a persistent critique."[3]

In the lead chapter, Sally Merry argues that popular justice may involve a "counterlegal order" arising from "spontaneous acts of collective judging and violence,"[4] but she also characterizes it as a "judicial institution located on the boundary between local ordering and state law" (32). She characterizes popular justice *culturally* (i.e., in the way it is represented) as similar to indigenous or local ordering, but *practically* as homologous to state law (35). Yet her four-part typology of popular-justice forms identifies two types (the reformist and the socialist) that are "more closely tied to state law than to indigenous law" (45), and two types (the communitarian and the anarchic) that are closer to indigenous ordering (45–49). Within this typology, the experience of Papua New Guinea is represented as falling under both the "statal" reformist form and the "local" communitarian form. Merry concludes that "by and large, popular justice tends to reinforce and entrench relations of power rather than to transform them," but she also claims that "the argument that informal justice is an expansion of state control by nonstate means is only one side of the story" (61).

Merry and Milner may claim that the ambiguities in their approach result from the ambiguous character of the phenomena they seek to represent, but it is surely the test of a theoretical method that it can adequately locate in analytical terms the phenomena it is used to investigate. It should explain rather than simply embody or reflect ambiguities. In the authors' account, popular justice is trapped on a borderline between the statal and the local, forcing it to look both ways at once, but that borderline is a *theoretical* construct, and it needs interrogation and critique if we are to understand the phenomena under investigation.

At its heart, the theoretical problem is one of reconciling a dominant constructivist/structuralist approach with a necessary residual emphasis on agency.[5] Popular justice is primarily conceived within the dominant structures of law and state, but such an approach fails to make space for conflict and change, and therefore has to be supplemented with reference to struggle and opposition from beyond the law and state. However, because of the dominance of the constructivist approach, such a supplement can only take the form of a primary, essentially unconditioned, moment of agency. Thus while popular justice is essentially parastatal, a space must also be granted for it to be "local" or "indigenous." Yet these latter "terms of innocence" can hardly in truth be said to have a real historical point of reference, and so they are quickly returned into the web of construction that predominates. Popular justice is either inchoate or given form by returning it into the arms of what it supposedly is not: the legal, the formal rational, the bureaucratic, the statal.

There is a general antinomial problem in the analysis of popular justice, which is well expressed by Fitzpatrick in a recent paper he prefaces with the challenge of William Blake: "Unorganised innocence: an impossibility."[6] It seems to me that all the antinomial terms I have described above are variations on the theme so neatly skewered by this Blakean epigram. In this paper, my focus will be on the form of the antinomy that has been most central to the popular-justice debate: the dichotomy between the formal and informal. I shall take this dichotomy to be central to Weber and the product of the neo-Kantian, essentially juridical worldview that informs his work,[7] and which therefore informs the popular-justice debate. Since Weber's view of law is fundamentally skewed, any view of popular justice that starts out from it will also be skewed. I shall argue that a Weberian conception of law and legal *formalism* generates a correlative antinomial conception of *informalism,* and it is this that lies at the heart of the problem of popular justice.[8] My argument will be that in order to conceptualize adequately the idea of popular or informal justice, we need to develop a methodology that can displace the concepts of formal law and justice that govern our thinking on popular justice. The failure to understand informalism stems from a prior failure to understand legal formalism.

What is to be put in the place of this antinomial problematic? One possibility is Foucault. Fitzpatrick's Foucault-influenced account should be read as a criticism of one dominant conception of popular justice rather than a rejection of its possibility *tout court,* for he ultimately wishes to affirm the possibility of alternative legalities.[9] But there are grounds for arguing, as I will in the next section, that the Foucauldian position on which he draws does not possess the theoretical resources with which to explain the phenomenon either. The use of Foucault, indeed, only replicates and sustains the problem of false dichotomies. In this regard, Foucault-inspired approaches only repeat mutatis mutandis the mistakes of the neo-Kantian approaches (usually directly or indirectly Weberian) they purport to supersede. Whichever of the two approaches is adopted, we are left with an untenable sense of "the informal," and it is this that leads to the kind of dichotomous and contradictory approach exemplified above.

I shall argue alternatively for a dialectical approach that draws upon Roy Bhaskar's recent realist renovation of dialectic, and my own work on criminal law and legal theory.[10] It is true that the idea of dialectic has already been canvassed in the popular-justice debate and found wanting, but I shall argue that the concept that was employed was in fact itself antinomial and failed to take dialectic seriously. It was the attempt to apply a concept of dialectics that was at fault, not the concept itself.

One consequence of the failure to understand popular justice save in antinomial terms has already been indicated: that it becomes virtually impossible to think the concept at all. A further result, more directly practical and political, is that popular justice is seen as fundamentally concerned with *social* goals rather than *individual* aspirations in the mediation of social relations. If form is opposed to substance, then before long, individual rights are opposed to social interests, and a simplistic opposition between the values of individual and social justice is established. In this particular version of antinomialism, popular justice is portrayed, either positively as affirming collective over individual ends, or negatively as a kind of "mob rule."[11] Either way, popular justice is portrayed as separate from and inimical to individual justice, but this, I shall argue, is a process that is immanent in the theoretical tools employed, rather than in the phenomenon itself. Popular-justice forms may or may not be, as a matter of historical or empirical account, anti-individualist in practice, but this should not be theorized as a logically necessary characteristic.

Ultimately, I wish to argue for what I think is a more subtle, historically and structurally more viable, account of the character of *both* legal *and* popular justice: one that can be more sensitive to the phenomena in question than an approach governed by antinomialism. I shall argue for an approach that recognizes social control systems as involving different, historically and structurally particular, *dialectical arrange-*

ments ("architectonics") of form/content relations: an approach that can supersede the antinomialism of formal/informal dualisms and thereby locate that "in-betweenness" central to the character of law.[12] In the final section of the essay I will seek to illustrate my approach with discussion of the debate on popular justice in one society, Mozambique, in order to show briefly what I think to be its strength. It must, however, be stressed that the primary aim of this essay is theoretical, and it is not possible to clarify all the questions it raises, or apply its perspective broadly, in relation to what is an extensive and differentiated empirical field. My argument will be that there exists a plurality of popular-justice forms. The aim of the essay is to make headway on a theoretical position that can adequately ground that plurality.[13]

The False Antinomies of Popular Justice: Weber and Foucault

The "original sin" is Weber's. Steven Spitzer, in his long, thoughtful, and important investigation of law and popular justice, sets out to "decipher the *dialectics* of formal and informal control,"[14] but he does so armed with the following *Weberian* standpoint:

> "Equality before the law" and the demand for legal guarantees against arbitrariness demand a formal and rational "objectivity" of administration. . . . If, however, an "ethos"—not to speak of instincts—takes hold of the masses on some individual question, it postulates *substantive* justice oriented toward some concrete instance and person; and such an "ethos" will unavoidably collide with the formalism and the rule-bound and cool "matter-of-factness" of bureaucratic administration.
>
> The propertyless masses are not served by a formal "equality before the law" and a "calculable" adjudication and administration, as demanded by "bourgeois" interests. Naturally, in their eyes justice and administration can fulfil this function only if they assume an informal character to a far-reaching extent. It must be informal because it is substantively "ethical" ("Khadi-justice"). Every sort of "popular justice"—which usually does not ask for reasons and norms . . . crosses the rational course of justice and administration.[15]

"Formal and rational" justice is opposed to "substantive" justice, formalism to informalism, and substantive ethics become a matter of the masses' irrational instincts. Weber's legacy was to link radical social change to what he called informalism, and to oppose popular justice to formalism, defined as the giving of "reasons and norms." In Weber's account, the connection between popular justice and mob rule is also foreshadowed.

Weber's disdainful conception of popular justice is not shared by Spitzer, whose aim is a nonjuridical, nonalienated state of being, but the use of the Weberian antinomy still structures his "dialectical" account. While his formal definition of dialectics reflects classical analyses,[16] his method ends up juxtaposing the Weberian antinomies in order to chart "the ways in which movements toward *formalism* and *informalism* contain *dynamics* that transform them into something very different from what they appear or are proclaimed to be" (172–73; emphasis added). Spitzer's dialectic is in practice Weber's antinomialism dynamized, and since the Weberian approach portrays popular justice as beyond "reasons and norms"—beyond *form*—this generates an inchoate basis for Spitzer's conception of popular justice. Thus when he comes to consider popular change in Maoist China, he is forced to talk of the "attack on 'old' legal form and the search for 'new' legal substance" (169).

The problem with this approach is that it artificially separates out issues of form and substance. The old form/new substance formulation elides the question of substance in relation to the "old" form, and the question of form in relation to the "new" substance, and this is not just a question of shorthand description. Weber's approach sanctions the view that form and substance can be separated and set against each other, that popular justice is a substance, an "ethos," that "does not ask for reasons or norms." It lacks precisely *form,* that which constitutes rationality. Spitzer's antinomial conclusion, that either we risk sticking in the reassuring mud of formalism or ride the tiger of informalism, is set up by his Weberian methodology.

In the light of Weberian antinomialism, Fitzpatrick's quotation from Blake is appropriate. "Unorganised innocence" is precisely what a concept of formal rationality posits as its other, whether this be viewed favorably or not. It is in either case an impossibility, and this is the thrust of Fitzpatrick's Foucault-inspired critique of accounts of the

Community Boards Program in San Francisco.[17] But how successfully would a Foucauldian approach avoid the false dichotomy of the formal and the informal that Fitzpatrick rightly criticizes?[18]

In Foucault, the informal is also constituted as the other side of a formal juridical realm. The juridical conception of action and actors operating with responsibility under law necessarily establishes as its opposite a nonlegal dimension in which multifarious powers, relations, and agencies operate. But this is not a realm in which the state lacks control. The informal is the area in which the disciplines operate, and in which power produces actions. The realm of law establishes formal controls upon a juridical subject, but these controls are supported both within and beyond the juridical realm by the productive power of the disciplines. Thus the informal aids and abets the formal. Far from being opposed to it, the informal secures the formal by offering other mechanisms of control: the two "are distinct but the same. . . . what is involved here is a homology."[19]

The immediate problem with this approach is that once again the possibility of popular justice is ruled out. Law backed by the disciplines squeezes out alternative counterlegalities so that we are driven beyond the modern state's realm of control to the nations of "the periphery," so-called, to find such things "in places where the vitality of alternative traditions and the relative absence of disciplinary power have restricted the ability of state law to present an adequate synopsis of power and society." Fitzpatrick ultimately suggests the necessity of "the denial of alternative law in Western societies, not because it has been rendered insignificant in modern society, *but because it is so significant*"[20] However, it is hard to see why this should be, given the dominance of disciplinary power. Popular alternatives appear to be only possible in "the periphery" because of the dominance of the Western lifeworld by the disciplines, and therefore impossible under Western conditions. How can it be otherwise in a world in which people are only the effects of power, the "elements of its articulation," unless the alternative is conceived, precisely, as the expression of "unorganised innocence"? Where power is all consuming, all that remains is either the "acceptance of the system" or an "appeal to an unconditioned event."[21]

The deep reason for this impossibility, I suggest, is that Foucauldianism, while apparently opposed to Weberianism, in an important way operates as its mirror image. For Weber, the formal or legal constitutes *the* mode of social organization in modern society, while the informal constitutes its logical and political opposite. With Foucault, there is a parallel dichotomization, albeit in different terms. Law-and-discipline repeat in different guise the form-and-substance antinomy. For Foucault, disciplines *underpin* the juridical forms, whereas for Weber, substantive rationality *threatens* formal rationality. The terms of the opposition are different, as is their relationship (the one complementary, the other antagonistic), but the opposition remains in place. In both, the defining term is *form:* form of law as guarantee of individualism, markets, and rationality (Weber), versus form as mask of individual rights and liberties (Foucault). Foucault replicates Weberian antinomialism.[22] Both in their different ways involve the kind of constructivism that marginalizes and renders inchoate oppositional agency.

Beyond Antinomialism I: Taking Law Dialectically

Others have remarked upon the failure of a "dialectical" approach to popular justice because of its "mechanistic" character.[23] Spitzer's work exemplifies the genuine problem of what a dialectical approach means and how it can overcome Weberian and other dichotomies. It will not be enough either to paint form and substance, or the formal and informal, with the colors of history and politics, or simply to invert one's political viewpoint—to shift one's commitment from "form" to "substance." We need to develop and apply a mode of dialectical analysis that foregoes antinomialism if we are to progress. In this section, I begin by outlining in schematic fashion what a concept of dialectic means, and then move to consider in the following sections what role it can play in a theory of the formal and informal, law and popular justice. As I have already stated, the key to unlocking popular or informal justice will eventually be found in an understanding of its Weberian antonym, legal formalism.

Dialectic and Critical Realism

The concept of dialectic has recently been developed by Roy Bhaskar as an elaboration of his critical realist philosophy.[24] A limited and necessarily schematic digression is necessary to locate this development.[25] The ramifications of Bhaskar's work are many and are only now beginning to be taken seriously.[26] For my purpose, the significant elements in his conception of the social sciences are those of *relationality* and *totality*. The former entails the possibility of discovering the internal connections, the relations, between apparently disparate phenomena such as forms of economic, political, and legal life. Sociology, looking for relations among phenomena, seeks through totalizing theoretical strategies to understand the nature of social totalities. Such a relational approach gives rise to a conception of sociology as "concerned with the structure governing the relationships which are necessary, in particular historical periods, for the reproduction (and transformation) of particular social forms." This approach entails a view that sociology is never "sociology-in-general, only the sociology of particular historically situated social forms,"[27] which means that the totalizing tendency in sociology is always toward the totalities embraced by and understood in history.

The aim of Bhaskar's most recent work is to develop this position by marrying it with the Hegelian dialectical tradition, but with the intention of going beyond the idealism and the unitarianism that govern and limit Hegel.[28] Bhaskar seeks a fuller understanding of the role of dialectics in thought, but also in history. For Hegel, dialectics involve a process of differentiation and negation, the positing of contradiction that is resolved in a further moment of integration. But in Hegel's approach, the new and deeper unity is always a return and restoration, for it is always already present in the initial separation. Hegelian dialectics never escape their starting point in an idealist monism that posits as the end state of the dialectical process a unity-in-diversity that is the product of mind.

An important starting point in Bhaskar's account is the decentering of mind and the insistence on ontologically real, emergent dialectical processes operating in society and history. To Bhaskar's existing account of (inter alia) the nature of social scientific knowledge and of social relationality and totality, he now adds what he calls a "second edge of development" that includes characteristically dialectical categories expressed in ideas of negation and negativity, contradiction, becoming and development (retrogression and decay), spatiality and temporality, mediation and reciprocity.[29] These represent only one part of a profound account of the role of dialectical thinking,[30] but it is the combination of a historical, relational approach to sociology with an insistence on the importance of dialectical processes (and understanding of those processes) that I wish to carry into the analysis of law and popular justice. In particular, I want to employ a concept of dialectic in the sociology of law in place of the antinomial approach I have described. To this end, I take from Bhaskar his account of *dialectical connection* and *contradiction.*

The essence of dialectical connection is the idea of the internal relatedness of elements, their inherent, "molecular," connectedness. A *dialectical connection* exists

> between entities or aspects of a totality such that they are in principle *distinct* but *inseparable,* in the sense that they are synchronically or conjuncturally *internally* related, ie both . . . or one existentially presuppose the other.[31]

It is the sense of existential presupposition that is missing in Weber's antinomial account of formal rationality. In that account, an ideal typical methodology insists upon the empirical and historical links between, and therefore the coexistence of, different conceptions or aspects of law, but not their real bonding in necessary social connections. The ideal-typical methodology of abstraction hypostatizes (and thereby misrepresents) one element in an internally bonded, real social relation, rupturing its fundamental interconnectedness. Formal rational law is wrenched apart from its substance in a way that denies an essential linkage; in the process the ideal type of rational legal form is both made possible and prioritized, while other forms, such as "popular justice," are both denegated and denigrated.

Linked to the idea of dialectical connection is that of *dialectical contradiction.* Contradiction per se involves a situation in which a premise or end cannot be satisfied save at the expense of another. Contradictions can be internal or external. Where they are internal, "a system, agent or structure, S, is *blocked* from performing with one system, rule or principle, R, because it is performing with another, R1."[32] A *dialectical contradiction* is a form of internal contradiction where the contradictory elements are inherently interconnected in the sense described above. Such a contradiction involves both internal relatedness and opposition in that one element of the dialectically related entities negates an element in another, or in their common ground. This sense of the internal relatedness or necessary interconnection of contradictory elements is, I shall argue, central to an understanding of

Western law. Of course, it is denied by any theory that portrays law's base in formal rationality, but once we have seen the difference that a dialectical understanding of Western, so-called formal rational, law makes, we will be in a much better position to understand informal or popular justice.

Dialectic and Law

To return to where we started with Bhaskar, his relationship with Hegel, there is an important parallel between his project of decentering mind in order to establish a realist conception of dialectics, and the decentering task that needs to be performed with regard to law. The positivism of the modern legal worldview was given sophisticated expression in the neo-Kantian thought of writers as (apparently) diverse as Kelsen and Weber. Legal neo-Kantianism took up the characteristics of unity and rationality threatened by the collapse of the Hegelian system,[33] and read them directly into law. Rather than seeing law as part of a dialectical progression of rational spirit through historical society, law became the immediate locus of reason. This nonmediated identification was understood philosophically through Kelsen's "pure theory" and was given a sociological turn by Weber. It is the ideal-typical, formal rational conception of law, on which is based the formal/informal antinomy, that we need to decenter.

What is required is a sociohistorical approach that can grasp the duality of law as a specific form of *historically constituted sociality*.[34] Such an approach reflects law's own claims, but at the same time critically explores and decenters them. It involves a respect for the "internal" presentation of legal concepts (their treatment *as if* they were formally rational), coupled with a historical and deconstructive exposure of the limits of such an approach. Such a deconstruction takes us into the "external" social and historical conditions of possibility of the internal presentation. It asks: what claims does law make, and how does it sustain them; what is wrong with the claims that law makes and the means of sustaining them; and in what social conditions and contexts does it become possible to seek to make and sustain them?

Central to this deconstructive and decentering project is the concept of dialectical connection. The very idea of law as a *specific form* of *sociality* endorses the idea that law can only be understood dialectically, in its intrinsic relatedness to what it is not. Law is generated by, and is an expression of, broader social and political relations, but in the image presented by lawyers, it is seen as independent, autonomous, and formally rational. In its practice, it is presented as possessing its own specificity, but there remains an important difference between self-image and purported specificity on the one hand, and the law's reality on the other. The insistence on fundamental interconnectedness, keeping falsely abstractive methodologies at bay, is one important means of holding onto *both* sides of this difference: of recognizing law's claims to specificity, while denying its independence.

A second key idea is that of dialectical contradiction, for it is this that both directly challenges the claim to independence, autonomy, and formal rationality, and reveals the interconnectedness of law and its social context. It is through tracing law's contradictions that we expose the claims of formal rational law and disclose the relations that underlie it. In this way, we get to understand the deeper historical logic that underlies the flawed self-understanding of law and legal ideology. So-called formal law is a contradictory, hence irresolute,[35] "molecular" compound reflecting the dialectically contradictory structure of the sociopolitical context that generates it. If we start from this point, we will find that our understanding of both formalism and informalism is qualitatively enhanced.[36]

I have already suggested that the formalism/informalism dichotomy can be traced back to the late-nineteenth-century positivist and neo-Kantian traditions in Western thought, which posited a conception of formal closure as the basis for stable and legitimate legal practice.[37] Because of this nexus between theoretical argument and legal practice, the academic construction and defense of legal formalism does no more than take the self-understanding and self-presentation of the lawyer, law's self-image, as the basis for a scientific theory. The law, as Stanley Fish puts it, "wishes to have a formal existence,"[38] but there is a fundamental gap between the wish and its fulfillment. Law needs to see itself as complete, as immune from social and moral interpretation, as "normatively closed," but the closure it achieves is always and only fictive. Legal formalism in this sense is never achieved. It is manufactured and needs constantly to be maintained—in part by legal theorists who, like practical lawyers, act *as if* legal formalism were true. In Fish's account, the "amazing trick" of the law is achieved rhetorically, by the actions of lawyers who continually act "as if" formal legal interpretation were possible, even as their own arguments reveal the "as if" to be the fiction it is.

In contrast to Fish's rhetorical resolution of the problem of law's formal possibility, I have developed elsewhere the argument that legal formalism is organized around the figure of the abstract legal subject. It is this figure that permits the instantiation of one moral and political discourse, the repression and exclusion of alternatives, and the denial that this is happening.[39] Repression and exclusion are intrinsic to legal subjectivity and rationality, but because that which is repressed continually returns, these need to be worked at constantly. This is a role of legal actors, including academics who seek to rationalize law's necessarily contradictory texts. One can understand the conjunction of academic reconstruction and legal practice that constitutes modern legal science as "praxiological," that is, as knowledge that is inherently tied to a particular historical practice, and therefore limited by the character of that practice.[40]

It is this praxiological character that involves lawyers in bridging the gap and contradiction between law's self-image and its sociopolitical reality. Formal law is concerned with achieving normative closure, but this involves discursively elaborate exclusions of alternative social, moral, and political discourses. Legal form is the imposition of one moral and political narrative about how people ought to behave, dressed in a language of formality that has to be constantly safeguarded against alternative moral and political possibilities. Judges and academic lawyers, in the name of legal subjectivity and formal rationality, operate as the border patrollers of this moral-political discourse. Its fictive character is revealed by the constant need to repair the boundaries against the corruptive invasion of alternative moral-political accounts—of legitimate and illegitimate uses of property, of violence, and of sexuality.

The key concepts in maintaining the possibility of closure are those of legal form and formal rationality: concepts organized around the ideology of the juridical individual, a homuncular figure whose abstraction and generality is the basis for maintaining law as a seemingly general and universal system of social control that is nonetheless politically, normatively, and historically specific and partisan. The "logical integrity" of the system, as opposed to its historical and practical stability, rests upon a decontextualized conception of the individual subject that stands at the center of its discourse. Through the manipulation of the individualist forms of the law, it maintains an appearance of universality in the face of the social, political, and moral conflicts in which it participates. To take two examples: in the area of criminal law, it is the idea of the abstract responsible subject operating within a legal code that blocks discussion of conflicting moral and political issues generated by that code;[41] and it is the abstract rights-bearing subject within a liberal private-property system—introduced by violence and deceit—who blocks the "customary" or "traditional" land and environmental rights of "first nation" or local peoples. These rights become "additional and competing" claims superimposed upon a system that largely excludes them in favor of an apparently more "complete," more logical system of property tenure.[42]

Legal individualism and formal rationality are modes of exclusion and repression. At the same time, it is through these conceptions that law establishes itself as the basis for a realm of freedom, in which the individual's rights and interests are constituted and guarded.[43] At the heart of law is a set of contradictions in which the abstract juridical individual stands "in the place of" socially contextualized individuality on the one hand, and "against" general social and political interests on the other. The liberal subject of law, the responsible citizen it instantiates and formal rationality adumbrates, represents both a figure of inclusion (the bearer of rights against the state) and exclusion (the bearer of imposed duties to respect laws to which "s/he has agreed"). Thus a system that blocks and excludes particular moral and political voices with one hand gives something back with the other: rights subjectivity within a liberal legal order.[44]

From Formal Law to Popular Justice

This limited sketch of the complex individualist core at the heart of Western legal systems indicates a contradictory combination of elements of form and content, in which the specifics of juridical form are dialectically related to the social and political context of liberal capitalist societies. Form is already inherently, "genetically," a mode of establishing and maintaining a particular social and moral content, and of barring alternatives. Thus legal form is set up as an exclusion of other forms and other contents. The crucial point for thinking about popular justice, however, is that this conception of law is also the basis for the exclusion of other *combinations* of form and content. So-called legal or formal justice is dialectically connected to the exclusion of what comes to be called "informal" or, sometimes "popular," justice, and what comes to be described in these "other" terms can only be so described because of the work of exclusion and construction that goes into the manufacturing of the particular form-content relationship that is modern Western formal law.

So-called formal-rational law is one way of organizing social-control processes around the presentation of particular moral and political norms under the figure of the abstract individual subject and the rule of law. Formal-rational law is *one* form, with its own particular organizational modes, an *architectonic*,[45] of a dialectical form/content relationship. But it sets itself up as something rather different: as "legal formalism" in contradistinction to other nonformal modes. So doing, it denies that it is the embodiment of particular contents, that it is a particular historical embodiment of a form/content relationship, and that its casting of other such embodiments into the wilderness of the inchoate and incomprehensible is a deeply political act.

If we permit the Western lawyer's "claim to form" to define and to exclude, different architectonics of justice, of judgment, and of law become understood only as negations of Western law, as its antinomy. Formal-rational law is part of a particular, historical practice that is underpinned by a specific philosophical (neo-Kantian) conception of rationality, one that apparently separates form from any particular content. Its claim to universality seeks to evade the charge that it is a particular, historically constructed, dialectical combination of formal *and* normative elements operating to exclude differently constituted architectonics of form and content. Weber's conception of law must be located as much in the camp of analytic jurisprudence as the sociology of law.[46] Yet the popular-justice debate operates and applies his constrictive historical categories as the basis for a supposedly adequate elucidation of the phenomena of popular justice. The irony in this should be clear: the popular-justice debate utilizes concepts for understanding a phenomenon that were originally developed to exclude and deny its very significance. Modern writers generally, though not uncritically, see more in popular justice of value than Weber did, but they work with one hand tied behind their back because they continue to employ his scheme. Small wonder, then, that the very idea of popular justice should prove elusive.

Beyond Antinomialism II: Dialectics and Popular Justice

I have argued that there has been a hijacking of the ideologically resonant conception of "formalism" by Western law, a conception that in this manifestation embodies social, economic, and political interests in one particular form/content architectonic. Popular justice must be seen as its antinomy, as what Western law is not, that is, as "informal." This means that it becomes impossible to think seriously about the organizational architectonic of form/content relations in so-called popular-justice systems, and about their disparity and diversity. Popular justice is always defined against a fiction and therefore is taken fictionally in itself. Only occasionally do researchers who are thoroughly immersed in the social relations they investigate, together with the particular mediation mechanisms that they generate, comment on the inappropriateness of the Western epistemology. In a study of popular justice in Mozambique, Gundersen makes the point very well when she writes that

> very few, if any, of the systems described under the heading of "informal justice" are informal in the sense that they are formless. What have sometimes been labelled "informal" systems of law may be systems which exhibit *different* forms in comparison with one type of system which is used as a reference, namely Western-style formal courts of law.[47]

She rightly cautions against the "ethnocentrism" in such an approach, though less polite words could be used. It is the idea of differential juridical architectonics embodying particular dialectical form/content relations that I see as the key to developing an understanding of popular justice, and *different* popular-justice forms. It is beyond the scope of this essay to apply such an idea in detail to any particular version of popular justice, but I will indicate with an example the force of this method in comparison to the antinomial approach adopted by one leading writer.

In Albie Sachs's account of Mozambiquan popular justice, the phenomenon is cast in the form of a moment of ideal innocence:

> The people solve their problems, applying progressive new kinds of norms, and it's the people themselves, organised, that do this, they express power. . . , and they achieve a very large degree of involvement and support from the community in general. . . . [It is] a very rich experience, and a wonderful one . . . to see justice transformed into a true instrument of community expression.[48]

Sachs does not, however, integrate this identification of a "truly" popular moment with his acknowledgment of the role of the Frelimo-organized (and therefore state-sponsored) "dynamizing groups" in sponsoring and promoting popular justice, or the leading role of the vanguard party in establishing the social and democratic principles of the popular tribunals, although he acknowledges the importance of both.[49] Nor does he explain why creating popular justice in Mozambique should require a synthesis of *three* distinct and contradictory dimensions: the "liberating and freedom-enhancing aspects of community-based law" (the moment of true community expression), the need for strictly imposed state law "to defend the gains of independence and the new society," and the application of "what some refer to as internationally accepted norms of justice," that is, "procedural rights and guarantees, commonly referred to as human rights."[50] Sachs points out that the demand for procedural rights was initially generated by the theory and practice of the Frelimo party-state, and not by self-interested Western liberal institutions,[51] but he does not explain how the experience of a third world revolutionary state could give rise to so contradictory an amalgam of state-encouraged social action ("popular participation"), state-imposed power, and state controls on itself. The result is a set of paradoxical conclusions about law, the state, and emancipation.

In the wake of the taking of state power by a third world revolutionary party, idealist talk of popular justice is perhaps to be expected. But it must be tempered by the recognition that there will be, to the extent that the new state can exercise power, a necessary interconnection between the state and popular social relations. Lines of political power will exist, will be created and maintained, between the people and the state. State power will be exercised in particular and contradictory ways in relation to the social forces and movements that give their support to and/or are governed by it. The social forces that give their support to the new state are at once the historically placed agents of social change, partners in progressive social struggles for development and against colonialism, and the objects of what may become a centrist bureaucratic power with its own interests, capable of acting both against and with its people.[52] In this contradictory context of cooperation and conflict, procedural rights appear paradoxically as both a necessary protection *against* the state, and as barriers to progressive and liberating change led *by* the state. Similarly, as I shall argue below, community-based law (popular justice) can genuinely have a liberating quality, but only because it is *not* wholly community based, but comes in significant part *from the state.*

Law and popular justice in Mozambique had a necessary but ambiguous place shaped by the context of third world revolution. They lay between the urban and the rural, the "traditional" and the "modern," the politically progressive and the reactionary, the authoritarian and the liberatory aspects of a complex social context. Popular justice was not presocial, primary, or innocent. It was always complexly located in relations with the state and the underlying social structure. To say this, however, is not to say that it was compromised, captured, or that it failed to "escape" the state, because such judgments measure the concept of popular justice against what is an impossible, ideal standard.

The apparent paradoxes of popular justice in Mozambique were a product of its dialectical situation within a contradictory field. It was exercised in and through a relationship with the state and the conflicting social forces at play. It is only if we can see that popular justice in such situations involves a combination of "popular," "statal," and "legal" mechanisms that we can see that popular justice is always situated and particular, and often what its name suggests it ought *not* to be: dialectically combined with law and state. That is what popular justice is, so that to talk of it as either a form of state power, or as a locus of local power, is to miss the point: that state and local power were inherently inseparable. There was no "borderline" between state power and indigenous order on which agencies of popular justice were located: such agencies always already instantiated dominant social and political relations in the society as a whole, expressing them in particular form/content architectonics of mediation and judgment.

Consider more particularly the Mozambiquan experience of popular justice in the liberation of women. For Sachs and Welch, popular tribunals (or, as they also describe them, "state courts"—*sic!*) "drawn directly from the local community" have been important in supporting women's rights by "balanc[ing] out to a considerable extent the advantages which men enjoy in the society."[53] They include at least one woman, and are related to the work of the OMM, the Organisation of Mozambiquan Women. New socialist principles of marriage affirming the freedom and equality of the woman were applied, according to the authors, "without strain" on the basis of the

> concept of a voluntary union based on equality and the free assumption by the partners of rights and responsibilities. Although the judges might not always have expressed themselves exactly in these terms, these were the principles that underlay their decisions.[54]

Yet in a society in which traditional social relations governed nine-tenths of the population living on the land, and where the authors acknowledge the need to eliminate "the structures of women's oppression,"[55] it is not possible that the popular tribunals would not reflect the contradictory social forces at play. A propaganda and practice of modern marriage generated in the early liberated war zones by Frelimo, and later in the urban centers, had to compete with arrangements reflecting the ideas and structures of the traditional patriarchal peasant society. In later fieldwork, Gundersen confirms that popular-justice tribunals operated to provide mediatory *compromises* between traditional and new views of the roles of husband and wife; that there accordingly *was* strain in their practice; and that *women* members of tribunals, appointed by the OMM, often reflected traditional values in their assessment of how women should behave.[56] The strain produced by this process of mediation and control was evidenced by the coercive, state-enforced character of these "popular" decisions.

Given the ideal understanding of popular justice as "a true instrument of community expression," it is hard to grasp the fact that tribunals could only embody emancipatory norms because they reflected principles established and promoted *by the Frelimo party-state.* Thus the transformative and liberating aspects of the popular tribunal came from the state. This seeming paradox can only be understood in terms of the structures, forces, and ideologies in operation in the society at large, and therefore embodied and expressed through its forms of mediation and control. Popular justice as a progressive social practice in Mozambique was rooted in a set of dialectical relations in society that were translated into a particular architectonic of form and content at the level of the tribunal. That architectonic was marked by procedural informalism[57] and dialogue, with coercive mediation available, and it was coupled with (and enabled) the clash of contradictory political and social positions that were expressed but contained, not resolved or overcome, within it. Popular justice, though never popular in the ideal sense suggested by Sachs, was progressive and evolving. It conjoined social forces and political power to produce a developing complex combination of juridical forms and contents. The three dimensions of socialist legality that Sachs identified, with all their contradictions, can only be understood if we discard the innocent, presocial conception of the popular, and put in its place a historical and structural understanding of social relations within the third world revolutionary state. Only from such an understanding can we move to contemplate the contradictory forms of regulation such a society instantiates. This involves thinking relationally about the social totality that constitutes the contradictory crucible in which the juridical—*any* set of juridical relations, "first" or "third" world, "East" or "West"—is formed.

Conclusion

I began this essay by opposing an abstract method of looking at issues of legal form that is only able to see issues of form and content, the formal and the informal, and so on, in antinomial terms. I argued instead that a better method would insist on the differential, internally organized, character of form/content relations in different contexts. Such a method would recognize the dialectical relationships within such architectonics of law, justice, and judgment, and also between them and the social, political, and historical contexts whence they arise and which they mediate. Such a view can then lead to a mode of analysis that can better understand the phenomenon of popular justice in itself. What emerges is the idea of specific, internally related combinations of form and content, locally molded as they relate to, and develop from, particular moral and political contexts and histories. Law is always to be read, therefore, in terms of what it defines itself against, as therefore always occupying the relational space between its self-definition and its definition of what is other to it. It is this relationship of "in betweenness" that accounts for its antinomial irresolution.[58]

What I am arguing for is the concept of a dialectical understanding of architectonics of form and content as a means of understanding both popular justice *and* Western law. Such a conception would be the basis for a wide-ranging comparative analysis of what we understand as law. With regard specifically to popular justice, such an approach would give a much more nuanced analysis of its character and dynamics than we are at present able to provide. The diversity of contexts within which different "popular" architectonics of justice occur means that popular justice cannot have the homogeneous quality that the antinomial approach necessarily gives it. Once we get beyond "either/or" thinking, we can give credit to the crucial differences between different popular-justice forms. It has always seemed odd that forms of justice generated by quite different social contexts such as exist in late capitalist, revolutionary socialist, postrevolutionary, and postcolonial societies should all be lumped together under the same heading of the "popular." Yet if we define Western law as legal formalism, this is encouraged and has profound effects on our ability to understand other "non-Western" juridical relations. Attempts to typologize will inevitably lead into the kind of problems outlined above in relation to Milner and Merry. Understanding popular democratic forms through an antinomial prism, we are driven to a theoretical characterization of them as informal, whereas they are better understood as "differently formed."

The legal pluralist nomenclature in particular adds confusion to a difficult area. Even Gundersen, in her exemplary Mozambique study, falls foul of this terminology. She is alert to the importance of holding onto an empirical concept of the informal (meaning a minimum of procedural requirements),[59] while insisting that to describe what is merely different in its form as informal is misleading. She also correctly stresses the connection between form and content in assessing the character of a system of justice. Yet she still endorses the term *informal* to describe "a normative system outside the formal legal system." This leads her to argue,

> The local popular tribunal [in Mozambique] can best be conceived as an institution located in the borderland between the formal and the informal systems of law.[60]

If popular tribunals should be seen as differently formed from the Western-style formal court of law, how can they also be said to exist *between* the formal and the informal? How is the metaphorical terrain between the formal and the informal to be described or delineated: what is the specific character (form?) of this borderland?

What is at stake here, however, is not just our understanding, though that is clearly a first step to anything, but also practice. If we see popular justice as simply informal, then it can be portrayed as incipiently authoritarian, for there are no formal mediations to protect the individual from the collective. Popular justice becomes equated with "mob rule," a position central to the old Weberian standpoint, as we have seen. There is no means of protecting people from the revolutionary monster they have created; in Spitzer's phrase, it is a matter of "grabbing the tail of a passing tiger."[61] Accepting this dichotomy, one is then drawn back uncritically onto the terrain of Western legal formalism, as in Sachs's call for "respect for human rights," what he grandiosely calls "part of the patrimony of humankind as a whole." In the process, as he says, socialist legality "becomes less rather than more demarcated from bourgeois legality,"[62] and, one might also suggest, socialist society becomes rather less demarcated from bourgeois society.

Yet as Sachs himself recognizes, the need to rule through consensus meant that citizen's rights were already on the agenda for a socialist Mozambique, and such rights could therefore be understood as part of the practical patrimony of the Mozambiquan revolution, not as something to be parachuted in from outside to an otherwise "informal," non-rights-based system. To portray citizen's rights as exogenous to a socialist system is clearly to delegitimize that system in the name of other social and economic systems, which are unlikely in the long term to advance or empower the majority of the people in a third world society like Mozambique. And that, after all, is what popular justice is supposed to, and can, be about.

Western legal concepts, like other forms of Western aid, do not come without strings attached. Societies that seek to encourage development on the basis of self-determination encounter many difficulties. There is no need to add to these by a Western mode of analysis that fails to understand, on the juridical level as regards the concept of popular justice, what self-determination might mean. I return to where I began, with de Sousa Santos. If we are to understand popular or community justice, we must interrogate the liberal concept of autonomous law, which not only places itself on a pedestal, but also ordains that other modes of social regulation must fail, conceptually and practically. The conceptual vagueness in our understanding of popular justice is a corollary of liberal law's understanding of itself as firm and clear. If we tackle that understanding by placing relationality, infirmity, and unclarity at law's center, we can move beyond it to open up the different geohistorical and sociolegal worlds that have existed, and will continue to exist in our presents and futures.

NOTES

This paper originally appeared in *Social and Legal Studies* 5 (1996): 383–404. I must thank all those who commented on it at various seminars, but especially Davina Cooper, Robert Fine, Peter Fitzpatrick, Nicola Lacey, and the two anonymous reviewers for *Social and Legal Studies*. The paper has been updated and amended for this collection.

1. B. de Sousa Santos, "State, Law, and Community in the World System: An Introduction," *Social and Legal Studies* 1 (1992): 132.

2. The sense of antinomy I wish to convey is something like "a self-contradiction by accepted ways of reasoning [that] establishes that some tacit and trusted pattern of reasoning must be made explicit and henceforward be avoided or revised' (Quine, qtd. in T. Honderich, *The Oxford Companion to Philosophy* [Oxford: Oxford University Press, 1995], 40). Antinomy, I argue, is deeply embedded in Western thinking about law (A. Norrie, "Closure and Critique: Antinomy in Modern Legal Theory," in *Closure or Critique: New Directions in Legal Theory*, ed. Norrie [Edinburgh: Edinburgh University Press, 1993]). See also A. Norrie, "'Simulacra of Morality'? Beyond the Ideal/Actual Antinomies of Criminal Justice," in *Criminal Law: Principle and Critique*, ed. A. Duff (New York: Cambridge University Press, 1998).

3. S. Merry and N. Milner, *The Possibility of Popular Justice* (Ann Arbor: University of Michigan Press, 1993), 4–5, 7, 9.

4. Ibid., 31.

5. This point is owed to P. Fitzpatrick, "Missing Possibility: Socialisation, Culture, and Consciousness," paper presented at Law and Society Association Summer Institute, June–July 1995.

6. P. Fitzpatrick, "The Impossibility of Popular Justice," *Social and Legal Studies* 1 (1992): 199–215.

7. Norrie, "Closure and Critique."

8. There is a problem specific to critical analysis in using concepts such as "law" and "popular justice," or "formal" and "informal" justice, because such analysis must both use such categories as they are presented in experience (for what they are), and seek to establish their historical conditions of existence and

limits (what they are not). The latter problematizes the concept to reveal its inadequacy and incompleteness, while not denying its practical significance. Hence every use of terms like these should carry the academic equivalent of a government health warning, perhaps in the form of scare quotes, to show that one is handling them critically. For exploration and explanation of the methodological issues raised by a critical realist analysis of social forms, see R. Bhaskar, *The Possibility of Naturalism* (Brighton: Harvester, 1979); W. Outhwaite, *New Philosophies of Social Science* (London: Macmillan, 1987); and D. Sayer, *The Violence of Abstraction* (Oxford: Blackwell, 1987).

9. P. Fitzpatrick, "The Rise and Rise of Informalism," in *Informal Justice?* ed. R. Matthews (London: Sage, 1987), and "Impossibility of Popular Justice."

10. R. Bhaskar, *Dialectic: The Pulse of Freedom* (London: Verso, 1994); A. Norrie, *Crime, Reason, and History* (London: Weidenfeld and Nicolson, Butterworth, 1993); Norrie, "Closure and Critique"; Norrie, "Criminal Justice, the Rule of Law, and Human Emancipation: An Historical and Comparative Study," in *Law and Crisis in the Third World*, ed. S. Adelman and A. Paliwala (London: Hans Zell, 1993); Norrie, "The Limits of Justice: Finding Fault in the Criminal Law," *Modern Law Review* 59 (1996): 540–56; Norrie, "Between Structure and Difference: Law's Relationality," in *The Emergence of Law through Economy, Politics, and Culture*, ed. R. Bergalli and D. Melossi, Onati Papers 1 (Onati: International Institute for Sociology of Law, 1997; Norrie, "Legal and Moral Judgment in the General Part," in *Criminal Legal Practices*, ed. S. McVeigh, P. Rush, and A. Young (Oxford: Oxford University Press, 1997); Norrie, "Simulacra of Morality."

11. Compare S. Spitzer, "The Dialectics of Formal and Informal Control," in *The Politics of Informal Justice*, ed. R. Abel, vol. 1 (London: Academic Press, 1982); M. Cain, "Beyond Informal Justice," *Contemporary Crises* 9 (1985): 335–73; J. Allison, "In Search of Revolutionary Justice in South Africa," *International Journal of the Sociology of Law* 18 (1990): 409–28; A. Sachs and G. Welch, *Liberating the Law* (London: Zed, 1990).

12. Darian-Smith and Fitzpatrick, introduction to this volume; Norrie, "The Limits of Justice" and "Simulacra of Morality."

13. Cain, "Beyond Informal Justice," is a bold attempt to develop such a position, but it suffers from an overemphasis on standpoint and political function, and an insufficient analysis of the essential forms of, for example, "professionalized justice."

14. Spitzer, "Dialectics of Control," 171; emphasis added.

15. M. Weber, *From Max Weber: Essays in Sociology*, ed. and trans. H. Gerth and C. W. Mills (London: Routledge, 1991), 220–21.

16. Spitzer, "Dialectics of Control," 169–70.

17. Fitzpatrick, "Impossibility of Popular Justice."

18. M. Foucault, *Power/Knowledge: Selected Interviews and Other Writings*, ed. C. Gordon, trans. C. Gordon, L. Marshall, J. Mepham, and K. Soper (Brighton: Harvester, 1980), 98; Foucault, *The Foucault Effect*, ed. G. Burchill, C. Gordon, and P. Miller (London: Harvester, 1991), chap. 2. Fitzpatrick's most recent work

(e.g., "Passions Out of Place: Law, Incommensurability, and Resistance," *Law and Critique* 6 [1995]: 95–112) makes clear his own current distance from these positions. They remain important, however, within the theory of popular justice, and that is why I consider them here.

19. Fitzpatrick, "Impossibility of Popular Justice," 202.

20. Fitzpatrick, "Rise and Rise," 196, 197; emphasis added.

21. These are the invidious alternatives posed to Foucault by an anonymous questioner (Foucault, *The Foucault Effect,* chap. 2). Foucault's argument is that a progressive politics does not meet this choice if it is devoted to examining inter alia the "possibilities of transformation" accorded by the "mode of existence of discourses" (70). But what transformation is possible if discourses, like individuals, are inscribed by the workings of power? Either discourses conform to the laws of their own production, which means acceptance of the system, or one must have recourse to an outside, unconditioned event.

Foucault wrestles with different aspects of this dilemma in several places in his later work. Freedom, for example, is explained as the internal condition for the working of power, but in his description of its "intransigence" and "recalcitrance," he almost places it beyond power's reach. When he writes of an "agonism" between power and the "intransitivity of freedom" and describes this as "inherent in all social existence" (Foucault, "Afterword: The Subject and Power," in *Michel Foucault: Beyond Structuralism and Hermeneutics,* ed. H. Dreyfus and P. Rabinow [Brighton: Harvester, 1982], 223), as part of an argument for promoting "new forms of subjectivity" (216), he comes close to undermining his own premise that subjectivity suggests "a form of power which subjugates and makes subject to" (212). A similar ambivalence seems to be at work in "What Is Enlightenment?" in *The Foucault Reader,* ed. P. Rabinow (Harmondsworth: Penguin, 1984), 45–50. With regard to resistance, Foucault claims that "great radical ruptures" are possible, yet resistance "is never in a position of exteriority in relation to power" (*History of Sexuality,* vol. 1: *An Introduction,* trans. Robert Hurley [Harmondsworth: Penguin, 1981], 95). See further P. Dews, "The *Nouvelle Philosophie* and Foucault," *Economy and Society* 8 (1979): 127–71; Fitzpatrick, "Passions Out of Place."

22. In his 1972 discussion of popular justice with Maoists, Foucault writes that the "idea that there can be people who are neutral in relation to the two parties, that they can make judgments about them on the basis of ideas of justice which have absolute validity, and that their decisions must be acted upon, I believe that all this is far removed from and quite foreign to the very idea of popular justice. In the case of popular justice you do not have three elements, you have the masses and their enemies. Furthermore, the masses . . . do not rely on an abstract universal idea of justice, they rely only on their own experience [and] purely and simply carry [their decisions] out (*Power/Knowledge,* 8–9). This is no different from Weber's position, though Foucault is an enthusiast for popular justice; indeed, he rather heroically "out-Maos" the Maoists, who argue, correctly in view of what I say below, that a state apparatus, and controls on it, are a prerequisite for popular justice in a third world revolutionary society.

23. Cain, "Beyond Informal Justice"; Fitzpatrick, "Rise and Rise."

24. Bhaskar, *Dialectic.*

25. The key books leading to his work on dialectic are R. Bhaskar, *A Realist Theory of Science* (Leeds: Leeds Books, 1975), *The Possibility of Naturalism,* and *Scientific Realism and Human Emancipation* (London: Verso, 1986). See also Outhwaite, *New Philosophies;* and Collier, *Critical Realism.*

26. A. Collier, *Critical Realism* (London: Verso, 1994), chap. 7.

27. Bhaskar, *The Possibility of Naturalism,* 56.

28. Bhaskar, *Dialectic.*

29. Ibid., chap. 1.

30. Beyond this second level of analysis, Bhaskar also proposes third and fourth levels, concerned with "totalising motifs of totality" and practice as "active and reflexive engagement within the world." These levels do not concern us here.

31. Bhaskar, *Dialectic,* 58.

32. Ibid., 56.

33. Norrie, "Closure and Critique."

34. Norrie, "Closure and Critique," "Between Structure and Difference," and "Critical Legal Studies," in *The Philosophy of Law,* ed. D. N. MacCormick and B. Brown, Routledge Encyclopedia of Philosophy (London: Routledge, 1998).

35. Darian-Smith and Fitzpatrick, introduction to this volume.

36. What follows is a limited account of certain core concepts. A more developed approach would recognize the additional enhanced "social" roles of the state in the twentieth-century Western state and the fragmenting effect this has had on legal forms (see, e.g., R. Cotterrell, *Law's Community* [Oxford: Oxford University Press, 1995]).

37. R. Cotterrell, "English Conceptions of the Role of Theory in Legal Analysis," *Modern Legal Review* 46 (1983): 481; Norrie, "Closure and Critique."

38. S. Fish, "The Law Wishes to Have a Formal Existence," in Norrie, *Closure or Critique.*

39. Norrie, *Crime, Reason, and History.*

40. Ibid., chap. 11; Norrie, "Closure and Critique"; cf. Bhaskar, *The Possibility of Naturalism.*

41. Norrie, *Crime, Reason, and History,* 37–47, 77–81, 106–7, 129–33, 161–63, 188–91.

42. See, e.g., J. Kelsey, *Rolling Back the State: Privatisation of Power in Autorea/New Zealand* (Wellington: Bridget Williams, 1993), pt. 4; A. Higgins, "Land and Freedom," *Guardian,* October 17, 1995; P. Fitzpatrick, *The Mythology of Modern Law* (London: Routledge, 1992), 82–85, 89.

43. Norrie, *Crime, Reason, and History,* chap. 11.

44. Vivid examples of this process often emerge in colonial and postcolonial contexts in which liberal capitalist institutions are introduced to replace existing social orders. Thus in British India, colonial law conspired with Indian patriarchal power to exclude the moral and political voices of women, as in

R. Guha's powerful account, "Chandra's Death," in *Subaltern Studies V: Writings on South Asian History and Society,* ed. Guha (Delhi: Oxford University Press, 1987). But it also sought to protect women in the name of liberal values, as in the efforts to abolish *sati,* the ritual immolation of a widow on her husband's funeral pyre (D. Stein, "Burning Widows, Burning Brides: The Perils of Daughterhood in India," *Pacific Affairs* 1988:465–85). Today, Indian feminists utilize the law as a means of developing and protecting women's freedom, while recognizing the social and political limits associated with that freedom (A. Stewart, "Debating Gender Justice in India," *Social and Legal Studies* 4 [1995]: 253–74).

45. Norrie, "Legal and Moral Judgment," "Simulacra of Morality."

46. Norrie, "Closure and Critique."

47. A. Gundersen, "Popular Justice in Mozambique: Between State Law and Folk Law," *Social and Legal Studies* 1 (1992): 260–61.

48. Sachs and Welch, *Liberating the Law,* 123.

49. Ibid., chap. 5; cf. A. Isaacman, and B. Isaacman, "A Socialist Legal System in the Making: Mozambique," in Abel, *Politics of Informal Justice.*

50. Sachs and Welch, *Liberating the Law,* 15–16.

51. Though Sachs does not point out the codetermination of current rights discourse by Western self-interest and a technocratic elite within the Mozambiquan state (J. Hanlon, *Mozambique: The Revolution under Fire* [London: Zed, 1994]; P. Utting, "From 'Orthodoxy' to 'Reform': Experiences of Dependent Transitional Economies," *United Nations Research Institute for Social Development,* 1989, 15–16). In 1989, Frelimo formally abandoned its Marxist-Leninist ideology and supported IMF-backed economic-recovery plans and the principle of a mixed economy. These developments took place against the backdrop of a brutal, externally sponsored civil war that closed down democratic participatory options, forced reliance on Western economic-aid donors, and encouraged market reforms (V. Brittain, "A State Remade to the United Nations' Design," *Guardian,* August 6, 1994).

52. G. White, *Revolutionary Socialist Development in the Third World* (Brighton: Harvester, 1983); Norrie, "Criminal Justice."

53. Sachs and Welch, *Liberating the Law,* 17.

54. Ibid., 101.

55. Ibid., 97.

56. Gundersen, "Popular Justice in Mozambique."

57. While it is necessary to hold onto the idea of informalism as an empirical description of a particular kind of procedural context, it is crucial to separate this usage from that which designates a particular form/content architectonic as informal (cf. Gundersen, "Popular Justice in Mozambique").

58. Norrie, "The Limits of Justice," "Simulacra of Morality."

59. See note 57.

60. Gundersen, "Popular Justice in Mozambique, " 261.

61. Spitzer, "Dialectics of Control," 200.

62. Sachs and Welch, *Liberating the Law,* 16.

Rabies Rides the Fast Train: Transnational Interactions in Postcolonial Times

Eve Darian-Smith

Introduction

The high-speed railway link, and the Channel Tunnel through which it rushes under the sea, have been declared at the forefront of technological progress and engineering expertise. As part of the Trans-European Network of transport, they dramatically encapsulate hopes for a new era of European economic integration and transnational political cooperation.[1] In the words of the French president François Mitterrand, "the Channel Tunnel . . . is nothing less than a revolution in habits and practices; . . . the whole of Community Europe will have one nervous system and no one country will be able indefinitely to run its economy, its society, its infrastructural development independently from the others."[2]

Despite these positive speculations, however, the Channel Tunnel dramatically highlights England's popular anxiety in being a member of the European Union (EU). Though the Channel Tunnel was officially inaugurated on May 6, 1994, and is in effect a fait accompli, information about the tunnel, and the high-speed rail link joining London to Paris and Brussels, continues to pervade the media.[3] Such publicity excites popular reactions that are by any standards out of proportion to the problems concerning the railway's actual route though the English

An earlier version of this essay appeared in a Special Issue on Law and Postcolonialism, edited by Eve Darian-Smith and Peter Fitzpatrick in *Law and Critique* 6, no. 1 (1995). Reprinted by permission of Deborah Charles Publications.

county of Kent, which lies between the coast and London, and its disruption to local Kentish residents and their claims to a rural environment. While these intrusions are certainly not trivial, they do not fully explain the widespread and seemingly irrational unease that embellishes the Channel Tunnel's impact with forecasts of terrorism, apocalyptic fires, and most dramatic of all, a sudden influx of the dreaded rabies disease.[4] In Julian Barnes's wonderful description of the tunnel's inauguration:

> It was as if, lining up behind Mitterrand and the Queen as they cut the tricolor ribbons at Calais, were packs of swivel-eyed dogs, fizzing foxes, and slavering squirrels, all waiting to jump on the first boxcar to Folkestone and sink their teeth into some Kentish flesh.[5]

In the first section of this essay, I interpret the English fear of rabies as a metaphor embodying distinct cultural meanings and messages.[6] Understanding the rabies phenomenon in this way helps unravel contradictory English reactions toward the EU. For the national excitement and apprehension about rabies and the fast train on which it supposedly rides is, I argue, inextricably linked to England's imperial history. Such imagery recalls both the glory of nineteenth-century Britain and the fall of its colonial regime. Situating talk about rabies (and railways) in a historical context is one of many possible ways to locate a postcolonial legacy that lives on in the construction of English attitudes and identities. What I hope to show is how this legacy is also implicitly present in Britain's relations with other Western nations and hence significant in the shaping of England's European future.

In the second section, I examine the meaning of transnationalism, further exploring the salient, but often unremarked upon, overlapping connections between postcolonialism and the forms of Europe's unfolding. Taking what Homi Bhabha calls "a post-colonial perspective" as my cue, I argue that it is not surprising that England is caught between both acclaiming and fearing the intervention of Europe. The postcolonial perspective, according to Bhabha, emerges from "the colonial testimony of Third World countries and the discourse of 'minorities.'"[7] What this perspective does is recognize the modern nation-state's pretensions toward universalism, given the state's fundamental need to posit itself as a rational, sovereign entity in contrast to external others.[8] Being part of a European transnation expands England's economic and political opportunities. At the same time, England's postcolonial experiences counter this imagined amalgamation by positing multiple discourses and critical revisions that challenge the presumption of England's universal "hegemonic 'normality.'"[9] In other words, locating postcolonial experiences occurring within the nation in a larger transnational landscape suggests that many English people perceive their country's very identity as an enduring, singular state entity to be at stake.

In the construction of the English national identity, law is, according to Anthony Carty among others, a particularly important dimension.[10] Hence this chapter explores how EU law may be presenting alternative legal avenues and, inadvertently, sanctioning competing legal voices not contained by the state. This discussion, then, seeks to go beyond the more visible negotiations between people and law, and probe how transnational activities may be bringing into question how law, as embodied through the nation-state, represents a credible narrative of impartiality.[11] Local-level responses to the Channel Tunnel in Kent, through which the high-speed rail link runs, react to the breaking down of national narratives by and through the EU's "colonization." I suggest that as a result of the Channel Tunnel, there may be emerging in Kent, to borrow again from Bhabha, the conditions by which to establish a "hybrid location of cultural value." This expression refers to the porous quality of state entities and the transformative potential in the crossing of cultural and political borders within a given location.[12] Critical to this emergent "hybridity," I argue, are the legal infrastructures through which Kent is being reimagined as part of a primary European region rather than the peripheral "garden" county of England.[13]

Rabies

Rabies, or in French *la rage,* has a unique and long history. Conjuring up images of other deadly diseases such as cancer and AIDS, rabies also evokes premodern imagery in its association with the medieval terror known as the bubonic plague. It is believed the disease was first introduced into England by Julius Caesar's invading legions in 54 B.C. It caused many deaths up until 1902, when it was finally eradicated. In the years since then, there have been periodic outbreaks, such as when

328 infected French dogs were brought back to England by returning soldiers after World War I. According to official records, for over sixty years there have been no deaths from rabies in Britain, one of the few countries in the world to be rabies-free. This is achieved through rigorous customs controls and quarantine laws. Any animal coming into the country has to be quarantined for six months.[14]

Rabies is a terrifying disease. It is transmitted to humans by bites and scratches from rabid foxes, rats, bats, and more insidiously domestic dogs and cats. The disease attacks the central nervous system and salivary glands, leading to lunacy and seizures. In the perfunctory words of a publicity document on rabies published by Eurotunnel, the joint Anglo/French company in charge of the Channel Tunnel's construction, "Once clinical signs of the disease develop (convulsions, frothing of the mouth, hydrophobia or fear of water and hallucinations) there is no known cure and death is inevitable."[15] For an animal-loving population such as the English claim to be, images of warm and cuddly creatures being the carriers of death are potent and captivating. At the Eurotunnel Exhibition Center in Folkestone, which sells a vast range of gimmicks and promotional information about the tunnel, the report about rabies is one of the biggest sellers. As seems to be the case with most things portending death, people are fascinated.

The British government has not been able to ignore the media hype about a possible rabies outbreak in the wake of the tunnel's construction. This is hardly surprising, considering it has for years been responsible for "sometimes horrendous anti-rabies propaganda," said Bradley Viner, a well-known Middlesex vet.[16] According to Mark Jones, a representative of the London and Essex International Quarantine Pound, the "main worry is that animals will slip in through that bloody tunnel or past lazy customs officials, although no one at the Ministry of Agriculture is admitting it."[17] Eurotunnel, not surprisingly, denies these risks. Its claim is that the Channel Tunnel provides just one more form of transport among many existing ones, and is no more likely to be used by animal smugglers than the enormous number of ferries, hovercraft, and planes that cross the Channel daily. This view was supported by others such as Christopher Gay, chief executive of Canterbury City Council, who stated that those people fearful of mass influx of rabid foxes represented a "lunatic fringe."[18] Yet despite much evidence that no animal would travel thirty kilometers along a dark, cold, and foodless tunnel,[19] the British government was not satisfied with this argument and in 1987 made Eurotunnel incorporate defense measures into the construction of the tunnel. Lord Pennock, then chair of Eurotunnel, in the House of Lords debates about the Channel Tunnel Bill remarked that

> because of the sensibilities of the great British public, noble Lords can rest assured that we shall have deep pits, electrified fences, electronic sensor devices and everything known to man to make sure that there are no foxes running through the 50 kilometers at whatever miles per hour they care to make it.[20]

As a result, a complex electronic system has been installed to catch any adventurous animals, comprising

> a *security/perimeter fence,* with animal proof mesh buried below ground, surrounding the terminals. There will be surveillance to detect the passage of animals at terminal entrances.
>
> a *high-security fence* around the tunnel portals, with animal-proof mesh buried below ground, and an environment at the portals which will be hostile to animals. In addition, there will be *round-the-clock surveillance.*
>
> *electrified barriers* at each end of the undersea sections of all three tunnels, preventing the passage of animals in the unlikely event that they have passed through the first two *lines of defence.*[21]

Despite conflicting reports about the tunnel's involvement in a rabies epidemic, it is clear that the fast train will not pose a significant threat above that already existing. Animal smugglers can use the already existing boat and air cross-channel networks. And even the most daring, cunning, and determined foxes and rats will find it difficult to travel thirty kilometers underground, passing by "round-the-clock surveillance" and a "high-security" electrified fence. Ultimately, the scare is unsubstantiated and speculative. However, lying beneath the surface of the rabies debate is a more profound and deeper logic sustaining the bulk of English anxiety. In a political climate that makes open xenophobic attitudes intolerable, and nostalgia for a "lost" empire repugnant, I suggest another interpretation of the public obsession with rabies.

Rabies, for many English people, represents a form of invasion.[22]

As the Conservative MP Norman Tebitt noted in 1990, "The blessing of insularity has long protected us against rabid dogs and dictators alike."[23] More recently, dog fancier Raymond Seitz, U.S. ambassador to Britain, noted insightfully, "It's about sanctuary and the invulnerability of Britain. It has a strong psychological hold."[24] The current absence of rabies in Britain, then, reinforces the nation's unique superiority, in both military and cultural respects. After all, it is the only European country to be cleansed of rabies. This absence of disease upholds the virtues of a rational and law-abiding citizenry, as well as the country's ability to legally control its ports and borders. Sovereign law, an essential ingredient in the makeup of the English identity, is sustained. And it is law that allows Britain to structure its defensive stand against the deadly disease that, according to media publicity, is being spread by unrestrained "third world" migrations into Europe and particularly into France, and is now creeping westward toward England. In the words of the official Eurotunnel publication on rabies, the disease runs "virtually unchecked" in foreign (postcolonial) countries.[25] In India alone, an estimated twenty thousand people die annually from rabies. In Europe over the past twelve years, thirty-six people have died (although ten of these people contracted the disease in Africa or in the Far East). In 1991, one continental European died, but that person had picked up the disease when traveling in Mexico. The implicit messages are that rabies is associated with "developing" countries and ethnic peoples, and, despite an EU scheme to stamp out the disease, it is unlikely rabies will ever be fully eradicated.

What the threat of rabies excites, then, is the sense that Britain must remain vigilant. Unable to impose round-the-clock surveillance and erect electric fences against incoming "foreigners," rabies provides an acceptably neutral explanation for the maintenance and reinforcement of border controls. Rabies makes customs enforcement critical, and spatial boundaries of inclusion and exclusion essential. The threat of rabies sustains the logic that the pure political and social body of England, visually manifested as a feminine Britannia, requires protection against intruding infection *and* the imposition of an alternative European "nervous system" as described by Mitterrand.[26] By implication, a temporal rationale operates, suggesting that society should stay as it is in order to withstand the invasion of a contagious, anomalous, and lawless force. Implicitly, Britain should remain steadfast as a united, homogenous, "white" nation. Change—at least toward that of a more open and borderless Europe—is denounced at the same time that the EU makes claims to such change as the basis for its existence.

What makes rabies a particularly powerful metaphor is its difference from all other viruses. Unlike AIDS, which is peculiar to contemporary society, rabies represents the returning to England of a premodern "black death" that alienates and objectifies by physically transforming the victim into raving, frothing, lunacy.[27] Still, there are connections between the diseases. According to a local rector in Rochester, Kent, rabies presents real concerns, but, he says, these are exaggerated.

> The Channel Tunnel is a violation of our island integrity—a rape. Building it was a triumph of power and money over ordinary people and the English countryside. People think it might give us rabies in the same way as a rape victim might catch AIDS. I suspect something like this is happening at the psychological level.[28]

Rabies and AIDS, unlike cancer, are both caused by an invasion of an "infectious agent that comes from the outside."[29] In this way, as Susan Sontag notes, descriptions of epidemics become conflated with ideas of otherness, providing an explanation for why "xenophobic propaganda has always depicted immigrants as bearers of disease."[30] "[T]here is a link between imagining disease and imagining foreignness. . . . Part of the centuries-old conception of Europe as a privileged cultural entity is that it is a place which is colonized by lethal diseases coming from elsewhere."[31] Jean Baudrillard adds a twist to this perceived threat of external invasion. Baudrillard is primarily concerned with AIDS in his writing about the viral and virulent excesses involved in current society's "endless process of self-reproduction."[32] Nonetheless, he offers greater insight into the seemingly irrational terrors evoked by the threat of rabies by highlighting the insidious and imminent forces of "radical otherness" and disorder now emerging from within. In an insightful discussion about the impact of the colonized, Baudrillard writes:

> It lies in their power to destabilize Western rule. . . . It is now becoming clear that *everything* we once thought dead and buried, everything we thought left behind for ever by the ineluctable march of universal progress, is not dead at all, but on the contrary

> likely to return—not as some archaic or nostalgic vestige (all our indefatigable museumification notwithstanding), but with a vehemence and a virulence that are modern in every sense—and to reach to the very heart of our ultra-sophisticated but ultra-vulnerable systems, which it will easily convulse from within without mounting a frontal attack.[33]

Terror of the "enemies within" is heightened at a time when the mythological sense of being British has lost some of its vitality, and the country is culturally and politically fragmenting.[34] The influx of postcolonial peoples since the 1950s and 1960s has been instrumental in developing two general versions of Britishness, which in a way reflect two different trajectories of modernity; the first is regressive, conservative, and based on the presumption of a stable unified culture; the second is motivated by the tense, and at times bloody, overlapping of cultural histories and traditions, which in their link to class and ethnicity, challenge the very notion of British homogeneity.[35] While the repeated successes of the Conservative Party throughout the 1980s and 1990s suggest the dominance of the regressive type of British identity, its vulnerability was highlighted by increasing minority dissidence in recent years. This has been illustrated by the dramatic defeat of the Conservatives in the general elections in early May 1997. In the volatile and distrustful political and social environment of Britain in the past decade, it is hardly surprising that in the fight against rabies, the Conservative British government required three lines of defense and an electrified fence to be built inside the tunnel, and, moreover, that a large number of the English public refused to believe that this was adequate.[36]

Railways

While fear of rabies can be viewed as representing English peoples' heightened sensibility of the internal disintegration of their own nation, does the high-speed rail link on which rabies supposedly rides modify this interpretation?

Railways are symbolic of a national heritage and hold a special place in the English imagination.[37] In no other country would you find the number of hobbyists spending hour after hour "trainspotting," outlaying enormous expenditure on Hornby model railways, or participating in amateur clubs that maintain old engines and run steam-train rides. One only has to walk into almost any bookshop and see the abundance of literature on railway history in order to realize the extent of this national interest.[38]

Within Britain, railways played a dramatic role by functionally and symbolically altering the relationships between cities. By 1848, one could travel by rail from Edinburgh to London. The reduction of travel times between towns and places led to an "enormous shrinkage in the national space" and instrumentally united the British nation.[39] The first railway line was laid in the industrial north between Manchester and Liverpool. As railways developed and transformed the "whole surface of the land," they visually brought home to the wider population the impact of the Industrial Revolution.[40] And with the opening up of job opportunities, and the rising economic power of the middle class, came capitalism's accompanying ideology of individualism that fundamentally disrupted the rural, and in a sense still feudal, social fabric.[41] "The railway was the embodiment of the new equalitarian civilization of the towns."[42]

Particularly in country areas, the coming of the railway was often met with violent and bitter opposition.[43] In arguments that are strongly reminiscent of today's local reactions against the high-speed rail link to London, it was claimed that the new railway lines would carve up the fields like a knife and "brutally amputate every hill on their way. So that communications between the towns might be improved, the ancient communications of the countryside were ruthlessly sacrificed."[44] Against these localized objections, the railway engineers and entrepreneurs stood firm. Apart from satisfying private investors, they saw their mission as one of improving the visual landscape. In 1837, the historian Arthur Freeling wrote that these engineering projects were things that "in their moral influence must affect the happiness and comfort of millions yet unborn."[45] According to another critic, the engineer's "will to conquest appears to be dominated by a deep 'sense of moral obligation to put the conquered territory to productive use.'"[46]

This moral overlay helped rationalize the extension of rail across Britain throughout the nineteenth century, and introduce it to its wider empire. Perceived as a feat of universal progress, rail represented a revolution in international transport necessary to bring the rest of the world within European reach. The railway was the agent and primary generator of Britain's informal nineteenth-century colonial expansion by helping to stake out Britain's imperial territories, opening up its colonial markets and resources, and promoting investment and immigration.[47] Providing the means for both overseas integration and territorial annexation, railways were critical in shaping the colony-metropole relationship in almost every colonial context.[48] Moreover, the enormous use of railways in the second half of the nineteenth century as a means of opening up new colonies in South America and southern Africa explicitly marks a shift in the imperial vision away from a protectionist policy over dominions toward a free-trade economy of rampant exploitation.

In this way, railways integrally affected the internal politics of Britain. As has been pointed out, railroads were as much a part of the nation's development as they were of empire building.[49] Analogous to the way Britain's internal railroads altered the distance between town and country, and hence the spatial organization of work, leisure, and domesticity, Britain's overseas railroads affected the spatial relations between the imperial power and its peripheral colonies. For as much as railways were a feature of Britain's nineteenth-century colonial expansion, they were also in a large way responsible for the empire's eventual demise. For instance, in the 1890s, Cecil Rhodes built rail lines north from Kimberley to Bulawayo and Salisbury (Harare) in a bid to take control of the territory that is now the Republic of Zimbabwe. However, once built, the railroad became the focus of a claim to independent power on the part of the settlers, giving first Rhodes's British South Africa Company (which was chartered to exploit the mineral resources of the region) and then, after 1923, the self-governing colony of Southern Rhodesia "more with which to bargain against the metropolis."[50] This quickened a shift in the balance of power between the imperial metropole and peripheral colony. "The railways proved crucial not only in the creation of the empire and efforts to maintain it, but also in shaping the successor states that replaced it."[51] Railways, then, provided a catalyst through which to mobilize anti-English sentiment and resistance.

This brief discussion of Britain's imperial railway experiences suggests how the rabies metaphor may be embellished by the image of the fast train on which it rides. As suggested above, the somewhat irrational public fear of rabies can be interpreted as embodying the English people's heightened sensibility of the internal disintegration of their own nation in the face of an encroaching New Europe. At the same time, the rabies fascination sustains the need for the island state's legal defense against external intervention. Thus the rabies scare expresses disillusionment in the establishing of ethnic harmony, which is intimately tied to England's future open borders with mainland Europe. What the image of the fast train does is to intensify this fear. By alluding to England's rail heritage, the fast train evokes historical images of the railway's capacity to carve up the countryside, alter relations of distance between cities, towns, and villages, and ultimately centralize the industrial nation. But in the fast train's linking London to Paris and Brussels, these evocations of a national past are fundamentally distorted. New ground networks emphasize a theme of connection that is distinctly different from, yet reminiscent of, Britain's expansionist imperial history. This longer historical perspective provides the background to English anxiety in the tunnel railway's potential to generate transnational territorial integration. In the context of Europe's transport network and the penetration of the island nation, the fast train materially highlights a turning point in the shifting spatial relations between the EU's Brussels capital and an increasingly peripheral England.

Transnationalism

The fast train in Europe brings to the fore the issue of transnationalism, which is often interpreted as heralding the breakdown of the nation-state. Against this, I suggest that somewhat paradoxically, transnationalism, which marks forces moving beyond and geographically transcending state boundaries, at the same time affirms that ideas of nation-state and national borders exist, and, to the extent that they can be transcended, are fixed. Transnationalism draws its meaning from, and so intrinsically reifies, a modernist theory of nation building. In short, nationalism and transnationalism, in ways similar to colonialism and postcolonialism, are distinct but aligned processes.[52]

This is not to argue, however, that the increasing scale of transnationalism does not pose particular problems and issues. Rather, my concern is in exploring the intersections between law and transnational activities, where the reification of modernist conceptions as they relate to law become overtly problematic. In this way I want to consider a presumption often made in transnational studies, which is that legal systems, while responding and adapting to new pressures, are nonetheless holistic, coherent, and state-bound. Transnational activity raises jurisdictional issues of cross-border legality. But in connecting new legal configurations such as immigration and trademark legislation, I suggest that what also needs to be explored is the very authority of law through which these new connections are made. Since transnationalism involves not only a confrontation of the nation-state with external forces, but also a confrontation of those external forces with the internal diversities within any one nation-state, how may transnational activities pose new questions about the nature of law, its sources of legitimation, its power of inclusion and exclusion, and its ready conflation with particularized territories?

A brief examination of the creation of the nation-state in the nineteenth century suggests parallels with current transnational formations. The rise of the modern nation-state was essentially an imperialist project, requiring the idea of a distant other to consolidate internal state divisions. No country better exemplifies this need than Britain, where the "protective shield of empire" was critical. The otherness of Europe, and even more so the colonial other, came to be popularized and domesticated, forming a central ideological force in smoothing over internal political and cultural divisions and shaping everyday conceptions in the production of an authentic "British" community.[53] Following this argument, transnationalism can be interpreted as a neoimperialist process, requiring as much as any form of nationalism an abstracted other through which to define itself as a coherent force. But in contrast to nationalism's location within the nation, in the transnation there is a greater willingness to acknowledge the integral presence of the other within.[54] Hans Magnus Enzensberger, in an essay entitled "Reluctant Eurocentrism," discusses this converse position:

> [I]f a cultural other is no longer available, then we can just produce our own savages; technological freaks, political freaks, psychic freaks, cultural freaks, moral freaks, religious freaks. Confusion, unrest, ungovernability are our only chance. Disunity makes us strong. From now on we have to rely on our own resources. No Tahiti is in sight, no Sierra Maestra, no Sioux and no Long March. Should there be such a thing as a saving idea, then we'll have to discover it for ourselves.[55]

The European Union is a conspicuous example of both trans-state formation and the potential of transnational "ungovernability." Driven by the need to redefine faltering member-state economies, national resources are being united in order that Europe may become a viable world power. In this way the EU embodies a new ambitious phase of global integration and cooperation. According to Charles Tilly, as seen from Eurasia, there have been numerous waves of political and economic globalization since the tenth century. Today's phase of globalization is certainly not the same as its historical predecessors, with technology and speed of communications characterizing its distinct difference. Nonetheless, there are parallels between today's globalization and that experienced in the past century, which resulted in the rise of the modern nation-state in conjunction with "a rush for empire."[56]

These historical parallels become more concrete in the context of the EU's fast-train network. In the discussion above, it was pointed out that in the second half of the nineteenth century, Britain quickly realized the capacity of railways to consolidate its colonial empire. Railways were used for the purposes of territorial annexation, primarily by imposing lines of integration on often fragmented and diverse conquered communities. In the context of the Channel Tunnel fast train, there is a clear sense that a transnational rail network is vital to enhance European integration. Mitterrand's comment that "the whole of Community Europe will have one nervous system," and that no one country will be able to run independently from the others, is a strong reminder of the hopes of an interconnected transport system.

Drawing upon insights from its postcolonial heritage, what England most fears about this transport system linking it to the mainland, and hence weakening of its national borders, is not a sudden influx of rabies. Rather, the greatest anxiety for the English people and the British government is that the train, what de Certeau called that "tireless shifter" in the production of relational change,[57] will alter spatial relations and the balance of power between the island nation and mainland Europe. And in this transitional reshuffling, the train may facilitate new political discourses and focus critical revisions of the significance of national governments to control their transport and economy. Already the high-speed rail link, institutionalized through British, French, and EU law, contests the presumption of England's legal autonomy within its island-bound jurisdiction.

Kent

In recent years there have been dramatic changes in Kent, the English county most immediately affected by the building of the Channel Tunnel and the high-speed rail link. Many natural features of the Kentish landscape have been permanently obliterated or marred. Road traffic has increased enormously. Noise and pollution are emerging as significant social problems. Unemployment has risen, and an estimated ten thousand Dover ferrymen will lose their jobs by the end of the decade. The list of problems associated with the Channel Tunnel goes on and on.

But running across the breadth of dissatisfaction among Kentish communities, there emerged in the later 1980s and early 1990s a general disillusionment in the then Tory government and its outmoded nationalist sentiments. Many people believed that under Thatcher, the government failed to hear local voices and consult Kent opinions. This was highlighted in 1986 when the government chose to push through the Channel Tunnel Hybrid Bill, which denied Kent residents the right to demand a public inquiry into the need for the Channel Tunnel.[58] Residents were only allowed to raise objections concerning the tunnel's implementation, not its existence. But despite the House of Commons Select Committee's receiving a record 4,866 petitions, these objections were cursorily heard in six days. Public reaction to this treatment was strong, with groups such as ACTS (Against Channel Tunnel Schemes) stating in its press release entitled "Breakdown of British Democracy," "As Mrs. Thatcher becomes progressively like Hitler, her bullies become like the Gestapo."[59] Representative of numerous letters to local papers, Arthur Percival wrote, "The Select Committee is in danger of going down in history as a monument of flagrant injustice," and it should "call for a full inquiry where ordinary people's voices can be heard and not stifled."[60] These views were endorsed at the level of local government, and groups such as the Dover Chamber of Commerce offered free legal representation to residents in an action before the European Court of Human Rights against what it believed was an irresponsible British government.[61]

It appears that the building of the Channel Tunnel has imposed a wedge of discontent and division between the government and Kent residents. Arguably, a sense of Kentish identity has been strengthened as a result of the perceived neglect by the rest of the country from within, and attack by mainland Europe from without. Of course, a more detailed study is needed to substantiate this claim.[62] Nonetheless, a strong sense of locality and place as well as concern for the environment pervades local Kentish communities, intensified by firsthand experiences of disruption. The leader of the Canterbury Conservation Volunteers, a local environmental group, supports this interpretation. "In the past few years," she writes, "there has certainly been an explosion of public interest in conservation issues, and I'm sure the Channel Tunnel has played its part in convincing local people that they have to do something before the Kent Countryside gets swallowed up. . . . The development generated by the Tunnel will be a major catalyst to this trend."[63]

At the same time, EU intrusion has opened up new economic and political opportunities for Kent that bring to mind de Certeau's musing about the train as a mobile symbol both separating and connecting people.[64] Known historically as the "Garden of England," Kent has long enjoyed the reputation of being a "sleepy" and peripheral agricultural peninsula. This has now been modified by Kent County Council's declaring an additional title for Kent, the "Gateway to Europe." There are increasing attempts through private businesses, tourism, education schemes, cultural links, twinning of cities, and student exchanges to establish new connections with mainland Europe.

Yet it is Kent County Council's local government activities that most stand out. Not only does it have an office in Brussels, but it has been instrumental in establishing what is called the Euroregion, an institutional framework that facilities transfrontier cooperation primarily concerned with managing the high-speed link between Kent, Nord-Pas de Calais, Flanders, Wallonia, and Brussels. Importantly, the Euroregion has independent legal status that eases collaboration between the French and Belgian legal systems, but also gives Kent a measure of autonomy from central government.[65] This has been heightened by the Euroregion's attracting 35 million pounds in regional funds. Whether this will help increase a sense of Kentish identity along the lines of established Scottish and Welsh nationalisms is highly unlikely. But it is important to note that the infrastructural possibilities for a heightened awareness of Kent as a new form of regional entity not categorized as English nor contained by the state do exist.[66] Kent county stands somewhat independently from the rest of Britain as part of a frontier region with France and Belgium and as a co-recipient of

Union funds. In extending the natural coastal borders through EU law, Kent County Council has reconfigured its spatial territory and the local county's political, economic, and social positioning.

In the short term, the Channel Tunnel and the high-speed railway link have certainly highlighted England's legal deficiencies and administrative bungling in governing the railway's impact. In the long term, the greater issue may be that the train heralds alternative visions of egalitarianism and justice promulgated through legal procedures such as France's higher land compensation payments to affected property owners, and the EU's more stringent enforcement of environmental regulations. More directly, Kent's participation in the Euroregion presents an alternative and arguably more accessible channel for local government control and legal reform. The exciting but disquieting potential for these transnational visions is that they may undermine the English law's "mythic foundations" from within, by calling into question and resisting its claims for being neutral, impersonal, and universal.[67]

Legal Jurisdictions

Fear of the idea of a more integrated Europe reflects the English fear for the country itself. And nowhere is this anxiety so well articulated as in the context of law and the issue of national legal sovereignty. The EU represents a new and more powerful legal order binding its member states. Where Union law applies, it has, notes Mary Robinson, a former president of Ireland, in effect brought into the national English system "a written constitution through the European back-door."[68] She goes on to say that "in recent years there has been a realization that there must also be a possibility of different groups using the wider European framework, but using it in a way that penetrates right down to the local level. . . . I think there is a very strong movement at European level for more regional and local taking of decisions."[69]

The EU's constitutional challenge dislodges the ideology of England's legal autonomy. Importantly, Europe creates an increasingly powerful legal forum through which Scottish, Welsh, Irish, and other, less territorially defined nationalisms may reform their relative positioning and significance inside and outside Britain. Neal Ascherson, a Scottish journalist and author, notes that "Europe is somehow a way of

Scotland getting into the world."[70] Thus in shaking up legal relations within the country, the EU also introduces new moments of cultural and political opportunity. Splinter groups within Britain can, in particular circumstances, now make direct appeal to Brussels and side-step the centralized hierarchy of state power. Admittedly, these appeals are somewhat limited. Nonetheless, the breakup of Britain by its multinational elements envisaged by Tom Nairn in the late 1970s is now supplemented by other forces of fragmentation.[71] Regionalism as a substitute for ethnonationalism is increasingly being exploited through the EU 's regional and structural fund schemes, alongside the potential of the principle of subsidiarity and new institutions such as the European Committee of Regions.[72] It is these localized spatial reconfigurations of transnational activity, which both subdivide and extend the borders of England, that disrupt a modernist reading of law and legal meaning.

But how does this argument correlate with my earlier claim that nationalism and transnationalism should be considered not as opposed political processes, but rather interconnected and mutually sustaining? In pointing to how the nation-state is undergoing internal and external transnational challenges, I do not mean to suggest that as an institution it is on the way out. On the contrary, the heady cry of the nation-state's demise is now being revised and countered, particularly in Europe.[73] Rather, what I argue is that it is not appropriate to analyze national versus transnational processes as if they are distinct, opposing, and mutually exclusive. Nor is it appropriate to presume that law is coherent, holistic, and state-bound. In the very connectedness of national and transnational processes, what should be recognized are the complex political and cultural shifts that underlie the contradictions of the coexisting endurance and vulnerability of law as an expression of national unity. In other words, that the state may well continue to override all other political structures is not questioned in my argument. But I ask how the state can maintain that position despite coexisting nationalisms and regional ventures both within and outside its borders that increasingly make use of multiple sources of legal legitimation. In short, strategies both endorsing and resisting transnationalism, and through such strategies the reflexive modification of what constitutes a legal system and legal sovereignty, may increasingly have to be recognized as problematizing our understandings of law.

Conclusion

In this discussion, I have treated the perceived threat of rabies, and the fast train on which rabies rides, as a powerful and complex metaphor. Its central significance is its representation of an insidious disease that will infect the English island, and herald speedy change in the form of a European transport invasion. I have argued that underpinning the metaphor's potency is the continuing significance of England's post-colonial heritage. Particularly important is the understanding that railways promoted both the rise of the British Empire and its eventual demise.

Reacting against and through this postcolonial legacy, what many English people fear is that the EU's high-speed rail link will "colonize" the nation and alter its spatial, legal, and political relations with Europe. This means a national subordination to EU law and, more importantly, suggests the internal fragmentation and reconstitution of what is defined as England against mainland Europe. In the county of Kent, the completion of the Channel Tunnel and early construction on the high-speed rail link to London have generated legal challenges and changes. In particular, the Kent County Council's involvement in the control of the tunnel through the creation of the Euroregion uniting it with Nord-Pas de Calais, Flanders, Wallonia and Brussels points to the development of more accessible channels for local government control and legal reform through the EU. I have stressed that infrastructural possibilities do already exist for heightening awareness of Kent as a new form of regional entity not categorized as English or contained by the state. In short, the tunnel and rail link are practically illustrating an instance of the wider jurisdictional limitations of British, and more specifically English, law.

The historical parallels between an imperial Britain and a transnational Europe are illuminating and insightful. While the two entities cannot be equated, like Britain, the EU today is primarily an economic and commercial venture, with fluid, vulnerable, and contested borders. Like Britain, the EU seeks to consolidate multiple nationalisms, not so much through internal cohesion, as through imposing a single institutional frame, legal system, and citizenry that creates exclusivity against the rest of the world. Unfortunately, the EU, like Britain, has not fully reconciled the promise of modernity to transcend cultural differences with its failure to do so. And so the EU may in the future have to cope with painful conflicts that accompany an institutionalization of democracy without either populist consensus or territorial solidity. Perhaps, as has often been argued, there are no easy solutions, and cultural and political struggles at the level of state, region, and city are inevitable in Europe. If this is the case, it is no wonder that the British government and many English people do not view the Channel Tunnel, symbolic of the EU's neoimperialist integration and territorial annexation, with the same optimism as their European counterparts. England's postcolonial legacy is forever present and suggests the ominous internal presence of further social fragmentation. Rabies riding the fast train may be useful as an interpretative metaphor, but it represents real fears of impending radical change.

NOTES

I thank Peter Fitzpatrick for all his support, as well as Mathieu Deflem, Bernard Hibbitts, and John Comaroff for comments on earlier drafts. Research for this essay was supported by grants from the National Science Foundation and the Wenner-Gren Foundation for Anthropological Research.

1. J. Viegas and U. Blum, "High Speed Railways in Europe," in *Transport in a Unified Europe,* ed. D. Banister and J. Berechman (Amsterdam: Elsevier Science Publishers B. V., 1993), 75–90.

2. I. Holliday, G. Marcou, and R. Vickerman, *The Channel Tunnel: Public Policy, Regional Development, and European Integration* (London: Belhaven Press, 1991), 190.

3. On the French side, the rail link between Paris and Calais was completed as scheduled in early 1994. By contrast, English plans for the overland route, site of the London terminal, and construction of an international passenger terminal at Ashford were still at discussion stages at the beginning of 1994. By June, the British government had announced a shortlist of consortia bidding to build the fast rail link. However, it is not anticipated that the fast rail will be completed before 2002. What is surprising is the British government's apparent lack of embarrassment for such extreme administrative, political, and legal blundering, painfully highlighted by the French government's comparative efficiency.

4. In a national poll two months before the inauguration of the Channel Tunnel on May 6, 1994, the British population declared their unease, with nearly 70 percent claiming that they would never travel in a car under the sea.

5. J. Barnes, *Letters from London, 1990–1995* (London: Picador, 1995), 318.

6. For a comprehensive and fascinating discussion of the use of metaphors, particularly as they relate to law, see B. J. Hibbitts, "Making Sense of Metaphors: Visuality, Aurality, and the Reconfiguration of American Legal Discourse," *Cardozo Law Review* 16, no. 2, (1994), 229–356.

7. H. K. Bhabha, *The Location of Culture* (London: Routledge, 1994), 171.

8. Hibbitts, "Making Sense of Metaphors," 141.

9. Ibid., 171.

10. A. Carty, "English Constitutional Law from a Postmodernist Perspective," in *Dangerous Supplements,* ed. P. Fitzpatrick (London: Pluto Press, 1991), 182–206. See also L. Colley, *Britons: Forging the Nation, 1707–1837* (New Haven: Yale University Press, 1992).

11. See P. Fitzpatrick, *The Mythology of Modern Law* (London: Routledge, 1992).

12. Hibbitts, "Making Sense of Metaphors," 173.

13. E. Darian-Smith, "Legal Imagery in the Garden of England," *Indiana Journal of Global Legal Studies* 2, no. 2 (1995): 395–411.

14. This has caused anger among some people wishing to bring dogs into the country. But British customs officials have stood firm against implementing the vaccination system now used by Norway and Sweden. According to Winfried Mueller, from WHO Rabies Center in Tuebingen, "the British are probably right to wait and see how well the Scandinavians get along with their new system" (*Observer,* May 29, 1994, 18). The EU has somewhat modified these regulations by allowing dogs that have been vaccinated against rabies before entering England to forgo the six-month quarantine, so long as the dog has come from a registered commercial breeder.

15. Eurotunnel Publications: E253, *Rabies and the Channel Tunnel* (London: Channel Tunnel Group, 1990), 1.

16. *Los Angeles Times,* November 10, 1996, 23.

17. *London Student,* February 24, 1994, 10.

18. Christopher Gay, interview by the author, December 21, 1993.

19. A. J. Crowley, Minister of Agriculture, Fisheries and Wildlife, "The Passage of Wildlife through Road and Rail Tunnels," lecture delivered at the World Health Organization Consultation on Natural Barriers of Wildlife Rabies in Europe, Vienna, April 28–May 1, 1981.

20. Channel Tunnel Bill, second reading, 1987 col. 923.

21. Eurotunnel Publications: M3, *Eurotunnel Information Paper: Rabies and the Channel Tunnel* (London: Channel Tunnel Group, 1992), 1; emphasis added.

22. The last invasion of England occurred in 1066, and the country's historical independence is strongly defended and constantly evoked in the national imagination. Unlike other European nations, whose borders have been the subject of constant friction and in many cases have geographically shifted over time, the thought of potential invasion carries intense and particular meaning in Britain.

23. K. Walsh, *The Representation of the Past: Museums and Heritage in a Post-Modern World* (London: Routledge, 1992), 87.

24. *Los Angeles Times,* November 10, 1996, 23.

25. *Rabies and Channel Tunnel,* 3.

26. E. Martin, "Toward an Anthropology of Immunology: The Body as Nation-State," *Medical Anthropology Quarterly* 4, no. 4 (1990): 410–26. See also E. Martin, The End of the Body? *American Ethnologist,* 19, no. 1 (1992): 121–40.

27. S. Sontag, *AIDS and Its Metaphors* (New York: Farrar, Straus and Giroux, 1989), 45.

28. Letter to the author, March 16, 1994.

29. Sontag, *AIDS and Its Metaphors*, 17, 47–50.

30. Ibid., 62.

31. Ibid., 50.

32. J. Baudrillard, *The Transparency of Evil*, trans. J. Benedict (London: Verso, 1993).

33. Ibid., 137–38.

34. S. Hall, *The Hard Road to Renewal* (London: Verso, 1988), 8.

35. See for instance, I. Chambers, *Border Dialogues: Journeys in Postmodernity* (London: Routledge, 1990); P. Gilroy, *There Ain't No Black in the Union Jack* (Chicago: University of Chicago Press, 1991); H. S. Mirza, *Young, Female, and Black* (London: Routledge, 1992).

36. For a discussion of plagues and epidemics as signs of political and moral decline, see Sontag, *AIDS and Its Metaphors*, 54.

37. See, for instance, O. S. Nock, *The Railways of Britain: Past and Present* (London: B. T. Batsford, 1947), v.

38. The special fascination of trains has attracted theoretical discussion. Foucault has pointed out that "a train is an extraordinary bundle of relations because it is something through which one goes, it is also something by means of which one can go from one point to another, and then it is also something that goes by," M. Foucault, "Of Other Spaces," *Diacritics* 16, no. 1 (1986): 23–24. Michel de Certeau likens the train to a form of incarceration. As the rail carriage hurtles along, passing through abstract spaces and illegible frontiers, the traveler leaves behind his/her proper place and in a sense is suspended in time, separated from reality. The train "not only divides spectators and beings, but also connects them; it is a mobile sym-bol between them, a tireless shifter, producing changes in the relationships between immobile elements" (*The Practise of Everyday Life* [Berkeley and Los Angeles: University of California Press, 1984], 113).

39. N. Thrift, "Transport and Communication, 1730–1914," in *An Historical Geography of England and Wales*, ed. R. A. Dodgshon and R. A. Butlin, 2d ed. (London: Academic Press, 1990), 463. See also J. R. Kellett, *The Impact of Railways on Victorian Cities* (London: Routledge and Kegan Paul, 1969); N. Faith, *The World the Railways Made* (New York: Carroll and Graf, 1990), 58–70; W. Schivelbusch, *The Railway Journey: The Industrialization of Time and Space in the 19th Century* (Berkeley and Los Angeles: University of California Press, 1986).

40. C. Barman, *Early British Railways* (Harmondworth: Penguin, 1950), 9.

41. Faith, *The World Railways Made*, 59.

42. Barman, *Early British Railways*, 26.

43. Faith, *The World Railways Made*, 35–57.

44. Barman, *Early British Railways*, 25. See also J. R. Stilgoe, *Metropolitan Corridor: Railroads and the American Scene* (New Haven: Yale University Press, 1983).

45. Cited in Barman, *Early British Railways*, 35.

46. Cited in ibid., 35.

47. R. E. Robinson, "Introduction: Railway Imperialism," in *Railway Imperialism*, ed. C. B. Davis and K. E. Wilburn (New York: Greenwood Press, 1991), 2.

48. See generally the essays in Davis and Wilburn, *Railway Imperialism*.

49. Robinson, "Introduction: Railway Imperialism," 4.

50. W. T. Hanes, "Railway Politics and Imperialism in Central Africa, 1889–1953," in Davis and Wilburn, *Railway Imperialism*, 65.

51. Ibid., 44.

52. E. Darian-Smith, introduction to special issue on Law and Postcolonialism, ed. Darian-Smith and P. Fitzpatrick, *Social and Legal Studies* 5, no. 3 (1996): 291–99.

53. H. K. Bhabha, "The Other Question: Difference, Discrimination, and the Discourse of Colonialism," in *Literature, Politics, and Theory*, ed. F. Barker, P. Hulme, M. Iverson, and D. Loxley (London: Methuen, 1986), 153–56. See also Colley, *Britons*.

54. See P. Fitzpatrick, "'We Know What It Is When You Do Not Ask Us': Nationalism as Racism," in *Nationalism, Racism, and the Rule of Law*, ed. P. Fitzpatrick (Aldershot: Darmouth, 1995).

55. M. Enzensberger, *Political Crumbs* (London: Verso, 1990), 32–33.

56. C. Tilly, "Globalization Threatens Labor's Rights," Working Paper No. 182, Center for Studies of Social Change, New School for Social Research, 1994, 1.

57. de Certeau, *Practise of Everyday Life*, 113.

58. See Holliday, Marcou, and Vickerman, *The Channel Tunnel*, 39–41; also D. Hunt, *The Tunnel: The Story of the Channel Tunnel, 1802–1994* (Worcestershire: Images Publishing, Malvern, 1994), 182–84.

59. *Kentish Gazette*, October 10, 1986.

60. *Kentish Gazette*, October 3, 1986.

61. *Times*, September 16, 1986.

62. See E. Darian-Smith, *Bridging Divides: The Channel Tunnel and English Legal Identity in the New Europe* (Berkeley: University of California Press, 1999).

63. Letter to the author, January 19, 1994.

64. de Certeau, *Practise of Everyday Life*, 113.

65. See M. T. Sinclair and S. J. Page, "The Euroregion: A New Framework for Tourism and Regional Development," *Regional Studies* 27, no. 5 (1993): 475–83; S. Martin and G. Pearce, "European Regional Development Strategies: Strengthening Meso-Government in the UK?" *Regional Studies* 27, no. 7 (1993): 681–96.

66. See E. Darian-Smith, "Law in Place: Legal Mediations of National Identity and State Territory in Europe," in Fitzpatrick, *Nationalism, Racism, and the Rule of Law*. With respect to changes occurring in Scotland, see D. McCrone, "Regionalism and Constitutional Change in Scotland," *Regional Studies* 27, no. 6 (1993): 507–72.

67. See P. Fitzpatrick, *The Mythology of Modern Law* (London: Routledge, 1992).

68. M. Robinson, "A Question of Law: The European Legacy," in *Visions of Europe,* ed. R. Kearney (Dublin: Wolfhound Press, 1992), 138.

69. Ibid., 139.

70. N. Ascherson, "Nations and Regions," in Kearney, *Visions of Europe,* 20.

71. T. Nairn, *The Break-Up of Britain: Crisis and Neo-Nationalism* (London: Verso, 1977); see also J. Anderson, "Nationalisms in a Disunited Kingdom," in *The Political Geography of Contemporary Britain,* ed. J. Mohan (London: Macmillan, 1989), 35–50.

72. See for instance, H. W. Armstrong, "Subsidiarity and the Operation of European Community Regional Policy in Britain," *Regional Studies* 27, no. 6 (1993): 575–606; C. Harvie, "English Regionalism: The Dog That Never Barked," in *National Identities: The Constitution of the United Kingdom,* ed. B. Crick (Oxford: Blackwell, 1991), 105–18; R. Kearney, "Postmodernity, Nationalism, and Ireland," *History of European Ideas* 16, nos. 1–3 (1993): 147–55; D. Marquand, "Nations, Regions, and Europe," in Crick, *National Identities,* 25–37.

73. See A. S. Milward, *The European Rescue of the Nation-State* (London: Routledge, 1992).

Contributors

Antony Anghie	College of Law, University of Utah, Salt Lake City
Eve Darian-Smith	Department of Anthropology, University of California, Santa Barbara
Peter Fitzpatrick	Department of Law, Queen Mary and Westfield College, University of London, England
Rolando Gaete	Department of Law, South Bank University, London, England
Alan Norrie	School of Law, Kings College, London, England
Dianne Otto	Department of Law, University of Melbourne, Parkville, Australia
Paul A. Passavant	Department of Political Science, Hobart and William Smith Colleges, Geneva, N.Y.
Colin Perrin	School of Law, University of New South Wales, Australia
Jeannine Purdy	Western Australia
Annelise Riles	School of Law, Northwestern University, Chicago
Roshan de Silva	Law School, University of Kent, Canterbury, England
John Strawson	School of Law, University of East London, England

Index

Aboriginal peoples, 207, 213–22
Absolutism cultural, 5–8. *See also* Universalism
Aesthetics, 240
Ahmad, A., 22
AIDS, 283
Alterity. *See* Otherness
Alvarez, L. E., 154
Ambivalence, 24, 270; and law, 3
Americas, the, 40
Anderson, B., 20, 30, 31
Anthropology, 183
Antinomialism, 250
Anxiety, 19, 27, 277, 281
Apartheid, 213
Architectonics, of law and justice, 250
Ascherson, N., 292
Assimilation, 214, 215, 242
Australia, 210, 213, 217, 219, 220
Azim, F., 113

Barbarians. *See* Other, the
Barnes, J., 278
Baudrillard, J., 27, 127, 283, 284
Bauman, Z., 239
Bedjaoui, M., 148, 152
Bhabha, H., 2, 20, 26, 29, 137, 168, 278
Bhaskar, R., 250, 253, 257–60
Bill of Rights, American, 61
Blake, W., 252
Blanchot, M., 19
Bourdieu, P., 222
Bretton Woods Institutions, 153, 155, 158, 208
Brewster, A. B., 127
British colonialism, 113
Bropho, R., 206
Buddhism, 183, 187, 191. *See also* Mythology

Capitalism, 285
Carty, A., 279
Case Law: *Barnes v. Glen Theatre* (1991), 65; *Bethel School District v. Fraser* (1986), 80; *Chaplinsky v. New Hampshire* (1942), 62; *Ireland v. UK* (1978), 238; Land claims case (Fiji), 129, 130; *Mabo v. New Queensland* [*No.* 2] (1992), 219, 221; *Martin v. Struthers* (1943), 81; *Miller v. California* (1973), 65; *Miller v. Civil City of South Bend* (1990), 81; *Paris Adult Theatre I v. Slaton* (1973), 65, 80; *Roe v. Wade*, 241; *Roth v. United States* (1957), 65; *United States v. Carolene Products* (1938), 63; *Whitney v. California* (1927), 80
Cesaire, A., 207, 208
Chafee, Z., 79
Chakrabarty, D., 161, 162, 165
Channel Tunnel, 277, 280; resistance to, 290

Charter of Economic Rights and Duties of States 1974, 156, 165
Chomsky, N., 207
Civilization, 47, 53, 68, 70–75, 237; and barbarism, 47, 66, 69, 71, 72, 74, 75; margins of, 235; western, 67
Civilizing Mission, 50 104, 160, 223
Clifford, J., 22
Cold War, 148, 174, 233, 242; effect on American identity, 81
Colonialism, 52, 54, 89, 115, 150, 161, 208; British, 113; contemporary, 207; Fiji, 127, 129; internal, 219; and Islamic law, 114; justifications for, 100; and law, 100, 101, 103; and orientalism, 117; religious authority for, 92; Spanish, 91, 92, 95; and violence, 209, 218, 219
Colonization, 42; and European Union, 279
Common Heritage of Mankind, 156, 158
Communitarianism, 235
Community, 32, 170, 172, 173
Consciousness, 45, 46, 189
Constitutions: American, 61; Sri Lanka, 183, 186, 189
Constructionism, 20, 24, 252
Cosmology, Buddhist, 183, 187, 190–98
Critical Realism, 257
Cultural Difference, 90, 91, 102, 294
Cultural Relativism, 235, 236, 238

de Certeau, M., 289, 291
Decolonization, 152, 153, 160
Democracy, 145, 150, 159, 169–73, 175
Demonic, the, 192–96
Derrida, J., 19n.3, 64, 150
Despotism, 119, 120, 121
Development, 163; and law, 4
Dhamma, 191
Dialectics, 257, 258, 259
Diderot, D., 40, 43, 44–47, 49
Difference, 146, 165, 167, 170, 171, 172, 174
Dipavamsa, 193, 196
Discussion, 66, 67, 71, 72, 74, 75, 77, 78
Disease. *See* Rabies
Divine Law, 94
Donnelly, J., 236
Dow, A., 119, 120

East, the, 75, 76
Economic and Social Council, 163
Empire, railways, 285, 286, 294
Enlightenment, 148, 174, 237, 240, 242
Enzenberger, H. M., 288
Essentialism, 157, 166
European Committee and Court of Human Rights, 238
European Committee of Regions, 293
European hegemony, 149; hegemony challenged, 153, 155, 157
European identity, 71, 172
European integration, 289, 292
European Union, 277, 287, 289, 291
Euroregions, 279, 291, 292, 294
Eurotunnel, 280
Exclusion: and civilization, 75; and free speech, 61, 75. *See also* Marginalization
Exploitation, economic, 208, 209

Fanon, F., 127, 137, 172
Feminist Theory, 206
Fesl, E., 206
Fiji, 127, 129; Land Claims Case, 129, 130
Fish, S., 261, 262
Fitzpatrick, P., 205, 209, 217, 221, 252, 255
Foreignness, 283
Form/Substance, 255
Formal/Informal, 250, 252, 255, 270
Foucault, M., 210, 211, 216, 217, 250, 252, 256, 257; on discourse, 21, 51. *See also* Governmentality

Freedom of Speech, 61–64, 75
Free Speech, 65, 68, 78, 79
Frontier Region, 291
Fundamentalism, 235

Gadamer, H. G., 240
Genealogical, 64
General Agreement on Tariffs and Trade (GATT), 155, 208
General Assembly Resolutions, 154, 156
Geography, 66, 68, 69
Global, 128, 133, 134, 136, 137
Globalization, 52, 206, 235, 237, 244, 289; and law, 4
Global Village, 233, 244
Gong, G. W., 5
Gordon, A., 129
Governmentality, 151, 161–63, 167, 173, 174
Grady, S. G., 119
Grotius, H., 89
Group of 77 (G77), 147, 154, 158, 164, 165, 166, 169, 174
Guha, R., 159, 161, 166
Gunasekera, P., 185

Hague Convention 1907, 129
Hamilton, C., 113–19, 121, 122
Hartwig, M., 207
Hay, D., 204, 205, 213
Hedaya, 115, 117, 121
Hegel, G. W. F., 45, 46, 258
Heidegger, M., 183
Herder, J. G., 40, 42
Historiography, 167
Hobbes, W., 239
Howard, R., 5–10, 236
Human Rights, 123, 233, 234, 240, 244; as fundamentalism, 236, 237; and International Court of Justice, 243; and morality, 239; in Mozambique, 271; and *opinio juris*, 241; and universalism, 5–10
Hungary, 39
Huntington, S., 81
Hutchful, E., 208, 209, 213

Identity, 40, 49, 50, 78, 172, 184, 190; American, 80, 81; and anxiety, 20; British, 278, 279, 282, 284, 290; Buddhist, 182, 184, 190; cultural, 53; European, 71, 172; and exclusion, 55, 80; globalized, 55; and irresolution, 44; and postcolonialism, 1, 10; and savagery, 53; the west, 48, 81
Immigration, 283, 284
Imperialism, 148, 153, 166, 172, 173, 205
Imprisonment, 211–14, 216
Incommensurability, 40–43, 48–51, 53, 137, 147, 172, 173; failure of, 43
Indentured labour, 210
Independence, 150, 165
India, 113, 119, 146, 159, 160, 162, 164–66, 282; people of, 40, 41
Indigenous peoples, 20, 26, 206, 219; and exoticism, 25; and land, 25; and self-determination, 32, 33. *See also* Aboriginal peoples; United Nations Declaration on the Rights of Indigenous Peoples
Individualism, 263, 285
Indonesia, 243
Industrial Revolution, 285
International community, 145, 147, 148, 157, 160
International Court, 129
International law, 89, 104, 128, 133, 145, 151, 174; and colonialism, 89, 90, 91, 152; customary law, 151, 152; and democracy, 146; *jus gentium*, 94, 97, 101, 102; and justice, 156; law of war, 98, 99, 100; and liberalism, 145; *opinio juris*, 240, 241, 243; sources of, 151, 152
International Legal Order, 90; challenges to, 154, 158
International Monetary Fund, 155, 213

Invasion, 281, 283
Islam, 109, 111, 118, 120, 237; and Arab society, 111
Islamic law, 109–13, 121, 122, 235; and the impact of colonialism, 114; and women, 116

Jones, Sir W., 110, 113
Jurisdiction, 93
Jus gentium, 94, 97, 101, 102
Justice. *See* Popular justice

Kant, I., 236, 237, 240; neo-Kantian juridical worldview, 252, 260
Kapferer, B., 183, 197
Karma, 187
Kearns, T., 203
Kennedy, D., 152
Kern, S., 135, 136
Keruish, V., 222
Knowledge(s), 135, 136

Lacan, J., 27, 28
Land rights, aborigines, 220, 221. *See also* Fiji, Land Claims Case
Language, and exclusion, 188, 189, 190
Law, 2, 50, 66, 261, 293; and civilization, 48, 50, 54; and closure, 262; and colonialism, 110, 114, 135, 167; and the colonial subject, 218; and community (*see* Popular justice); and critique, 136; and culture, 130; as disciplinary, 217, 218 (*see also* Imprisonment); as discourse, 217, 218; divine law, 94; and equality, 218; and exclusion, 103, 262–64; hard law, 152, 155; and identity, 49, 282; and individualism, 263; international (*see* International law); and liberalism, 263; and nation, 293; natural law, 91–94; and passion, 50; and postcolonialism, 1, 209, 210, 222; and repression, 263; and resistance, 164; and savagery, 47; soft law, 151, 154, 155, 158; and transnationalism, 288; and universalism, 264; and violence, 203, 209, 210, 213, 216, 218, 219; of war, 98, 99, 100; Weberian conception of, 252; western law, 256, 260, 263, 265, 270
Legal formalism, 261, 262
Legal pluralism, 249
Legal positivism, 260
Legislation: Channel Tunnel Bill, 281; Channel Tunnel Hybrid Bill, 290; Official Language Act (Sri Lanka) 1956, 188; Pecuniary Claims Arbitration Procedure 1910, 129; Tamil Language (Special Provisions) Act 1958, 189
Liberal individualism, 170
Liberalism and law, 263; and justice, 151
Liberal legal theory, 249
Liberation Tigers of Tamil Eelam, 181
Local, 132–34, 136, 137, 252
Lyotard, J. -F., 19, 34n.1, 237

Mahavamsa, 193, 196
Marginalization, 146; and language, 188–90; of Tamils, 183, 184, 188, 189, 194, 195, 197. *See also* Exclusion
Marx, K., 209
Marxism, 4
Mayer, A., 109
McAfee, K., 207
Memory, 33
Merry, S., 250, 251
Methodology, 250, 259
Mexico, 40, 282
Mill, J. S., 65, 66, 67, 74, 78; and civilization, 67, 70; on India, 72, 73; on liberty, 64, 66, 68, 73, 74, 75, 77; on the savage, 67, 70
Milner, N., 250
Mitchell, T., 110
Mitterand, F., 289

Modern, 234
Modernity, 20, 149, 166, 168, 169, 171, 174, 234, 294; and indigenous peoples, 28, 29; and otherness, 39; and universalism, 235
Modernization, 4, 234
Moghul Empire, 113, 120
Monsters, 42, 53
Montevideo Convention on the Rights and Duties of States 1933, 149
Moody, R., 206
Mouffe, C., 171
Mozambique, 254, 265–69
Myth, Sinhalese Buddhist, 184, 186
Mythology, Buddhist, 186, 187, 193–97

Nairn, T., 293
Nancy, J. -L., 19
Narrative, 29
Nation, 21, 31, 133, 137; boundaries, 287, 288, 293; disintegration of, 287; and exclusion, 68, 74, 77, 283; origin, 30; nation state, 278, 288, 293; and universalism, 278, 288
National elites, 159, 164
Nationalism, 77, 159, 160, 164, 165, 292, 294; blood and soil, 25, 32; in Sri Lanka, 184. *See also* Transnationalism
Nativist narratives, 165
Nativist philosophy, 157
Natural law, 91–94
Nature-Culture, 47
Negritude, 157
Neocolonialism, 206, 208, 219
Neo-Kantian juridical worldview, 252, 260
New International Economic Order (NIEO), 154, 157, 158, 164–66
New World Order, 145, 174
Nibbana, 187
Nicaragua, 242
North-South divide, 158

Occident, 41. *See also* West, the
O'Dowd, L., 205
Omowale, A., 205, 213
Ontology, Sinhalese Buddhist, 183, 184, 191
Orientalism, 21, 22, 23, 110, 118, 149; legal orientalism, 109, 110, 119, 122, 123; and despotism, 119, 120, 121
Origin, 30
Other, the, 28, 44, 48, 49; colonized other, 20; the savage, 44, 54, 68; Tamil as other 190, 196, 197
Otherness, 20, 29, 168, 171, 172, 283, 288; temporal otherness, 70

Pagden, A., 41, 42
Pantin, D., 213
Papua New Guinea, 54, 251
Passeron, J. -C., 222
Passion, 47
Peasants, 40, 49, 52, 55, 164, 166–68; marginality of, 39
Periphery, 213
Perspective, 127, 131, 132, 134, 135–38
Popular justice, 249, 251, 253, 264; and formal law, 251; Weberian concept of, 250. *See also* Mozambique
Postcolonial, 146, 164, 165, 166, 173, 174, 284; legacy of, 278, 295; and modernity, 19; and otherness, 21
Postcolonialism, 1, 3, 205; and colonialism, 204, 205, 206; and identity, 1, 10; and nation; 147; and the West, 2
Postmodernism, 1, 137
Poststructuralism, 1, 137
Power, 22, 51
Prison. *See* Imprisonment
Pujavaliya, 196
Purvis, N., 151

Qur'an, 113

Rabies, 278, 279, 280, 283
Racism, 205, 208

Railways, 284–87; Trans-European Network, 277
Rajavaliya, 197
Rauch, J., 81
Regionalism, 293
Relationality, 258
Relativism: cultural, 235, 236, 238; human rights, 238, 239, 244
Religion, 91, 92
Renan, E., 33
Repetition, 26, 27
Resistance, 22, 39, 40, 51–54, 95, 98, 159, 168, 169, 171, 242
Reynolds, H., 219, 220, 221
Richard Jacobs, W., 206, 209
Rights, 61; and exclusion, 62; First Amendment, 62, 63; individual rights, 253
Robinson, M., 292
Rule of law, 2, 3, 49, 129
Russell, A. G., 209

Sachs, A., 266, 268, 269
Said, E., 6, 20–23, 66, 109, 149, 168, 205, 207. *See also* Orientalism
Santos, B. de Sousa, 249
Saracens, 99, 100
Sarat, A., 203
Sartre, J. P., 203
Savage, 47, 49; noble, 44–46
Savagery, 50, 53; and civilization, 48
Savages, 54, 68
Scale, 127, 128, 131, 132, 134–36
Schact, J., 110, 111, 112
Self-determination, 147, 159, 166, 169
Senghor, L., 157
Sensus Communis, 240
Shapiro, M., 79
Shari'a law. *See* Islamic law
Slaveholding, 42
Snyder, F., 204, 205
Social interests, 253
Sontag, S., 283
South Africa, 286
Sovereignty, 90, 91, 98, 100, 102, 103, 149, 292
Spanish colonialism, 40, 91, 92, 95
Spitzer, S., 254, 255
Spivak, G. C., 157, 162, 171
Sri Lanka, 54; colonialism, 181, 197; conflict, 182, 197; constitution, 185, 186, 188, 189, 192; federalism, 185, 186, 189, 190 ,198; Sinhalese-Tamil relations, 183, 186, 189, 190, 198
Statehood, legal criteria for, 149–51
Stereotype, 26
Strathern, M., 134, 135
Structural adjustment, 233
Subaltern, 146, 161, 164, 165, 167, 168, 171, 173
Subaltern Studies Collective, 146, 159, 160, 164–74
Sudan, 123
Sunna, 111, 113

Tamil separatism, 181
Technology, 233, 234
Terra nullius, 219, 221
Terrorism, 278
Thatcher, M., 290
Tibi, B., 237
Tilly, C., 289
Timor, East, 243
Totality, 258
Trade, 95
Transgression, 48, 51,53; and resistance, 52
Transnationalism, 287, 288
Trinidad and Tobago, 210–13, 218
Trusteeship, 97

United Nations, 148
United Nations Charter, 147, 151, 155, 160, 163, 173
United Nations Declaration on the Rights of Indigenous Peoples, 19–21, 24
United States, 61, 207, 208; commu-

nity mediation, 250; and human rights, 241; and Nicaragua, 242
Universal, 42, 45, 50; inclusion, 41
Universalism, 133, 135, 136, 234, 235, 241, 244; aesthetical, 240; and colonialism, 104; and human rights, 5–10; and particularism, 162
Universal law, 95, 102; divine law, 94; natural law, 91–94
Universal rules and norms, 96, 97
Uti possidetis juris, 150

Verwey, W., 156, 157
Violence, 26, 209. *See also* Colonialism, and violence; Law, and violence
Vitoria, F. de, 89–104

Wallerstein, I., 208
War, 97. *See also* Law, of war
Watkins, K., 208
Watson, I., 204, 206
Weber, M., 250, 252, 255, 256, 257
West, the, 5, 6, 19, 41, 48, 64, 66, 71, 75, 76, 81
West Indies, 210
Western law, 256, 260, 263, 265, 270
White, H., 41, 46
Williams, E., 221
Women: and Islamic law, 116; liberation of, 267, 268; subaltern, 173
World Bank, 155

Young, I. M., 170
Young, R., 22